The Encyclopedia of
SNAKES

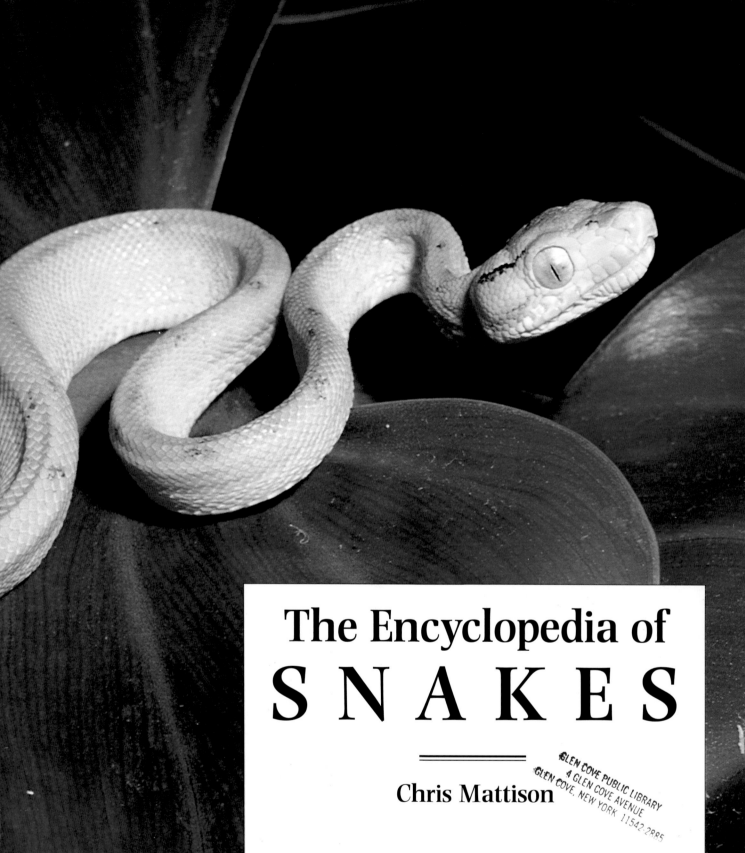

The Encyclopedia of
S N A K E S

Chris Mattison

Facts On File®

AN INFOBASE HOLDINGS COMPANY

To my parents,
Ron and Rose Mattison,
who nurtured my interest
in animals and books.

The Encyclopedia of Snakes

Copyright © 1995 by Chris Mattison
First published in the UK by Blandford,
an imprint of Cassell plc, London

Facts on File, Inc.
460 Park Avenue South
New York NY 10016

Library of Congress Cataloging-in-Publication Data

The Encyclopedia of snakes/Chris Mattison.
        p.   cm.
    Includes bibliographical references and index.
    ISBN 0-8160-3072-3 (alk. paper)
    1. Snakes.   I. Mattison, Christopher.
QL666.06E53   1995
597.96—dc20   95-2501

Facts on File books are available at special
discounts when purchased in bulk quantities for
businesses, associations, institutions or sales
promotions. Please call our Special Sales
Department in New York at 212/683-2244 or
800/322-8755.

Designed by Yvonne Dedman

Line drawings by Alan Rollason

Typeset by Keystroke
Jacaranda Lodge, Wolverhampton, England

10 9 8 7 6 5 4 3 2 1

This book is printed on acid-free paper.
Printed and bound in Hong Kong
by Dah Hua Printing Press Co. Ltd.

Title page: An Amazon tree boa, *Corallus enhydris*.

Contents

ACKNOWLEDGEMENTS

Such a large project as this book is never possible without the help of a number of individuals. People who helped by supplying specific information relating to their research, providing copies of papers they have written, or helped in other ways include the following (in alphabetical order):

Dr Claes Andren (University of Göteborg); Dr E. N. Arnold (British Museum (Natural History), London); Dr W. R. Branch (Port Elizabeth Museum, South Africa); Richard Clark; Dr L. Lee Grismer (La Sierra State University, California); Dr Robert Henderson (Milwaukee Public Museum, Wisconsin); Dr Colin McCarthy (British Museum (Natural History), London); Professor S. McDowell (Rutgers University, New Jersey); Dr Göran Nilson (University of Göteborg); Dr Nikolai Orlov (Russian Academy of Sciences, St Petersburg); Paul Orange; Mark O'Shea; Dr R. D. G. Theakston (Liverpool School of Tropical Medicine).

Literature searches were carried out at the libraries of the Universities of Nottingham and Sheffield.

Special thanks to Richard Trant, who loaned several volumes of rare books from his collection and also helped with the bibliography; to Mark O'Shea for access to parts of the manuscript of his forthcoming book *A Guide to the Snakes of Papua New Guinea*; to Frank Schofield, Adam and April Wright, and several other friends for locating or providing specimens for photography; to the photographers, listed on page 249, who gave permission for photographs to be used; and to the artist, Alan Rollason, for his excellent work on the line drawings. Gretchen Davison helped to check sections of the manuscript and assisted in many other ways. Thanks also to Audrey Aitken for reading the proofs, to the designer Yvonne Dedman and to Miranda Stonor and her colleagues at Cassell.

Introduction

In this book I have set out to describe and explain, in a readable way, the lives of snakes. In doing so, I hope that it will introduce the reader to the same sense of fascination and wonderment that I have felt when watching and studying them, whether in the field or in captivity.

The information has been obtained in a number of ways. Although I have drawn on personal experiences where I felt appropriate, a book of this type is not the place for original observations. Rather, it is a means of communicating information that numerous professional and amateur herpetologists have accumulated over the years. Many such observations have appeared in scientific journals and society publications that are not widely read by the general public and so the information they contain is often overlooked; I have attempted to extract those pieces of knowledge that are most likely to be of interest to amateur herpetologists, as well as to general naturalists who may wish to know more about snakes. In doing so, I acknowledge the massive contribution that has been made by innumerable researchers and writers upon whose efforts I have relied and whose findings I have plundered. I have given references in places, but only where a specific piece of information has been used or where I have drawn heavily from major review articles. I feel that the insertion of too many references disrupts the text to an unacceptable degree and often serves no useful purpose in a book of this type.

Some of the material consists of interesting 'snippets' relating to some of the more unusual or spectacular species or to their behaviour. Most of it, though, concerns underlying principles and generalizations that apply to all snakes, bearing in mind that it is not always possible to give simple, hard and fast rules about how snakes live: this reflects their diversity as well as the lack of knowledge about certain aspects of their lives.

Throughout, I have tried to adopt an evolutionary approach. Snakes have been moulded by natural selection. The array of shapes, sizes, colours and behaviour patterns that we see are the end products of this process and I believe that it is not possible to produce an account of them without continual reference to evolutionary forces and pressures: understanding these allows us to answer many of the questions about why snakes look and behave the way they do. I apologize in advance if some of this material seems complicated, although I have tried to present it in simple terms wherever possible.

Natural selection is the driving force behind evolution. Organisms evolve in response to changes in their physical environment as well as interactions with other organisms, of the same or different species, with which they share their environment. Most environmental changes are gradual and evolution keeps pace with them to produce ever more efficient answers to new problems.

Often, one species' loss is another one's gain. More recently, the human species has brought about far-reaching changes, the speed of which easily outstrips evolution. Organisms that have taken millions of years to become good at what they do, have no response to these changes. They are not able to adapt to new conditions in the space of a few generations and many of them, including snakes, are becoming rare or extinct.

Our reaction to this problem seems to vary with the type of animal concerned. Because snakes are among the most secretive and overlooked components of the biological diversity with which we share our world, relatively little attention has been paid to their conservation in the past – it is hard to love something you can't see!

Furthermore, there is an ingrained distrust of snakes, fuelled largely by ignorance, even though most are harmless and many are useful and beautiful to look at. There is some evidence that snakes, along with other aspects of nature, are becoming more 'acceptable'. I hope that this book will continue this trend by contributing towards a greater understanding of them and, through this, a greater appreciation.

1
The Origin and Evolution of Snakes

Snakes are reptiles. In other words, they belong to the order Reptilia, which also includes the turtles and tortoises, the crocodilians, an odd lizard-like creature from New Zealand called the tuatara, the lizards and the amphisbaenians. All these groups of animals are related, but some are more related than others. The most important assemblage, as far as snakes are concerned, is the order Squamata. This order is divided into three suborders: Ophidia, containing the snakes, Sauria, containing the lizards, and the Amphisbaenia. (Outside the tropics, the amphisbaenians, sometimes known as worm-lizards, are not well known: the 130 or so species are restricted to warmer parts of the world where they spend the greater part of their lives burrowing beneath the surface of the ground.)

◄ A typical snake – moderately slender, with an almost cylindrical body and a head that is distinct from its neck. The scales are arranged regularly on the body and in this species, a colubrid, *Lampropeltis mexicana*, they are also arranged in a regular fashion on the top of the head. Members of certain other families, especially the pythons, boas and vipers, may have numerous small scales covering the head.

DEFINING SNAKES

What makes a snake different from amphisbaenians and lizards? This is not quite such a ridiculous question as it may seem. In fact, it is not too easy to come up with a definition that includes all the snakes but excludes other members of the Squamata. Firstly, snakes have no legs – but neither do many lizards nor most amphisbaenians. Snakes have no eyelids but, again, neither do some lizards nor any of the amphisbaenians. Snakes have no external ear openings – again, neither do some lizards nor any amphisbaenians.

We can, however, use a combination of characteristics that will get pretty close to defining snakes. All snakes have a backbone (i.e. they are vertebrates) but lack limbs, eyelids and external ear openings. In addition, snakes have a specialized row of scales along the underside of their bodies, the ventrals, whereas lizards have various patterns of scales but never a single row. The scales of amphisbaenians are peculiar in that they are arranged in rings around the body, so that small species superficially resemble earthworms. On the question of legs, even those lizards that have lost their legs retain vestiges of the limb girdles, as do the amphisbaenians, whereas, although some families of snakes do retain vestigial pelvic girdles, none of them have pectoral girdles. Finally, snakes have unique skulls – the bones of their upper jaws are not united at the snout but are free to move away from one another, so allowing the passage of larger prey items than would otherwise be the case. This arrangement is not found in lizards or amphisbaenians. In the hand, snakes are supple and muscular whereas legless lizards tend to be more rigid.

Is it a snake?

Snakes are long, slender vertebrates without legs. This definition is not enough to separate snakes from some other groups of animals, though. Eels, for instance, are also long and slender and have no legs, but their scales are very small and they breathe through gills, which can plainly be seen just behind the head.

It is not so easy to separate legless lizards and amphisbaenians, from snakes. All are reptiles, their bodies are covered with scales and they all breathe through lungs. All these reptiles evolved limblessness for the same reason – to help them crawl quickly through dense vegetation or to burrow in loose soil. Limbs would, quite simply, get in the way.

All the amphisbaenians, except for three species in the genus *Bipes* are limbless (and *Bipes* only have front limbs). Limbless lizards, or lizards in which the limbs have been reduced to such a degree that they are all but absent, are found in seven families. The following chart will help to distinguish between snakes and other limbless reptiles, but by far the easiest way to differentiate them is to become familiar with species living in your area – the glass lizards of North America, for instance, do not look similar to any of the snakes found in the same region, nor does the European slow worm. The only possible confusion is the case of three flap-footed lizards from Australia, which are thought to be mimics of certain juvenile brown snakes of the genus *Demansia*.

▲ Although they look superficially similar to snakes, legless lizards, like *Ophisaurus ventralis* from North America, differ from them in several ways, including the presence of external eardrums and eyelids, a different arrangement of scales on their undersides and several internal anatomical characteristics.

▲ Most amphisbaenians also lack legs, but the arrangement of their scales into regular rings immediately distinguishes them from both snakes and lizards.

Snake, lizard or amphisbaenian?

1. Animal has four legs . . . . **Lizard**

   Animal has no legs . . . . *Go to 2*

2. Scales arranged in rings around body . . . . **Amphisbaenian**

   Scales overlapping and tile-like . . . . *Go to 3*

3. Eyelids present . . . . **Legless lizard**

   Eyelids absent . . . . *Go to 4*

4. Single row of wide ventral scales . . . . **Snake**

   Several row of small ventral scales . . . . **Legless lizard**

n understanding of the origin and evolution f snakes is an important aspect of the classi-cation of the living species into genera, milies and so on. Previously, biological assification was based more on the outward ppearance of organisms with little regard o their evolutionary history. (This would e rather like sorting library books by the olour of their jackets rather than their abject matter and is obviously a less useful vstem.) Modern classification is intended o reflect the relationships between species, enera and families.

There is a common assumption that nakes evolved from their closest relatives, ie lizards. Members of seven families of zards, including the Australian snake-zards (Pygopodidae), the skinks (Scincidae) nd the anguids (Anguidae), demonstrate tendency for their legs to become smaller nd many species have lost them altogether. eglessness has therefore evolved indepen-ently in several unrelated lizard families nd is likely to have occurred several more mes during the course of evolution. Snakes re thought to be derived from such a family f lizards, although the actual link is un-nown. Current scientific opinion favours lineage that includes the monitor lizards Varanidae) as the one from which snakes volved, although there are several possible lternatives. (As it happens, there are cur-ently no legless monitors but this does not xclude the possibility that they existed at ome time in the past.)

If we assume that all snakes arose from a ommon ancestor, it should be possible, in n ideal world, to work back, through the ossil record, and develop a 'pedigree chart' nowing the relationship between all the pecies and their ancestors. Unfortunately, ie fossil record, owing to its chancy and idiscriminate nature, is far too incomplete o enable this type of analysis to take place nd so the results of much careful research re, very often, inconclusive.

A number of different characteristics re used to classify snakes. These include eneral morphology; the arrangement of ones in the skull and other parts of the keleton, especially the presence or absence f a pelvic girdle, of hypapophyses (spike-ke projections pointing downwards from ie vertebrae), or of a coronoid bone (a small one in the lower jaw); the structure of ie hemipenes (the paired copulatory organs f male snakes) and microscopic and bio-hemical material such as the chromosome rrangement (karyotype) and protein analy-es. Obviously, only a very small proportion

of these tools is available to palaeontologists.

Most fossil snake material consists of vertebrae. Although the structures of verte-brae may differ between groups of snakes, it is rarely possible to distinguish between closely related forms from this type of material alone. Fossil skulls are more useful and are found from time to time but, even so, the absence of soft parts of extinct snakes will always make their relationships with living forms open to debate. Other problems include the small size, and therefore delicate

bones, of some of the more primitive snakes, such as the blind snakes and thread snakes which, though undoubtedly present in ancient times, rarely show up in the fossil record.

From what we do know, it seems that snakes first appeared between 100 and 150 million years ago, during the early Creta-ceous period. Between then and now, they evolved into the 2,400 or so species currently recognized as well as an inestimable number of other forms that became extinct in the mean time.

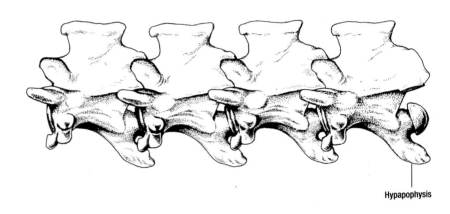

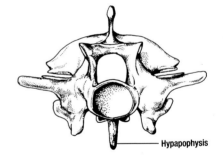

▶ The presence or absence of hypapophyses, especially in the lumbar region of the spine, is used as one of many diagnostic characters when classifying snakes. In some species, notably the egg eaters, *Dasypeltis*, which use them to saw through egg shells, these structures are enlarged.

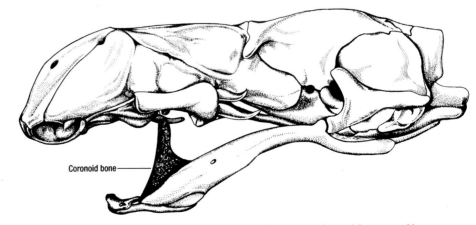

▲ The shape and size of the coronoid bone is subject to much variation, being quite large in primitive snakes such as the worm snakes and thread snakes and becoming progressively smaller, or absent altogether, in the more advanced snakes.

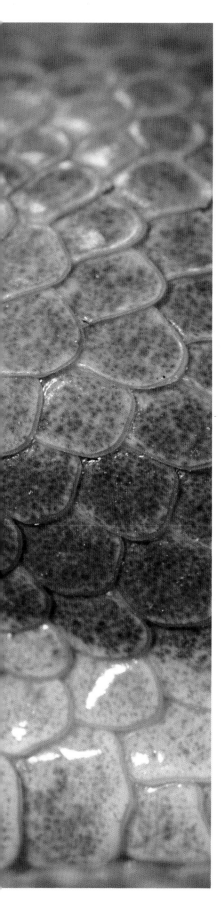

The earliest known snake is *Lapparentophis defrennei*. It shows no link with earlier snake-like reptiles and so its origin is a mystery at present. Its fossils have been found in what is now North Africa and it was a terrestrial snake. The next oldest remains are those of a marine species, *Simoliophis*, found in areas of Europe and North Africa that previously formed part of the sea bed. This species first appeared at the beginning of the late Cretaceous period (100 million years ago). By the end of the Cretaceous period (65 million years ago), however, the families to which *Lapparentophis* and *Simoliophis* belonged had already become extinct, but many more snakes had evolved, including representatives of at least two more families that later became extinct and at least two

◄ All snakes lack eyelids. Instead, they have a single transparent scale, known as the brille, covering each eye and the outer layer of this is shed with the rest of the epidermis.

▼ The members of certain primitive families of snakes retain vestiges of the pelvic girdle. In boas and pythons, and a few other groups, its presence is associated with small claws or spurs located on either side of the vent. Male boas and pythons use their spurs, which are often longer than those of females, to stimulate the females during courtship.

that still survive (the pipe snakes, Aniliidae, and the boas, Boidae). Fossil snakes from this era have been found in most parts of the world, showing that, by the time the dinosaurs became extinct, snakes had already diversified and become widespread.

After the Cretaceous period, snakes were in the ascendant: at least seven families were present, including the boas, which appear to have reached the peak of their speciation around this time and formed perhaps the dominant family. Colubrid snakes, which make up by far the largest number of species today, did not appear until the end of the Eocene period or the beginning of the Oligocene (36 million years ago) and began to diversify rapidly into numerous species during the Miocene period (22.5 to 5.5 million years ago). Their diversification coincided with the disappearance of several of the more ancient lineages of snakes, perhaps because the latter were unable to compete with the better adapted species that were evolving. The number of boids was also reduced at this time. Also appearing during the Miocene period were representatives of two other important families, the Viperidae (vipers) and the Elapidae (cobras and their relatives) and a smaller family, the Acrochordidae (file snakes).

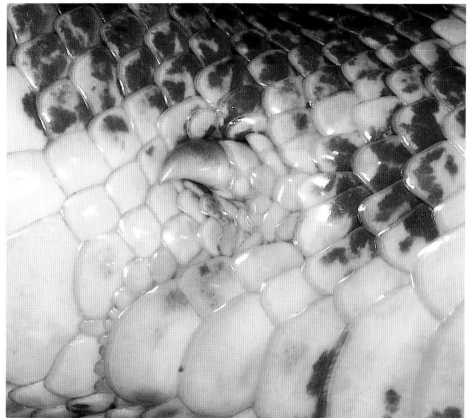

MODERN SNAKE CLASSIFICATION

The snakes living today, then, owe their existence to a rather complicated history of evolution, speciation and extinction going back over 100 million years. During that time, the shape of the land has changed out of all recognition. The present distribution of the surviving families is dependent, to some extent, on the time at which they evolved; old families tend to have a world-wide distribution whereas newer families have often failed to reach parts of the world that became isolated as a result of the break-ing up of the landmass, a process that had already begun when they first put in an appearance and continues to this day. Chapter 4 deals in more detail with the global distribution of snakes.

The classification of surviving snakes, though strongly linked to, and dependent upon, their evolution, is somewhat easier than that of extinct snakes. It is not straight-forward, however, because many species are imperfectly known whereas others seem to have conflicting characteristics, making it difficult to assign them to one family or another. Again, different degrees of impor-tance are assigned to various characteristics by different researchers. Many arrangements have therefore been put forward over the years, some of them differing only slightly from previous classifications while others are more revolutionary.

There are generally accepted to be 14 or 15 families of snakes but the 2,400 species are by no means equally divided between them. Two families contain only one species each, one contains two species while another contains three. On the other hand, the largest family, the Colubridae, which has no accepted common name, has, at present, over 1,500 species assigned to it. This family is most certainly derived from a number of ancestral lines and future research will undoubtedly divide it into a number of smaller families. At present, it is divided into subfamilies, some of which are better defined than others. A more thorough breakdown of the families and their genera is given in Chapter 10.

A major division is made between some very primitive snakes and the more advanced species. The most primitive species make up the families Anomalepididae, Typhlopidae and Leptotyphlopidae, which are composed entirely of small burrowing snakes with rudimentary eyes and smooth, shiny scales. They differ so widely from all other snakes that they are grouped together in an infra-order called the Scolecophidia. They feed mainly on the larvae and eggs of termites and ants and their jaws are not capable of

the same degree of extension as those of other snakes. Furthermore, they have few teeth, sometimes having none on the upper jaw or on the lower jaw, depending on which family is in question.

All other families of snakes are grouped together in the second infraorder, the Alethinophidia. The arrangement of these more advanced families, in which order they evolved and which are most closely related to which, has not been finally resolved. A few families are constantly moved back-wards and forwards as new evidence and new theories appear. The family Acrochor-didae, or file snakes, is one such enigma. All three species are totally aquatic, living in coastal waters and estuaries. Their scales are totally unlike those of other snakes and they have several other peculiarities that may be due to their ancestry but which may just as well be the results of their unusual life-style. Similarly, the two families that have one member each (the Loxocemidae and Aniliidae) and the Xeno-peltidae, which has two species, are so unlike other snakes that it is difficult to know quite where they fit into the evolu-tionary scheme. *Loxocemus* was thought for a long time to belong with the pythons, although being Mexican in origin it would be the only species in the group to be found outside the Old World. Other authorities consider it more closely related to another 'odd-ball', *Xenopeltis unicolor*, from south-east Asia, which it superficially resembles and it has been placed within the Xeno-peltidae at various times. The third single-member family is the Aniliidae. Its only member, *Anilius scytale*, comes from South America but it also bears a superficial resemblance to species in south-east Asia and it was for many years included with them in the Uropeltidae. The Uropeltidae, as now recognized, is confined to a group of burrowing snakes including the pipe snakes and the shield-tailed snakes.

We are much more familiar with members of the Boidae than with any of the snakes mentioned so far. In its broader sense, this family includes all the giant snakes – boas, pythons, anacondas and so on – as well as a number of small to medium-sized species. There is a case for regarding the pythons as a separate family, the Pythonidae, but a more conservative approach is to place the pythons in a subfamily of the Boidae. The West Indian 'boas' have now been accepted as constituting a separate family, the Tropidopheidae. Boas are found in North, Central and South America and on

the island of Madagascar, the pythons i Africa, south-east Asia and Australia. Th West Indian boas are, as may be expecte restricted to the Caribbean region. An impo tant difference between the boas and pytho is that the former give birth to live youn whereas the latter lay eggs. Some boas an pythons (but not West Indian boas) hav heat-sensitive organs situated around the upper and lower jaws. These help the to detect warm-blooded prey even in tot darkness.

All other snakes are regarded as mo recently evolved; they do not possess hin limb girdles as do the families dealt wit so far, nor do they have a coronoid bon They include the burrowing asps, Atract spididae, a small family of venomous, bu rowing snakes restricted to Africa and th Middle East, some members of which hav enormous fangs at the front of their upp jaws but few other teeth. Although former thought to be vipers, they are now regarde by most authorities as a separate fami and are highly adapted to living and feedin below ground. (Some herpetologists, how ever, consider that the burrowing asps a highly adapted colubrids and place the in the subfamily Atractaspidinae.)

The Colubridae is, by far, the largest fami of living snakes. Its 1,500 or so species hav moved into almost every possible ecologic niche and diversified accordingly. Only i Australia are its members not the dominar component of the snake fauna. Colubri are found in trees, on the ground, beneat the ground and in the water (althoug there are no exclusively marine species Colubrid snakes are typical in having mo or less slender, elongated bodies, larg scales covering their heads and large eye A wide variety of food is taken by the variou species, some specializing in certain pre e.g. snails, eggs, etc., while others are gene alists and eat almost anything small enoug to be swallowed. A number of species a venomous but their methods of deliverin the venom are not as well developed as the cobras or the vipers; only a few a dangerous to man. Their reproductive habi are also varied, with some species layin eggs and others giving birth to live young

The cobras and their relatives are place in the family Elapidae. This is usually take to include the sea snakes, kraits, mamba coral snakes and a host of Australian speci that have evolved to fill all the niches ma available by the scarcity of colubrids ar the lack of vipers on that continent. Elapic are the main family of snakes in Australi

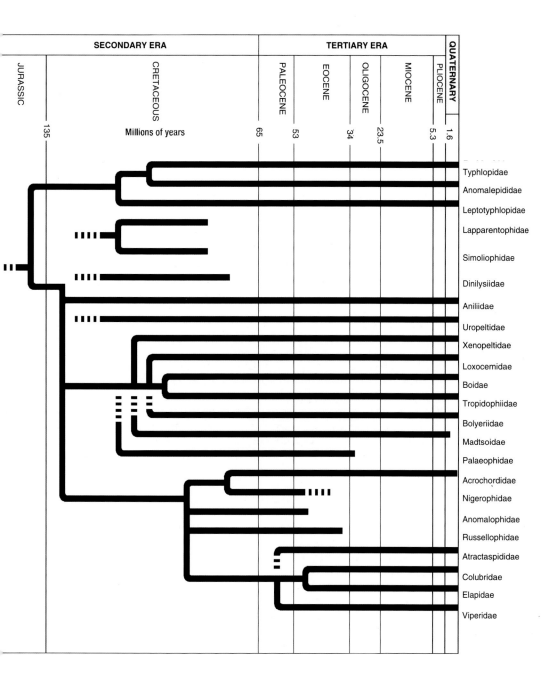

	SECONDARY ERA			TERTIARY ERA				QUATERNARY

JURASSIC	CRETACEOUS	PALEOCENE	EOCENE	OLIGOCENE	MIOCENE	PLIOCENE	QUATERNARY
135	Millions of years	65	53	34	23.5	5.3	1.6

Typhlopidae

Anomalepididae

Leptotyphlopidae

Lapparentophidae

Simoliophidae

Dinilysiidae

Aniliidae

Uropeltidae

Xenopeltidae

Loxocemidae

Boidae

Tropidophiidae

Bolyeriidae

Madtsoidae

Palaeophidae

Acrochordidae

Nigerophidae

Anomalophidae

Russellophidae

Atractaspididae

Colubridae

Elapidae

Viperidae

◀ A 'family tree' of the living and extinct families of snakes, showing the approximate time of their appearance in the fossil record and their relationships to one another. Some relationships are vague and these are shown by broken lines.

hich has the dubious honour of being habited by more venomous snakes than armless ones (although not all of them re dangerous to man). The cobra family characterized by hollow venom fangs xed at the front of their upper jaws and pecialized ducts that carry the venom from e venom glands to the tip of the fangs. obras may be aquatic, terrestrial, burrowg or climbing in habit and may lay eggs or ve birth to live young.

Vipers, Viperidae, are generally regarded as the most advanced snakes in evolutionary terms. They appear to have evolved after the Australian landmass broke away from the rest of the world and so were unable to reach there. Otherwise, they are widespread, and include the most northerly and most southerly occurring snakes as well as the species found at the highest altitude (in the Himalayas). Their fangs are relatively long and are hinged so that they can be

folded away when not in use. One group of vipers, found throughout America and in parts of Asia, evolved a pair of heat-sensitive pits between the eyes and the nostrils and are known as pit vipers. These pits are structurally different from those found in some boas and pythons and have certainly evolved independently. The members of one group of American pit vipers are easily recognizable for another unique characteristic, the rattle on their tails.

2
Morphology and Function

Although snakes are all long, slender animals lacking limbs, external ears and eyelids, there is considerable variation between them, enough in fact for over 2,400 species to be recognized on superficial characteristics alone. Animals of all kinds look the way they do, not by accident, but for a reason. Their size, shape, colours and markings suit them to the tasks they have to perform in order to survive and reproduce. Snakes are no exception.

◀ Most snakes have similar proportions to this American rat snake, *Elaphe obsoleta rossalleni*. This shape is used as the benchmark for a snake of 'normal' proportions throughout this book.

SIZE AND SHAPE

In order to live long enough to pass on their genes, snakes need to achieve certain goals. They must feed so that they can grow to maturity but, at the same time, they must avoid being eaten by other animals. In order to do either of these things, it will be necessary to move around, and so some form of locomotion must be developed – no easy task for an animal without legs. Depending on the habitat they find themselves in, locomotion may involve swimming, climbing or burrowing as well as straightforward crawling across the ground.

If our snake finds enough food and avoids all its predators long enough to reach maturity, it is then faced with the more esoteric problem of finding a member of the same species but of the opposite sex, and achieving a form of sexual union in order to bring spermatazoa and ova together.

All the functions outlined so far are, in a way, behavioural. Feeding, defence, locomotion, reproduction and so on all require the snake to make an action or a sequence of actions.

Other functions take place beneath the skin. Finding, subduing and swallowing prey, for instance, must be followed by digestion and assimilation if it is to have any purpose. Such functions depend on internal anatomy and biochemistry. Physiological and behavioural factors work in concert to allow the snake to function effectively.

These actions, of course, will be made easier if the snake is well equipped at the outset and this in turn depends upon genetic programming. This, then, is how evolution operates – animals that are well equipped tend to survive while those that are not tend not to. Because of this, any feature that helps to enhance an individual's chance of survival will become more common within a population and characteristics that have a negative or neutral effect will gradually disappear. We have to assume that, after thousands of generations, each species has reached a point in its evolution that works well – if it did not, it would have died out. We do not, however, need to assume that each evolutionary line has reached its pinnacle – snakes will probably go on evolving into even more efficient organisms for as long as there is somewhere for them to live.

Our basic assumption, then, is that each species of snake is the size, shape and colour it is because it has arrived at a good (but not necessarily perfect) design. Now we can look in more detail at each facet of that design, bearing in mind the evolutionary principles that control them.

Size and shape, together with colour and markings, help to give each snake its identity. They may also hold important clues to the life-style of the snake because certain habitats and conditions tend to limit or encourage the way in which snakes evolve.

Size

The statistic that is of most interest to the layman is that of length. Few zoological facts are in as much contention as those regarding the lengths of snakes: the exaggerations of fishermen are nothing compared with the stories of 15- and 18-metre-long (50- and 60-foot-long) pythons and boa constrictors reported by what would otherwise be regarded as fairly reliable explorers and biologists of the nineteenth century.

There is no denying that the lengths of snakes are notoriously difficult to estimate. Few of them stretch out straight in order to allow themselves to be measured accurately. Indeed, few of them could be expected to keep still while this was carried out. Portions of large snakes seen slithering away, glimpsed through gaps in the dense vegetation in which they often live, can be misleading, even to careful observers. Snakes that are killed are often too large and heavy to be transported from the place of their death to a place where their size can be measured accurately. In any case, snake carcasses and skins can be stretched by anything up to 20 per cent, perhaps more, either deliberately or inadvertently.

The 'big six'

Altogether, there are six species that may b[e] loosely termed 'giant snakes'. Two of the[se] live in South America, there are anoth[er] two in Asia, while Africa and Australas[ia] have just one each. Tall stories are divide[d] between the species although the two larg[est] snakes found in South America seem t[o] have more than their fair share.

■ The anaconda, *Eunectes murinus*

On the grounds of weight alone, there [is] almost no doubt that the South America[n] anaconda is the world's largest snak[e]. Length seems more important to the recor[d] breakers, however, and it is in this depar[t]ment that controversy occurs.

The largest anaconda ever reported wa[s] 18.9 m long (62 ft) killed by Colonel Perc[y] Fawcett, of the Royal Artillery, in Braz[il] in 1907. This gigantic snake was sho[t] while trying to escape up a riverbank. Ther[e] is considerable doubt surrounding th[e] episode, though, not least because it ha[s] been estimated that a snake of this hug[e] size would be unable to support its ow[n] bulk (although this in itself is inconclusiv[e] because the anaconda is a semi-aquati[c] species that is buoyed up by water whe[n] swimming).

Other gigantic anacondas include on[e] shot in 1910 by Lange along the Jivari Rive[r] in Peru and claimed by him to have measure[d]

▼ The anaconda, *Eunectes murinus*, the largest snake in the world.

6.5 m (54 ft) in length. Another one, reputedly of similar size, was seen, but not killed, by the explorer de Graff in 1927.

A more down-to-earth report concerns a specimen of 37 ft 6 in (11.4 m) in length, shot in Colombia in 1944, and this record was accepted for many years. Like several others, it has been repeated by successive authors, thereby gaining some degree of credibility. This particular specimen was killed by a prospecting party led by a geologist, Roberto Lamon. When the party returned to photograph and skin the snake (having eaten their lunch in the mean time!) they found it had gone. Presumably it had recovered and crawled or swum away. Another record is that of 11.6 m (38 ft), killed by Indians during an expedition by the Brazilian General Rondon (who later lent his name to Rondonia, a large region of Amazonian Brazil).

Reports of specimens in the 9–10.7 m (30–35 ft) size range are more plentiful and include several that cannot be easily dismissed because they have involved scientists whose reputations for reliability are otherwise unchallenged. For instance, a 10.4 m (34 ft) anaconda was shot in British Guiana by Vincent Roth, director of the national museum. Mr R. Mole, a naturalist who made many important contributions to the natural history of Trinidad, reported a 10 m (33 ft) example there in 1924 and Dr F. Medem, from Colombia University, reported a specimen measuring 10.26 m (33 ft 8 in) killed in the Guaviare River.

It is worth noting that, compared with the reticulated python, the anaconda makes a poor captive, being bad tempered and often failing to feed adequately. For this reason it is not so often displayed in zoological gardens, despite its obvious attractions.

The reticulated python, *Python reticulatus*

The reticulated python has a wide range over much of south-east Asia. It could well be the longest snake in the world, although it is much more slender than the anaconda. Strangely, there are far fewer dubious stories concerning the length of this species than the anaconda, and they tend to concentrate more on its appetite for human prey rather than its size.

Oliver mentions a specimen of 10 m (33 ft) that was killed by locals in Celebes and measured accurately by a civil engineer, but there was no evidence. A number of captive specimens have approached 9 m (30 ft), and there are several authenticated reports of reticulated pythons of around the 8.5 m

An easy way of measuring snakes

Measuring snakes presents various problems, not least of which is that of keeping them still. The following method can be used to good effect. First place the snake on a thick pad of foam rubber and gently lay a piece of glass over the foam, trapping the snake. Using a marker pen, draw a line on the glass, starting at the snake's snout and following its midline all the way to the tip of the tail. Now release the snake and return it to the wild (or to its cage).

You can measure the length of the line in one of two ways: either use one of the small gadgets sold for measuring distances on maps or, if this is not available, lay a piece of string along the line and measure it after it has been straightened out again.

The advantages of using this 'squeeze box' method are twofold. Firstly, the snake will not have been stretched, as sometimes happens when attempting to straighten out a snake and, secondly, the snake is less likely to be stressed. If the snake is a poisonous or bad-tempered individual, the operator is also less likely to be stressed! Unfortunately, although the method works well with the great majority of species, it can only be used with medium-sized snakes, up to 1 m or 1.5 m (4 or 5 ft) in length.

Snakes that have been photographed in the field can be measured without using a squeeze box. Photograph the snake alongside an object of known length – a ruler, field guide, etc., then release the snake. If you are using slide film, project the processed transparency on to a large piece of board or paper, moving it backwards and forwards until the object of known length is the correct size. Now draw a line along the length of the snake, on the paper. Measure in the same way as the line on the squeeze box. If you are using print film you will have to compare the length of the object to its image on the film and correct for scale after you have measured the snake (or project the negative).

The shed skins of snakes should not be used to obtain a measurement as they will be, on average, 10 per cent longer than the snake they came from. A series of skins from the same snake as it grows, together with the dates on which the snake produced them, can provide a good indication of its growth rate, however, and makes an interesting project for young snake keepers.

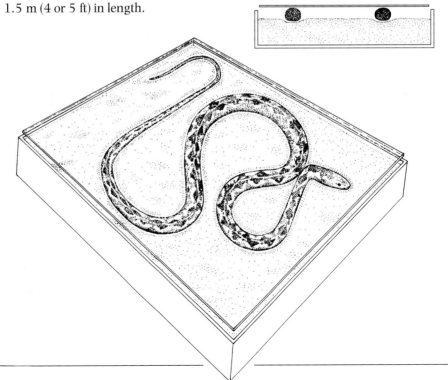

▲ The reticulated python, *Python reticulatus*, the longest snake and the largest Old World species.

► The Indian python, *Python molurus*, may grow to almost 6 m (20 ft).

include a specimen in the collection of the Bombay Natural History Society measuring 5.84 m (19 ft 2 in) and weighing 90.7 kg (200 lb), shot by the Maharajah of Cooch Behar in Assam, and two of 5.8 m (19 ft) shot in Sri Lanka. Other, slightly less easily verified, accounts mention specimens of 6.7 m (22 ft) and 7.6 m (25 ft) although there is always the danger, when dealing with this species, that confusion between it and the reticulated python may occur as they share parts of their respective ranges.

■ The African python, *Python sebae*

The African python, sometimes also known as the rock python, is the only really large snake present on the African continent. Although its size has been stated as 7.6 m (25 ft), FitzSimons in his *Snakes of Southern Africa*[2] states that '. . . it is most unusual nowadays to find a snake exceeding 20 feet [6.1 m], while the average length of adults can be put at 13 to 15 feet [4–4.6 m] . . .' He goes on to record that 4.6–4.9 m (15–16 ft) captive specimens can weigh up to 54.4 kg (120 lb).

(28 ft) mark. These include a live specimen of that size in the possession of an animal dealer, John Hagenbeck, in 1905, reported by Colonel Frank Wall in his book *Snakes of Ceylon*.[1] This snake weighed 113.4 kg (250 lb). Another one, measuring 7.6 m (25 ft) and weighing 138.3 kg (305 lb) was the largest snake ever displayed at the National Zoo, Washington, and is now in the United States National Museum. The discrepancy between the weights of this and the Hagenbeck specimen could easily be accounted for by the relative condition of the two snakes or by sexual dimorphism, female snakes normally being bulkier than males of a similar length.

■ The Indian python, *Python molurus*

This species occurs in two forms, *Python molurus molurus* and *P. m. bivittatus*, the latter sometimes referred to as the Burmese python. A third form, *P. m. pimbura*, is restricted to the island of Sri Lanka (formerly Ceylon) although it is not always recognized as a distinct subspecies. It seems that any of the three forms can grow into giants and, although the average adult size for this species is probably around 3.7 m (12 ft), there are a number of reliable records giving details of specimens approaching 6 m (20 ft).

For instance, Wall, in the book mentioned above, states that 'specimens of 18 feet [5.5 m] are not very uncommon . . .', and goes on to list several well-documented specimens exceeding this size, from the Indian mainland and from Sri Lanka. These

▼ The African python, *Python sebae*, is the largest African snake.

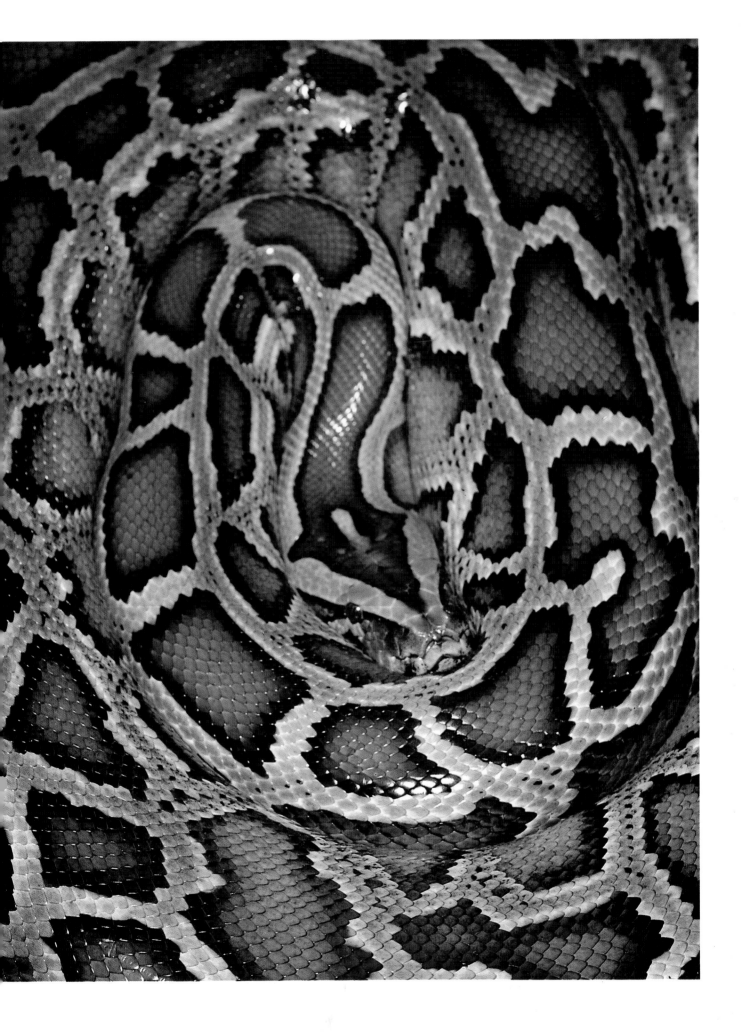

■ The amethystine, or scrub python, *Morelia amethistina*

This Australasian species presents something of an enigma. Although adults average only 3–3.7 m (10–12 ft) or less, there are a few reports of specimens far exceeding this size. These include one of 8.5 m (28 ft) killed at Greenhill, Cairns and measured by L. Robichaux in 1948. This snake was reported by Worrell,[3] while another, more modest one, of 7.2 m (23 ft 8 in), was measured by S. Dean and reported by Pope.[4] Since these records were made, a new species of giant python, the Oenpelli python, *Morelia oenpelliensis*, has been describ[e]d from Arnhem Land, Australia, to further a[dd] to the confusion.

▼ The amethystine python, *Morelia amethistina*, from New Guinea and Australia, where it is the largest snake.

■ The common boa, *Boa constrictor*

The common boa is not, and never has bee[n] regarded as the largest species of sna[ke] except by the most uninformed section [of] the public. At the same time, no oth[er] snake has captured the public imaginati[on] to quite the same extent, and the tales [of] returning nineteenth-century explore[rs] were considered incomplete unless th[ey] included an account of a close encount[er] with one of these gigantic serpents.

Just how big *does* the 'boa constrict[or]' grow? Until recently, the record size of t[he] species was widely accepted as being 5.64 [m] (18 ft 6 in). This length was attributed [to] a specimen killed in Trinidad sometim[e] during the Second World War by a malar[ia] control work party under the command [of] a Mr Colin Pittendrigh. Unfortunately, a[nd] as is so often the case, the carcass of t[he] huge snake could not be preserved und[er] the prevailing conditions, although t[he] record was widely accepted and reporte[d] initially by Oliver[5] and, subsequently, [by] many more authors.

In a recent article, Hans Boos, a notab[le] Trinidadian herpetologist, has thrown lig[ht] on this episode, and casts some dou[bt] not on the size of the snake killed by [Mr] Pittendrigh, but on its identification.[6] [It] appears that Mr Pittendrigh had exclud[ed] the possibility that this snake was a[n] anaconda, *Eunectes murinus*, on the groun[ds] of inappropriate habitat. Hans Boos h[as] found a number of anacondas near to whe[re] the Pittendrigh snake was killed. Furthe[r]more, eyewitnesses have given retrospecti[ve] descriptions that seem to be more in keepi[ng] with the coloration of the anaconda.

On balance, then, it would appear th[at] the snake in question could well have be[en] a large anaconda rather than a commo[n] boa. This likelihood is made all the mo[re] feasible when it is considered that the ne[xt] largest boa constrictor found on the islan[d] measured only 3.35 m (11 ft) (and wou[ld] therefore have weighed probably less tha[n] half Pittendrigh's specimen) whereas o[n] the adjacent mainland (Venezuela) t[he] maximum recorded size, given by Ro[ze] (1966),[7] is 4.2 m: this translates to just ov[er] 13½ ft, a mere bootlace compared with a[ny] of the other 'big six'. Only one other reco[rd] is larger than this (disregarding all t[he] reports that can probably be traced ba[ck] to the Trinidadian specimen) and this is o[ne]

The common boa, *Boa constrictor*, is fairly well ~~~wn the league table of giants, rarely exceeding a ~~~ngth of 4 m (13 ft) and usually remaining ~~~bstantially shorter than this.

~ 4.5 m (just over 14½ ft), given by Amaral ~ the maximum size the species attains in ~azil.[8]

~~~everal conclusions can be drawn from ~~~ese varied and scattered records concern-~~~g large snakes. Firstly, it appears that, as ~~~pected, many of the reports concerning ~~~e largest specimens are unsubstantiated ~~~nd fail to stand up to careful scrutiny. This ~~~uch is to be expected, human nature ~~~eing what it is. Furthermore, all these large ~~~ecies, with the exception of the amethy-~ine python, are bulky animals, with a ~~~oportionately large girth compared with ~~~her, more familiar species. A coiled snake, ~ith a girth the size of a man's thigh, for ~~~stance, could quite easily be estimated to ~~~easure ten metres or more when in reality

it may measure less than six, especially if it is a gravid female or an individual that has recently fed.

A slightly worrying aspect is the amount of time that has elapsed since any very large snakes have been reported. Recent books and articles have been unable to improve on records provided by authors such as Wall and Oliver: their statistics are often repeated, but rarely exceeded, by later authors. Does this mean that snake slayers of today are more honest or more careful in their measurements, or have all the large snakes disappeared during the last 50 years or so? The truth is probably a combination of both. Early observers from uncharted jungles had nothing much on which to base their reports, so a large snake may just as well have measured 18 m (60 ft) as 9 m (30 ft) if its body was not available for in-spection.

On the other hand, some of the more reli-able records of the first half of this century still stand. Authors such as FitzSimons state

that 'it is most unusual *nowadays* to find snakes exceeding 20 feet [6.1 m]', suggesting that at one time snakes of this size may have been more commonplace. There can be no doubt that human pressures act in several ways against the chances of snakes reaching large sizes. Mainly, there are fewer remote areas left. Snakes encountered during the course of road building, prospecting or other pioneering activities are likely to be killed on sight, preventing them from reaching their full size – and, of course, the bigger they are, the less chance that they will escape notice.

It may be, then, that we will never see wild snakes the like of those killed by Fawcett, Lange, Lamon, and the Maharajah of Cooch Behar (even allowing for any exaggerations they may have made).

It does seem likely, though, that a captive snake will eventually reach the 9 m (30 ft) target. As conditions in zoos and private collections have improved, the maximum sizes of several of the smaller species of snakes have been easily exceeded by captive specimens. This probably stems from a better and more reliable feeding regime coupled with protection from natural diseases, parasites and predators.

Costs and benefits of large size

Being large confers a number of advantages, not least the ability to avoid predation and to eat a wider variety of prey. At the same time, large snakes need to eat more than small ones. Even though snakes can survive on remarkably small amounts of food, finding enough prey to keep a 130 kg (300 lb) body and soul together is no easy task, especially for an animal that is not very mobile and must, to a great extent, sit and wait for its meals to come blundering by. Large snakes, then, must live in areas where suitable food is relatively abundant.

In addition, their large bodies take longer to warm up than small ones and, being cold-blooded, they cannot become active unless their body temperature is raised to a suitable level. For this reason, they are restricted to warm parts of the world. In practice, the regions where both these requirements are met fall within the tropics. Here, the ambient temperature is suitable and there is a reasonable chance of finding food every few days.

Of our 'big six', the anaconda and the reticulated python are more or less restricted to tropical rainforest regions. The Indian python is also largely a forest species although it may also be found in open country, especially around farms and villages. The huge distribution of the boa constrictor falls

mainly within rainforest, in South and Central America, but it does range north into the semi-desert thorn scrub habitat in parts of northern Mexico. The African python and the amethystine python are generalists. They may be found in grasslands, scrub, along river courses and in forests.

The 'dwarfs'

Going to the other extreme, the smallest species of snake measures about 10 cm (4 in) and belongs to the family Typhlopidae, or blind snakes. It is hard to say exactly which species of blind snake is the smallest because several are about the same size and, in any case, it would be difficult to know if

▲ The tropical Central and South American snakes belonging to the genus *Imantodes* are among the most slender species: this is *I. lentifera*

any of the measured animals were full grown when they were measured – blind snakes are secretive, burrowing snakes of which only a tiny proportion of each specie is likely to be available for sampling. There are many other species of snake in the 10–30 cm (4–12 in) size range.

Shape

Just as snakes vary in size, so they vary in shape. Compared to most other animals, all are long and thin of course, but some are longer and thinner than others. There some degree of correlation with habitat here as arboreal species tend to be more slender and have longer tails, and are therefore lighter relative to their length. Example include the long-nosed tree snake, *Ahaetull nasuta*, the twig or bird snake, *Thelotorn capensis* and, especially, the blunt-headed tree snake, *Imantodes cenchoa* and its relatives. The two arboreal boids, *Corallus canin* and *Chondropython viridis*, may not seem to fit into this pattern, being more stoutly built than most arboreal snakes, until they are compared with the other boids, when it will be seen that they have evolved fair way towards the long-and-slender

◄ A thread snake, *Leptotyphlops dulcis*, from Texas. All thread and blind snakes are diminutive the smallest snake belongs to one of these families but its exact identity is difficult to establish because some are known only from a few specimens.

ndition. Certain terrestrial species are so long and slender. These include the tive, fast-moving hunters, often diurnal ecies such as the whipsnakes, *Coluber* and *asticophis*, and the sand snakes, *Psammophis*. her terrestrial species may be short and out, however. These consist of the sit-d-wait predators such as several vipers, tably the Gaboon viper and puff adder, *tis gabonica* and *Bitis arietans*, some ustralian elapids, especially the death ders, *Acanthophis* species, and three pythons, *jthon regius*, *P. anchietae* and, most notably, *curtus*, the blood or short-tailed python, hich may be the world's chunkiest snake.

There is also variation in the shape of akes' cross-sections. Burrowing snakes nd to be cylindrical whereas terrestrial ecies are more or less flattened on their ntral surface – this gives them an creased area over which to grip and push ainst the ground when they move. rboreal snakes, apart from being slender, ay be flattened from side to side (e.g. *rallus*), as are aquatic species, especially e most highly adapted forms such as the a snakes. A few species, such as the African e snakes, *Mehelya* species, the kraits, *ungarus* species and, to a lesser extent, the merican indigo snake, *Drymarchon corais*, e triangular in cross-section with their rsal midline forming a prominent ridge ong the length of their bodies. The purpose this shape is unknown.

▼ Variations in the cross-sectional shapes of snakes: (a) cylindrical, as found in many burrowing and semi-burrowing species; (b) triangular, a shape whose function is uncertain but which is found in several widely separated species such as the African file snakes, *Mehelya* and the American indigo snake, *Drymarchon corais*; (c) dorsally flattened, a shaped found in many heavy-bodied species, such as the larger vipers, and which is often exaggerated when these and other species bask; (d) laterally flattened, as found in many arboreal snakes, such as the tree boas, *Corallus*, and others, and also in aquatic species such as the sea snakes.

▲ Heavy-bodied snakes are found mainly among the vipers, boas and pythons. This example is a Pacific boa, *Candoia aspera*, the thickest of a trio of closely related species.

(a)

(b)

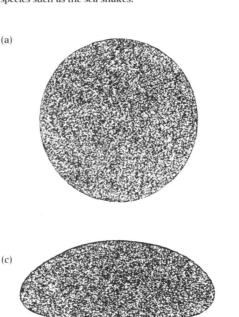

(c)

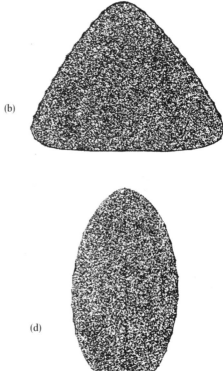

(d)

COLOUR

Snakes come in just about every colour. Some species, such as the North American green snakes, *Opheodryas*, are uniform in their coloration whereas the pattern of others, such as the Gaboon viper, *Bitis gabonica*, are almost unbelievably intricate. Many diurnal snakes are striped, whereas nocturnal or crepuscular species tend to be banded. Some vary from one individual to another, even when they are from the same clutch of eggs, and a few start off one colour and then change as they grow. These colour schemes, convenient though they are for identification, are not there for the benefit of herpetologists. Each has a role to play in helping the snake to survive. Furthermore, their role in survival may be primarily defensive, as in camouflage, or physiological, in increasing the absorption of heat or protecting vital organs from excessive radiation.

▶ Snakes' scales are often highly iridescent, as in the aptly named sunbeam snake, *Xenopeltis unicolor*, from south-east Asia.

▼ Another brilliantly iridescent species is the rainbow boa, from South America; this is the Brazilian subspecies, *Epicrates cenchria cenchria*.

w colour is produced

lours, as we perceive them, may be used in three different ways. Two of them are due to structural factors – the physical properties of the surface – and the other due to pigments in the scales and is therefore chemical in nature. The cells that are responsible for colours are known collectively as chromatophores.

ments

mentary colour is caused by groups of chromatophores containing coloured chemicals, situated within the scales. They are mainly at the junction of the dermis and the epidermis. This is the most familiar form of coloration and gives a wide range of hues. A number of different pigments have been isolated from snakes, some more commonly than others. Melanin is almost universal in occurrence and gives rise to several different colours: black or dark brown (eumelanin), light brown and yellow (phaeomelanin), or grey. The cells containing melanin (melanophores) are irregularly branched, with arms reaching out in all directions. The arms of one melanophore will overlap with those of many of its neighbours, forming a complicated matrix. The pigment itself is in the form of granules and these may be spread throughout each cell, in which case the area will appear dark, or concentrated towards the centre of each cell, in which case the area will appear light. Other pigments may be present: some yellows, reds and oranges are produced by carotenoids, and white is produced by guanine, a pigment that is a metabolic by-product. Combinations of different pigments can clearly give an almost infinite palette of shades and hues.

terference colour (iridescence)

descence is a feature of many species. It is not caused by pigments but by the physical properties of light. The outer layer of a snake's scale is thin and transparent. When light strikes it from an angle, it is split into its spectral components and each wavelength produces a different colour. Depending on the nature of the surface, and of the underlying colours, this produces an iridescent effect. As the snake moves (or as the observer's position moves) the colours appear to change. All snakes with smooth scales are, to some extent, iridescent, but some are more so than others. Iridescence is most noticeable in black or dark coloured snakes. The species that are best known for this type of coloration include the Asian

sunbeam snake, *Xenopeltis unicolor*, the rainbow boa, *Epicrates cenchria*, and several other boids.

Tyndall scattering

This type of coloration is quite common throughout the animal kingdom. It owes its effect to the scattering of light by small particles, known as iridophores. These consist of stacks of purine crystals embedded in cells, which reflect and refract light in a particular way. Short wavelengths of light, at the blue end of the spectrum, are affected more than the others and so the colour produced is blue. (The sky appears blue for exactly the same reason.) In certain species of snakes, a layer of cells containing small reflecting particles is found well below the surface of the scales. If the effect they produced worked alone, the snake would be blue and there are a few blue snakes, notably among the South American pit vipers belonging to the genera *Bothriopsis* and *Bothriechis*. Usually, however, the blue effect is combined with a layer of yellow chromatophores, known specifically as xanthophores. These cells overlie the cells containing the iridophores and, together, they produce green (holding a piece of yellow cellophane up to the blue sky produces exactly the same effect). Green is a much more common colour in snakes than blue because it helps to camouflage those snakes that live among vegetation. Green snakes are found in many families and many parts of the world and include the emerald boa, *Corallus canina*, the green

tree python, *Chondropython viridis*, several arboreal pit vipers, such as *Trimeresurus* species and a great many colubrids, mainly arboreal species.

Patterns of snakes

Although some snakes are uniform in colour, many have markings consisting of spots, blotches, stripes and bands of different colours or shades. These are created by different patches of scales taking on the various colours and can be caused by groupings of different pigments. This is most easily understood by studying the coloration of the many colour mutants that are widely bred in captivity. In amelanistic corn snakes, for instance, the black pigment is missing and the full red areas can be easily seen. Furthermore, the red saddles on the back of these snakes are much brighter than they are on normally coloured individuals because the red areas are usually overlain with a diffuse layer of black pigment (melanin). In anerythristic individuals, on the other hand, it is the red pigment that is missing and the extent of the black areas can be better appreciated. To take just one more example, the albino form of the black ratsnake, *Elaphe obsoleta obsoleta*, retains light red or pink blotches along its back, even though normal adults are plain black; this is evidence that the black pigment, melanin, does not replace

▼ Where mutations occur, a variety of colour variants are possible. In this example, a black rat snake, *Elaphe obsoleta obsoleta*, all the black pigment is lacking, leaving only the underlying light red pigment that would normally be masked.

► The colour patterns of snakes are made up of a mosaic of pigments, some of which are not obvious. Here, small spots of black pigment, melanin, are distributed locally on the otherwise pale green scales of an emerald boa, *Corallus caninus*. This gives the appearance of darker green areas surrounding the white dorsal markings.

other pigments as the snake matures but obscures them.

The patterns of many species need not only be caused by a combination of pigmentary colours but can result from structural and pigmentary coloration. Many species have a superimposed iridescent sheen overlying their deeper, more solid colours, and even in uniformly coloured snakes, such as the green species referred to above, the exact shade of green varies according to how much or how little melanin overlies the iridophores and xanthophores.

Genetic control of colour

Colour, like other characteristics, is under the control of genes. These behave in the usual Mendelian fashion, whereby a gene may be dominant or recessive and the quota of dominant and recessive genes will control the colour. This applies to cases where species exist in more than one colour form as well as to artificially selected mutant strains. When a normally coloured snake is carrying a recessive gene for amelanism, for instance, its condition is known as heterozygous. There is no way of telling, superficially, that it carries the mutant gene because that gene's opposite number is normal. An amelanistic snake, on the other hand, must carry two mutant recessive genes (otherwise it would not look amelanistic).

Genes programme for the formation of xanthophores as well as pigments. Since the xanthophores change the blue coloration to green by filtering the light coming back from iridophores, the absence of xanthophores results in blue snakes. These are not common but have been recorded for at least two species, the green python, *Chondropython viridis*, and the eastern diamondback rattlesnake, *Crotalus adamanteus*.

Colour changes

Snakes may change their colours in two ways. A few species are capable of limited colour change throughout a fairly short period of time. This aspect is not very well documented but a few examples can be mentioned. A small form of common boa, popularly known as the Hog Island boa, can

change the tone of its coloration quite significantly. This usually occurs at night when the snake becomes paler, with a more washed-out pattern. A similar situation exists in the Oenpelli python from northern Australia, which is brown during the day and pale silvery grey at night. The Round island boa, *Casarea dussumieri*, the Pacific boa, *Candoia carinata*, and several of the small West Indian *Tropidophis* species are also capable of limited colour change, always from dark during the day to light at night.

Another example of colour change, but on a different time scale, is that of the female Madagascan tree boa, *Sanzinia madagascariensis*, in which females become noticeably darker when they are pregnant, presumably to optimize the absorption of radiation and thus speed up the development of their embryos. In a similar vein, there is some evidence that other species of snakes become darker during cooler weather, including the Australian taipan, *Oxyuranus*, and the brownsnakes, *Pseudonaja*, also from Australia. All these examples concern dark or light coloration and therefore melanin is the pigment involved. It can be surmised, then, that the colour changes are brought about by melanin granules being mobilized within the melanophores, as is the case with animals in other groups that are well known for colour changes, such as cha eleons, fishes and cephalopods.

Colour change on a longer time scale is rather better known. There are a great many species in which the juveniles are differently coloured or marked from adults of the same species. In its simplest form this transition involves an overall darken-

ing of the colours. The milksnakes, *Lampr peltis triangulum*, are good examples, whe the brightly coloured hatchlings gradua become duller as they grow, and th eventually turn almost uniform black some subspecies, for example in *L. andesiana*. Here, melanin production mu continue throughout the life of the snak gradually suffusing its surface with blac and obscuring the underlying pattern. T various subspecies of the North America rat snakes, *Elaphe obsoleta*, also under colour changes as they mature. All su species start off grey or light tan with number of darker saddles running alor the length of their backs. As they gro the saddles become less obvious and eve tually fade altogether. Depending on t subspecies, other markings may devel and the overall coloration may chang The one exception is the grey rat snake, *E. spiloides*, in which the saddles are retain throughout the life of the snake and t colour and markings of juveniles are mu the same as those of the adults. Oth rat snakes, including a European specie *E. quatuorlineata*, also undergo changes which juveniles are blotched but adu are uniformly coloured or striped.

There are several other, more drama examples of colour change. The best kno are those of the emerald tree boa, *Corall caninus*, and the green tree python, *Chond python viridis*. These two species show remarkable degree of convergence in th appearance and behaviour (a topic discuss in more detail elsewhere) and even exte this to colour change. Both species are brig green as adults but juvenile pythons a usually bright sulphur yellow, occasiona

ck red or brown, whereas juvenile
erald boas are usually orange but may
o be yellow or brown. The change in
pearance usually occurs quite quickly,
ually within the first year, and is presum-
ly the result of the production of new
gments due to unknown triggers. Juvenile
adagascan tree boas, *Sanzinia madagas-
riensis*, are also red at birth and change
the normal greenish coloration before
ey reach one year of age. No totally satis-

factory explanation has been proposed
for this remarkable convergence, involving
as it does species from South America,
Australasia and Madagascar. Each of the
species concerned is arboreal, but each is
rather bulkier than most other arboreal
snakes. The most likely explanation is
that the colour change corresponds to a
change in habit, with young snakes perhaps
occupying different positions within the
forest canopy.

**Natural populations with aberrant
coloration**

Because coloration is under genetic control,
it is always possible that mutations will
arise. Under normal circumstances, these
would soon fall prey to predators and the
frequency of such mutant genes would be
kept at a low level within populations. In
certain situations, however, the mutation
can provide a benefit that outweighs the
disadvantages.

Producing normal offspring from albino parents

Although colour is controlled by genes,
here need not be a single gene
controlling each colour: in fact, this is
almost never the case. Pigments such
as melanin are the end result of a
chain of biochemical steps in which
here are several intermediate products. Chemicals act on each of these
intermediate products in turn,
transforming them to the next product
in the chain. Genetic defects can affect
any of the steps in the chain.
Amelanism, for example, can be caused
in several ways, with the process being
blocked at one of several stages. So, if
we take two amelanistic snakes that
have different defective genes and
breed them together, the resultant
offspring will be normal.

To explain this more easily, let
us assume that a chemical, Y, is
responsible for converting a pigment
precursor, A, to a second precursor,
B. Then a second chemical, Z, is
responsible for converting B to the end
product, pigment C (melanin in our
example). Now, the first snake has the
gene for manufacturing chemical Y but
the gene for producing chemical Z is
defective. The second snake has the
gene for manufacturing chemical Z but
the one for producing chemical Y is

defective. There is a breakdown in the
biochemical pathway in both snakes
and so they appear amelanistic.

If they breed together, however, the
first snake will supply their offspring
with the gene for producing chemical Y
and the second snake will supply them
with the gene for producing chemical Z.
The offspring will have functioning
genes for producing both chemicals and
the biochemical pathway has been

▲ The cornsnake, *Elaphe guttata*, has may
colour varients including albino.

restored – two amelanistic snakes have
bred together to produce normal-
looking offspring.

In 'real life' the pathway will not be
as simple as this: there may be many
steps in the process of producing a
pigment, but the general principle is
the same.

Melanism

Most examples concern melanistic populations, especially of snakes living in abnormally cold conditions. Thus certain populations of some European viper species, including adders, *Vipera berus*, asps, *V. aspis* and Spanish vipers, *V. seoanei*, have a tendency towards melanism, as do some populations of the eastern garter snake, *Thamnophis sirtalis sirtalis*, in several localities around Lake Erie in Ontario, Canada, and elsewhere in the more northern parts of the subspecies' range. All these snakes live in cool regions, either by virtue of their distribution at northerly latitudes or because they inhabit mountains. A similar situation exists within populations of the tiger snake, *Notechis scutatus*, in Tasmania. These snakes show great variation in their colour and markings, but uniform black individuals are more frequent in the cooler west, south-west and montane parts of the island. Black populations, sometimes regarded as a separate species, *N. ater*, also occur on some of the small islands in the Bass Straits. In other cases, melanism has become fixed in variable, or polymorphic, species. These include the eastern hognose snake, *Heterodon platyrhinos*, which may have dark spots on a yellow, brown or reddish background but which also occurs as a plain black form. Similarly, in the aptly named variable kingsnake, *Lampropeltis mexicana thayeri*, there is a variety of colour patterns, one of which is plain black.

Albinism

Albinism is rather more difficult to live with than melanism: whereas melanistic snakes may not be quite as well camouflaged as normally coloured individuals, pure white ones are definitely not. Although the occasional adult albino does crop up, the majority of them must perish long before they reach the stage where they can reproduce and pass on their albino genes. In fact, there is just a single known example of a naturally occurring albino population. This is in Japan, where albino rat snakes, *Elaphe climacophora*, live in and around the city of Iwakuni, along with normally coloured members of the species. The snakes are protected by the Japanese Government as a national monument and a captive breeding programme has been initiated in order to maintain the population of albinos, which were declining.

In captivity, of course, the risks of predation are non-existent and so colour mutations are able to survive, provided they are healthy in other respects. In this way large captive populations of selected colour forms have been built up by snake breeders, and these include strains in which one or more pigment is lacking altogether, e.g. amelanistic (lacking black pigment), anerythristic (lacking red pigment) as well as total albinos, which lack all pigment. Where all the pigment is lacking but the xanthophores are present, the snake will take on a yellowish coloration, as in some strains of pythons.

Other colour variations

Other variations in colour and pattern within a species fall into the categories of polymorphism, where two or more types of coloration are present in a population, and sexual dimorphism, where males and females are differently coloured or marked. These phenomena are dealt with elsewhere under defence (page 125) and sexual dimorphism (page 161).

Snakes' skin is completely covered with scales of various types. The skin and scales together form the integument. This must perform a number of functions.

The skin

Although snakes are covered with scales, part of their integument consists of skin. When the snake's body is distended, after a large meal, for instance, this interstitial skin can be easily seen and, indeed, it is the areas of skin between the scales that give the snake's body its flexibility. Other than this important function, snakes' interstitial skin is unremarkable, except in a few cases where it is coloured differently from the scales and is used in displays to intimidate predators. The twig snake, *Thelotornis capensis*, for example, inflates its neck when annoyed, exposing a large black marking on its interstitial skin. The boomslang *Dispholidus typus* in which the interstitial skin may be blue, has a similar display as do some of the bronzeback snakes, *Dendrelaphis* from south-east Asia.

The scales

Reptile scales are formed from thickened area of the epidermis. In this respect, they are unlike the scales of fishes, which can be removed individually without damaging the skin.

▼ Snakes' scales are formed from thickened areas of skin and are therefore integral with the skin, unlike fishes' scales, which can be easily scraped off. Here, the skin is stretched, pulling the scales apart so that they do not form a continuous covering.

Scale polishing

nakes of a few species 'polish' their
scales with a secretion that they obtain
from their nostrils. Species in which
this type of behaviour has been
observed include the Montpellier snake,
Malpolon monspessulanus, from south-
rn Europe, its close relative M.
moilensis from North Africa, and four
species of sand snakes, Psammophis,
om Africa and the Middle East.

In Malpolon the oily fluid is secreted
ia a small aperture on the outside of
he nasal flap. Polishing is carried out
y moving the head up and down over
s flanks and its ventral scales, about
00 times, moving progressively along
s body as it goes. In this way, the
ecretion is applied in a continuous
ig-zag line along almost the entire
ength of the ventral surface, with the
nake turning its body over slightly to
llow contact between its snout and its
nderside. Each side of the head is used
n alternative sequences.

During warm weather, Malpolon
monspessulanus polishes itself regularly,
hroughout the day. During cool
weather, polishing seems to be
estricted to the periods immediately
fter shedding its skin, and just after it
as eaten.

The hissing sand snake, Psammophis
sibilans, polishes itself in a similar
manner although its movements are
more complicated. The head passes
ver the back of the snake to polish the
cales on the opposite side of its body,
e. the right nostril comes into contact
ith scales on the snake's left flank,
ipes the scales backwards and
orwards and then moves over to the
ther side. As it works its way down
he body, the scales on the ventral
urface and on the flanks, on both sides
f its body, are covered. At the same
me, each section of its body is raised
n turn to allow the nostril to contact
he snake's underside.

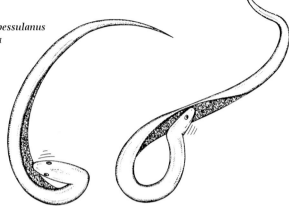

► Scale polishing in *Malpolon monspessulanus*
(redrawn from Steehouder, *Litteratura
Serpentium*, Vol 4 (3/4)).

▼ *Malpolon moilensis* from Egypt

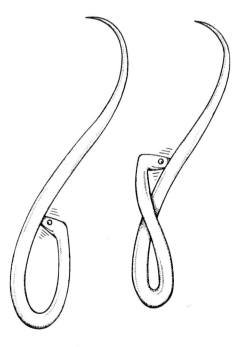

Scale polishing in *Psammophis sibilans*
edrawn from Steehouder, *Litteratura Serpentium*,
ol 4 (3/4)).

The other species of sand snakes in
which polishing has been observed
are *P. condanarus*, *P. schokari* and
P. subtaeniatus. Their methods and
movements are similar to those of
P. sibilans, but with minor variations.

The purpose of this behaviour is not
known with certainty but it may help
to reduce water loss. It is well known
that the permeability of snakes' scales
is partly dependent on the amount of
lipids secreted, because these oily
substances help to seal the scales and
prevent the passage of water across
their surface.

On the other hand, it has also been
suggested that scale polishing is
concerned with chemical
communication; the aromatic
substances produced in the nasal
glands are smeared over the body so
that the snake marks the ground over
which it crawls.

All snakes are covered in scales, but their shapes, textures and arrangements vary greatly. They fulfil several purposes. They form a good degree of physical protection from general wear and tear when the snake moves across rough surfaces, etc. At the same time, the use of small units of armour allows greater flexibility than would large bony plates and snakes depend heavily on flexibility during locomotion and when subduing their prey. Elasticity is also important when swallowing.

Certain scales are used in locomotion, when their edges are hooked over irregularities in the surface (see Locomotion, later in this chapter).

The scales of most snakes also contain the cells that give the snake its characteristic colour and markings, which are especially important in defence, such as camouflage, warning coloration.

Permeability of the skin

Although scales must help to prevent dehydration, this may be a less important function than was formerly believed; desert species have a high degree of resistance to desiccation, but rainforest species do not – even though both types are covered in broadly similar arrangements of scales. This would seem to indicate that other mechanisms are of greater importance in this function.

Permeability may also alter throughout the snake's active season. This is thought to be due to the secretion of lipids, which reduce permeability. Permeability may be under the physiological control of the snake to some extent, although this has not been proved. Of the species tested, the most permeable skin is that of the file snake, *Acrochordus granulatus*, which is ten times as permeable as that of diamondback rattlesnakes, for example. This is thought to help prevent the snake from drying out – the skin attracts water which moves through the small canals between the granular scales. This forms a kind of water jacket, helping to prevent the snake from drying out if it becomes trapped in small, drying pools left by the receding tide (Lillywhite and Sanmartino, 1993).[9]

Another species with a very permeable skin is the semi-aquatic queen snake, *Regina septemvittata*. Snakes from dry environments tend to have less permeable skin, as would be expected, although habitat does not always correlate exactly with permeability. The skins of different species of sea snakes, for instance, have differing permeabilities (Dunson and Freda, 1985).[10]

Shedding the skin

Snakes' scales consist of two layers, an outer that is presented to the outside world and an inner layer which forms continually beneath the outer layer and which will take its place when the outer layer is shed. Between these two layers is a thin layer of clear cells that enable the other two layers to separate during shedding. Prior to shedding, the snake secretes an oily substance into this space in order to facilitate shedding; its markings become obscure and the eyes appear opaque or blue. The epidermis is normally shed in one piece, with the snake starting the process by rubbing its snout on a rough object then removing its old skin by crawling through vegetation or against a rock, bark or other rough surface. Once the skin has been shed, the old inner layer becomes the new outer layer and a new inner layer begins to develop.

The pigment cells are not contained in the epidermis but in the dermis, a layer of connective tissue that lies beneath the epidermis. Therefore, the shed skin is not coloured, although it may contain traces of the pattern in the form of faint dark markings. Because the new skin has not been subjected to the wear that the old one was, the colours of the snake are often much brighter than they were prior to shedding. In species in which the colour changes throughout the life of the snake, these changes are often more noticeable directly after shedding, even though they actually occur gradually.

Frequency of shedding depends on many factors. As shedding is to some extent dependent on growth, young snakes tend to shed more often than adults because they grow more quickly. As their growth rate slows down, so does the frequency of shedding. All snakes shed occasionally, however, even those that have all but stopped growing. In temperate species that go through a resting period, or hibernation, during the winter, shedding often takes place early in the spring almost as soon as they become active. Sexual activity is often heightened during the days immediately following this 'vernal' shed.

Female snakes often shed their skins just before laying eggs or giving birth to live young. This 'pre-laying' shed takes place at a predetermined time before laying, eight to ten days in most rat snakes and kingsnakes, for example, and is therefore very useful in predicting the date of egg laying. In other species, such as boas and pythons, there is an identifiable pre-laying shed but the

timing may not be as constant. Sor females go through another shed shor after laying, the post-laying shed.

Snakes that have been injured often sh frequently, sometimes shedding several tim in rapid succession even though they ha not eaten between sheds. This is presumal under hormonal control and serves to spe up the rate of healing.

The shed skin of a snake is moist a supple immediately after shedding, due the oily substance present, and the new sk of the snake may be similarly slightly tacl After a few hours, however, this wea off and the shed skin becomes brittle. Sh skins are appreciably longer than the snak from which they have come away, by to 20 per cent.

The rattlesnake's rattle

The rattle on the tail of rattlesnakes, gene *Crotalus* and *Sistrurus*, is formed from t successive remains of the scale covering t extreme tip of the tail. In most snakes, t scale is conical and the epidermis coveri it comes away with the rest of the sh skin. In rattlesnakes, however, the termi scale is shaped like an hour-glass, with constriction somewhere around its cen line. After the first shed, the skin arou this terminal scale becomes thicker th normal. When the young snake sheds the second time, this scale is torn away fr the old skin, because it is held in place the constriction. Now a new skin is form around the tip of the tail but it shrir away from the piece of old skin so tha is attached only loosely. When the sna sheds again, the second layer is preven from coming away, the tail has two se ments, one inside the other, and the cy starts over again. Eventually, a number segments are built up, the oldest towa the end of the tail and the freshest towa its base. Each segment, then, represent shed skin, but, although the snake may sk four or more times each year, rattles t consist of more than six or seven segme

▼ The rattlesnakes' rattle consists of pieces of thickened skin, left behind each time it sheds.

Prior to shedding their skin snakes secrete an
y substance between the old outer layer of
dermis and the inner layer (which will become
new outer layer). This substance is opaque,
using the snake's markings to become dull and
eyes to appear milky. This snake is a Central
merican rat snake, *Elaphe flavirufa*.

The outer layer of skin of a common boa is
led back from left to right as the snake crawls
t of it. Snakes usually shed their epidermis in
e piece.

▲ The horns over the eyes of the North African desert horned viper, *Cerastes cerastes*, are modif[i] scales. Their function is uncertain but other vipe[r] from similar desert habitats also share the same characteristic.

◄ Hognose snakes, of which this is the southern[n] species, *Heterodon simus*, have a modified rostra[l] scale that is used in digging.

are rare because the material is brittle and the tip, including the button, is usually broken off, leaving only the most recently formed rings. The purpose of the rattle is discussed in Chapter 6.

Types of scales

Snakes' scales are not all of the same type. There is variation between species and between different parts of the same species. In some families of snakes, notably the colubrids and elapids, large plate-like scales cover the head and these are arranged in a more or less consistent pattern and are easily identifiable. They are therefore of value in helping to identify species.

These head scales are given names by which they can be recognized. The diagram shows the position of these for a typical example. One of the most conspicuous is

the rostral scale; this is a single large scale positioned on the end of the snout and in many species it is enlarged or modified to provide a tool for burrowing, as in the shovel-nosed snakes, *Chionactis*, and the hognose snakes, *Heterodon*. Other specialized scales found on the head of snakes include the horns over the eyes of some species. These may comprise a single, thorn-like scale as in the African desert horned viper, *Cerastes cerastes*, and the horned adder, *Bitis caudalis*, a cluster of pointed scales as in the many-horned adder, *Bitis cornuta*, and the eyelash viper, *Bothriechis schlegelii*, or they may be formed from a single raised scale, as in the American sidewinder, *Crotalus cerastes*, or a group of them, as in *Pseudocerastes*, from the Middle East.

Other species, most notably the rhinoceros viper, *Bitis nasicornis*, have a cluster

of enlarged, pointed scales on their snou[t] while in other species, the snout is extend[ed] into an upturned rostral appendage, [a] nose horn comprising numerous sm[all] scales over a bony or fleshy protuberan[ce] this feature is especially frequent amo[ng] but not restricted to, the vipers, nota[bly] the European nose-horned viper, *Vip[era] ammodytes* and its relatives. The fishi[ng] snake, *Erpeton tentaculatum*, of south-e[ast] Asia is unique in possessing a pair of 'te[n] tacles' attached to the end of its sno[ut] For many years these were thought [to] perform as lures since the snake is aqua[tic] and feeds exclusively on fish. It has sin[ce] been shown, however, that the structu[re] could not be wriggled about in the w[ay] that would be necessary for a success[ful] lure. Neither can they be used as orga[ns] of touch as they have no nerve endin[gs]

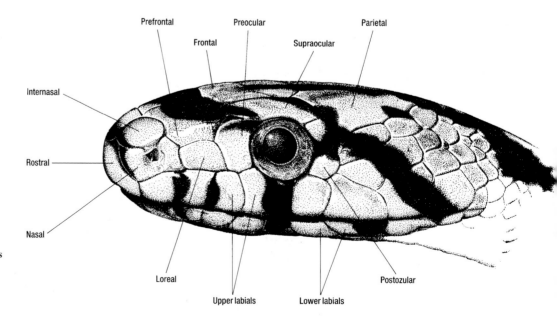

▶ The arrangement of the scales on the heads of snakes tends to be fairly constant within species and can be used as an aid to identification.

Prefrontal · Frontal · Preocular · Supraocular · Parietal · Internasal · Rostral · Nasal · Loreal · Upper labials · Lower labials · Postozular

The eyelash viper, *Bothriechis schlegelii*, from
[Cen]tral America, has a cluster of spine-like scales
[ove]r each eye. A few other species share this
[cha]racteristic, including the eyelash boa,
[Tra]chyboa boulengeri, which comes from the
[sam]e part of the world.

The rhinoceros viper, *Bitis nasicornis*, has an
[ela]borate cluster of scales on its snout. Again, their
[fun]ction is not known.

▼ (below left) A small group of Eurasian vipers,
such as the nose-horned viper, *Vipera ammodytes*,
have a prominent fleshy 'horn' on their snout. In
other species it is not so obvious.

▼ (below right) The horns or 'tentacles' on the
snout of the fishing snake, *Erpeton tentaculatum*,
probably play a part in its camouflage, by
disguising its outline.

It seems likely that they serve the rather more mundane purpose of disguising the outline of the snake's head when it is waiting motionless to ambush its prey. The cryptic longitudinal markings on the body of the snake, and its coloration, further support this theory.

Other strange nasal projections are seen in the three Madagascan snakes belonging to the genus *Langaha*. These single organs are also thought to enhance crypsis as the snakes are long and slender and frequently rest motionless among vines and thin branches. Unaccountably, in *L. alluaudi* only females are so adorned, while in *L. nasuta* the males have a straightforward soft fleshy spike on the end of their snouts whereas the females have a more elaborate affair in which the projection is modified into a series of lobes and serrations.

Scales on the dorsal surface of the bodies of most species tend to be diamond shaped and overlap like the tiles of a roof. They are organized into regular rows that can be counted and used as an aid to identification. Their tips may be rounded, as in the *Typhlops* species, or more pointed. The hairy bush viper, *Atheris hispida*, where the apices of the scales are drawn out into raised, spiky tips, is an extreme example of pointed scales. Further variation in the scales is provided by keels. These structures run along the mid-line of the scales and may be prominent, slight or absent altogether. There tends to be some degree of consistency within closely related species although some genera contain species with keeled scales and others with smooth ones. Keeled scales probably help to improve traction under certain circumstances and they are commonly found among the semi-aquatic natricine colubrids and the fishing snake, *Erpeton*, for instance. Other aquatic species, however, lack keels.

▲ The scales of the hairy bush viper, *Atheris hispida*, are elongated and pointed, with their tips curled up, giving the snake a rough, hairy appearance.

◄ The scales of many snakes have keels – ridges running down their centres – which can be useful in identification. Keels may be very obvious, as here, or they may be hardly visible, as in some of the rat snakes. Other species have completely smooth scales.

In the saw-scaled vipers, *Echis*, and the desert vipers belonging to the genus *Cerastes*, the large keels are modified so that they can be rubbed together to produce a rasping sound and this behaviour is mimicked, with similar results, in some of the egg-eating snakes, *Dasypeltis* (see Chapter 6, page 129).

Snakes with smooth scales may be able to move more rapidly through vegetation, loose sand, etc., as their polished surfaces produce less drag. This type of scalation is commonly seen in burrowing or semi-burrowing snakes, although species from other habitats may also have smooth scales. The three species of snakes belonging to the family Acrochordidae are unusual in having small granular scales. This is thought to be an adaptation to the totally aquatic life-style of these strange but interesting species, and may help them to hold slippery fish, which form their main prey, in their coils. Algae frequently grows over the surface of these scales and this undoubtedly helps to enhance their camouflage.

The scales covering the belly of all snakes are arranged as a single row, a feature that separates them from lizards. These ventral scales usually correspond to the position and number of ribs (except in the Typhlopidae) and commonly number more in females than in males of the same species. They are not always constant, however, and the ventral scale counts are usually given as a range, or two ranges (one for males and one for females) for each species. The ventral scale immediately in front of the cloaca is known as the pre-anal scale and it may be single or divided, depending on the species. Similarly, the scales beneath the tail, known as the subcaudals, may also be single or divided. Even in species with divided subcaudals, it is not unusual to find one or more single subcaudals scattered among the more typical ones.

In the locomotion department, snakes have a fairly obvious handicap – their lack of legs. In this they are almost unique among the terrestrial vertebrates. Considering the range of habitats in which they are found, however, the problem of leglessness appears not to have placed too many restrictions on their ability to move around.

In practice, snakes have evolved a number of distinct types of movement, the method used sometimes depending on the size of the snake and sometimes on the substrate over (or through) which it is moving. Most species can switch from one type of locomotion to another as the circumstances demand, but others are more specialized and only perform efficiently in their own particular environment.

Serpentine crawling

The most common form of snake locomotion is that seen when a small or medium sized snake is travelling across rough ground. It consists of a side-to-side wriggling, sometimes known as lateral undulation. An identical form of movement is used when moving quickly through dense undergrowth or branches. Simply speaking, the snake uses the sides of its body to push against small irregularities in the surface of the substrate. At any given time, various points along the body of the snake are pushing simultaneously against a number of fixed points. As the snake moves forward, new parts of the body are continuously coming into contact with the same points and so all parts of the body follow the same line and the snake moves forward steadily with an almost fluid grace. During swimming, the same sequence of events takes place but the body of the snake pushes against the resistance of the water.

Concertina locomotion

Concertina locomotion is most often seen in burrowing snakes but can also be observed when a more typical species is crawling through a tube or along a narrow space between two immovable objects. First, the head and the front part of the body are extended forward, while the back half is curved several times to provide an anchor. In a burrow, for instance, this brings a number of points to bear on the sides of the burrow. Once the head and front part of the body are fully extended they, in turn, are used to gain purchase on the surface in the same way so that the back part of the

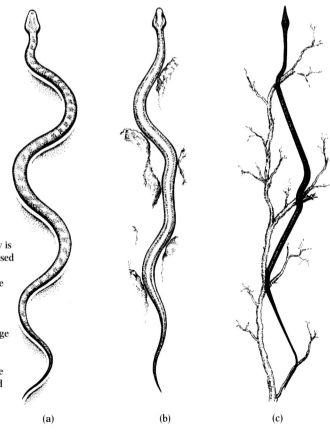

▶ (a) Typical serpentine locomotion, in which the body is wriggled from side to side, is used by snakes crossing an uneven surface. Successive loops of the body push against small irregularities. (b) A similar method is used to crawl over rough surfaces except that large objects such as rocks, etc. are used to provide the anchor points. (c) Arboreal snakes use branches to give purchase and are often capable of spanning large gaps due to their body shape.

(a)   (b)   (c)

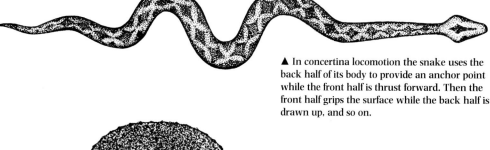

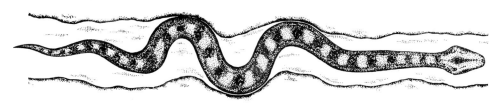

▲ In concertina locomotion the snake uses the back half of its body to provide an anchor point while the front half is thrust forward. Then the front half grips the surface while the back half is drawn up, and so on.

◄ The body of some species, notably the rat snakes, *Elaphe*, is an effective compromise between their terrestrial and arboreal habits. The edges of the ventral scales are strongly keeled, providing a ridge that is useful in gripping the bark of trees when climbing.

▲ When moving along existing underground tunnels, snakes use a method of locomotion that is similar to concertina locomotion, except that the sides of the tunnel provide purchase for one section of the body while the rest moves forward.

▼ In rectilinear crawling, alternative sections of the ventral skin and scales are moved forward relative to the rest of its body. The snake progresses in a more or less straight line (like a caterpillar). This method is used mainly by large, heavy-bodied species such as pythons, boas and some vipers.

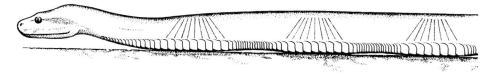

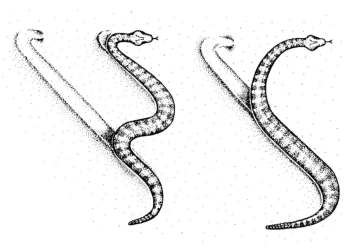

► Sidewinding is used by a number of snake species that live on loose sand and soil. The snake moves sideways in a series of looping movements and leaves a characteristic track. Many sidewinding species are specialists that use it almost exclusively but sometimes other species may revert to a type of sidewinding when circumstances dictate.

body and the tail can be drawn up. T[he] sequence is repeated as many times as necessary.

A similar type of movement is used [for] climbing rough surfaces, such as the bark [of] trees. In order to increase their efficien[cy] some species, such as the North America[n] rat snakes, *Elaphe*, have a pair of ridg[es] running along their bodies near the edge [of] their ventral scales and this ridge provid[es] additional grip.

Yet another variation of the technique [is] used by the burrowing snakes belongi[ng] to the family Uropeltidae (shield tails). [In] these species, parts of the vertebral colum[n] can be bent into a series of curves wh[ile] the sides of the body remain parallel. Th[is] causes the body to become shorter a[nd] thicker, so the snake can jam itself betwe[en] the walls of its burrow with one part of [its] body while another part is thrust forward [or] drawn along behind.

Rectilinear crawling

Some heavy-bodied snakes, especially bo[as] and vipers, abandon the usual serpenti[ne] method altogether and use the edges of t[he] scales on their undersides as anchor poin[ts] to pull themselves forward. Smaller snak[es] may also use this method if they are unab[le] to get enough purchase to thrust diagonal[ly] against the substrate, as in serpentine loc[o]-motion. During the final stages of stalki[ng] their prey, many snakes edge forwards in [a] more or less straight line, using a variati[on] of rectilinear locomotion so as not to ale[rt] their intended victim.

The operation consists of stretchi[ng] forward and hooking the edges of the scal[es] over small irregularities, then pulling t[he] body up to this point. Alternate parts [of] the body will be stretching and pulling [at] the same time, and the muscles then rel[ax] and contract in a series of waves runni[ng] along the length of the snake. The anim[al] moves in a straight line with none of t[he] characteristic sideways wriggling usual[ly] associated with snake locomotion.

Sidewinding locomotion

Sidewinding is a specialized form of locom[o]-tion usually associated with a particul[ar] group of snakes. It is used by specie[s,] notably vipers, that live in areas of loos[e,] windblown sand. Interestingly, there a[re] snakes in North America, South Americ[a,] North Africa, southern Africa and centr[al] Asia that sidewind, suggesting that t[he] technique has evolved independently o[n] several occasions.

Sidewinding is rather like concertina locomotion in that one part of the body acts as an anchor while another part is moved forward. Starting from a resting position, the head and neck are raised off the ground and thrown sideways, while the rest of the body provides purchase. Once the head and fore part of the body are again on the ground they in turn act as an anchor while the rest part of the body catches up. Almost as this is happening, though, the head and neck are flung sideways again, resulting in a continuous and remarkably effective looping movement across the sand. The snake moves at about 45° to the direction in which it is pointing and leaves a trail of characteristic markings in the sand.

Speed of movement

Speed of movement is related to method but is not totally dependent on it. Basically, snakes move as fast as they need to. Thus, active diurnal hunters move rapidly, using the serpentine crawling method of locomotion, whereas large heavy-bodied vipers, which tend to ambush their prey, are often sluggish and may use rectilinear crawling to move around.

The speed at which a snake can travel is open to debate and, like the length of snakes, is often exaggerated. The green mamba is often quoted as one of the fastest snakes; it has been accurately timed at 7 miles (11 km) per hour. It seems likely that several other species, such as whipsnakes and racers, *Coluber*, coachwhips, *Masticophis*, Australian whipsnakes, *Demansia*, and the sand snakes, *Psammophis*, can equal this speed, at least over short distances. Even so, the possibility that any snake could chase and overtake a reasonably fit human is highly unlikely.

Structures associated with locomotion

Locomotion is achieved with the help of a series of muscles, arranged diagonally along each side of the snake. The ends of these muscles are attached to ribs, sometimes joining adjacent ribs but mostly joining ribs that are some distance apart. It is the particular pattern of contraction and relaxation of these muscles, used by the snake, that controls the type of locomotion that is performed. For instance, if muscles on one side of the snake are contracted at the same time as the equivalent muscles on the other side are relaxed, the body will be bent. If, on the other hand, opposite sets of muscles are contracted and relaxed in time with one another, the snake's body will remain more or less straight.

Since snakes have so many ribs, over 400 pairs in some cases, the co-ordination of these muscles can become very complex with, sometimes, one part of the body doing one thing while another part does something entirely different.

In order for the snake to be able to bend and coil its body, the vertebrae (equivalent to the number of ribs) must be capable of a high degree of sideways flexibility and a simple ball and socket arrangement allows this to occur. On the other hand, the amount of twisting movement must be limited because the spinal cord runs through a canal along the top of each vertebra and must be protected: if the vertebrae had complete freedom to spin independently of one another, the nerves inside the spinal column would be wrung like a piece of cloth. For this reason, each vertebra has a number of wing-like processes that interlock loosely with the corresponding processes on the adjacent vertebrae. This limits the amount of twisting.

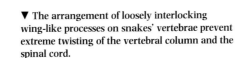

▼ The arrangement of loosely interlocking wing-like processes on snakes' vertebrae prevent extreme twisting of the vertebral column and the spinal cord.

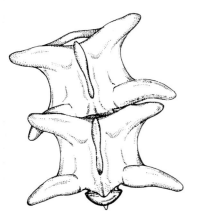
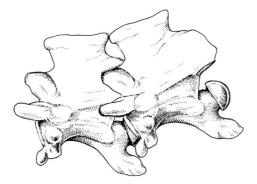

Animals interact with their surroundings by processing information and acting upon it. The information arrives in various forms and so the keener the senses of the animal, the more quickly and efficiently it will be able to respond. Snakes are no exception to this but differ from other vertebrates in the way in which they rely on their various senses. Several novel senses are found uniquely in the snakes and these may have evolved in response to their poor eyesight.

Sight

Although all snakes are predators, their organs of sight are not very efficient. This anomaly may stem from their origins as primitive burrowing reptiles, evolved from burrowing lizards. Burrowing animals have little use for eyes and they tend to degenerate over a long period of time – various insects, amphibians and fish that live in caves and other totally dark conditions demonstrate very well how this may come about. Similarly, primitive burrowing snakes, such as those belonging to the Typhlopidae and Leptotyphlopidae, which spend the greater part of their lives beneath the surface, have only rudimentary eyes, covered with a scale and, at most, capable only of distinguishing light from dark.

Having returned to the surface, and therefore a well-lit habitat, at a later date in their history, the more advanced snakes had to re-invent the eye and, although this was achieved, many of the more sophisticated features had been lost for ever. In particular, it appears that only one genus of snakes, *Ahaetulla*, are able to focus by changing the shape of their lens: all other species must focus by moving the lens backwards and forwards, as in a camera. This more ponderous method provides a more limited degree of focusing ability. In addition, the cells that line the retina, known as rods and cones, and which enable vision to take place under a range of light intensities, are not as well organized in snakes as they are in most other vertebrates, and many snakes lack one or other of these types of cells altogether. The net outcome is an inability to see detail and, in particular, the inability to notice stationary objects. Sensitivity to movement is enhanced, however, and the wide field of view, provided by the position of the eyes on either side of the head, allows snakes to notice activity that may indicate danger or a potential meal. The eyes of snakes have limited mobility except for a few species, notably the vine snakes belonging to the genus *Oxybelis*, which can swivel their eyes

▲ The scale covering the eye, the brille, is a specialized scale found in all but the most primitive snakes. It is shed periodically with the rest of the epidermis. This western sand snake, *Psammophis trigrammus* from southern Africa, has just begun the shedding process.

to search for prey, danger, etc., while still maintaining a motionless position. Others, including blood pythons, *Python curtus*, also swivel their eyes but to a lesser extent.

Predictably, the species that have evolved the most efficient visual equipment are diurnal hunters, such as the whipsnakes and garter snakes. Diurnal hunters such as these are usually recognizable by means of their large circular pupils. Nocturnal hunters, such as the lyre snakes, *Trimorphodon*, and the cat snakes, *Telescopus*, also have large eyes, but with vertically elliptical pupils that close down to narrow slits during the day.

A few species, notably the long-nosed tree snakes, *Ahaetulla* (formerly *Dryophis*), of which there are eight species in Asia, and the twig snakes, *Thelotornis*, (two species in Africa) have large eyes and horizontally elliptical, or keyhole-shaped, pupils. This arrangement has evolved to give the snakes a high degree of binocular vision and is

associated with a long narrow snout along which the snake can look in order to judge distances. They may further enhance their binocular vision by swaying from side to side when lining up their prey. These snakes are active by day and stalk their prey, consisting of agile lizards, by sight. They need to judge distances carefully and to strike accurately because they are unlikely to get a second chance.

In addition to their inefficient eyes, snakes lack eyelids, a feature that separates them from all but a few lizards. Instead, most species have a single large scale covering the eye, sometimes known as the brille or spectacle. This protects the eye from damage and is shed at intervals along with the rest of the scales. Some primitive snakes lack a brille and the eye is covered by one or more conventional scales.

Hearing
Snakes are popularly thought to be deaf. This is not strictly true because, although they lack external signs of ears, they do retain the vestiges of the sound-transmitting equipment in the form of a small bone, the stapes. This bone is in contact with the quadrate bone, which in turn articulates with the lower jaw. As the lower jaw is often in

contact with the ground, sensitivity to vibrations must be extremely acute. In addition, low frequency airborne sounds may also set up vibrations and these can probably also be detected by snakes.

One of the implications of a lack of hearing, of course, is that vocal communication between individuals is not possible, as it is in frogs and toads, for instance. Therefore the sounds that certain snakes do produce – hisses and rattles – have evolved in order to communicate with other kinds of animals as warnings.

Smell
The lack of keen sight and sensitive hearing has led to the development of other, more specialized sense organs in snakes. One of these is the Jacobson's organ, found only in snakes and in some groups of lizards. The Jacobson's organ works in conjunction with, and in addition to, the nostrils and the olfactory part of the brain. It consists of a pair of sacs lined with sensory cells, situated in the front of the palate. The sacs open to the roof of the mouth via a pair of narrow ducts and their inner ends are connected to a separate branch of the olfactory nerve.

When a snake wants to investigate its surroundings, it flicks its tongue out rough a notch in the upper jaw known as e lingual fossa. The tongue picks up scents the form of airborne molecules and is en withdrawn into the mouth. Here the in tips of the forked tongue are inserted o the opening ducts of the Jacobson's gan, the molecules are identified, and the ormation is passed to the brain. Active akes use their tongues constantly and obably rely on their Jacobson's organ as ch as, if not more than, their nostrils. hen not in use, the tongue rests in a fleshy eath on the floor of the mouth.

at-sensitive pits

e senses already described are present some extent in all snakes. Certain groups, wever, have evolved additional sense gans that are unique in the animal king- m. These are specialized heat-sensitive s found in the boas, pythons and pit vipers. vipers belong to the subfamily Crotalinae, metimes regarded as a full family, Crota- ae, and include the rattlesnakes, *Crotalus* d *Sistrurus*, as well as members of several er genera. Due to the distant relation- ips between boids and vipers, and the ferences in the structure of their pits, they ist have evolved independently.

The structure of the pits was first described long ago as the early nineteenth century, hough the first experiments to establish eir purpose were made in the 1930s, first a pit viper by Noble in 1934,[12] then on a thon by Ros in 1935, then on pit vipers ain by Noble and Schmidt in 1937.[13]

Basically, the pits are lined with a layer epithelial cells containing a number of ermoreceptors. Nerves from these receptors k the pits with the brain. The pits of the vipers are rather more sophisticated an those of boas and pythons. They nsist of two compartments, an inner one d an outer one, divided by a membrane. e inner one is connected to the outside rough a narrow pore-like channel that ens just in front of the eye. This serves equalize the air pressure on either side of e membrane and also records the ambient nperature of the air. Heat originating m a warm-blooded animal is detected ly by the outer surface of the membrane,

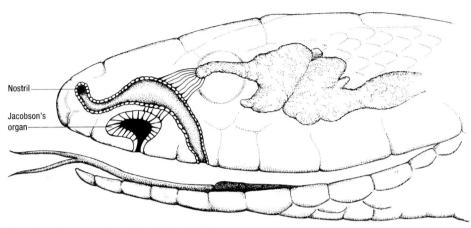

▲ Jacobson's organ is situated in the front of the head and opens on to the roof of the mouth where the tips of the tongue can be inserted into its opening. Nerves from the organ connect it to the olfactory lobe of the brain.

▶ Snakes' tongues can be extended even when their mouths are closed, through a notch in the upper jaw known as the lingual fossa.

When activated, the tongue is extended for some nsiderable distance and flickered around in the in order to pick up scent molecules. These are n carried back into the mouth and transferred the Jacobsen's organ. This snake is a mutant m of the American rat snake, *Elaphe obsoleta*, which the pigment is lacking.

▼ Emerald boa, *Corallus caninus.*

In boas, pits are found in three genera only, *Corallus*, *Epicrates* and *Sanzinia*. When present, they are situated in the labial scales. The pits may be large and extensive, as in *Corallus*, or there may be just a few shallow pits, as in *Epicrates*. Species that feed on warm-blooded prey – mammals and birds – tend to be better equipped than those that feed on lizards and frogs, although the common boa, *Boa constrictor*, is an exception because it lacks pits even though it feeds primarily on warm-blooded prey. The Pacific boas also lack pits as do all the members of the subfamily Erycinae – the sand boas, *Eryx*, the rosy boa, *Lichanura trivirgata*, and the rubber boa, *Charina bottae*. Lack of pits in these species is thought to be a result of their separation from the main boa stock before heat-sensitive pits evolved. Also,

being burrowing species, the pits would be likely to become clogged with debris.

In pythons, the pits are found within the labial and, sometimes, the rostral scales. Once more, the occurrence of pits is not constant throughout the family. Members of the genera *Python*, *Morelia* and *Chondropython*, for instance, are well endowed, others, such as *Liasis*, have only a small series of shallow pits while some, such as the burrowing python, *Calabaria reinhardtii*, and the two members of the Australian genus *Aspidites*, lack pits. The latter feed largely on cold-blooded prey, including other snakes, and so pits would be of limited use to them, whereas *Calabaria* is a burrowing snake in which facial pits would probably be more of a hindrance than a help as it worked its way through loose soil, as in the erycine boas.

▼ Rosy boa, *Lichnura trivirgata.*

▼ Children's python, *Liasis childreni.*

Facial pits in vipers

The pit vipers have evolved the most effective pits. In these species, found in North, Central and South America and in Asia, the heat-sensitive pits take the form of a single large organ on each side of the head, roughly situated just below a line between the eye and the nostril and slightly nearer the nostril. The pits are edged with small scales and directed forwards. They were originally thought to be ears, then additional nostrils – pit vipers are still known as *cuatro narices* (four nostrils) in parts of Latin America.

Experiments have shown that at least some species are sensitive to changes in temperature of as little as 0.001°C (0.002°F). Using these organs, the location of prey, or enemies, can be accurately assessed, even in total darkness. This implies that

▲ Milos viper, *Macrovipera schweizeri*, a 'typical' viper, without pits.

messages obtained by each pit can be compared and that the snake can use this information to judge not only the position of the prey but also its range, rather in the same way that animals with binocular vision can judge distances.

and the snake is thus able to differentia between convected warm air, such as warm breeze, and a radiant object.

A hunting pit viper is therefore w equipped to detect prey. Vibrations m alert it first, then identification is ma using the tongue and Jacobson's organ. closer range the pits provide the necessa information to enable it to strike accurate even in total darkness. A blind rattlesna for instance, scored direct hits on its pr 48 out of 49 times, a success rate th was comparable to that of rattlesnal that could see. When its pits were cover however, its success rate fell to 4 out of attempts. Furthermore, when prey w hit accurately, the more vulnerable he or thorax were the areas most likely to penetrated by the fangs.[14] This gives a go indication of the accuracy with which vipers can strike, using only their facial p

Before leaving this subject, it is wor noting that experiments conducted Breiderbach (1990) have shown that wa objects can also be detected by vip

▼ Southern Pacific rattlesnake, *Crotalus viridis helleri*, a pit viper.

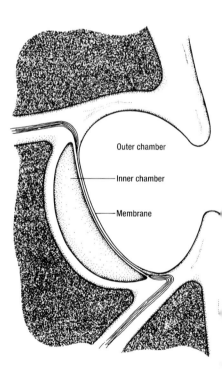

▲ Heat pits in the pit vipers are fairly simple structures. The base of the chamber is lined with thin, sensitive membrane that detects temperatu differences. These are then relayed to the brain b nerves, which are accommodated in channels in the maxillary bone. By moving the head, the amount of heat detected in each pit can be balanced so that an accurate strike can be made even in total darkness.

Outer chamber

Inner chamber

Membrane

ithout facial pits. They were able to differentiate between warm and cold objects
and struck at warm objects.[15] It is not
known how this is achieved, nor how their
accuracy compares with that of the pit
vipers. One would suspect that their abilities
are far more limited.

Scale tubercles and pits

In snakes, and in most families of lizards,
there are certain scales with areas where the
cuticle is thinner. Because nerve endings are
concentrated in the region immediately
under these areas, it seems almost certain
that they are sense organs of some description. Their purpose, however, is still largely
unknown although we can make certain
theoretical assumptions. Two types of organs
are recognizable: tubercles and pits.

Tubercles are very small, 1–2 mm in
diameter, and each consists of a rounded
elevation, or pimple, surrounded by a circular depression. Beneath the tubercle, the
epidermis is raised to fit into its underside
and the nerve ending lies just below the
epidermis. Pits are larger than tubercles,
up to 3 mm in diameter and may be oval
rather than circular. The cuticle is thinner
at the bottom of the pit and this is the area
where nerve endings are situated.

Tubercles

Tubercles are the most common, both in
terms of the numbers of snakes on which
they are found and also in terms of numbers
of scales that have them. So far they have
been found on every snake examined
for them but they are not equally numerous
on all of them. On the primitive snakes,
Typhlopidae, Leptotyphlopidae and Anomalepidae, they are found only on the
forward parts of the head, with hardly any
traces on the body or tail. Some of the other
primitive snakes have plenty of tubercles,
however. *Xenopeltis* and *Loxocemus* have
them on the head, body and tail, as do
the members of the Uropeltidae, the shield-
tailed snakes, which also have large
numbers on the specialized rough scale on
the end of their tails. Among the boas and
pythons, there is more variability, with
some species having many tubercles while
others have them only in certain areas: in
Eryx(?), for instance, they are found only
on the head. In the higher snakes –
colubrids, elapids and vipers – tubercles are
found on the head, especially on the rostral
and labial scales. They may extend on to the
dorsal and ventral scales but are usually less
numerous here than on the head.

▲ Small tubercles are found on certain scales of
most snakes, especially those around the head, and
can clearly be seen in this *Tropidophis melanurus*.
Although their function is uncertain, they may
play a part in the sensory system or in chemical
communication.

The general assumption is that tubercles
are more numerous in areas of the body that
come into contact with objects as the snake
moves around. Unless this is coincidental,
it would appear to lead to the conclusion
that the tubercles are organs of touch.

Similar structures were found on scales
near the vent of male rough earth snakes,
Virginia striatula. Because they are confined
to males, these secondary sex characteristics are thought to help the male to locate
the female's vent during courtship and
mating. Ridges and bumps have also been
noted in the same area of male snakes
belonging to a variety of other species, including garter snakes, water snakes and
a coral snake, and their function is presumably similar.

Pits

Unlike tubercles, pits have been found only
on the higher snakes. They are not found
in all species, however, and appear to be
absent in elapids, for instance. Caution is
required in this area, though, because
anatomists have often failed to realize the
importance of pits (and tubercles) and they

have only been looked for in a small proportion of snakes. Where they do occur, pits are
more numerous on the head, especially
around the snout, than they are on other
parts of the body. Furthermore, where pits
and tubercles are found on the same scales,
they tend to be found on different parts
of these scales. On the body, pits are found
mainly on the tips (apices) of the scales and,
for this reason, are sometimes known as
apical pits.

Even less is known about the function of
the pits than of the tubercles. One theory is
that they are light sensitive. Evidence for
this is that they tend to be lost in burrowing
forms.

Other researchers have proposed that the
pores, and other thin areas on the scale,
allow an oily substance to exude on to the
outer surface of the scales; this would then
act as a barrier to water. Alternatively, the
pits may exude substances which play a
part in chemical communication, helping
snakes to find and identify one another and,
possibly, to mark territories.

INTERNAL ANATOMY

The internal anatomy of snakes is little different, in effect, from that of other vertebrates. The emphasis in this section will therefore concentrate on the areas in which snakes differ from typical vertebrates, and in the way in which the organs are arranged in such elongated animals.

As in other animals, the organs can be unravelled, figuratively speaking, into a number of sets, each set constituting one of the basic anatomical systems.

Digestive system

The digestive system starts with the mouth and it is here that most of the modifications have taken place. The oral glands, that secrete a cocktail of substances to enable the snake to swallow its food more easily and to begin the process of digestion, are well developed. They consist of glands in the tongue, below the tongue and in the lips. The latter, more correctly known as labial or parotid glands, are especially large in some species and the substances they secrete contain strong digestive juices.

Certain colubrid snakes are, to some extent, venomous. Their venom is delivered to enlarged teeth towards the rear of their mouth and so they are commonly known as rear-fanged species. The venom in these species is produced in the Duvernoy's gland, which is a modified salivary gland but rather different in structure from the venom glands of vipers and elapids. The gland, which varies in size from species to species, empties into a central duct. This duct opens near the rear fangs, in a fold between the base of the teeth and the lips. The teeth of some species have grooves running along their lengths and the saliva, or venom, is drawn along these by capillary action.

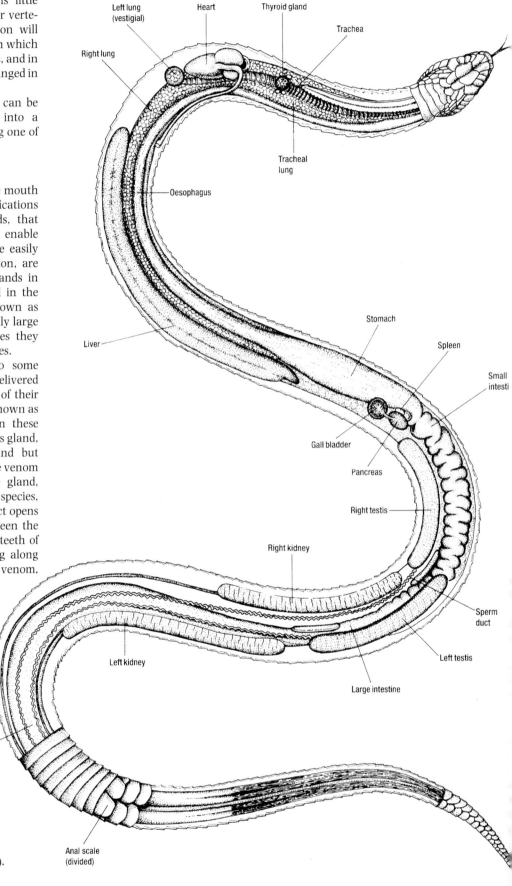

► Internal anatomy of a snake (simplified).

he composition of the modified saliva
ies. It may secrete only mucous cells, in
ich case there is no venom whatsoever:
cies producing this type of secretion do
 have enlarged rear fangs. On the other
d, it may contain enzymes that help
reak down proteins and, depending on
ir strength, snakes producing this type
ecretion may be classed as venomous.
ey include the boomslang, *Dispholidus
us*, twig snakes, *Thelotornis*, and an
an species, *Rhabdophis tigrinus*, all of
ich have caused fatalities in humans, as
ll as numerous other colubrids that may
duce mild symptoms in man but which
 more effective against their normal
y.

n some of the higher snakes, the elapids
 vipers, the digestive secretions have
lved into a powerful form of venom.
om glands, when present, originate
n the upper labial glands and open by
ns of a narrow duct into the grooves or
ities of the poison fangs. The venom
nds may be greatly enlarged and, in
e species, extend for a considerable
ance along the body of the snake. They
 surrounded by muscles known as the
sseter muscles, which are used to
eeze the venom gland, forcing the
om that is stored there through the
om ducts to the fangs. In this way they
er from the fangs of rear-fanged snakes
 the poisonous lizards, *Heloderma*, in
ich the venom is drawn along the fang
capillary action. Also, in *Heloderma* the
on fangs are in the lower jaw.

he tongue of snakes is not used in
llowing. Its function has been altered
hat of an aid to smell, and it is used in
junction with the Jacobson's organ,
ich has already been described.

he throat and oesophagus of snakes are
hly muscular, for forcing food items
n towards the stomach, and greatly
endable, in order to accommodate large
y. The oesophagus becomes gradually
er about one-third of the way along the
y of the snake until it opens out to the
nach. This consists of a wider, muscular
ion of the gut where additional secre-
s attack the food. The pancreas and gall
der are situated at the further end of the
nach. The lower intestine is slightly
ed, but not as much as in animals with a
re conventional shape; this is possible
ause all snakes are carnivorous and so
y do not require the long and convoluted
 found in herbivorous or omnivorous
mals. The lower intestine merges into the
rectum, which finally opens to the cloaca
and finally the vent, where the remains of
undigested food are voided.

Respiratory system

Although respiration in snakes is fundamentally the same as in other air-breathing
vertebrates, a high degree of modification
has been necessary in order to enable the
necessary apparatus to fit into their bodies.
In the vast majority of species the left lung is
either very small or absent altogether, with
only the Boidae having a sizeable left lung.
The right lung, on the other hand, is greatly
extended backwards and may, in aquatic
species, extend for almost the entire length
of the body; in these species, the far end
of the lung, known as the saccular lung,
has only limited ability to extract oxygen
but is used instead for air storage and as a
buoyancy organ.

An additional organ is found around the
windpipe of some snakes, where the vascular
lining of the lung extends forwards. This
structure, known as the tracheal lung, gives
additional capacity. This can be important
not only for aquatic species but also where
feeding behaviour prevents breathing.
The snail-eating snakes belonging to the
genera *Dipsas* and *Sibon*, for instance, have
large tracheal lungs. These species specialize
in eating snails, a habit that involves bury-
ing their heads in the shells while they
extract the soft parts. Tracheal lungs may
also help other snakes to continue breathing
when large items of prey are swallowed. As
the food passes down the body, parts of the
lung are compressed and do not function
well; by extending its length, the tracheal
lung ensures that at least one part of the lung
can be expanded normally at all times.

Also connected with the need to continue
breathing when large items of food are
being swallowed, the opening of the windpipe, the glottis, takes the form of a muscular
tube that can be thrust forward from the
floor of the mouth and held open despite
the pressure exerted by the food.

Snakes do not have a true voice but may
produce a hiss by expelling the air rapidly
from their lung. This sound can be especially
loud and startling in some species, such as
the American gopher snakes, *Pituophis*,
and hognose snakes, *Heterodon*. This sound
is produced when air rushes across a special
membrane in the glottis, causing vibration.

Circulatory system

The circulatory system is similar to that of
other animals except that the heart has
three chambers, not four as in mammals
(or crocodilians). The pulmonary part of
the system, taking blood to the lungs for
gaseous exchange, is more important in
reptiles than it is in amphibians, for
instance, which rely, to a large extent, on
gaseous exchange across the surface of their
skin. The arrangement of the aorta, the
large artery leaving the heart, is modified in
snakes and may be variable throughout the
families.

Excretory system

The main modifications here concern the
lack of a bladder and the placement of
the kidneys. Snakes do not excrete urea
in the form of urine. As an aid to water
conservation, especially important to those
species that live in an arid environment,
snakes reclaim almost all the fluid from
their system and excrete their nitrogenous
waste material in the form of uric acid, a
semi-solid white material that contains the
minimum amount of fluid necessary to
carry it out of the body.

The kidneys are greatly elongated and
staggered within the body cavity, so that
the left kidney is significantly more forward
than the right one.

Nervous system

The nervous system serves the sense
organs, as described earlier in this chapter.
Peculiarities in the system are confined to
the organs that are not present in most
other animals, such as the branch of the
olfactory nerve that goes to the Jacobson's
organ and to the heat-sensitive pits in those
species that have them. Additional nerve
endings are found immediately below the
scale pits and tubercles, so far found only in
snakes, and of which the exact functions are
unknown.

Otherwise the system is more or less
conventional. The spinal cord extends the
whole length of the backbone. The system
as a whole is somewhat less complex than it
is in higher animals, as snakes lack many of
the appendages that would normally be
served by the nervous system. Having said
this, some of the more primitive species
have a network of nerves that would
normally go to the hind limbs if they had
them – good evidence that the ancestors of
snakes had legs.

Reproductive system

The most important step that enabled
reptiles to move away from the water was
the development of a shelled egg, and some

species later evolved viviparity to further their adaptation to the terrestrial environment. Either method of reproduction requires internal fertilization and, although some amphibians practise a simple form of this, in reptiles it is well developed, with the evolution of a paired copulatory organ in males, the hemipenes, and of a shell gland in the females of those species that lay eggs.

The female reproductive system

Female snakes normally have a pair of ovaries, staggered like the kidneys so that they can be accommodated into the elongated body. In some snakes the left oviduct is missing. Snake eggs are large because they contain enough yolk to nourish the developing embryo until it hatches as a fully formed juvenile. The eggs mature in the ovary, where yolk is produced. Yolking, or vitellogenesis, is dependent on the condition of the female – if she is underweight it will not occur and the eggs will develop no further. The eggs mature simultaneously and break through the wall of the ovary into the body cavity. Here they are collected by the funnel-shaped end of the oviduct (the infundibulum) and then move into the oviduct. Fertilization takes place here, either by sperm introduced while the mature ova are waiting in the oviduct or by sperm stored from a previous mating, possibly several months previously. A specialized structure or chamber, the seminal receptacle, situated towards the posterior end of the oviduct, is used to store the sperm. In oviparous species, the shell is formed in the lower part of the oviduct, just before the eggs are laid.

The male reproductive system

Male snakes have paired testes, staggered like the ovaries and the other paired organs. Long coiled tubes, the seminiferous tubules, lead from the testes, carrying sperm to the ureter, where they are stored in a bladder-like structure. The ureter opens into the cloaca where another structure, the papilla urogenitalis is situated. A groove transports the sperm from this structure to the base of the hemipenes. Each hemipenis lies at the base of the tail, normally inverted and forming a thick area that may be used to visually determine the sex of the snake. The hemipenes can also be everted in living snakes by applying upward pressure at the base of the tail. In addition, the opening of the inverted hemipenes can be seen beneath the pre-anal scale and its length can be probed with a narrow instrument. At copulation, blood is forced into the hemipenes and, at the same time, a muscle pulls the hemipenes out of the tail. Only one hemipenis is used to copulate – individual snakes appear to favour either the left or right organ although either can, theoretically, be used.

The hemipenes have no enclosed sperm duct but rather an external groove that ends in a lip surrounded by a fleshy rim. When the hemipenis is inserted into the cloaca of the female, the groove forms a channel along which the sperm can travel. The surface of the hemipenis is covered with spines and projections, often arranged in rosettes. These are thought to help the male snake to locate the cloacal opening of the female and to fix the hemipenis in place once copulation has begun. The hemipenes of some species are branched and in these species the female's cloaca is also branched. Similarly, if the hemipenes are covered with spines, the female's cloaca has a thicker wall than in those species in which spines are reduced or absent. Dissection of females has shown that in every case the internal shape of the cloaca corresponds closely to the shape of the hemipenes of males of the same species. The system therefore forms an isolating mechanism, preventing unrelated species from mating and the shape and structure of the hemipenes are of considerable interest to taxonomists as they form part of a 'lock-and-key' mechanism. Although males can only usually mate effectively with females of the same species, the mechanism is not as effective as it was once thought to be as hybrid snakes are not uncommon under the artificial conditions of captivity, and naturally occurring hybrids are also found from time to time.

In tropical snakes the testes are probably active throughout the year, but in temperate species they usually produce sperm during the height of the active season, in summer and early autumn. The snakes then enter hibernation with plenty of stored sperm which is used the following spring during the breeding season. There are a few exceptions to this arrangement, however, where the males produce the majority of their sperm in the spring and use it later in the same year. This system has only been shown for a few species, although it may be more widespread.

The skull and skeleton

The skeletons and skulls of snakes have been extremely modified, especially in the more advanced families and it is possible, to some extent, to trace the evolution of the

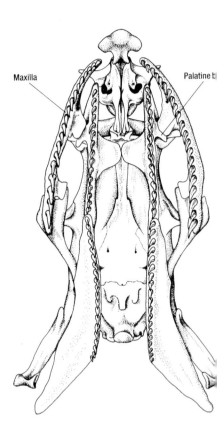

Maxilla ——————— Palatine b

▲ The structure of the skull showing tooth-bea bones. The exact arrangement of the tooth-bea bones varies from snake to snake (and a few species lack teeth) but snakes are typically well endowed with teeth on both their maxillary an palatine bones.

suborder by examining their progres modifications.

The skull

Compared with their closest relatives, lizards, the skulls of snakes are far m delicate and loosely articulated. This co as a result of their feeding habits. Whel most lizards have rigid jaws that can ch and dismember their prey, snakes swal it whole, without chewing. This wo restrict them to eating small animals wel not for the elasticity of the jaws and the s around them. Not all snakes are capabl stretching their jaws to great dimensio however. The thread snakes, Lept phlopidae, have reduced mouths and v short lower jawbones. The jaws of blind snakes, Typhlopidae, the pipe sna Aniliidae, the shield tails, Uropeltidae, the sunbeam snakes, Xenopeltidae, capable of only a little more movement terms of numbers of species, however, th families comprise only a small proportio snakes. In more advanced snakes, the bo

he skull are capable of more independent
vement and the mouth can be opened
ch wider in order to accommodate prey
t has a diameter far greater than that
he snake's head.

his is possible because the bones of the
er and lower jaws are loosely connected,
er than being fused to one another and
he cranium, or braincase. This allows
m to move outwards as well as back-
ds and forwards, independently of the
of the skull or of each other, helping
m to pull prey into the mouth while at
same time moving out of the way so that
n be swallowed. To avoid damage to the
in when large prey is forced through the
uth, the bones on the roof of the mouth
extended and strengthened. The two
ves of the lower jaw are not connected at
front (chin) but are joined by an elastic
ment, allowing them to move away
n one another, further increasing the
acity of the mouth.

teeth

number and arrangement of snakes'
h vary greatly according to the species;
ne have practically no teeth at all while
ers have numerous teeth as well as teeth
everal different types. Typically, snakes
e teeth along the ridge of the lower jaw,
maxilla (the outer portion of the upper
), the palatine bones (long bones that
along the roof of the mouth inside the
xillary bones) and the pterygoid bones

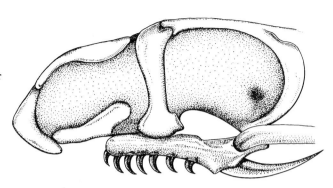

▶ Xenodontine snakes have a
hinged arrangement in their
jaws, shown diagrammatically
here. Their enlarged rear fangs
can be swung forward and may
be used to puncture their prey or
to give a better grip. In general,
these snakes are not regarded as
dangerous although they may
possess a Duvernoy's gland.

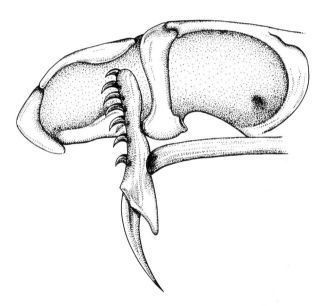

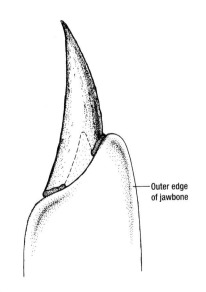

— Outer edge
of jawbone

he teeth of snakes are of the pleurodont type
ey do not rest in a socket but are attached
e angled top of the jawbone on which they
set.

(paired bones that are fixed to the palate at
the front and the quadrate bones at the
back).

Their teeth are of the pleurodont type.
This means that they are attached to the
inner edges of the jawbones, rather than on
top of them. They are replaced throughout
the life of the snake: replacement teeth
develop at the bases of the existing ones,
ready to be swung upwards and sideways
when the old tooth is shed. Shed teeth are
often swallowed, sometimes because they
have become embedded in prey, and can be
found in the snake's faeces.

Many typical snakes, i.e. most colubrids,
have teeth that are more or less equal in size
and shape. This type of dentition is known as
aglyphous (without fangs). Others, though,
have specialized dentition. Opisthoglyphous
snakes have one or two pairs of enlarged
teeth towards the back of their mouths
and are commonly known as rear-fanged.
All rear-fanged snakes are colubrids or
atractaspids, and the fangs are associated
with the presence of Duvernoy's glands,

described on page 113. Because of the position of these fangs, and the usually low
potency of the venom, they are not normally
regarded as dangerous to humans, although
a few species have caused deaths. Where
enlarged fangs are present in the back of the
mouth, there is invariably a gap in front of
them. This is known as the diastema and
allows the enlarged fangs to be deeply
embedded in the prey.

Some species of colubrids, usually
referred to the subfamily Xenodontinae
(meaning strange teeth), have an unusual
arrangement whereby two rear fangs are
attached to the back of the upper jaw. When
the mouth is closed, the teeth are positioned
horizontally, but when the mouth is opened
wide the upper jaw swings into a more
vertical position, and the teeth are brought
into play. These snakes, which include the
well-known hognose snakes, *Heterodon*, of
North America as well as the lesser known
genera *Lystrophis*, *Waglerophis* and *Xenodon*
from Central and South America, feed
largely on toads, which often inflate their

► In vipers, the fangs are located on a shortened maxilla, which is mobile. When at rest, the fangs lie under the roof of the mouth and are covered with a fleshy sheath but when the snake strikes, the maxilla, and therefore the fangs, is rotated forward, due to the pushing action of the pterygoid and transpalatine bones. Each fang has a hollow channel, through which the venom is forced.

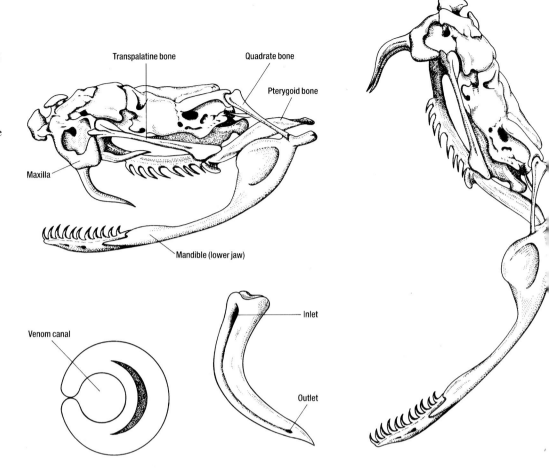

bodies when faced with a predator. The purpose of the enlarged teeth may therefore be to puncture the bodies of the toads, making them easier to swallow. If the fangs were arranged vertically on the jaw, the snake would be unable to close its mouth without injuring itself.

Other snakes have modified teeth at the front of their jaws. The members of the Elapidae, comprising the cobras, mambas, kraits, coral snakes and related species, have short venom fangs attached to the maxillary bones. These fangs are hollow, with an inlet at the base and an outlet near the tip. During envenomation, venom is ducted to the inlet and forced through the small hole at the tip of the fang. The only exceptions are the spitting cobras belonging to the genera *Naja* and *Hemachatus*, in which the outlet is situated in the front of the fang, somewhat above its tip, so that when pressure is applied to the venom gland the venom is forced through it at high speed.

The fangs of the vipers are even m[ore] highly modified. They are hollow, like th[ose] of the elapids, but tend to be longer, allo[w]ing the venom to be injected further i[nto] the prey. In order to accommodate the[m in] the mouth when it is closed, the maxilla[, to] which they are attached, is hinged in suc[h a] way that the fangs are folded backwa[rd] along the roof of the mouth, when not [in] use. Both the elapids and the vipers hav[e a] diastema immediately behind their ven[om] fangs.

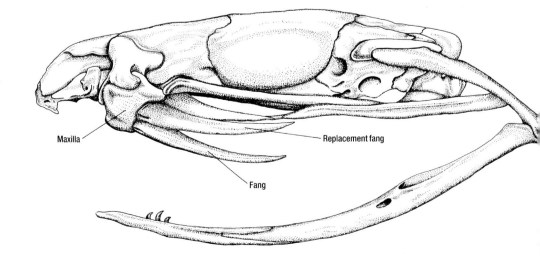

► The burrowing asps, *Atractaspis*, have hinged fangs with a high degree of movement, allowing them to strike in the confines of a burrow. Most other teeth are lacking, however.

Snakes of the family Atractaspididae ve a variety of fang arrangements. In *ractaspis*, which is the largest genus, e fangs are attached to the maxilla. The xilla, prefrontal and frontal bones all erlock in a unique manner and the fangs ve only a limited degree of movement. ey can be swung sideways and are used th a stabbing motion, without the neces- y of opening the mouth fully. This is ught to be an adaptation to hunting ile in underground tunnels and burrows. *ractaspis* has lost all the other teeth in its per jaw and those in the lower jaw are atly reduced. Related species have fangs the back of their mouths while others ve fixed fangs at the front.

When snakes' teeth are examined micro- opically, they are found to have a pair ridges running along their length. In ne species that eat reptile eggs, such as *odon*, these are very pronounced and are ught to be used for cutting through the gshells. *Dinodon* species are popularly own as 'kukri' snakes in recognition of ir knife-like teeth. Certain other species ve additional shallow ridges, fluting, striations along the length of some of ir teeth, with the deepest grooves being vards the base of the teeth. These uctures are found mainly in aquatic and ni-aquatic, fish-eating species, such as file snakes, *Acrochordus*, and the homa- osine colubrids such as *Enhydris*, and are ught to help the snakes to penetrate hard scales and therefore grasp their y more firmly. Similar structures have n found on the teeth of snakes that eat rthworms and molluscs, where they may o aid penetration (Vaeth, Rossman and oop, 1985).[16]

e skeleton

akes' skeletons consist very simply of a ill and a number of precaudal and caudal rtebrae. The precaudal vertebrae each ar a rib but there is no breast bone, or rnum, and so the free ends of the ribs connected to each other, and to the rsal and ventral scales, by muscles. ese are important in locomotion and in nstriction. The vertebrae themselves numerous, sometimes numbering over O and the number is slightly variable, en within species.

Each vertebra has a central portion, or ntrum, which is shaped like a short inder with one convex and one concave l. These ends articulate on the corre- onding ends of the centra that adjoin

them. Above the centrum is a neural arch, an arch of bone through which the spinal cord runs. A number of spines or processes jut out from this basic structure, and these also articulate with their counterparts on neighbouring vertebrae. The hypapophyses, which are downwardly-projecting processes, are not found throughout the suborder – they are absent altogether in the Typhlopidae and Leptotyphlopidae, for instance, and are often missing from burrowing species in other families. They are invariably present in aquatic snakes, however, although their exact function is not clear. In the egg-eating snakes, *Dasypeltis*, the hypapophyses on the first few vertebrae extend down into the throat and are used to break through the shell of birds' eggs on which these species feed.

The caudal vertebrae, which make up the tail, are simplified and do not have ribs attached to them. In a few snakes, belonging to the genera *Scaphiodontophis* and *Coluber*, the vertebrae of the tail may break as a defensive mechanism, although they may lack the fracture plane running across the vertebrae that is found in many families of lizards.

No snakes have pectoral girdles but those of some of the more primitive families, namely the Typhlopidae, Leptotyphlopidae, Aniliidae, some Uropeltidae (subfamily Cylindrophinae), and Boidae, have vestigial pelvic girdles. The absence of pelvic girdles in some of the other primitive families, such as the Anomalepididae and the remaining Uropeltidae (subfamily Uropeltinae), when they are present in the far more advanced boas and pythons, is rather strange, but may be accounted for by the fact that male boas and pythons use the spurs, which are vestigial legs attached to the pelvic girdles, during courtship. For this reason they may have been retained, whereas where they are not required they have been lost.

1. Wall. Frank (1921), *Ophidia Taprobanica or the Snakes of Ceylon*. H. R. Cottle, Government Printer, Colombo, Ceylon (Sri Lanka).
2. FitzSimons, V. F. M. (1962), *Snakes of Southern Africa*. Purnell and Sons Ltd., Cape Town.
3. Worrell, E. (1958), *Song of the Snake*. Angus and Robertson, London.
4. Pope, C. H. (1961), *The Giant Snakes*. Routledge and Kegan Paul, London.
5. Oliver, J. A. (1958), *Snakes in Fact and Fiction*. The Macmillan Company, New York.
6. Boos, H. (1992), 'A note on the 18.5 ft Boa Constrictor from Trinidad', *Bulletin of the British Herpetological Society*, 40:15–17.
7. Rose, J. A. (1966), *La Taxonomia y Zoogeografia de los Ofidios en Venezuela*. Universidad Central de Venezuela, Caracas.
8. Amaral, A. do (1978), *Serpentes do Brasil*. Ministry of Education and Culture, São Paulo, Brazil, 1977.
9. Lillywhite, H. B. and Sanmartino, V. (1993), 'Permeability and water relations of the hygroscopic skin of the file snake, *Acrochordus granulatus*', *Copeia*, 1993(1):99–103.
10. Dunson, W. A. and Freda J. (1985), 'Water permeability of the skin of the amphibious snake *Agkistrodon piscivorous*', *Journal of Herpetology*, 19(1):93–98.
11. Ros, M. (1935), 'Die Lippengruben der Pythonen als Temperaturorgane', *Jenaisch. Zeit. für Natuerwiss*, 70:1–32.
12. Noble, G. K. (1934), 'The structure of the facial pit of pit vipers and its probable function', *Anat. Rec.*, 58, supp. p. 4.
13. Noble, G. K. and Schmidt, A. (1937), 'The structure and function of the facial and labial pits of snakes', *Proc. Am. Philos. Soc.*, 77(3):263–288.
14. Kardong, K. V. and Mackessy, S. P. (1991), 'The strike behaviour of a congenitally blind rattlesnake', *Journal of Herpetology*, 25(2):208–211.
15. Breiderbach, C. A. (1990), 'Thermal cues influence strikes in pitless vipers', *Journal of Herpetology*, 24(4):448–450.
16. Vaeth, R. H., Rossman, D. A. and Shoop, W. (1985), 'Observations of tooth surface morphology in snakes', *Journal of Herpetology*, 19(1):20–26.

3
How Snakes Live

Snakes, like other organisms, do not live their lives in isolation. They have to interact with other animals, which may be of the same species, in which case they could be mates or rivals, or of other species, in which case they could be potential prey or predators. These are biological factors, to be dealt with in the next section. They also interact with the physical environment – factors such as heat and cold, wet and dry, light and dark. These are dealt with first.

◀ Tropical snakes, such as *Philodryas viridissimus*, from Amazonia, have little need to bask because ambient temperatures are close to their preferred range.

THE PHYSICAL ENVIRONMENT

As already described, the senses monitor both biological and physical environments, and the snake reacts as necessary, using involuntary or voluntary actions. Involuntary actions consist of the physiological processes that operate to maintain the *status quo*, or homeostasis, within the body and may be supplemented by behavioural activities such as moving from one place to another. Voluntary actions comprise behavioural responses – movement, altering the body shape or posture and bringing additional sense organs into play.

Thermoregulation

Reptiles are unable to produce much of their body heat internally, as can the birds and mammals, but rely almost entirely on external sources, a system known as ectothermy (as opposed to endothermy). For many species, especially those from cooler climates, this dominates their daily and seasonal activity patterns and is the key to understanding how snakes live.

Even though they are commonly labelled 'cold blooded', snakes, like other organisms, need to attain certain body temperatures in order that the natural processes of muscle activity, nerve activity, digestion, spermatogenesis and so on can take place. Snakes regulate their body temperature by a combination of behavioural and physiological responses. The behavioural responses are by far the more important, however, and the physiological ones act more as fine tuning.

Despite their reliance on external sources of heat, most snakes are not completely at the mercy of their environment, as is sometimes thought. Research has consistently shown that snakes' body temperatures are frequently higher than those of their surroundings, especially at the beginning of the day when they are warming up, but that they may also be cooler than their surroundings should these become dangerously hot. Many species are able to keep their body temperatures within very narrow 'operating bands' during their active periods, often within 1°C (2°F) of their preferred body temperature. Furthermore, they are able to do this despite the fact that their long, slender bodies, which are not covered with fur, feathers or other insulating material, are not ideally suited to retaining heat.

Operating temperatures

As has already been said, snakes have a preferred body temperature that they attempt to maintain through behavioural activities. If the temperature falls too low the snake will freeze to death (lethal minimum) and, conversely, if it gets too high the snake will die from heat exhaustion (lethal maximum). Other important values are the critical minimum and maximum temperatures – these occur when the snake loses the power of locomotion and is therefore unable to move to a more favourable location. The precise temperatures vary according to the species and, possibly, other factors such as whether the snake has fed recently, if it is reproductively active, or if it is about to shed its skin. Within a wide-ranging species it can often be shown that individuals from the cooler parts of the range can tolerate lower temperatures than those from warmer parts of the range, although their preferred body temperatures may be identical.

In the past, two methods have been used to establish the preferred body temperature for a snake. Active snakes can have their temperature taken in the field when they are found fortuitously, or they can be kept under controlled conditions in which they are offered a choice of temperatures. Both these methods are useful but they have the drawback that it is necessary to disturb the snake, and therefore to subject it to stress, in order to obtain results. More recently, telemetry systems have been used.

These work by implanting a miniatu[re] electronic radio transmitter into the body [of] the snake, then using a receiver to moni[tor] its signal. With the right equipment, t[he] system can be used to give a continual rea[d] out of the snake's body temperature, [as] well as its whereabouts, over a long peri[od] of time. Body temperatures for resting [as] well as active snakes can then be obtain[ed] without undue disturbance.

The results produced by pooling all the[se] methods seem to show that snakes of m[ost] species prefer to keep their body temper[a] tures at or around 30°C (86°F) – rath[er] warmer than is often thought. Their activi[ty] range is wide, however, with temperatur[es] as low as 10°C (50°F) and as high as 40[°C] 104°F) having been recorded from acti[ve] snakes. The pattern that emerges from the[se] figures is that snakes can become acti[ve] well before their bodies have warmed up [to] their preferred, or ideal, level – this mak[es] sense, of course, because resting snakes [in] shaded underground retreats, for instan[ce] would otherwise remain where they we[re] and never get the chance to warm the[ir] bodies up. Having become active, they th[en] try to reach their ideal body temperatu[re] as quickly as possible and, having do[ne] so, ensure that it does not rise more th[an] a few degrees above this. Lethal high te[m] peratures are much closer to the preferr[ed] temperatures than are the lethal low on[es] and so avoidance of extremely hot con[di] tions is always more urgent than avoidan[ce] of cold ones.

Although snakes are not ideally design[ed] to conserve heat, being without fur [or] feathers, they can improve the efficien[cy] with which they absorb and retain heat [by] using a number of strategies. Their lon[g] slender bodies have a high surface-to-weig[ht] ratio and, since heat is absorbed over the[ir] surface, they can increase heat uptake [by] stretching out. By flattening their bodi[es] they will improve the surface-to-weig[ht] ratio even more, and at the same time the[y] allow radiant heat (i.e. from the sun) to f[all] on a greater proportion of their skin. T[he] underside of their bodies will also be in clos[e]

▼ Temperature 'landmarks' in thermoregulation of a typical snake. The stippled area covers the normal activity range, the preferred temperatures are those between which the snake tries to maintain its body temperature, the critical minimum and maximum are the temperatures at which it loses the power of locomotion (and hence the option of retreating to somewhere more suitable) and the lethal minimum and maximum are the temperatures at which it dies.

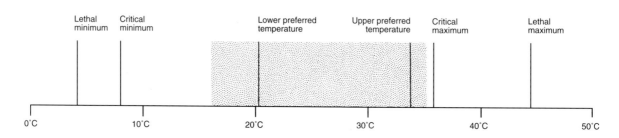

In order to warm up quickly, snakes may flatten their bodies against a warm substrate, as this viper, *Macrovipera schweizeri*, is doing.

contact with the substrate and this, too, may increase heat absorption by conduction.

Basking snakes do not always expose themselves to full view and many bask out of sight by lying beneath flat rocks (or, in artificial situations, under pieces of tin and other debris) where they can absorb warmth without running the risks of predation.

Nocturnal snakes often bask early on during their period of activity by flattening themselves against a rock or warm sand. Where surfaced roads pass through their habitat, snakes may bask on the road, often to their cost (but also to the benefit of herpetologists, who frequently use this fact to sample the snakes in a large area quickly and easily).

Conversely, heat can be retained by reducing the surface-to-weight ratio. This is achieved by coiling, the tightness of the coils acting as an accurate mechanism to regulate heat loss. In extreme cases, snakes may coil into an almost spherical mass and by doing so they reduce the surface-to-weight ratio to its lowest possible value and keep heat loss to an absolute minimum. Taking this a stage further, a large number of snakes, coiled up together, would be able to conserve heat more efficiently by forming a coiled mass: their aggregate surface-to-weight ratio would be relatively smaller than if each one coiled separately. This does seem to happen under certain circumstances, particularly during temporary periods of cold conditions, when snakes may be found coiled around one another.

Evidence that aggregations of snakes are the result of a desire to conserve heat is largely circumstantial. For instance, only northern species of rattlesnakes congregate in large numbers in dens while pythons and boas tend to be found together only in cooler parts of their ranges. Saving heat by aggregating would, of course, be only a temporary advantage because over a long period of time, as in hibernation, all the heat would be lost anyway. In the early spring, though, the inhabitants of a rattlesnake den may emerge to bask for short periods each day and, by aggregating during the following night, they could prevent their temperature from falling too low, so enabling them to be active earlier the next day. The

more individuals that were involved, the greater would be the effect and therefore benefit. It is worth noting that the members of such an opportunistic aggregation need not all be the same species and, indeed, large numbers of snakes, comprising three or four different species, have been discovered on a fairly regular basis (although heat conservation is not always necessarily the prime motive for these aggregations – see under 'Water balance', page 61).

Colour also plays a part in heat absorption. It is well known that black objects absorb heat much better than light coloured ones and so snakes living in cooler climates have a tendency to be black or dark in colour. In Australia, for instance, two of the most characteristic southern genera, the copperheads, *Austrelaps*, and the tiger snakes, *Notechis*, both of which are represented on Tasmania, have darker than average species, often black, in the southern portions of their ranges.

This difference is not restricted to entire species, however; sometimes individuals from temperate parts of the range are darker in colour than those from warmer areas, where a species has a wide range. For instance, black examples of the common garter snake, *Thamnophis sirtalis*, are found in isolated colonies towards the northern

▼ The black tiger snake, *Notechis ater*, comes from south-eastern Australia, where its black colour helps it to absorb heat more quickly, a distinct advantage in the relatively cool places in which it lives.

limits of the species' range, in Canada and northern USA, and European adders, *Vipera berus*, have a similar tendency to be darker in the more northern parts of the species' range, especially in Scandinavia and northern Britain. (Populations living on islands may also contain a high proportion of black individuals, but for reasons other than thermoregulation.)

There is growing evidence that snakes living in regions with distinct warm and cool seasons may even change colour slightly in order to improve heat absorption during cool weather and also to prevent overheating during hot weather. So far, only Australian snakes belonging to the Elapidae have been shown to do this but it is possible that snakes in other parts of the world have evolved similar mechanisms.

Female Madagascan tree boas, *Sanzinia madagascariensis*, take on a darker, more sub-dued coloration during pregnancy – again, this is almost certainly due to the need to improve heat absorption, in this instance because the growing embryos will develop

▲ Pregnant females need to absorb as much warmth as possible to speed up the development of their young: female Madagascan tree boas, *Sanzinia madagascariensis*, achieve this by changing to a darker shade of green during pregnancy.

▼ Snakes with black heads, such as Gould's black headed snake, *Unechis gouldii*, can expose only their heads when they begin to bask. This ensures that warmth reaches their brain and sense organs quickly, making them less vulnerable to predators.

re quickly if the female keeps her body
rmer and so speed up pregnancy. It would
interesting to know if other species
ve evolved this seemingly highly efficient
haviour.

Still on the subject of colour, an unusually
h number of snakes have black heads.
eems possible, or even likely, that these
akes expose their heads while keeping
 rest of their bodies under cover. The dark
mentation will help the head to absorb
t, which can then be shunted, via the
od, to the rest of the body. The advantages
this system would be that the brain and
sense organs, practically all restricted to
 head, would be the first parts of the body
begin operating efficiently, so the snake
uld be alert to danger before it took the
k of exposing itself completely. Black-
aded species are found in many parts of
 world: to take just a few examples at
dom there are several Australian species,
h as the black-headed python, *Aspidites
lanocephalus*, and Gould's black-headed
ke, *Unechis gouldii*, as well as the American
ck-headed snakes, *Tantilla* species, the
host indistinguishable Middle Eastern
cies *Rhynchocalamus melanocephalus*, and,
 a lesser extent, the European smooth
akes, *Coronella* species and hooded snake,
croprotodon cucullatus.

Conversely, snakes living under hot con-
ons are often pale in colour in order to
ect heat (although this may also result
m camouflage). Because they move about
close contact with the substrate, which
often extremely hot, their undersides
 also pale in colour and this may also
p to prevent them from overheating,
wing them to remain active longer than
y would if they had dark undersides.
 species that hunt diurnal lizards, for
tance, this is an important consideration.
Despite the efficiency with which snakes
 able to regulate their body tempera-

tures, it is inevitable that some fluctuations
will occur. These take two forms.

Daily thermoregulatory patterns

Firstly, there will be a daily pattern, and the
degree to which this swings up and down
will depend on whether the snake comes
from a tropical or temperate region. If it
comes from a temperate region, the amount
of fluctuation will depend on the time of
year – in early spring and late autumn there
will be greater fluctuations than during
midsummer and midwinter because the
day/night temperature differences will be
greater. Superimposed upon these daily
fluctuations will be the overall seasonal
fluctuations; again, these will be greater for
species from temperate regions and some
tropical species may be able to maintain
fairly constant temperatures throughout
the year.

The actual process of gaining heat from
the surroundings varies with the species and
with the season (in temperate species, at
least). It is simplest to first consider a typical
diurnal species, such as a garter snake,
Thamnophis, or a European grass snake,
Natrix. Tricks used by these species to raise
the body temperature include stretching
out the body while flattening and tilting it
towards the source of heat (usually the sun),
in order to expose as much surface area as
possible. These snakes tend to be black or
dark in colour and this helps them to absorb
radiant heat more effectively. Heat-gaining
activities take place in the morning, the
exact time depending on the season – in
early spring the snakes may not emerge
until midday and retreat again a few hours
later. On overcast days they may not emerge
at all. By midsummer, though, they may
be able to gain enough heat by basking for
just a few minutes early in the morning.
Basking snakes may begin by exposing only
their heads.

Having attained the ideal body temperature, the snake will then go about its
usual activities, including foraging for food,
searching for a mate and so on. If these
activities take it into cooler places, it may
bask again later in the day in order to 'top
up' its body temperature. As evening falls,
the snake will seek shelter, often underground, and by coiling its body it will
reduce the surface-to-volume ratio so that
heat loss is kept to a minimum. In this
way, its body temperature next morning
may be only slightly below its preferred
level, even though the ambient temperature
may have fallen quite drastically.

Nocturnal, crepuscular or secretive
species are not able to bask in the sun.
Instead, they may flatten their bodies against
a material such as rock, which retains heat.
This will extend their period of activity
into the night, even though the ambient
temperature may already have fallen below
their preferred level. They will need to seek
shelter again before their bodies cool down
to the critical temperature so that they are
not exposed to possibly lethal temperatures
during the coldest parts of the night.

In a way, comparing the thermoregulatory
behaviour of diurnal and nocturnal snakes is
putting the cart before the horse. More often
than not, the activity pattern of the snake is
controlled by the prevailing temperature
in the place that it lives. Thus in cold regions
snakes are likely to be diurnal, whereas in
hot places they are more likely to be nocturnal or crepuscular. Very often nocturnal
species are active at night *because* of temperature considerations: they live in areas
where daytime temperatures would be lethal
for them.

▼ A diurnal, active snake's body temperature may
be above or below the ambient temperature:
alternating periods of basking and sheltering help
it to maintain a fairly stable level.

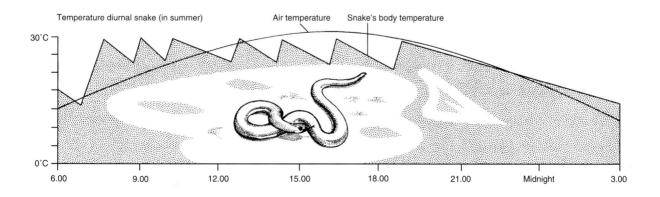

Temperature diurnal snake (in summer)　　　　　　　Air temperature　　Snake's body temperature

30°C

0°C

6.00　　　9.00　　　12.00　　　15.00　　　18.00　　　21.00　　　Midnight　　　3.00

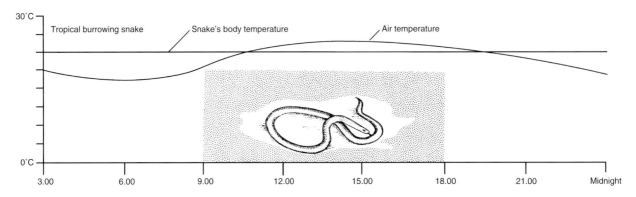

▲ Nocturnal tropical snakes, or burrowing species, have little opportunity to adjust their body temperatures and so they tend to be similar to the ambient temperature most of the time.

In tropical regions, where daily temperature fluctuations are smaller, snakes may not need to gear their periods of activity so closely to periods of suitable temperature. The availability of their food, and the time when it is most easily found, may be more important. Even in the tropics, however, ambient temperatures at ground level, under the forest canopy, can often be appreciably lower than the preferred temperatures of the snakes that live there and so it is wrong to assume that these species have higher preferred temperatures than temperate ones. On the other hand, they will almost certainly be less tolerant of cold temperatures (because they have not needed to evolve a system for coping with them) and so the critical and lethal minimum temperatures are likely to be rather higher than those of temperate snakes.

Seasonal thermoregulatory patterns

In places where there are significant temperature differences from season to season, snakes' activity patterns may also change. So, whereas diurnal snakes are rarely active at night, so-called nocturnal snakes are often active during the day at certain times of the year. During cooler parts of the year, they may be more active at dawn and dusk, i.e., they become crepuscular, or even during the middle part of the day, i.e., they become diurnal. Western diamondback rattlesnakes, *Crotalus atrox*, for instance, are usually found at night but during the spring they become active in the late afternoon and forage during daylight hours, returning to

▶ A western diamondback rattlesnake, *Crotalus atrox*, in a typical ambush situation in the late afternoon of a sunny April day. This species is mainly nocturnal but is active during the day early in the year, when the nights are too cold for it to hunt.

ir retreat early in order to escape from the
l night-time temperatures. These shifts
their activity patterns are in response
ly to temperature considerations.

\s the days become shorter and cooler,
kes may be active for only a short spell
h day and on especially cold days they
y not emerge at all. Whenever there is a
longed cold season, they will cease to
active altogether. They enter a period of
mancy, sometimes known as hiberna-
1, although this is not the same as hiber-
ion in mammals since they may well
ome active for short periods throughout
winter if conditions permit.

ome snakes prefer to hibernate in damp
iations, possibly to avoid the dangers of
iccation during cold weather. Groups
hibernating snakes have been found in
ded burrows and in old farm wells, for
iance, and there are cases where snakes
e become completely frozen. Some species
well adapted to cope with extremely
d spells of weather and, even if they do
ome frozen, most will recover once they
e warmed up again.

Cool season behaviour varies with species
l the places they live. Species from areas
h cold winters retreat to hibernation
s, where they may congregate with
er snakes of the same or different species.
ese dens are commonplace among rattle-
kes in the northern latitudes of North
herica and with the European adder,
era berus, and certain other members
he same genus, whereas other species of
se same genera, living in warmer places,
ernate individually or in small groups.
e dens may be located within the normal
ivity range of the individual snakes, or
y may be some distance away, forcing
snakes to migrate to and from the dens
the autumn and spring. Other species
snakes hibernate individually, usually
hin their home range. Individual hiber-
ion sites include cavities in rocks, old
ent burrows and holes at the base of
es. Some small species are often found in
ndoned ants' nests, either singly or with
er snakes. In warmer areas, snakes may
y need to shelter temporarily, during
rt cold spells of weather, and are active
ween these periods.

ncreasing temperatures in the spring
l eventually penetrate their hibernacula
l arouse them. Many species emerge
n communal dens to bask in its vicinity
a few hours each day. Mating may occur
his time, with the males using sperm
t was produced during the previous

Life in the cold

Animals living in extremely cold
environments need to evolve some
means of surviving subzero temperatures. Birds and mammals, being
endotherms, manage by producing
heat internally, maintaining their body
temperatures at a suitable level
regardless of the prevailing conditions.
Cold-blooded animals, however, do not
have this option and must evolve an
alternative strategy, or die.

Throughout the animal kingdom,
two such strategies have evolved:
'supercooling' and 'freezing tolerance',
Supercooling allows the body fluids
to fall below their freezing point
without the formation of ice; freezing
tolerance is an ability to withstand
formation of ice in the body.

In supercooling, substances in the
system, known as cryoprotectants, act
as antifreeze to prevent the formation
of ice within the body's cells: in other
words, they lower the freezing point of
the body fluids. One of the most
common cryoprotectants is glycerol
and related substances, found in many
species of insects and fishes that
inhabit waters that regularly freeze.

Freezing tolerance is an adaptive
ability that allows the formation of ice
in the body's cells without lethal
consequences. It is an alternative to
supercooling but may also work in
conjunction with it.

Because the body fluids contain
dissolved salts along with water, their
normal freezing point is below 0°C
(32°F), but only just: experiments have
shown that reptiles' body fluids have
a freezing point of −0.6°C (30.9°F).
Snakes living at the extremes of
their range may experience sudden
temperature drops to values below this
and so they would die if they did not
have some mechanism to counteract
it. One such species is the red-sided
garter snake, *Thamnophis sirtalis
parietalis*, which is the most northerly
occurring species in North America
and is found up to 60°N in parts of
Canada. This species hibernates in
communal dens, sometimes numbering
several hundred individuals.

In a series of experiments to establish
the tolerance of this species to cold, T. A.
Churchill and K. B. Storey lowered the
body temperatures of the snakes to
freezing point and below (*Can. J. of
Zoology*, 71(7):99–105). They found
that, in the autumn, garter snakes
could survive short periods at −5.5°C
(22.1°F) and longer periods, up to three
hours, at −2.5°C (27.5°F). During this
time, their body fluids contained up to
40 per cent of ice. After 10 hours, their
body fluids had an ice content of over
50 per cent and only about half
survived: after 24 and 48 hours, the ice
content had risen to 70 per cent of their
total body fluids and none survived. In
the middle of winter, however, their
results were somewhat different: they
could only survive temperatures down
to −1.2°C (29.8°F).

In order to find out which strategy
the snakes were using to counteract
freezing, they investigated samples
from the organs of the frozen snakes.
They did not find glycerol in any of the
organs they checked, but they did find
increased levels of glucose in the liver
and increased levels of lactate in the
heart. Otherwise, there was no sign of
these or other common cryoprotectants
in the snakes' organs. What they did
find, however, was abnormally high
traces of an amino acid, taurine,
which is known to have a role in
freeze-tolerant molluscs.

From these results, it seems likely
that red-sided garter snakes can
withstand freezing conditions due to
their ability to tolerate the formation of
ice in the body fluids for short periods.
This ability is greatly enhanced in the
autumn, but by midwinter it no longer
exists. The implications of this study
are that this species has evolved a
strategy for surviving short-term
freezing by a combination of
supercooling and freezing tolerance in
the autumn, when it may be caught
out by sudden frosts while it is still
active above ground, but its survival
during hibernation is dependent on
finding suitable sites below ground that
protect it from long-term freezing.

summer and stored over the winter. As the weather warms up the snakes disperse and their daily thermoregulatory patterns take over once more.

Limitations

So far, we have considered snakes that have some degree of choice as to where they go and what they do – they can bask, coil, shelter or disappear down a deep, cool burrow. There are groups of snakes, however, that do not have all these options. They include many fossorial species such as the blind snakes and the thread snakes, and fresh-water and marine water snakes. All these species have very limited opportunities to regulate their body temperatures. Burrowing snakes may be able to move up and down through the substrate to allow a limited amount of thermoregulation to take place, but there is no evidence that they actually do this. Similarly, water and sea snakes could move through the layers of water in order to thermoregulate, but, again, they appear not to have taken up this option. The colour of some sea snakes may help them to absorb radiation more quickly and therefore elevate their body temperature above that of the seas they live in and this has been shown for at least one species, *Pelamis platurus*, which spends its time at the surface of the water and has a dark dorsal surface. Most other sea snakes live at deeper levels, however, and so their coloration is likely to be controlled by factors other than thermoregulation.

How do burrowing and aquatic snakes regulate their body temperatures, then? The probable answer is that they do not. All the species studied so far had body temperatures about the same as their surroundings. This restricts them to parts of the world where ambient temperatures approach their preferred body temperatures: strictly burrowing and aquatic snakes are found only in tropical regions or are restricted to pockets of land outside the tropics where temperatures are relatively warm and stable.

The advantages of ectothermy

It is worth making the point here that, although ectothermy is often looked upon as a limitation, or as evidence of a primitive, poorly developed life-style, nothing could be further from the truth. Indeed, reptiles owe their success in many parts of the world, where they are the dominant group of vertebrates, to ectothermy. Warm-blooded, or endothermic, animals such as mammals and birds rely heavily on heat produced via their metabolic processes. In other words, a

▲ Aquatic marine snakes, such as the pelagic sea snake, *Pelamis platurus*, have limited opportunities to thermoregulate. For this reason, they are only found in warmer parts of the world.

large proportion of their food (perhaps as much as 90 per cent) is diverted away from growth, maintenance and reproduction, and channelled into heat production. For this reason, they need to feed frequently and so are restricted to places where they can be sure of a regular food supply. Reptiles, including snakes, on the other hand, require food only to maintain themselves and to grow and reproduce if possible. This enables them to survive on a small fraction of the food that would be required by a bird or mammal of the same body weight.

The desert is the most obvious example of an environment where food is scarce and there are advantages to be gained from being able to survive on very little. Reptiles, including snakes, are often the most obvious form of vertebrate life in such places and many species are so thoroughly adapted to life in the desert that they have evolved specialized methods of locomotion and so on.

The disadvantages of ectothermy

Despite the above, ectothermy has certain drawbacks. Firstly, it restricts reptiles to parts of the world where the daily temperatures reach fairly high levels for at least part of the day. Species living close to the Arctic Circle, in Scandinavia and Canada, have very limited periods of activity, often only

three or four months of the year. They m take many years to attain sexual matur and females may breed only every tv three or four years, using the 'fallow' ye to build up enough fat to produce offspri Furthermore, because large bodies ta longer to warm up than small ones, sna living in cold environments cannot afforc grow too big: all the larger species of sna are found within, or very nearly within, tropics.

Although snakes' low metabolic ra help them to survive on very little food, th is a trade-off in terms of energy. Endother with their high metabolic rates are able sustain work over a long period becau their breathing and heart rates can cont ually supply oxygen to the muscles. O after a relatively long period of exertion the muscles build up an oxygen de Snakes, on the other hand, with their l metabolic rates, build up an oxygen d very quickly. Although they can continue operate by breaking down stored chemic in the muscle cells (anaerobic metabolis this will also be of limited duration becau there is only a limited amount of mater that can be processed. For this reas they may be capable of short bursts activity, when chasing prey or escap from predators for instance, but they sc 'burn out' and must rest until they ha replenished their systems.

In practice, snakes overcome this probl by rarely venturing far from their retre and, in particular, only the most act species are seen out in the open, away fr suitable cover.

ysiological thermoregulation

hough behaviour is by far the most
portant means that snakes use to thermo-
ulate, there are occasions when physio-
ical processes help to maintain, or even
se, their body temperatures. The most
iiliar example of this is that of brood-
, pythons. It has been known for many
rs that female pythons coil around their
s during incubation. Although this
iaviour also serves to protect their eggs,
rmoregulation is at least as important.
the Indian python, *Python molurus*,
iperatures taken within the coils are
ially noticeably higher than those of the
rounding air. The way in which they
duce this extra heat is not completely
wn, but brooding females twitch or
ver regularly while they are brooding and
se muscle contractions seem to generate
ugh endothermic heat to raise the body
iperature slightly (just as shivering in
mmals helps to keep the body warm).
hough other pythons also shiver during
oding, temperature rises have only been
nitely established for the one species.
ne species manage to warm their eggs
leaving them to bask, then returning to
nsfer warmth from their bodies to the eggs
is, of course, is a behavioural rather than
hysiological activity.

Apart from brooding pythons, physio-
ical thermoregulation in snakes has not
n thoroughly investigated. The general
ling is that such mechanisms would be of
le use to small species because they lose
t to their surroundings too quickly. In
ge species, however, the metabolic rate
I the heart rate have been shown to
inge according to the conditions. These
inges could help the snake to warm up
ckly and then to retain its body heat
ger. In this way, it would increase the
ie it could be active, both at the beginning
I the end of its activity period.

spiration

piration in snakes is, in most ways,
ilar to respiration in birds and mammals,
luding ourselves. There are a few modifi-
ons and practical differences, however.

lungs

ierally speaking, the reptile lung is an
rovement on the amphibian lung – it has
e because amphibians can also breathe
ugh their skin whereas reptiles cannot.
ecause of their elongation, the left lung
nakes is either greatly reduced or effec-

tively absent. The capacity of the right lung
may be increased to compensate and, in
some species, there is an additional 'tracheal
lung' formed from a forward extension of
the right lung.

The actual process of breathing – getting
air in and out of the lungs – is done simply
by expanding the rib cage, as in mammals,
so that air is pulled into the lungs by suction
and pumped out again when the muscles
operating the ribs relax. Snakes can often be
seen moving the throat up and down as
though they were pumping air. Although
amphibians use this technique to get air
into the lungs, snakes seem to use it only to
draw air into the nostrils and so enhance
their sense of smell.

Gaseous exchange

Compared with mammals, there are basic
differences in the biochemical processes,
brought about by the slower metabolism of
snakes and their shape. The lungs are not
as efficient as those of birds and mammals,
and, in particular, they are not good at
eliminating carbon dioxide, the main waste
product of respiration. The excess carbon
dioxide left in the poorly ventilated lung
enters the bloodstream and combines with
water to form carbonic acid. This then
breaks down to bicarbonate ions. Because
of their inefficient lungs, reptiles have
needed to adapt to a higher concentration of
bicarbonate ions in their bloodstream.

Gaseous exchange is also affected by
temperature – at higher temperatures oxygen
is absorbed much more quickly. The effect of
this is that snakes breathe very occasionally,
and use very little oxygen, when they are
cold. As they warm up, so does their respiration rate. Even so, snakes and other reptiles
use much less oxygen than would a bird or
mammal of equivalent size and, in extreme
cases, snakes can survive without oxygen
for several hours.

In ectothermic animals, metabolism, and
therefore the rate at which oxygen is used
up, is also dependent on activity. As one
would expect, sleeping and resting snakes
breathe less often than ones that are looking
for food or are otherwise active.

The sea snakes are a special case. They
need to be able to stay submerged for as long
as possible otherwise they would spend too
much time repeatedly coming up to the
surface in order to breathe. Studies have
shown that most species come to the surface
to breathe every half hour or so, but that
they may stay submerged, voluntarily, for
up to two hours. Although their basic

anatomy is the same as that of terrestrial
snakes, sea snakes' lungs have a greater
capacity. There is a large tracheal lung,
extending well forward. The part of the lung
extending backwards (the saccular lung) is
not functional but forms a large air store.
Its wall is thick and muscular, unlike the
saccular lung of other snakes, and so the air
can be forced forwards into the functional
part of the lung (bronchial lung) where its
oxygen can be extracted.

Sea snakes are also unusual in the amount
of gaseous exchange that can take place
across the surface of their skin. Despite the
scaly covering, some species are able to
absorb up to one-fifth of their oxygen requirement in this way, a far greater proportion
than any land-dwelling species.

Although the aquatic wart or file snakes,
Acrochordus, are not related to the true sea
snakes, they also have extended saccular
and tracheal lungs to increase their capacity
and they can also absorb oxygen through
their skin. In addition, the granulated file
snake, *A. granulatus*, has a greater volume of
blood, relative to its size, than other snakes.

Water balance

All reptiles are covered with scales and this
was one of the factors that helped them to
leave the aquatic environment to which
amphibians are still more or less tied. Reptiles'
skins are not completely waterproof, however, and about two-thirds of their water
loss takes place through the skin. It is interesting that the scales themselves are not
significantly better at retaining water than
the skin between them – a few mutant
snakes lack scales altogether and these specimens have been shown, experimentally, to
be just as good at retaining water as normal,
scaled, individuals.

Because of the relative impermeability of
their skins, snakes are not capable of soaking
up water in the same way that amphibians
do. Therefore they must drink from time
to time or obtain water from their food.
Freshwater aquatic and semi-aquatic species
and rainforest species have a ready and
abundant supply of drinking water. At the
other extreme, desert species are often
unable to drink for long periods of time and
so water obtained from food is most important for them. Similarly, sea snakes do not
have access to fresh water, although species
belonging to the subfamily Laticaudinae
come ashore occasionally and have been
observed drinking from rainwater pools that
form in rocky crevices during rain and from
drops of rainwater on foliage.

After their scaly skins, the most important weapon in snakes' battle to conserve water is their excretory system. Unlike mammals, snakes convert their nitrogenous waste products to uric acid. This is a crystalline substance that can be excreted as a white paste-like substance containing almost no water. This greatly helps species from arid or marine environments to survive with little water.

Behaviourally, snakes may reduce the rate at which they lose water from their bodies by coiling. As in heat retention, this reduces the amount of surface area they expose and, thereby, the area over which evaporation can take place. In addition, if a number of snakes coil together, each individual will reduce its exposed surface area even further. Large aggregations of small, temperate snakes such as the red-bellied snake, *Storeria occipitomaculata*, are thought to have this purpose, while as long ago as 1936 Noble and Clasen showed that DeKay's snake, *Storeria dekayi*, and Butler's garter snake, *Thamnophis butleri*, lost less weight when huddled together than when they were separate, the difference almost certainly being due to differences in water loss.

It should be noted that not all snakes are equally good at saving water and their efficiency depends very much on their natural habitat – it has been estimated that rainforest species lose water about 100 times more quickly than desert ones. This, of course, is a function of evolution – mechanisms for saving water only evolve where there is a need.

Salt balance

The bodies of animals need salt in order to carry out their various functions. The most important salts are sodium and potassium although there are smaller quantities of a number of other salts, all obtained through the diet. The amount of salts in the system must be regulated and this is normally performed by the kidneys. The kidneys work to remove salt when there is too much and to conserve it when there is too little. In this respect, snakes are no different from other animals, although the actual concentrations of salts obviously varies.

Snakes living in the sea, however, are faced with a tricky problem; the salts in their bodies are at a lower concentration than in their surroundings, i.e. the sea in which they live. Through osmosis, there will be a tendency for water to flow out of their bodies until the concentrations are equal-

▲ The three species of acrochordids, such as the Arafura file snake, *Acrochordus arafurae*, have several adaptations that suit them to a totally aquatic lifestyle, including a larger lung capacity than other snakes.

► Colubrids belonging to the subfamily Homalopsinae frequently enter brackish or salt water and they have a gland for removing excess salt from their systems. It is situated in the roof of their mouth and therefore differs from the salt glands of the true sea snakes. The bockadam, *Cerberus rynchops*, is a typical homalopsine snake and is found in mangrove swamps and estuarine waters along the northern coast of Australia.

d. This would cause them to dehydrate
l so must be prevented. The problem is
st simply dealt with by making the skin
impermeable to water as possible and, as
ected, marine snakes have much less
meable skins than other snakes.

Sea snakes' food, consisting almost
irely of marine fish, is salty, and excess
t is therefore bound to accumulate in
ir systems. This must be excreted in some
y, but, unlike its mammalian counter-
t, the reptilian kidney is not able to
rete salts at a higher concentration than
present in the blood. An alternative
thod must be found to dispose of the
ess salt and this has evolved in the form
specialized glands, not found in other
kes. In the sea snakes, sea kraits and
rt snakes, this gland is situated under the
gue, and is therefore known as the sub-
gual gland. A duct leads from the gland
he sheath that surrounds the tongue so
t every time it is pushed out of the mouth
mall quantity of highly salty water is
hed out first.

The homalopsine water snakes (which
members of the Colubridae) do not have
ublingual salt gland but have indepen-
tly evolved a salt gland in the roof of their
uths. The one or two species of natricine
ter snakes that enter brackish water,
ably *Nerodia fasciata compressicauda*, seem
to have evolved a salt gland at all and
y presumably live within their bodies'
tolerance by only entering pure sea
ter for short periods of time and by drink-
plenty of fresh water.

The biological environment comprises the
organisms that live in the same place and
which have some bearing on the snake's
life. Because plants do not figure in the diet
of snakes, they have less of an impact than
they do in herbivorous groups of animals.
Plants are important, however, in providing
cover for snakes of all sizes, and piles of dead
vegetation are very often used by snakes as
egg-laying sites. Plants, including trees,
harbour the animals that snakes prey on
and so they are important, indirectly, in this
respect. Finally, plants buffer physical environmental factors, such as temperature and
humidity, by providing shade, absorbing
water and so on.

Some aspects of the biological environment are dealt with elsewhere: animals that
may form the prey of snakes are discussed in
Chapter 5, those that may in turn prey upon
them are dealt with in Chapter 6, and those
of the same species, that may be mates or
rivals, are covered in Chapter 7.

Interactions that do not involve eating,
being eaten, or mating, may be termed social
behaviour, and they can take place between
members of the same species or of different
species.

Social behaviour

Social behaviour is about interactions
between individuals – how they space
themselves in the environment, how and
why they communicate with one another
and whether they live as individuals or as
communities.

Studying the social behaviour of secretive
animals such as snakes obviously presents
many problems to researchers. Whereas
birds and mammals can be observed from
a distance, these methods are not generally
available for snakes. Furthermore, snakes
do not communicate with each other by
sound, nor by visual display, at least as
far as we know. The social behaviour
of snakes is limited, therefore, and such
information as we have often arrives fortuitously, as when pairs of mating or fighting
snakes are happened upon by chance or
when an aggregation of snakes is uncovered
accidentally.

It is generally accepted, then, that snakes
are not social animals. They are almost
unique in the vertebrate kingdom in not
showing any regular form of grouping, and
of being essentially non-territorial. Aggregations of snakes appear to be incidental:
they are formed in places where the environment is particularly favourable for one
reason or another or they huddle together

to conserve heat or water, as mentioned
earlier. These are not really social activities
because the groups may contain snakes of
various ages, sexes and species and may
occur at almost any time of the year: they
do not show any consistent patterns. There
appear to be few if any interactions between
the individuals of such aggregations although
they must obviously tolerate one another at
close quarters.

Mating aggregations have been observed
in certain species. These are often, though
not always, species in which large numbers
of individuals hibernate *en masse* and the
best known example is probably that of red-
sided garter snakes, *Thamnophis sirtalis parietalis*, in Manitoba, where huge numbers
of individuals have been found in 'mating
balls' immediately after their emergence
from hibernacula. Other examples concern
species that do not hibernate: small groups
of male diamond pythons may remain with
a female for about four to six weeks during
the breeding season, for instance. Other
observations seem to indicate that one or
more males will track down and follow a
'ripe' female for several days or even weeks
and that these animals can often be found in
close proximity to one another at this time.

Hibernacula, or dens, normally contain
members of the same species, although
mixed aggregations of snakes are not uncommon. Where good sites are hard to find,
all the snakes from the surrounding areas
may converge on them. Lang (1969)[1] found
that abandoned ant mounds are widely
used as hibernacula in Minnesota, and,
over a two-year period, eleven ant nests
yielded 2,019 red-bellied snakes, *Storeria
occipitomaculata*, 276 smooth green snakes,
Opheodryas vernalis, and 131 eastern garter
snakes, *Thamnophis sirtalis*. A single mound
contained a total of 299 snakes, including
all three species. Snakes from these sites were
estimated to have travelled 150–300 m
(160–320 yds) from the areas where they
were active in the summer. In another survey,
Carpenter (1953)[2] dug out ant mounds in
Michigan, and up to seven species of snakes
were found in a single mound. These
included two species of garter snakes, *Thamnophis sirtalis* and *T. butleri*, ribbon snakes,
T. sauritus, water snakes, *Nerodia sipedon*,
smooth green snakes, *Opheodryas vernalis*,
red-bellied snakes, *Storeria occipitomaculata*,
and a De Kay's snake, *Storeria dekayi*.

Other snakes may occasionally co-habit
with other types of reptiles, as in the case of
the Florida indigo snake, *Drymarchon corais
couperi*, which is often associated with the

▲ Female prairie rattlesnakes, *Crotalus viridis*, congregate in well-defined 'rookeries' when they are pregnant.

burrows of gopher tortoises, especially in the winter months when cool weather may drive it underground for a few days at a time.

Other types of aggregation involve the movement of snakes to particular areas for purposes other than hibernation or mating. Examples of these are rather scarce, although it has been noted that females of some species are found close to one another immediately before laying eggs or giving birth. Reichenbach (1982),[3] for example, described an aggregation of about 150 pregnant female garter snakes, *Thamnophis sirtalis*, in a small area at an abandoned brick factory in Ohio. The snakes were found under pieces of corrugated metal sheet scattered over the site and these are thought to have attracted the snakes because they provided good basking sites. Males were present but in much smaller numbers. In another case, Graves and Duvall (1993)[4] discovered that female prairie rattlesnakes, *Crotalus v. viridis*, in Wyoming moved to specific areas when they were pregnant. These 'rookeries' were always in rocky places and may have enabled the females to warm themselves more easily.

▶ Hatchling snakes usually disperse as soon as they hatch, although adverse weather may cause them to remain in the vicinity of their clutch mates for a short time.

It is safest to assume, in the absence of more evidence, that aggregations such as these occur when suitable basking or egg-laying sites are in short supply or when they are concentrated in a fairly small area. With egg-laying species, the correct soil type, or soil with the right moisture content, may attract gravid snakes.

Populations

The structure of snake populations has be studied in only a small number of speci Certain deductions can be made from th studies, however.

Mortality

Most population studies have shown t mortality among medium-sized, tempera species is highest during the snake's fi year. This is because small snakes are m prone to predation; because they are l large enough to store sufficient food to them through long periods of starvatic because they dehydrate more easily th large snakes (due to a larger relative surf area); and because they are generally l experienced at coping with the trials life. Once they approach sexual matur their prospects improve and morta among adult snakes may account for or a small proportion of the population ea year.

Abundance

Like many other aspects of their biolo the density of snake populations is hard measure, due to their secretive habits. T proportions of males, females and juveni within a population is even more diffic to establish for the same reason.

gh densities of snakes often occur sea-
lly, due to their gravitation towards or
y from hibernation or aggregation sites.
ther times, there appears to be little or
attern to the way in which they space
nselves out in the environment; densities
uate from time to time and from place
ace as they move hither and thither.

timates of population numbers can
etimes be made by mark and recapture
nods, where a number of snakes are
ured and marked. Some idea of numbers
be obtained by calculating the propor-
of marked individuals that crop up in
equent collections. Unfortunately, for
method to be accurate, a relatively large
ber of snakes need to be marked, and
e must be a good number of recaptures.
r precautions need to be taken in order
void errors in the calculation and better
lts are obtained if the study is conducted
a long period of time.

sing this technique, population densities
igh as 1,849 snakes per hectare (748
cre) have been established for the ring-
snake, *Diadophis punctatus* (Fitch,
5),[5] 1,289 snakes per hectare (522 per
) for the striped swamp snake, *Regina*
i (Godley, 1980),[6] and 729 snakes per
are (295 per acre) for the worm snake,
hophis amoenus (Clark, 1970).[7] It is
h pointing out that these are all
ively small snakes, two of which are
etive and feed largely on worms and
r soft-bodied invertebrates (which are
lly in plentiful supply), and the other
lleni) is a semi-aquatic species in which
lations are necessarily concentrated
suitable habitat. The vast majority
ark and recapture studies have shown
lations to be much less dense than
e figures, very often less than one snake
ectare, or two snakes per acre. Further-
e, hardly any tropical snakes have
studied in this way. When the same
ies has been studied at different times
ifferent places, widely different results
be obtained. This serves to illustrate
problems associated with population
ies of this kind.

pulation numbers probably fluctuate
year to year, according to the amount
od available and, subsequently, on the
oductive success of the adults. Some
ies are relatively short-lived, sometimes
surviving for a year or two, and their
lations are more likely to change dras-
ly in response to environmental factors
those of long-lived species. Whereas
uations in population numbers may

The ideal sex ratio

The sex of an animal's offspring is determined by the sex chromosome, one (either an X or a Y chromosome) is being carried in the male's sperm and the other in the female's egg. Eggs contain only X chromosomes. If the sperm carries an X chromosome the offspring will be female and if a Y chromosome it will be male. The offspring are therefore equipped with either a pair of XX chromosomes, in which case they will be females, or with an XY combination, in which case they will be males. Theoretically, male parents could influence the sex of their offspring by producing more of one type of sperm than the other. Females could also influence the sex of their offspring by selectively killing one type of sperm before fertilization of their eggs took place.

Except in a few unusual cases, the sex ratio among most species of animals, including snakes, is found to be roughly 50:50. Since male snakes do not help the female to raise the young, they do not need to form pair bonds and are therefore free to mate with as many females as they can find. So, because a single male can mate with any number of females, it may seem that a system that favoured a large number of females and a few males would be more sensi-ble. Furthermore, in many mating systems, dominant males mate with several females whereas small or subordinate males never get to mate at all. Why should such a system have evolved?

R. A. Fisher offered the explanation in his 1930 book *The Genetical Theory of Natural Selection* (Clarendon, Oxford). The key to understanding this problem is to realize that animals do not act 'for the good of the species' but for the good of themselves. More accurately, their *genes* act for the good of themselves: each gene within an animal's system wants to find itself duplicated in as many of that animal's offspring as possible.

Consider a hypothetical population where females outnumber males by 10 to one. Each female breeds for 10 years and produces 10 eggs: her reproductive potential is 100 offspring, each of which

shares half of her genes and half of their father's. Each male, however, will mate with 10 females, on average and so his reproductive potential is 1,000 offspring, each of which will contain half of his genes: males will be 10 times more successful at proliferating their genes. The best strategy now would be for each female to produce more male offspring (because this would give them the largest possible number of grand-children). The sex ratio will begin to swing towards a 50:50 split until, eventually, the population will contain an equal number of males and females.

Since males are so valuable in terms of producing grandchildren, will the sex ratio become biased towards males? The answer is no, because if there is a surplus of males, not all of them will get the chance to mate. All the females will produce young every breeding season, all other things being equal, but some of the males will not. If the pendulum swings too far in favour of males, there will be advantages in producing females.

In practice, populations do not oscillate between abundances of males and females: the selective pressures of producing one sex or the other are equally balanced and, over time, a stable system will have arisen.

Although there are exceptions to this rule, in social animals, and in species in which the sexes are different sizes, these do not seem to apply to snakes. Of the 2,500 or so snake species, the two sexes occur in roughly equal numbers. Skewed sex ratios, in which one sex or the other predominates, have been established in only five species, and the differences are only slight in some of them. *Apparent* skewed ratios some-times show up when male and female snakes have different habits: males may be more active than females, for instance, or they may be more brightly coloured, as in some vipers, and then are more likely to be caught. Again, some batches of newborn or newly hatched snakes may contain more of one sex than another but this is invariably due to chance: if a large enough sample was available, the sex ratio would correct itself.

▲ The Japanese rat snake, *Elaphe climacophora*, appears to be unusual among snakes because populations contain more females than males.

mirror fluctuations in food supply, steady declines can often be attributed to habitat changes, usually due to human activities. These, too, are difficult to measure but can often be noticed even by casual observers. Increases in population may also be due to habitat changes and have been noted in a few cases, as, for instance, when species colonize areas that have become irrigated, or when introduced species proliferate in a new environment.

Sex ratios

Apart from population numbers, it is interesting to look at the proportion of males and females within a population. The flowerpot snake, *Ramphotyphlops braminus*, is a female-only species (see page 147, Chapter 7) and can be ignored here. Otherwise, male and female snakes would be expected to occur in equal numbers at hatching. Since they are usually of similar size, there is no advantage in producing a higher proportion of one sex over another.

This appears to be the case in all the species that have been studied, with just a few known exceptions. Four of these exceptions involve species in which males predominate: the copperhead, *Agkistrodon contortrix* (in which there are twice as many males at birth as there are females), the four-striped rat snake, *Elaphe quadrivirgata*, the Australian tiger snake, *Notechis scutatus* and the gopher snake, *Pituophis melanoleucus*. It is difficult to offer an explanation for these figures. The fifth exception is that of the Japanese rat snake, *Elaphe climacophora*, in which females predominate at hatching. Again, it is hard to explain why this should be so and the possibility of small sample sizes producing a false picture should not be discounted.

In later life, sex ratios can differ from those that are found at hatching or birth, due to sampling error, dispersal of one sex or another, or differential mortality, where one sex is more likely to die early in life than the other.

Rarity

The opposite of abundance is, of course, rarity. Unfortunately, the term 'rare' can have several meanings, depending on its context. It can be applied to snakes that have a restricted range such as a small island, or those that have a much larger range over which they are thinly scattered.

At the same time, rarity can be an artifact of human powers of observation – species that 'rarely' interact with mankind or which live in inaccessible places. Many tropical snakes, for instance, are known from only a handful of specimens; this does not necessarily mean that they are rare because, very often, they live in regions that are little visited by herpetologists. Maps that show their distribution may have more to do with the distribution of herpetologists than with the snakes. This is a major problem because the areas where there are a lot of snakes – Amazonia, central Africa, south-east Asia – tend to have few herpetologists. Areas where there are many herpetologists, on the other hand, tend to have few species of snakes.

It is also important to distinguish between total rarity and local rarity. Most species become rare towards the edges of their range, though they may be common else-

where. In Britain, for instance, the sm[o]
snake, *Coronella austriaca*, is extremely r[]
although it is quite common over muc[h]
continental Europe.

There are three other reasons for sn[a]
to be naturally rare. Firstly, all animals [t]
operate towards the top of the food ch[]
are likely to be rare. As energy flows up[]
food chain, about 90 per cent of it is los[]
each level. By the time it reaches the hig[h]
levels, there is precious little left to sup[]
the animals that forage there. Snakes [may]
be positioned at various stages in the [food]
chain. Many species are small and []
on small animals, such as invertebra[]
which are plentiful. These snakes are li[]
to be common (though often overloo[]
because they are small and secretive). La[]
species, however, operate much close[]
the top of the food chain and one w[]
expect them to be rarer.

Secondly, some species are so hig[]
specialized, in terms of their food prefere[]
or some other requirement, that t[]
numbers are severely limited by the am[]
of that particular resource. Some sn[]
are incredibly specialized: the African []
eaters; species that feed only on amp[]
baenians; species that lay their eggs in []
nests, for instance, and there will alw[]
be an upper limit to their popula[]
densities.

Thirdly, the species that have evolve[]
isolation are likely to be rare. This ap[]
especially to island species, such as []
many endangered snakes of the West In[]
and other island groups throughout []
world (see Chapter 4). It also applie[]
species that evolve on ecological 'islan[]
such as isolated mountain ranges. A sim[]
situation prevails among species wh[]
ranges have become fragmented thro[]
the appearance of a physical barrier []
dispersal, either natural or man-m[]
Since snakes have very limited abilitie[]
cross hostile habitats, their opportun[]
to break out of restricted habitats are []
Not only is their habitat limited, but []
colonies may be founded by few individu[]
leading to a lack of genetic variation wh[]
itself makes them vulnerable. For insta[]
the pit vipers, *Bothrops insularis*, from []
small Brazilian island of Queimada Gra[]
may be dying out due to the appearanc[]
the population of a lethal gene. This g[]
causes some snakes to be intersexes – t[]
have characteristics of both males []
females and are sterile. Without the op[]
tunity to outbreed, they could be doome[]
extinction through inbreeding.

we look at communities of snakes, most
hem seem to consist of a relatively small
nber of very common species and a
er number of rare ones. Allowing for the
ewhat selective nature by which snakes
found, the most reasonable explanation
this is that common species are well
pted to the environment and are usually
d to be generalists, especially with
rd to their food requirements. The rare
cies, on the other hand, are often
ialists, with limited resources available
hem. The habitat, and the resources it
tains, have been divided up, over time,
veen a number of species, but it has not
n divided equally. Specialists scratch a
ng by eating items that the common
ies either overlook or are not equipped
eal with. In addition, species that occur
ow densities are less likely to attract the
ntion of predators than abundant
cies. The predators will not only form

search images of the more common species
but may also acquire behavioural and
morphological adaptations that are aimed
at those species. Certain species exploit
this system by being polymorphic: they are
trying, in effect, to become two or more rare
species instead of one common one. (Polymorphism is discussed in Chapter 6.)

Although there is no evidence that the
species richness of snake communities is
controlled by predators, there are precedents
in other branches of biology. It is well known
that grazing, which is a form of predation
(on grass), produces a rich community of
plants that often includes many rare species.
Among animals, it has been found that
when predatory starfish were removed from
a community, the number of species in the
community fell from 15 to eight. Predators
of snakes may 'make room' for some of
the rarer species by controlling the numbers
of the more common ones.

1. Lang, J. W. (1969), 'Hibernation and movements of *Storeria occipitomaculata* in Northern Minnesota', Contributed papers to the 12th annual meeting of the SSAR, in *Journal of Herpetology*, 3(3–4):196–197.
2. Carpenter, C. C. (1953), 'A study of hibernacula and hibernating associations of snakes and amphibians in Michigan', *Ecology*, 34(1):74–80.
3. Reichenbach, N. G. (1982), 'An aggregation of female garter snakes under corrugated metal sheets', *Journal of Herpetology*, 17(4):412–413.
4. Graves, B. M. and Duvall, D. (1993), 'Reproduction, rookery use, and thermoregulation in free-ranging, pregnant *Crotalus v. viridis*', *Journal of Herpetology*, 27(1):33–41.
5. Fitch, H. S. (1975), 'A demographic study of the ringneck snake (*Diadophis punctatus*) in Kansas', *Univ. Kans. Mus. Nat. Hist. Misc. Publ.*, 62:1–53.
6. Godley, J. S. (1980), 'Foraging ecology of the striped swamp snake, *Regina alleni*, in southern Florida', *Ecol. Monogr.*, 50:411–436.
7. Clark, D. R. (1970), 'Ecological study of the worm snake, *Carphophis amoenus*', *Univ. Kans. Publ. Mus. Nat. Hist.*, 19:85–194.

are snakes

number of snakes are known only
om very few specimens, but they are
ot necessarily rare – some live in
eas that have been little visited and
hers are very secretive species. Some
ecies, however, are on the verge of
xtinction, usually because they have
ry limited distributions, often islands,
d have suffered greatly from habitat
struction.

The following examples are a few of
e species that are considered rare, for
rious reasons.

ustralian thread snakes Four species
e known from single specimens:
amphotyphlops margaretae,
. micromma, *R. troglodytes* and
. yampiensis. A fifth species,
. kimberleyensis, is known from two
ecimens. Four of the five come from
e north-western region of Australia,
e 'Kimberley', which is difficult to
xplore and where many interesting
nimals have been discovered in recent
ears. The other species, *R. margaretae*,
from the arid interior of Australia.
hread snakes are small, secretive
rrowing species that are easily
verlooked.

▲ Rough-scaled python, *Morelia carinata*.

The rough-scaled carpet python
This species, *Morelia carinata*, was
described in 1981 from a specimen
collected ten years previously, in 1971.
It also lives in the Kimberley region
of Australia. A second specimen
was found in 1987 and a third in
1993.

Cropan's tree boa *Xenoboa cropanii*,
sometimes included in the genus
Corallus, was first described in 1954
from south-eastern Brazil. Only three
specimens are known.

Tropidophis fuscus This species, which
has no common name, was described
in 1992 from two specimens, found in
Cuba. No further specimens have been
found to date.

Round Island boa *Casarea dussumeri* is
found only on Round Island, which
has an area of only about 1 sq km
(250 acres). In 1983 it was estimated
that only 75 individuals remained and
it is probably the world's rarest snake.
A captive breeding programme has
been instigated to try to increase its
numbers with a view to reintroducing
it at a later date.

4
Where Snakes Live

The distribution of snakes can be looked at on two scales. Global patterns of distribution are interesting because they tell us about the evolution and spread of the major families and also, incidentally, add to our knowledge of the geological history of the earth's landmasses. On a smaller scale, it is plain to see that different snakes tend to live in different habitats. These two viewpoints are not exclusive, and the distribution of a particular species will depend on an interplay between the global distribution of its near relatives and the availability of a suitable habitat.

◄ Long, slender snakes are characteristic of tropical rainforests, where their light weight can be supported on thin branches and their elongated shape helps them to span gaps between branches. The blunt-headed treesnake, *Imantodes cenchoa* is a fine example.

HABITATS

Snakes are found in most types of habitats. Where they are not found, the climate is normally the limiting factor – very cold places, such as tundra, the polar ice caps and very high mountains lack snakes because they are untenable for large ectotherms requiring a relatively high body temperature in order to operate.

With regard to habitat type, snakes can either be classed as generalists (those species that are found throughout a region within a number of different habitat types) and specialists (those species that are invariably found in a particular type of habitat). The distinction is not clear cut, though, and species may show differing degrees of specialization.

Tropical forests

Tropical forests are found in Central America and the Caribbean region, South America, Africa, Madagascar, India, south-east Asia and northern Australia. The threats to their existence, through logging, agricultural development, pollution, etc., have been well publicized and need no further comment here. It is estimated, however, that removal of large expanses of tropical forests will have eliminated, or critically depleted, about half of the world's species of plants and animals, including snakes, by the end of this century.

Ecologists recognize several different types or subdivisions of tropical forests, depending on altitude, amount of rainfall and plant types. The distribution of snakes within these categories has not been thoroughly established and the habitat must be dealt with in its entirety for the time being.

Tropical forests are well known for the richness of their flora and fauna. Snakes fit this pattern, attaining their greatest diversity in tropical forests. A number of factors

▲ Tropical rainforest, a rich habitat that has been fully exploited by snakes from several families and with a wide variety of lifestyles.

◀ Many arboreal snakes are greenish in colour. *Chrysopelea paradisii* comes from south-east Asia and is known as the 'flying snake' because it sometimes glides from tree to tree.

contribute to this. Firstly, temperature rarely a problem because most tropi regions remain at a fairly constant, mod ately high temperature throughout year, despite the closed canopy. They o a wide scope of microhabitats, includin range of niches for arboreal, terrestrial, se aquatic and burrowing snakes. Some these niches are only available because the prevailing, near optimum temperatu allowing snakes to be active even thou they have limited or no opportunities bask.

Tropical forests offer abundant cover, b for secretive species that hide among under vegetation and forest debris, cryptic species that 'hide in full view', ecially some of the green arboreal species. y is not normally a problem either, with abundance of other animals to eat, ging from the smallest invertebrates up medium-sized mammals and including phibians, birds, bats and other reptiles. eral snakes from this habitat have devel- d specialized diets, such as land molluscs, have evolved appropriate adaptations. addition, many tropical forest species feed smaller snakes, creating a complex food that may never be unravelled.

Contrary to popular belief, snakes are not ily found in large numbers in tropical ests. Collections often show great species ersity but numbers of each species may be y low. For example, in a recent expedition Belize, Central America, Stafford (1991)[1] orded 12 species but, of these, six records sist of single specimens, two records sist of two specimens and another con- s of three specimens. Only one species, *stigodryas melanolomus*, was classed as nmon. This almost certainly reflects the iculty of finding snakes in this type of bitat – during clearance operations, such road building and logging, snakes are n found to be incredibly numerous.

Of 15 currently recognized families of kes (and taking the Colubridae as a gle family) all are represented in tropical ests except two: the Bolyeriidae and the rochordidae.

mperate forests

contrast to tropical forests, temperate ests are not rich in snakes, either in terms species or numbers. The cool climate of perate regions is compounded by the opy cover and such species that are nd in this type of habitat are usually tricted to lightly wooded areas, forest ges and clearings.

Black rat snakes, *Elaphe o. obsoleta*, for mple, are found around the edges of ests in temperate parts of North America. s habitat preference appears to be corre- d with birds' nesting habits, which vide a favoured source of food for the kes. Owing to agricultural practices, the ount of this habitat is decreasing, leading reduction in the numbers of the snakes.

nakes that are adapted to cold environments, as the adder, *Vipera berus*, may sometimes be d on the edges of woods or in clearings.

Deserts

Deserts are found in North and South America, Africa, Asia and Australia. The largest expanse includes the Sahara and a series of other deserts extending eastwards across the Arabian peninsula and into central Asia. In North America, deserts cover much of the south-western United States and northern Mexico. All together, arid and semi-arid regions cover about 30 per cent of the earth's surface. Although they are defined as areas in which there is a deficiency of water, their characteristics vary from place to place, according to temperature and altitude. Thus there are the sand deserts, such as the Sahara, the Atacama and the Namib, characterized by dunes, and stony deserts like the Sonoran

▲ Deserts are the home of many species of snake which are ideally suited to withstand their low productivity. Different types of deserts attract different species and communities: the gravel de of the Sonoran complex is home to a large numb of rattlesnakes as well as diurnal and nocturnal colubrids, a boa, an elapid and a thread snake.

◄ Dunes provide a different type of desert environment for another set of species. Extensive dune systems are found in several parts of the world: these form part of the Namib Desert.

and Chihuahuan Deserts. Each of th presents peculiar problems to the pla and animals that have colonized them. N all deserts are hot places: most have w temperature fluctuations from day to ni and some experience severely cold winte

Deserts are among the best habitats which to find and observe snakes. T species richness and numbers of individu are in sharp contrast to the situation other groups of animals, especially bi and mammals. The reason that they are successful here is partly related to th ectothermy; because they do not use part of their food intake to produce he snakes can exist on much less food tha bird or a mammal of equivalent size, ab one-fiftieth of the amount, according some estimates, and they can survive l periods without any food. This is obviou helpful in areas where the food supply limited and unreliable.

The lack of water that character deserts is overcome partly by snakes' sc

► The American sidewinder, *Crotalus cerastes*, which is perfectly adapted to deserts containing substantial areas of windblown sand, through i locomotion and coloration.

skins, which help to limit the amount of water lost, and partly by their excretory systems, which produces waste in the form of uric acid, a semi-solid requiring very little water to carry it out of the body. In addition, their relatively small size and long, slender shape are beneficial when it comes to avoiding lethally high temperatures (and lethally low temperatures) as they can easily crawl into small crevices among rocks or down rodent burrows, where temperatures are tolerable. Their low food requirement, and therefore their need to forage only occasionally, allows them to shelter from the heat or cold for as long as is necessary. Furthermore, their well-developed sensory systems, especially their ability to detect vibration,

the tongue and Jacobson's organ, and the heat-sensitive pits of several species, make them well adapted to nocturnal foraging when necessary.

Desert snakes may be found among a number of families, especially the Colubridae and the Viperidae but including, to a lesser extent, members of the Boidae, including pythons, the Elapidae and even the Leptotyphlopidae.

Grasslands and savannah

Grasslands are distributed throughout the mid latitudes, often known under local terms such as steppe (Asia), prairie (North America), veld (South Africa) and pampas (Argentina). Many of them cover vast areas

and some have been created, or enlarge by human activity or by natural fir destroying the forest cover. Savannah the term used for tropical areas of low ve; tation, including grasses, and may form link between deserts and tropical fores Grassland and savannah covers about or quarter of the world's surface.

Many grasslands are extensively cu vated or grazed by livestock and this not beneficial to reptile life. Periodic fir either natural or due to human int vention, hinder the establishment of via populations of snakes, either directly by eliminating their food supply, as do spraying with pesticides. It seems like however, that snakes have never fu

The effects of changing habitats

Even subtle changes in habitat can lead to changes in the species found in a given area. In a survey undertaken in 1987 and 1989, Mendelson and Jennings looked at the effects of habitat alteration in south-eastern Arizona and adjacent south-western New Mexico (*Journal of Herpetology*, 26(1):38–45). They compared their findings with those of a survey which took place about 30 years previously.

The area comprises a mixture of semi-desert grassland and desert scrub

but, since the first survey was carried out, much of the grassland has been replaced with scrub, altering the relative proportions of the two types of habitat. In addition, large numbers of cattle watering troughs have been installed in the area.

Altogether, 23 species of snakes were found, although many of these occurred in very low numbers. The most significant species were two species of rattlesnakes, the western diamondback and the Mojave, *Crotalus atrox* and *C.*

scutulatus, the gopher snake, *Pituophis melanoleucus* and the chequered garter snake, *Thamnophis marcianus*.

By comparing the numbers of each species found, as a percentage of the total number of snakes, it was possible to show how the snake community had altered; the garter snake had become much more common (9.7 per cent of the total snakes found compared to 1.1 per cent in the previous survey), almost certainly due to the presence of the cattle troughs, which attract breeding amphibians such as spadefoot toads, *Scaphiopus*, on which the garter snakes feed. Western diamond back rattlesnakes had increased slightly, from 15.0 per cent to 18.4 per cent of total snakes found but the Mojave rattlesnake had declined dramatically, from 45.5 per cent to 17.5 per cent. The gopher snake had increased slightly, from 14.1 per cent to 16.9 per cent.

These figures show that, as the semi-desert grassland gives way to desert scrub, the western diamondback rattlesnake benefits at the expense of the Mojave species. The garter snake, and perhaps the gopher snake, on the other hand, probably benefit from increased ranching activity.

◀ **Western diamondback rattlesnake,** *Crotalus atrox.*

exploited open grasslands in the same way that they have other habitats, although the reasons for this are not altogether clear. Overall temperatures may not be high enough in many of these regions and food supply may be sparse, while lack of cover may increase the chances of predation, especially from birds of prey.

Although snakes are not widely found in this type of habitat, there are exceptions, especially in Africa, where the African rock python, *Python sebae*, for example, is almost limited to open situations, although only where rock outcrops provide satisfactory cover. In North America, species such as the hognose snakes, *Heterodon*, one or two species of rattlesnakes, *Crotalus*, and some forms of the gopher snake, *Pituophis melanoleucus*, are found in prairies although they are not limited to them. European grasslands are not extensive like those in other parts of the world, often being divided into fields and meadows by hedges and walls, providing some cover and protection from extremes of temperature. Several species of *Vipera* may be found in such areas, as may the rat snakes, *Elaphe*, and the whipsnakes, *Coluber*. All of these species tend to be generalists, rather than grassland specialists.

Swamps and marshes

Swamps and marshes may be found throughout the world wherever the water table is close to the surface. They may be permanent, as in the Florida Everglades, or temporary, either drying out seasonally or becoming inundated with water, as in the Pantanal. In addition, the fringes of lakes, ponds, rivers and streams often provide a significant amount of semi-aquatic or marsh-like habitat. Mangrove swamps

(above) Extensive grasslands, sometimes known [as p]rairies (as here, in New Mexico) or savannahs, [som]etimes have a rich and varied snake fauna.

(centre) Australian grasslands are especially rich [in] snake species.

[A] typical grassland snake, the amethystine [pyt]hon, *Morelia amethistina*, in habitat in Papua [Ne]w Guinea.

Most aquatic snakes feed, naturally enou
on fish, although some also eat fish e
and invertebrates.

The homalopsine colubrids (poss
forming a separate family, the Homalo
dae) all come from south-east Asia, and
totally aquatic in habits, living in fre
water ponds and lakes. Some of them n
enter the sea occasionally. Of the th
species belonging to the Acrochordidae
file snakes, two live in fresh water a
the other in brackish coastal or estuar
waters.

The most highly adapted aquatic spec
however, are the sea snakes and sea kra
normally classified as subfamilies of
elapids but sometimes placed in two fami
of their own, the Hydropheidae (sometir
spelled Hydrophiidae) and the Laticaudic
containing 47 and five species respectiv
The sea snakes have the widest distributi
covering the coastal waters from sou
eastern Africa, across India and south-e
Asia to the northern coasts of Australia
single species, *Pelamis platurus*, extends t
range to the west coast of Central and Sou
America as it is pelagic, drifting in the up
levels of the ocean, often in large groups
'slicks'. The other species inhabit shallow

form a particular type of habitat, associated
with coasts and estuaries in favourable
tropical regions.

These types of habitats are widely used by
snakes. One of their main prey types,
amphibians, dwells there, and fish are also
available more often than not. Tropical
and subtropical swamps are more heavily
utilized than temperate marshes, due simply
to the benefits of higher temperatures. The
natricine colubrids, such as the European
Natrix and the North American *Nerodia*
species are especially associated with damp
habitats, but very many tropical snakes
may also be found in damp situations.

Mangrove swamps are inhabited by a number of rather specialized snakes, including a
species of file snake, *Acrochordus javanicus*,
and some marine snakes, which forage
around them at high tide. Certain natricine
snakes that feed on crustaceans are also
found here.

Aquatic habitats
Aquatic habitats may be freshwater or
marine. Purely aquatic snakes are more
or less confined to the tropics because water
acts as a heat sink, preventing snakes from
maintaining body temperatures very much
higher than the water surrounding them.

seas, often around coral reefs or mangrove forests, where food is plentiful.

The sea kraits are found in coastal waters around south-east Asia and the south-western Pacific islands. They are less aquatic than the true sea snakes, needing to come on to land in order to lay their eggs. One species lives only in a land-locked, brackish lagoon on Rennell Island, one of the Solomons group.

Mountains

Montane environments occur throughout the world, often surrounded by other types of habitat such as forest, desert or grass-lands and therefore becoming ecological islands. They present snakes with the serious problem of low temperatures, either perma-nently or seasonally. Tropical mountains are usually covered with forests, such as cloud forest, and a few of the species from lower altitudes may find their way into moderately high altitudes here, but mountain tops above the tree line at any latitude, are not heavily populated by snakes.

Of all the snakes, the vipers have most exploited the montane habitat. *Agkistrodon himalayanus* has been reported at an altitude of 4,900 m (16,000 ft) in the Himalayas, the highest recorded for any species of snake, although it is more commonly found between 1,500 and 3,000 m (5,000 and 10,000 ft). *A. strauchi* lives at elevations of up to 4,267 m (14,000 ft) in Tibet and

▶ Mountains present certain problems to snakes, not least of which is the fact that they tend to be cold for at least part of the year. Nevertheless, there are many species that are restricted to mountain ranges in different parts of the world. Small vipers are especially well represented.

▲ The twin-spot rattlesnake, *Crotalus pricei*, is found only in or near scree slopes, known locally as talus slides, in isolated mountain ranges in the southern United States and northern Mexico.

A. monticola is found between 3,600 and 4,000 m (12,000 and 13,000 ft) in Szech-wan, China. *A. halys* goes up to at least 4,000 m (13,000 ft) in central Asia and *A. intermedius* to at least 3,000 m (10,000 ft) in the desolate Lar Valley of Iran (now flooded), along with *Vipera latifi*. Three *Vipera* species from Europe, *V. berus*, *V. aspis* and *V. ursinii*, may reach 2,900 m (9,500 ft) in parts of their range.

In North America, the highest ranging species is the Mexican dusky rattlesnake, *Crotalus triseriatus*, recorded at more than 4,300 m (14,100 ft) in central Mexico. Several other rattlesnakes can be found at altitudes ex-ceeding 3,000 m (10,000 ft), including the Pacific rattlesnake, *C. viridis*, in California and Arizona, the cross-banded mountain rattlesnake, *C. transversus*, the

twin-spot rattlesnake, *C. pricei*, the r-rattlesnake, *C. lepidus*, and the small-hea rattlesnake, *C. intermedius*, in Mexi Willard's ridge-nosed rattlesnake, *C. willa* and the blacktailed rattlesnake, *C. moloss* reach almost to 3,000 m (10,000 ft) Arizona and adjacent parts of Mexico.

In Africa yet another viper, the b adder, *Bitis atropos*, is found up to 3,000 (10,000 ft). Other species may reach sim altitudes in the mountains of central a East Africa but these areas are poo explored herpetologically. Similarly, in South American Andes, altitudinal reco are poorly documented but, again, it wo seem that vipers fill the montane nic with *Bothriopsis albocarinata* and *B. altic* occurring at around 3,000 m (10,000 ft Ecuador.

an and disturbed habitats

...nough the encroachment of the human ...ies in all its forms is nearly always ...strous to wildlife, including snakes, ...e man-made habitats can, in excep-...al circumstances benefit certain species. ...st notably, the influx of vermin, in the ...n of rodents which accompany human ...elopment, provides a ready source of ...d for some of the larger snakes, provided ...y can escape the attention of the human ...abitants. Harmless snakes are tolerated ...ome parts of the world for this reason. ...er commensals, such as insects, attract ...ll lizards, especially geckos, and these, in ...n, are preyed on by numbers of snakes.

...gricultural development in the devel-...d world is usually accompanied by the ... of chemical pesticides and herbicides ...ich do nothing to enhance the habitat ...ar as snakes are concerned, but in devel-...ng countries, where low-tech agriculture ...till carried out, snakes may again be ...rated or even encouraged due to their ...eficial effects on rodent populations.

...udging by the numbers of snakes that are ...n found in them, abandoned dwell-...s often provide good refuges for snakes ...ng in otherwise featureless habitats. ...ey may be attracted by the cover afforded ...the structures themselves or, again, by ...ulations of rodents that live in such

...a rapidly expanding urban areas, good snake ...tat may be surrounded by development. Where ... occurs, small populations of snakes become ...ted but can linger on for some considerable ...e. This is a southern Pacific rattlesnake, *...alus viridis helleri*, photographed on a small ...in a Californian suburb.

places. Flooded quarries and gravel pits can provide additional habitats for aquatic and semi-aquatic snakes, and at least one population of the queen snake, *Regina septemvittata*, has moved into an abandoned quarry on one of the islands in Lake Erie following an increase in the numbers of crayfish since the quarrying stopped. In Britain, many abandoned gravel pits, often stocked with fish for the benefit of anglers, have healthy populations of grass snakes, *Natrix natrix*.

◄ Deserts are especially prone to habitat destruction and there is less chance of regeneration than there is in rainforests, for instance. Agriculture, involving irrigation, spraying, road building and human settlements, is one of the main threats.

ADAPTATIONS TO HABITATS

Each type of environment can be regarded as a set of circumstances, or problems, that must be faced. Natural selection is the process through which animals arrive at a design that best suits them to the various circumstances they find themselves in. Under a given set of conditions, individuals with qualities that are best suited to those conditions are the most likely to survive and pass on their genes. This is the driving force behind evolution, in which each population gradually changes in many subtle ways until it resembles its ancestors less and less. It adapts to its surroundings.

Habitats, then, tend to shape the animals that live in them. The size, shape, colour and other anatomical and behavioural modifications become the 'signature' of snakes from a particular type of habitat. The reason for this is quite simple. Two species of snakes, faced with identical problems, are quite likely to solve them in the same way, regardless of which part of the world they live in or what family they belong to. They come to share certain characteristics and may even look like one another. Where this produces very close similarities between unrelated species, the term 'convergent evolution' is used.

There is a corollary to this, of course. Where closely related populations find themselves in differing conditions, they will each adapt to their own circumstances. Over a period of time they will begin to look different from one another and at some stage these differences will have reached the point where we could call them different species. This process is known as 'adaptive radiation'.

Although many snakes show very few extreme modifications, there are certain characteristics that can be identified as being more frequently seen in snakes from a certain type of habitat.

Snakes in trees

Arboreal snakes are most common in tropical and subtropical countries where over half of the species may live in trees. Here, temperatures are suitable for snakes even in the shade and, in addition, the high rainfall favours a dense growth of tall vegetation, giving arboreal animals plenty of scope.

Arboreal species are found mainly among the Colubridae, Viperidae, Boidae and the Pythonidae and in some regions they may account for 50 per cent or more of the snake fauna. There is no obvious explanation for the lack of elapids (with exception of the

▲ The eyelash viper, *Bothriechis schlegelii*, occ in several forms, of which this 'lichen' coloratio perhaps the most remarkable.

mambas) among arboreal snakes, in spite of their close relationship with, and similarity to, the colubrids.

The most highly modified species are those that are totally arboreal, or nearly so. Many other species which spend differing amounts of time in trees and bushes may show certain of the characteristics of arboreal snakes, or may show the characteristics in less obvious ways.

Highly arboreal snakes have long, thin bodies, and long tails that are usually prehensile. Their bodies are often flattened from side to side; this gives them extra rigidity in the vertical plane, allowing them to cantilever out to bridge gaps between branches. Their heads are often long, with pointed snouts. Some of the tree snakes that are bulkier than average, such as the boids and some vipers, are nevertheless thin compared with their close relatives. Lightness of weight is an important consideration, especially for species that may need to crawl along thin branches in order to reach their food, and also helps the snake in stretching from one branch to another. The slender shape also helps some species to remain hidden when resting among vines, twigs and thin branches. The main disadvantages of a long, thin shape are the inability to store food or to produce large clutches of eggs. The tropical distribution minimizes these problems, however, because

food is usually abundant throughout year in the tropics and breeding may t place for all, or most of, the year.

Nearly all arboreal snakes are green brown in colour, obviously in order escape detection, either by predators prey, or both. In most, the underside lighter in colour than the dorsal surfac pattern known as counter shading, seen in fishes. The principle behind thi that light will fall on the dorsal surfa making it appear lighter, whereas underside will be in shadow, making appear darker; when viewed from the s the expected three-dimensional image be hard to discern. Many species have lor tudinal lines, especially through the in order to enhance their camoufla and some of the more spectacular ones h patterns that simulate mossy or lich covered branches.

The eyes of arboreal snakes are typic large with vertical pupils, characteristi nocturnal hunters. Those belonging to genera *Ahaetulla* and *Thelotornis*, howe have horizontal keyhole shaped pupils t help them to judge distances well Chapter 2, pages 39, 40). Because prey easily be lost if it is not firmly grasped, m

Convergent evolution and parallel evolution

...akes living in different parts of the ...orld are often very similar to one ...other, or they may share certain ...usual characteristics. These ...aracteristics may be related to ...fence, feeding, reproduction, or to ...her facets of their lives, and their ...milarities may be limited to one or ...o features – the pattern of their ...arkings, the shape of their snout, ...eir method of reproduction, etc. ...other cases, the similarity may ...compass several aspects of the ...akes, to the extent that unrelated ...ecies from different parts of the world ...n be difficult to tell apart without ...ose examination.

...Species that look alike usually live in ...milar habitats, and have similar life-...les: they have similar ecological ...quirements. Each species has had to ...lve the same problems in order to ...rvive, and each has arrived at the ...me solution.

...Where the species are descended ...om a common ancestor they may ...ve many shared genes, retained in ...e population because they are ...luable; the term 'parallel evolution' is ...en used for pairs or groups of species ...this type.

...If groups of species come to resemble ...ch other more closely than their ...cestors did, however, the term used

is 'convergent evolution'. Species that show convergent evolution do not share the same genes: their characteristics have evolved independently. Convergence can sometimes pose problems in the field of classification because similarities in appearance, or in certain characteristics, do not necessarily imply that the species that have them are closely related.

There are many examples of convergent evolution among snakes but it is perhaps best illustrated by the emerald tree boa, *Corallus caninus*, from South America, and the green tree python, *Chondropython viridis*, from Australasia. These species look like one another and are about the same size. They also behave in a similar fashion, draping themselves over horizontal branches and hanging their heads down in order to ambush their food. The young of both species have different colours from the adults. Although they are both boids, they are not very closely related, and are placed in different subfamilies.

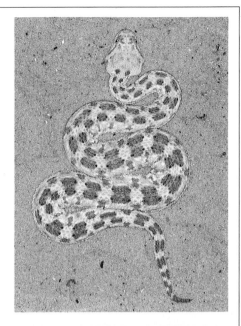

▶ Desert horned viper, *Cerastes cerastes* (top) and the American sidewinder, *Crotalus cerastes* (bottom).

▼ The emerald boa, *Corallus caninus* (left), and the green tree python, *Chondropython viridis* (right).

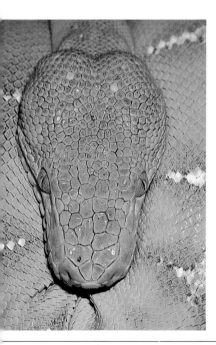
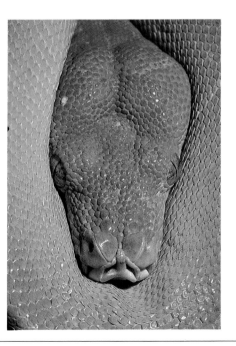

A second example, from a totally different habitat, concerns sidewinding snakes. Desert dwelling vipers from North America and Africa, typified by the sidewinder, *Crotalus cerastes*, Peringuey's viper, *Bitis peringueyi*, and the desert horned viper, *Cerastes cerastes*, all have the same characteristic method of locomotion, known as side-winding and described on page 38, Chapter 2. Furthermore, all these species are, again, roughly the same size and coloration. Although they are only distantly related, their chosen habitats are similar – loose, windblown sand and dunes over which sidewinding is the best method of moving. Sidewinding has also evolved in several lesser-known species from South America, the Middle East and central Asia.

▲ Snakes of the genus *Ahaetulla* have elongated, horizontal pupils and, hence, binocular vision. This allows them to judge distances accurately, a useful asset when climbing and striking at their prey.

arboreal snakes have long teeth, especially useful for penetrating the plumage of birds, while others are venomous species, either front- or rear-fanged, that hold their prey while their fast-acting venom takes effect.

Of the 'occasional' arboreal snakes, the rat snakes, *Elaphe*, show a further adaptation. Some species, those more inclined to climb, have a well-defined ridge at the junction of their ventral and dorsal scales, so that each ventral scale has a corner on each side. This is used to gain purchase on rough vertical surfaces such as the bark of trees. A similar arrangement exists in the arboreal boas and pythons, *Corallus* and *Chondropython*, which have laterally flattened bodies so that the ventral scales are narrow and also form ridges, although not as well defined as those of the rat snakes.

Burrowing snakes

Snakes that burrow are found mainly in tropical and subtropical regions because, like arboreal species, their opportunities to raise their body temperature above that of their surroundings are limited. Burrowing snakes are found in every family except the Tropidophiidae and the Acrochordidae. Several families, such as the Anomalepidae,

Leptotyphlopidae, Typhlopidae, Aniliidae and Uropeltidae, contain *only* burrowing species. The degree to which they burrow, and therefore the degree to which they have evolved morphological adaptations, vary. Many species are exclusively burrowers – they spend all or most of their lives beneath the ground. Other species, however, burrow only on occasions and may regularly be found on the surface. These species burrow to avoid danger or extremes of heat or cold,

to lay their eggs or to find their prey, an their adaptations to burrowing may no obvious from their outward appeara The type of substrate in which they also plays its part in the direction in w adaptations occur. Species that burro loose, drifting sand, for example, will rather different from those that tu through harder soils.

The confirmed burrowers, or tunne are those species that spend their whole underground, only occasionally emer on to the surface. They can be characte by a number of anatomical features. heads are not well defined from their bo and either their eyes are small or they be very simple and covered with scales. bodies are cylindrical in cross-section their scales are smooth and shiny. tails are short and, in some species, en a short spine or more elaborately mod scales. The three most primitive famil snakes, the Anomalepididae, Typhlop and Leptotyphlopidae, show all these cha teristics, as do members of the Uropelt in which the tails of some species en an oblique plate-like scale covered small spines. All the snakes in these families have skulls that are heavily and which are more rigid than thos most other snakes, to help them to

▼ *Typhlops diardi*, from Asia, is a member of family containing only burrowing snakes. Its e are rudimentary, it has smooth, shiny scales a cylindrical body.

way through the substrate. This limits
size of food they can engulf, although
is not normally a problem as they all
nvertebrates, mainly ants and termites
e case of members of the three primitive
lies, and earthworms in the case of
shield-tails. Both *Xenopeltis* species, and
cemus bicolor, which is the sole member
s family, have cylindrical bodies, small
and smooth, shiny scales, especially
peltis, which are beautifully iridescent
n seen in sunlight.

rrowing members of other families
w varying degrees of adaptation. The
owing boids all belong to the subfamily
inae, and include the rubber boa,
ina bottae, in North America and the
boas, *Eryx*, in Africa, Europe and Asia.
e species also follow the typical pattern
urrowing snakes, as does the only truly
owing python, the monotypic *Calabaria*.
owing examples among the colubrids
not so easily categorized. A number of
ies burrow for their food and they may
w slight modifications, especially to the
es of their snouts.

ther species, though, are sand and soil
mmers', moving effortlessly through
e particles in a serpentine manner.
se species have smooth scales and
ally flattened, streamlined skulls in
r to reduce friction or drag as they move
ugh the substrate, and sharp, upturned
es to their rostral scales. Many of them
brightly banded, although the link
een this and their burrowing habits is
well understood. Species of this type
found in several parts of the world and
n closely parallel one another in general
earance. They include the shovel-nosed
es, *Chionactis*, and the sand snakes,
meniscus, in North America, *Prosymna*
Elapsoidea in Africa and *Neelaps* and
selaps in Australia.

he gopher and pine snakes, *Pituophis*,
e slightly modified snouts and at least
e species use these to excavate burrows
chambers in which to lay their eggs.
ral other colubrids, from various parts
e world, have similar modifications to
r snouts, often to enable them to root
food that may be buried just below the
ace. These are not burrowing snakes,
tly speaking.

he burrowing elapids include species
South America (the coral snakes),
ca, Asia and Australasia. These species
burrow in order to hunt their food
ch, in some species at least, consists
st exclusively of other burrowing

▲ Like several species that live in sandy or dusty
places, the Namaqua dwarf adder, *Bitis schneideri*,
hides itself by shuffling beneath the surface.

reptiles. As a rule, they do not form their
own burrows but follow their prey along
tunnels that are already formed. Their
adaptations to a subterranean life, therefore, are limited to the smooth shiny scales,
small eyes and cylindrical bodies. The
burrowing asps, or atractaspidids, are all
burrowing species but, again, it seems
probable that many of them move through
the burrows that were made by their prey.
Some species have a unique adaptation
connected with their feeding habits: their
fangs can be moved laterally and made to
project from the side of their mouth even
when it is closed. This enables them to stab
their prey without opening their mouths,
which would be difficult in the confines of a
burrow.

A different type of burrowing is undertaken by a number of desert species, especially
those from sandy areas. These species are
'shufflers', working their way down below
the surface by rocking their bodies to and
fro. For this to be effective, the body must
be flattened, or capable of being made so
by spreading the ribs. The flanks are then
drawn into a sharp edge, and are easily
pushed into the substrate, which eventually
covers them. Unlike most burrowing snakes,
these species have keeled scales and are to be
found almost entirely within the Viperidae,
and include the sidewinder, *Crotalus cerastes*,
from North America, the desert horned
vipers, *Cerastes* species, from North Africa
and the Middle East and the carpet, or saw

scaled vipers, *Echis*, from Africa, the Middle
East and western Asia. Burrowing in these
species serves the purpose of concealment, as
they rest with just their eyes, and horns if
they have them, showing on the surface.
From this position they are well placed to
ambush their prey.

Aquatic snakes

Most snakes (including arboreal and burrowing forms) can swim quite well but
some are totally aquatic or almost so.
These include all three species of file snakes
(Acrochordidae), certain colubrids, especially those belonging to the subfamilies
Homalopsinae and, to a lesser extent, the
Natricinae, and the sea snakes and sea
kraits, Hydropheinae and Laticaudinae,
which are either classified with the elapids
or placed in families of their own. Only one
viper, the cottonmouth, *Agkistrodon piscivorus*, is normally associated with water.

Adaptations seen, to a greater or lesser
extent, in aquatic species, include the placement of the eyes and nostrils towards the
top of the head, and a laterally flattened
body and, especially, tail. The purposes of
these modifications are fairly obvious: the
nostrils enable the snake to breathe without
breaking the surface, the upward pointing
eyes enable it to watch for predators from

WORLD PATTERNS OF DISTRIBUTION

above and the flattened tail helps to propel it quickly through the water.

Other adaptations include keeled scales (although these are not confined to aquatic and semi-aquatic species), which may help them to swim more easily. Heavily keeled scales are especially characteristic of the natricine colubrids, many of which are semi-aquatic, but are not always present in aquatic snakes. The scales of the file snakes, for instance, are rough and granular, and are thought to help them to grasp fish when they coil around them.

The aquatic marine species have salt glands, either beneath the tongue (in the file snakes and the marine elapids) or in the roof of the mouth (in the homalopsine colubrids).

Other adaptations are less obvious and are concerned with the mechanics of diving. Because these species remain submerged for considerable amounts of time, the capacity of the lungs has increased. In addition, part of the lung functions as an organ of buoyancy. In the case of a file snake, *Acrochordus granulatus*, an abnormally large amount of blood circulates, further adding to its diving efficiency. It has roughly twice as much blood as a land snake of similar size and the blood can hold more oxygen than that of other species of snakes. This is of great value because it allows the file snake to remain submerged for longer and, in particular, to remain hidden in underwater burrows during the day, when it is inactive. Furthermore, the file snake may be unique among marine species in being a 'sit and wait' predator, so its ability to remain motionless underwater for extended periods is of special importance.

Even where suitable habitats exist, snakes may be absent altogether, or certain families may be found whereas others are not. In other places, several families are represented. Then again, closely related species may be separated by several thousand miles (of ocean for instance). The distribution of snakes, and the ways in which they have dispersed and speciated, are potentially among the most fascinating aspects of their biology.

On a local level, species owe their distribution to their urge to spread into neighbouring areas as their population grows. A growing population is accompanied by an expanding range. A shrinking population, in contrast, often goes hand in hand with a contracting or fragmenting range. During successful periods, populations grow until they become overcrowded and this forces some animals into fresh areas. During less successful periods, areas are vacated, but these are not always the most recently populated ones. In this way, the range of a population changes almost imperceptibly and often in tune with changing environmental conditions. Some species adapt to new conditions better than others and they become widespread, often at the cost of more specialized species. The ranges of some species may become smaller and smaller until they disappear altogether – they become extinct.

Obviously, the spread of populations will, sooner or later, be stopped at physical barriers such as oceans, deserts, mountains, etc. Barriers for one species, however, may be dispersal corridors for others, depending on their habitat preferences. Over long periods of time, barriers and corridors change position as a result of geological activity. For example, snakes reached Madagascar from the African mainland before the Mozambique Channel was formed. Similarly, North and South America were once separated and so the opportunities to disperse up and down the continents were limited until relatively recently.

When snakes first appeared, over 100 million years ago, the shapes of the landmasses were very different from how they are now. The southern continents, South America, Africa and Australia were joined together and, in addition, the pieces that were later to become Madagascar, India and south-east Asia, were attached to them. The northern continents, North America, Europe and northern and central Asia, formed the other large landmass. Dispersal of terrestrial animals was therefore much

easier than it is now and families that w radiating into different habitats were to move into many different parts of t respective 'continents'. Because of this, snake fauna of North America has n in common with that of Europe and cer Asia than it does with South Ame which shares similarities with the soutl continents – Africa, southern Asia Australia.

Only the more primitive families snakes, early ancestors of the surviv families, had evolved at the time w some of the large landmasses were jo together. By the time the more fam families began to appear, the shape the landmasses were already beginnin change. Some families evolved after cer pieces broke away and so their oppo nities to disperse were more limited t those that evolved when they w together.

Although it is not possible to give a c pletely accurate account of the sequenc events, the relationships between the sr families, and their distribution, can to fill in at least some parts of the ti table. For example, the absence of viper Australia indicates that this family evo after Australia broke free from the la landmasses. Conversely, the presence boas on Madagascar shows us that family had already evolved before So America and Africa parted company.

An overview of the world's geogra regions, in relation to the distribution snakes or, more particularly, snake fami is most easily undertaken by dealing v the continents in turn.

North America
The North American snake fauna inclu five families. Of the primitive snakes, t are a few species of *Leptotyphlops*, and species of boas, the rubber boa, *Cha bottae*, and the rosy boa, *Lichanura triving*

The colubrid fauna of North Americ relatively rich in species although c three subfamilies are present. These the colubrines (typical colubrids such kingsnakes and rat snakes, *Lamprop* and *Elaphe*), natricines (semi-aquatic sn such as garter and water snakes, *Th nophis* and *Nerodia*) and a few specie xenodontines (a poorly understood of colubrids that includes the hog snakes, *Heterodon*, among others). genera *Elaphe* and *Coluber* are also preser Europe and Asia while *Nerodia* of N America is very closely related to *Natr*

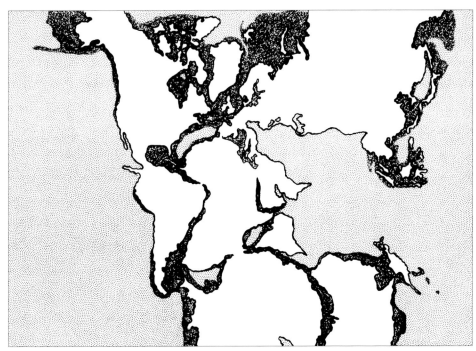

hen snakes first evolved, the major land-
es were joined, allowing certain groups to
d into many new areas. As the landmasses
d apart, however, opportunities for dispersal
more limited and this explains the isolation of
n small families. The dark areas represent the
nental shelves.

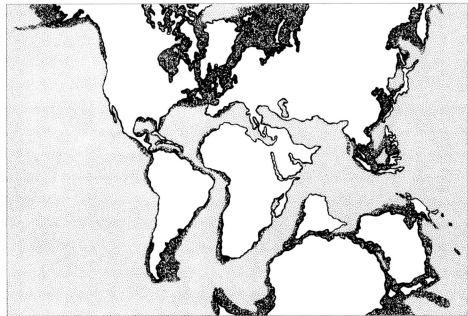

pe and Asia. These links are due to
ancient connection between North
rica and Eurasia. South America has
atricine snakes, showing that its con-
ion to North America is, by contrast,
ively recent.

North America, as elsewhere, the colu-
s have radiated into many ecological
es. There are burrowing, terrestrial
semi-aquatic species, and a few arboreal
. The wide variety of habitats and
atic zones has also helped to bring about
rsity, with more species being found
rds the south of the continent than
e cold northern parts. Especially rich
s include the subtropical swamps of
hern Florida and the south-western
rts.

apids are present, but only just, in
form of a small number of coral
es, *Micrurus* and *Micruroides*: these are
ominantly tropical snakes that are
numerous in Central and South
rica.

pers, on the other hand, are well repre-
ed in North America but only in the
of pit vipers such as members of
genera *Agkistrodon* and, especially, the
esnakes, *Crotalus* and *Sistrurus*. Isolated
ntain ranges in the south-west help
oost the number of species because
are home to a number of specialized
es, especially small rattlesnakes.

America.

Central and South America, including the Caribbean region

All three families of primitive burrowing
snakes, the Typhlopidae, Leptotyphlopidae
and Anomalepidae, are well represented in
South America. Other primitive families that
are found here include the pipe snake, *Anilius
scytale*, the only member of the Aniliidae,
the Boidae and the Tropidophiidae. Of the
latter two families, the greater numbers of
their species are found on the West Indian
islands, although they are represented on
the South and Central American mainland
by some wide-ranging species, especially *Boa
constrictor* and *Epicrates cenchria*. *Loxocemus
bicolor*, the only member of the Loxocemidae,
is found in the southern parts of Central

Central and
South America.

America, although its origins are something of a mystery.

Although there are many colubrid snakes, most belong either to the Colubrinae or the Xenodontinae. In addition, there are a number of poorly known species whose relationships have not been assigned yet. Some of these species are wide ranging, but others have very limited distributions. A number of colubrids are highly specialized, including the members of the Dipsadinae, which eat only molluscs.

The South American elapids consist entirely of coral snakes belonging to the genus *Micrurus*, of which there are many species. Vipers of the subfamily Crotalinae include a rattlesnake, large terrestrial pit vipers such as the bushmaster, *Lachesis muta*, and a great many arboreal species.

Europe

This region has a great deal in common with North America, as has already been noted. It also contains small numbers of species from neighbouring regions that, between them, help to increase the number of families represented: these include the Typhlopidae and the Boidae, in the form of a single species of blind snake, *Typhlops vermicularis*, and a single sand boa, *Eryx jaculus*. In addition, a single species of pit viper, *Agkistrodon halys*, also enters Europe, technically speaking, although its range only includes a very small part of extreme eastern Europe.

The dominant elements of European snake fauna, then, are the colubrids and vipers. The colubrids include the colubrines and the natricines that have close relations in North America, and some rear-fanged species that may have invaded from North Africa and/or the Middle East: the cat snake,

Telescopus fallax, which is found in south-east Europe, and the Montpellier snake, *Malpolon monspessulanus*, and the hooded snake, *Macroprotodon cucullatus*, which are found in south-west Europe. None of these is dangerous to man. All the European colubrids are terrestrial or semi-aquatic. A few species climb occasionally but there are no specialized arboreal species.

Vipers are well represented in terms of species, and are found in the far north as well as the southern part of the continent, around the Mediterranean region.

North and central Asia and the Middle East

For the purposes of snake distribution, northern and central Asia are similar to Europe because there is no barrier to dispersal between them and they all have similar temperate climates. They have many genera in common, therefore, although the pit vipers, *Agkistrodon*, and the sand boas, *Eryx*, are somewhat better represented in northern and central Asia than they are in Europe.

The Middle East has a more distinctive snake fauna, largely because of its position, making it accessible to species from Africa as well as southern Asia. The predominant

North and central Asia, and the Middle East.

habitat is desert, and so many species are desert specialists.

The families Typhlopidae and Leptotyphlopidae are each represented by a single species and there are two boids, the sand boas *Eryx jaculus* and *E. jayakari*. The Colubridae of the region consists mainly of typical terrestrial species such as those belonging to the genus *Coluber*, as well as some smaller, more secretive species and rear-fanged species such as *Telescopus*. A single species of burrowing asp, *Atractaspis engaddensis*, is also found here, as is a single

species of elapid, the Egyptian co *Walterinnesia aegyptia*.

The vipers are present in the forr two species of horned vipers, *Cerastes*, carpet vipers, *Echis*, the false horned v *Pseudocerastes* and several members o genus *Vipera*, which occur mainly in more mountainous parts of the region.

Southern and south-east Asia

This region, which includes all of tro Asia, is very rich herpetologically. Tw the three primitive burrowing families present in numbers, only the Anomalep being absent. The boas are represente one or two sand boas that reach t warmer parts and the pythons are well resented by several large species. Two o three species contained in the Acrocho are found here, as are both xenope *Xenopeltis unicolor* and *X. hainanensis.* Uropeltidae is also endemic to this regi

The Colubridae is very well represe and includes several subfamilies (per families in reality) that are not found where. These include the Calamari Homalopsinae, Pareatinae and the X derminae. Other colubrids found in sout and south-east Asia include very n colubrines and natricines as well as se genera whose relationships with c colubrids are not altogether clear. Colu from this region include burrowing, te trial, arboreal and aquatic species.

Many species of elapids are also f here, including several cobras and k but many smaller, less conspicuous sp as well. The pit vipers are widely dispe and include the genera *Agkistrodon* *Trimeresurus*. The true vipers are represe by Russell's viper, *Vipera russelli*. Fea's v *Azemiops feae*, which forms a sepa subfamily, Azemiopinae, is found in mountains of southern China.

Southern and south-east Asia.

Europe.

very successful snake

he adder, or northern viper, *Vipera rus*, is one of the world's most ccessful snakes. It has the largest eographical range of any terrestrial ecies (only the sea snake *Pelamis aturus* can theoretically be found over wider area) and is found from Britain d Scandinavia, through much of ntral Europe, across northern Asia far east as the Pacific Ocean. Here it ccurs on the island of Sakhalin, north Japan. In the southern parts of range it is restricted mainly to ountain ranges but elsewhere it has almost continuous distribution, ving in a wide variety of habitats, cluding moors and heaths, meadows, oodlands and marshes. Despite the uge range, there are only three bspecies: *V. b. bosniensis* is found parts of the Balkan region and *b. sachalinensis* is the form on akhalin Island and on the mainland extreme eastern Asia: elsewhere, the ominate form, *V. berus berus* is to be und.

Not only is the adder the most idespread snake, it also occurs further orth than any other species, having en recorded to a latitude of 69°N in candinavia, well inside the Arctic rcle. In northern parts of its range it is e only snake to be found and in any other parts it is the most mmon species.

Apart from differences between the bspecies, the adder shows little ariation throughout its range, though the ground colour, and the ntrast between the zigzag markings d the background, may vary slightly. here is a rare form in which the zigzag replaced by a continuous vertebral e, and also a totally black form. lack specimens have a velvety ppearance and sometimes crop up in therwise normal colonies but more mmonly they make up a substantial oportion of certain populations wards the north of the range and, ore especially, on some of the small

islands in the Baltic Sea, where it is common. It seems that the dark coloration enhances their ability to warm up quickly and that this more than compensates for the cost of poor camouflage.

That an ectothermic animal should be so successful in the cold, northerly

regions it inhabits is due to a suite of adaptations: small size, dark coloration and viviparous breeding habits. In parts of the range it may be forced to hibernate for eight months of the year, often emerging in the spring when patches of snow still lie on the ground. Truly a snake for all seasons.

Africa and Madagascar

There are several members of the Typhlopidae and the Leptotyphlopidae in Africa, mainly south of the Sahara. These families are not found on Madagascar, however. Boas are found on the African mainland in the form of sand boas, *Eryx*, and on Madagascar as three species of typical boas, belonging to the endemic genera *Acrantophis* and *Sanzinia*. Pythons, of the genera *Python* and *Calabaria*, are found only on the African mainland.

Africa and Madagascar.

Although colubrids are well represented, both on the African mainland and on Madagascar, the relationships of many genera are not clear. In some cases, there appears to be a link with species from South America, as there is with the boas. Most of the Madagascan genera are endemic to the island.

The family Atractaspididae, which has created many problems for classifiers but which seems to be closely related to the Colubridae, is found almost entirely in Africa, the only exception being the one species that reaches the Middle East. African and Madagascan colubrids include burrowing, terrestrial, semi-aquatic and arboreal species, many of which are highly specialized.

There are many genera of elapids, including several *Naja* species, and the mambas, *Dendroaspis*, which are notable for being the only arboreal cobras. There are no elapids in Madagascar.

A similar situation exists within the Viperidae, where a number of typical, terrestrial vipers, including members of the genera *Bitis*, *Causus* and *Echis*, are found throughout most of the continent in a variety of habitats but have not spread to Madagascar.

Australasia

New Zealand is easily dealt with because it has no snakes. Australia, however, is well endowed although few families are present. Of the primitive burrowing snakes, members of only the Typhlopidae are present. The Pythonidae, however, is very well represented and Australasia appears to have been one of the centres of evolution for this family. Pythons of one sort or another are found throughout the continent. Two of the three species of file snakes also occur here.

The colubrids are poorly represented, however, with a few species found in the north of Australia and in New Guinea. This fact, together with the complete absence of any vipers, is due to the separation of the Australasian landmass early on in that continent's history. There are very many elapids, including terrestrial forms, some of which have filled the niches normally occupied elsewhere by colubrids and vipers. Many members of both subfamilies of the marine elapids, the Hydropheinae and the Laticaudinae, are found around the warmer coastlines throughout the continent.

Australasia.

The islands of the Pacific region have diverse snake fauna and hold many resolved riddles relating to the dispersal snakes. Although their snake fauna predominantly Australasian, the prese of the boid genus *Candoia* is puzzling as the are no other boas in the region. *Candoia* may have spread by rafting from the South American mainland, following the ocean currents in the same way as did the iguan also found in the Pacific region. Boas

---

Animals on islands

The importance of island size in species diversity has long been recognized. Habitat diversity is obviously relevant but area *per se* may be the overriding factor. The 'Equilibriums Theory' proposed by R. H. MacArthur and E. O. Wilson, in their book *The Theory of Island Biogeography* (Princeton University Press, 1967), attempts to explain this in the form of a mathematical model, as follows.

The number of species living on an island at any given time is thought of as an equilibrium between immigration of new species and extinction of species already there. As the number of species on the island increases, there are fewer new immigrants so the numbers of additional species gets smaller until it reaches zero (when all the mainland forms are present). As the number of species increases, however, the rate of extinction increases, partly because there are more species that can

potentially become extinct and partly because, with a greater number of species, competition is likely to increase Eventually, new immigrants will be arriving at the same rate as old ones are becoming extinct. Now an equilibrium has been reached and the number of species will remain constant.

On large islands, the rate of immigration will be greater than on small islands, all other things being equal, because large islands are bigger targets. The rate of extinction will not be greater, however, and so it will take a longer period of time for the equilibrium to be reached. This will result in a greater number of species.

MacArthur and Wilson's model was not concerned specifically with snakes but snakes can be expected to follow the prediction at least as well as other animals (and better than some, such as birds, which can colonize and recolonize islands much more easily).

e-bearing and have long gestation periods,
act that would act in their favour should
pregnant female become marooned on
sam.

akes on islands

nds have long held a fascination for
logists and naturalists, due to their
en unique and unusual flora and fauna.
rwin's theory of evolution, for instance,
minated after a visit to the Galapagos
nds. Although these particular islands
have a small quota of snakes, other
nd groups are richer and potentially
ich more interesting herpetologically.
slands are also important due to the high
pportion of endemic species they support.
lated populations evolve in ways that
ly quickly separate them, both in appear-
ce and in behaviour, from the mainland
cks from which they arose. In fragmented
nd groups, each island may have one or
ore endemic species. The survival of these
pulations is vitally important because not
ly are they unique in their own right, but
ey are the results of natural experiments,
lding the secrets of evolution in their
es.

Unfortunately, island populations are
ecially vulnerable and the threats to their
vival are many. Small areas are very
ceptible to rapid environmental changes,
ecially habitat destruction by human
ncies. Introduced grazing animals, espe-
lly goats, contribute to and accelerate
s process alarmingly and have been
plicated in many extinctions, not just of
akes. Introduced vermin, such as rats and
s, find that species which have evolved in
absence of predators are easy targets
d they attack eggs, juveniles and adults,
ickly wiping out whole populations.
en introduced reptiles from other parts of
world can have negative effects, as in the
e of *Boiga irregularis* noted elsewhere
ge 91). Finally, many island forms are
interest to zoos and private collectors,
ecially when they become rare, and so
dangers of over-collecting are more
ious than they would be on mainlands.

Animals that live on islands, then, are
ecially prone to speciation and to extinc-
n. Other characteristics include greater
smaller size than their close relatives
the mainland. The giant tortoises of
Galapagos Islands and Aldabra are
d examples of gigantism among island
ns but there are examples among the
kes, too. The Chappell Island tiger
kes, *Notechis ater serventyi*, live on two

▲ Island species tend to be smaller than their mainland relatives: *Epicrates chrysogaster*, for instance, which comes from the Bahamas and the Turks and Caicos Islands, is among the smallest in its genus.

small islands in the Bass Strait between
New South Wales and Tasmania, Australia.
These tiger snakes are significantly larger
than the mainland tiger snakes, with total
lengths up to 240 cm (7 ft 10 in) compared
to 160 cm (5 ft 3 in) for the Tasmanian
form (*N. a. humphrysi*), their nearest
relatives. The reason for their large size is
almost certainly the unreliability of their
food supply. They feed predominantly on
sea bird chicks that are only present for
a few weeks of the year and they must be
capable of storing a large amount of fat to
tide them over the remainder of the year:
their large body size enables them to do so.
Similarly, the speckled rattlesnakes, *Crotalus
mitchelli angelensis*, from the island of Angel
de la Guarda in the Gulf of California, grow
half as big again as the mainland form,
whereas those on some of the neighbouring islands are dwarf forms. No ecological
studies have been carried out on these
populations and the selective pressures
that have pushed them in the direction of
gigantism and dwarfism, respectively, are
not known.

In fact, dwarfism in island snakes is a far
more common trait than gigantism and
very many small islands have populations
of snakes that are significantly smaller
than their nearest mainland relatives. For
example, the smallest species of *Epicrates*
boas on the West Indian islands, such as
E. chrysogaster and *E. exsul*, are found on
the smallest islands whereas the largest
islands (Cuba, Hispaniola and Jamaica)
have relatively large species. These are
interspecific differences but there are other
examples where the same species differs in
its size depending on where it lives.

The European nose-horned viper, *Vipera
ammodytes*, for instance, normally grows
to about 80 cm (2 ft 6 in) on the Greek
mainland but on several of the small islands
where it occurs it rarely attains 50 cm (1 ft
8 in) and becomes mature at around 30 cm
(1 ft). Other dwarf island populations are
found among the Boidae. In the Pacific
region, the subspecies of Macklot's python,
Liasis mackloti savuensis, that is restricted
to the small island of Savu in the Lesser
Sunda group, is significantly smaller than
the nominate form found on much larger
islands, and a form of the common boa, *Boa
constrictor*, from a group of small islands off
the northern coast of Honduras (possibly
extinct now) are considerably smaller than
mainland forms.

How do snakes reach islands? There are
several answers, and they depend to some
extent on the type of island. Some islands
are formed when part of the mainland
breaks away, through erosion for example,
or is separated by rising sea levels. Other
islands are formed by volcanic action or by
the emergence of coral reefs. Opportunities
for the colonization of each type of island
will obviously differ and there are three

basic methods by which snakes can reach them.

Firstly, they may already be present when the island is formed, when its connection with the mainland is severed. Secondly, they may reach isolated islands by rafting – precarious voyages made on uprooted trees and rafts of vegetation torn up from the mainland during storms and hurricanes. Thirdly, they may become introduced, either deliberately or accidentally by human agencies. The latter method is, of course, very recent.

Separation of islands through erosion and inundation is a gradual process – the isolation of the British Isles is an example. Many much smaller off-shore islands are also formed this way and they may be formed within lakes as well as in the ocean. Snakes already living on the section of land that becomes separated may continue to thrive there, assuming that conditions such as food supply continue to be suitable. Over long periods of time these populations may change, due either to chance or to selective pressures, and become separate races, sub-species or species. The age of the island will control the amount of speciation that has taken place – snakes living on ancient islands that have been colonized for a long time are likely to have evolved into different species and subspecies, whereas snakes living on more recently formed islands will be similar to their mainland counterparts.

Arriving on islands by rafting is a much more risky business. The chances of trees and other debris reaching an island is very slight indeed. Furthermore, the island on which the creatures land may not be capable of sustaining them, due to an unsuitable climate, lack of food or a multitude of other limitations. Even when a suitable habitat is available, a population of snakes will not become established unless at least one male and one female arrive together, or if a gravid or pregnant female is washed ashore. The assumption that island populations may be founded through the arrival of a clutch of eggs is an unlikely one because snake eggs are usually buried and, in addition, they have a low tolerance to salt water. Islands that have been colonized by rafting snakes are likely to lie in one of the main ocean current systems or to be situated opposite a large estuary. The islands of Trinidad and Tobago, for instance, have a rich snake fauna thought to be due, at least in part, to their position directly opposite the mouth of the Orinoco River on mainland South America.

Introduction of snakes by human agency is a recent phenomenon. Snakes may be carried inadvertently in cargoes of wood, food and other produce, or they may be deliberately introduced. There are few cases of deliberate human introduction because snakes are not among the animals with which humans normally like to co-habit. The case of the European Aesculapian snake, *Elaphe longissima*, may be an exception. This species had religious significance in Roman times and its patchy distribution in parts of central Europe may correspond to the localities of places of worship.

One example of accidental introduction, the brown tree snake, *Boiga irregularis*, on the Pacific island of Guam, is well documented. It arrived on the island, apparently entangled in the undercarriage of military aircraft and possibly among cargo. It took to its new home with such enthusiasm that, in a few years, it had spread over most of the island and was systematically wiping out the songbird population of the island and upsetting the natural balance between the lizard species found there.

Species that are introduced accidentally have the same problems to overcome as those that have rafted to islands – a reasonable number, of the right sexes, must be present in order for the population to expand and thrive. A single species of snake, the Braminy blind snake, *Ramphotyphlops braminus*, has overcome this limitation by being parthenogenetic: there are no males, and females begin to lay eggs as soon as they reach reproductive size. This greatly enhances their opportunities for extending their range and, sure enough, this species has a large and scattered distribution, having established itself far from its natural home. In addition, it is small and lives in soil, therefore escaping detection quite easily. In particular, it has been introduced along with potted plants, especially crops such as rubber and coconut, when these have been exported to other countries. Since the conditions required by the snake are the same as those required by the plants, it is likely to find itself in a suitable environment automatically. Its original home is India but it is now also found on several small islands in the Torres Straits, Christmas Island and Hawaii, as well as parts of South Africa, Australia, Madagascar, south-east Asia, Mexico and Florida. Its popular name in many of these countries is 'flowerpot snake' (see also page 147).

The snake fauna of any particular island will depend on several factors. The size of the island is obviously important. Large islands may have a range of habitats, making them suitable for a number of different types of snakes. They are also likely to sustain a good supply of other animals that snakes can prey on. Large islands also make easier targets for species that arrive by rafting. Small islands, by contrast, are likely to contain few habitats and are more susceptible to climatic and ecological disasters. They are more difficult targets for drifting debris to hit.

The distance from the mainland is another important factor. Islands closer to the mainland are more likely to be colonized than those at greater distances. Combining this aspect with island size, it is clear that large islands close to the mainland are likely to have a relatively rich snake fauna when compared with small islands that are a long way from shore.

These are not just theoretical assumptions. A number of studies have shown the pattern to apply, although the usual method is to include both lizard and snake species, not just snakes. Studies on West Indian islands of varying sizes and at varying distances from the mainland have shown that the figures are close enough to the predictions to be significant. In another example, of the 12 species of snakes found on at least one island in Lake Erie, there was a strong correlation between island size and numbers of species and between distance from the shore and number of species.

Island groups and their snake populations

Although it is not possible to catalogue all the small islands worldwide, or to list the snakes that inhabit them, it is interesting to select a few island groups and discuss the snakes that have managed to colonize them.

The West Indies

The West Indies are especially rich in reptiles, including snakes, and the origins of these species are hotly debated. The larger islands, Cuba, Hispaniola, Puerto Rico and Jamaica, are thought to have been part of the mainland of Central America at one time. The smaller islands, the Lesser Antilles, are oceanic, however, and rose from the sea through volcanic activity and were later capped by the growth of coral reefs. Snakes on the West Indies, therefore, may have arrived by two separate methods – by being present on the various landmasses prior to their separation from Central America, or by rafting. Other authorities maintain that reptiles arrived on all the islands by rafting

Ecology of an interloper: the brown tree snake on Guam

The brown tree snake, *Boiga irregularis*, a mildly venomous, back-fanged snake that is native to north-eastern Australia, New Guinea and several other islands in the South Pacific region. In the late 1940s it was accidentally introduced to the small island of Guam, which is one of the Mariana group, probably via cargoes delivered to the United States military base towards the south of the island. In the absence of natural predators, it gradually spread throughout the island until, by 1982, it could be found in almost every part except small areas of savannah, where it seems unable to live.

By the 1960s there was concern over the declining populations of several species of forest birds on Guam. This trend continued throughout the 1970s and 1980s until, by 1987, all 10 forest species were in serious trouble: some had not been seen for several years and were presumed extinct on the island and those that remained had retreated to a single small area, in the part of the island that was furthest from the point of the snake's introduction, and their populations were estimated to contain fewer than 100 individuals. Those that were thought to be extinct included two endemic species, the Guam flycatcher, *Myiagra freycineti*, and the Guam rail, *Rallus owstoni*, and a third endemic species, the white tern, *Gygis alba*, was restricted to the northern coastline.

Apart from the birds, brown tree snakes appeared to be feeding on small lizards, including skinks and geckos, were causing power cuts by climbing into overhead cables, eating domestic chickens and causing concern among the human population. Thomas Fritts and colleagues noticed that the snakes frequently attacked sleeping children, especially those aged between 1 and 3 months. Some of the injuries seemed to result from attempts to eat the children (*Journal of Herpetology*, 28(1):27–33).

Although the disappearance of the birds was closely correlated with the spread of the snakes, experiments carried out by Julie Savidge in 1987 provided additional evidence (*Ecology*, 68:660–668). She placed traps containing quails, *Coturnix coturnix*, in a variety of sites. In order to exclude terrestrial predators, such as rats, the quails were placed in mesh cages that were hung from branches. Three sites were in areas where forest birds had already disappeared and the population of snakes was known to be high; 75 per cent of all the quail had been eaten by snakes within four, seven and nine days. Two other sites were in areas where some birds still remained and which had only recently been colonized by the snakes; the predation rate was lower in these sites, probably because the snakes were still feeding on wild birds or because there were fewer snakes in areas where they were newly established.

Since the brown tree snake lives in a state of ecological balance in its natural range, why should it have wreaked havoc on Guam? Firstly, it has few predators on Guam and so its population has been able to grow unchecked. Secondly, the forest on Guam is less complex than forests elsewhere: most importantly, the canopy is lower and so birds are unable to find places to roost and nest where they are immune from attack. Thirdly, the availability of alternative prey, in the form of lizards, provides a reservoir of food that the snake can fall back on when birds are eliminated from an area; any attempt by the birds to re-establish themselves will be met by a fresh onslaught from the snake.

The events on Guam are the first and only example of a snake being responsible for the extinction of other species of animals and they are an important object lesson in the dangers of introductions, whether by accident or design. Ironically, snakes are usually among the victims of introductions: the brown tree snake seems to have turned the tables.

the separation from the mainland having occurred too early for reptiles to have taken advantage of it.

Whichever way the snakes arrived on their islands, a great deal of speciation has taken place and very many endemic species are found on various islands. Naturally, the larger islands have the greatest numbers of species, especially Cuba and Hispaniola, with 22 species each. Jamaica, a moderately large island, by comparison has only six species of snakes. This surprisingly small number cannot easily be explained, but extinctions in recent years owing to human disturbance of the habitat and the introduction of domestic livestock and mongooses could be contributory factors. Typhlopids, boas and tropidophids are the dominant groups in many cases. Cuba, for instance, has nine tropidophids, over half of the known species. Of the smaller islands, a huge proportion have endemic species or subspecies of snakes, many of which are classed as endangered. A number of these rare snakes are confined to small satellite islands that have remained relatively unaffected by the depredations of the mongooses, rats, cats and goats that have been introduced to the more sizeable islands.

In this context, snakes belonging to the genus *Liophis* have been particularly badly affected. *Liophis cursor*, formerly found on the island of Martinique, now survives only on a small island of 20 hectares (50 acres), while *L. ornatus*, from St Lucia, is now restricted to an island of only 10 hectares (25 acres). According to Henderson and Bourgeois (1993),[2] the main island populations of both these species have been extirpated by mongooses, *Herpestes auropunctatus*. Other species have fared only slightly better.

The Gulf of California

The islands within the Gulf of California form a discrete group and are of interest because they are surrounded by mainland on three sides. Several islands are less than 5 miles (8 km) from either the Sonoran coast or the peninsula of Baja California and were previously joined by land bridges. Other islands, though, are more isolated and are volcanic in origin and colonization of these can only have taken place by rafting (human introduction of snakes appears

► Speciation on the Cyclades Islands, Greece, has led to a number of endemic reptiles, including the Milos blunt-nosed viper, *Macrovipera schweizeri*, found on only three small islands.

to have occurred). The dominant genus [of] snakes on these islands is *Crotalus*, the [rat]tlesnakes, and a number of unique forms [are] found there. Eleven species are each [fou]nd on at least one island. One of these, [*C.] catalinensis*, is endemic to a single island [an]d has undergone some interesting [bio]logical changes, see page 128, Chapter [3,] and seven subspecies of mainland forms [are] restricted to one or more islands. Taking [the] snakes as a whole, the larger islands, [suc]h as Tiburón, have several species [whe]reas some of the small islands have only [one] or two.

Cyclades

[Th]e only sizeable groups of small islands in [Eur]ope are those of the Aegean Sea. Of [the]se, the Cyclades has the most diverse [sna]ke fauna. At least six taxa are endemic [to o]ne or more islands within the group: it is [not] clear at present which of these are full [spe]cies and which are subspecies as the [tax]onomy of the snakes from this region is [in t]he process of revision. Altogether, there [are] 13 species of snakes and the greatest [numbers] are found on the islands of Tinos [(eig]ht), Andros, Milos and Paros (six each) [and] Kea, Kimilos, Mykonos and Naxos (five [eac]h): these are all large islands. Nine [isla]nds have only one species each: these [are] all small islands.

Pacific islands

[Th]e Pacific island groups, of which there [are] many, have not been well colonized [by] snakes. Many of them are extremely [sca]ttered and isolated and they would make difficult targets for flotsam. The boas, *Candoia*, have already been mentioned (see page 89) in connection with the mystery surrounding their presence in what is otherwise python territory. The Solomon Islands, situated to the east of New Guinea, have representatives from six families, including the endemic genus *Salomoneleps*. Many island groups have no native snakes whatsoever and these include Hawaii, although the flowerpot snake, *Ramphotyphlops braminus*, has been introduced here along with several other islands in the region. Perhaps the greatest enigma is the presence of an elapid, *Ogmodon vitianus*, on Fiji. This snake, which has rarely been collected, appears to have no close relatives in neighbouring parts of the world.

Indian Ocean islands

The islands of the Indian Ocean, with the exception of Madagascar, tend to be small and isolated. This has meant that snakes have had difficulty in reaching them but there are a few species scattered among them. The Seychelles, for instance, has three species of snakes. One, the flowerpot snake, is an introduction but the other two, the Seychelles house snake, *Lamprophis geometricus*, and the Seychelles wolf snake, *Lycognathophis seychellensis*, are endemics. The house snake has close relatives on the African mainland but the wolf snake has no close relatives and is the only member of its genus.

▼ *Lycognathophis seychellensis* **is one of the three species endemic to the Seychelles Islands.**

1. Stafford, P. J. (1991), 'Amphibians and reptiles of the joint services scientific expedition to the Upper Raspaculo, Belize, 1991', *British Herpetological Society Bulletin*, (38):10–17.
2. Henderson, R. W. and Bourgeois, R. W. (1993), 'Notes of the diets of West Indian *Liophis*', *Caribbean Journal of Science*, Vol 29 (3–4):253–254.

5
Feeding

The feeding behaviour of snakes is of great interest because so many unique features are involved. These are partly due to the elongated body shape, which has several implications with regard to capturing, subduing and swallowing prey. This, together with the lack of limbs, has led to the evolution of specialized methods of prey capture and the means of overpowering it before it has a chance to inflict injuries. To this end, the shape and position of their teeth are modified and show great variation, linked to the type of prey and method of hunting employed. Many species have evolved venom and the apparatus with which to deliver it, although, again, there is great variation. In the final stages of feeding, the option of dismembering prey is not available and so it must be swallowed whole. This is made possible by modifications to the skull and skin. Finally, some species have the additional problem of finding enough food in areas that may be of very low food productivity, such as deserts.

◀ A boomslang, *Dispholidus typus*, a notorious rear-fanged snake from Africa, subdues and swallows a dwarf chameleon.

TYPES OF FOOD

All snakes are carnivorous. The range of prey that they eat, however, is very wide and it seems likely that, collectively speaking, snakes will eat just about anything that is alive (or has been alive) and that will fit into their bodies.

Methods of establishing the diet of snakes include dissection of preserved individuals, analysis of faeces, regurgitation of prey (either voluntary or induced), observations in wild and captive specimens, and implication. Of these, records of snakes in captivity must be used cautiously, while implied diets where, for instance, a snake is seen entering the nest of a bird or mammal, must also be carefully examined and backed up, if possible, by other evidence.

Specialists and generalists

Whatever the methods used, it is well established that some species eat a variety of prey types whereas others are specialists. Some species eat different prey at different stages in their lives. To a large extent, the prey that each species eats depends on availability and, where a species is found over a wide area, its preferred prey may differ if the occurrence of prey species vary within this range. The availability of an animal as prey depends not only on its occurrence in the same area as the snake but also on its habits and the ease with which it can be caught and eaten.

In order to exploit certain types of prey efficiently, morphological and behavioural modifications may be necessary. If this happens, the species concerned is likely to become a specialist and may be ill suited to take an alternative type of prey. The

egg-eating snakes belonging to the genera *Dasypeltis* and *Elachistodon* are good examples.

Other types of prey, though, may require similar handling – snakes that eat lizards will usually eat snakes as well and may also eat small mammals if they are available. These snakes, then, are generalists. There are more dietary generalists than specialists among snakes. This is exactly what we would expect: no species wants to exclude a potentially valuable type of prey if it is available, or even if it is available only occasionally. On the other hand, those species that have specialized have staked their existence on the availability of just one type of prey. Although this may make them more vulnerable to an erratic food supply, they are usually better placed and better equipped to deal with that particular type of prey than a generalist would be.

When 'deciding' to become a specialist or a generalist, a species has many factors to weigh up. To become a specialist, it is necessary to 'know' that the chosen food supply is going to be available regularly throughout the year, and there must be plenty of it. It will be easier for a specialist to become successful if its chosen food is one that is not already heavily exploited by generalists. These criteria seem pretty hard to meet, and this is probably why there are so few specialists.

Even so, snakes have tendencies to look for certain types of prey, even though they may not be restricted to them. These could be called 'preferred' prey types. The preferred prey of most species is fairly logical – they

prefer the type of prey that is most comm or most easily caught, in the places t frequent. If a particular prey is extrem abundant, a snake may appear to be spe izing in it, even though it would take o prey if it were also available. Many V Indian snakes eat *Anolis* lizards, for insta but many of them (perhaps all of th will also take other lizards and other typ prey – *Anolis* just happen to be incred abundant and are often the only item in stomachs of a series of such snakes. In of places, however, there are no predomin prey types and in these places we wo expect most snakes to take a range of p species.

The following accounts of snakes' d are broken down into prey types. To so extent, it is unavoidable that specia should get most of the attention (they t to be more interesting when it come: feeding habits) but it should be obvi from what has already been said t snakes will not always, or often, fit ne into one or more category of prey types.

Invertebrates

Starting at the bottom end of the sc the small burrowing snakes belongin the most primitive families, Typhlopi Anomalepididae and Leptotyphlopidae, h small diameters and small mouths. Un those of more advanced snakes, the jaw these species are fairly rigid and so food it must be small in order to be accommod Because they eat only small prey, they m eat a great number of them: this furt restricts their diet to species that can found in large numbers. In practice, th are the social insects, especially ants termites. Many records of the diets of th species are based on casual observati and make certain assumptions. Shine Webb (1990),[1] however, surveyed the of four Australian species of *Ramphotyph* by dissecting museum specimens and fo that 93–97 per cent of the stomach conte were ant pupae and larvae. Indivic snakes contained up to 1400 prey ite These species rarely ate termites or a ants. By contrast, White *et al.* (1992)[2] fo that the Hispaniolan species *Typhlops* *therus* ate mostly termites but also took a and larval beetles, and spiders. *Typh* *richardi* and *T. biminiensis* are also thou to eat termites on occasion.

Species of *Leptotyphlops* eat mo termites and are often found in ter nests. To protect themselves from att they smear themselves with a substa

Dietary preferences in western garter snakes

Steven Arnold studied the diet of the western garter snake, *Thamnophis elegans*, in an experimental situation (*Evolution*, 35:510–515). Inland populations of this species are aquatic and feed mainly on frogs, fish and leeches, whereas coastal populations are more terrestrial and feed mainly on slugs. In the laboratory, wild individuals from inland population refused to eat slugs, although the coastal ones accepted them. He then tested newborn individuals that had no prior experience of feeding and

found that 73 per cent of the coastal type would eat slugs compared to only 35 per cent of the inland type.

When coastal and inland individuals were mated in the laboratory, an intermediate proportion of their hybrid offspring accepted slugs. The implications of this experiment are that diet preferences are inherited, in the same way as colour or markings, and that individuals from mixed parentage will have characteristics that fall somewhere between those of each parent.

ost blind snakes, such as *Ramphotyphlops*
scens, feed largely on termites and their
e. It may be that by secreting pheromones
mitate those of the termites, they pacify the
rs and avoid serious attacks from them, as
een shown with certain *Leptotyphlops*
es.

produce in their cloacal glands; this
ains pheromones which 'switch off' the
essive behaviour of the soldier termites,
onstrating a long-term commitment to
particular diet.

any snakes eat insects and other inver-
ates. Some specialize in this type of prey
reas others eat them as additional
items. Earthworms are the staple diet
nany shield-tailed snakes (uropeltids)
as those belonging to the genera
ophis and *Uropeltis* of Sri Lanka and
hern India. North American colubrids
as the garter snakes, *Thamnophis*, also
earthworms, although some species
to eat them more than others: *T. butleri*
ought to specialize in them, at least to
e extent. The Mexican garter snake relies
vily on earthworms and leeches when
ng, moving on to fish and amphibians
t grows. Birth of the young, in July
August, coincides with the greatest
lability of these prey species and a
lar correlation has been found with
related species, *Thamnophis sirtalis* and
dia sipedon*. Ring-necked snakes, *Diadophis*,
ily eat earthworms in captivity although
e is no confirmation that this diet reflects

the natural state of affairs (and some forms
live in arid areas where earthworms would
be hard to find).

Slugs and snails present peculiar problems
due to the slime with which they cover
themselves and, in the case of snails, a hard,
indigestible shell. They are therefore not
widely eaten by snakes, except for certain
species that have evolved the means of
overcoming these problems. Slug- and snail-
eating snakes occur in several parts of the
world and are found among the members
of at least four subfamilies of colubrid
snakes. Usually the species involved tend
to specialize in these prey and eat little or
nothing else, although there are exceptions.
The North American red-bellied snake,
Storeria occipitomaculata, eats mainly slugs
and its congener, *S. dekayi*, eats them sometimes but also eats a wide variety of other
soft-bodied invertebrates. Rossman and
Myer (1990)[3] describe the methods of feeding of these two species. The snakes grasped
the soft bodies of the snails and pushed them
along the substrate until the snail became
wedged against a piece of rock. The snake
then twisted its head through 180° or more
and maintained this position until the snail's
muscles began to tire. The body of the snail
was then pulled from its shell and eaten.
The whole process took from 12 to almost
20 minutes. A third North American species,
the sharp-tailed snake, *Contia tenuis*, apparently also feeds on slugs but it is not known
if it also takes snails. *Storeria* and *Contia*
both have long teeth on their mandibles,
thought to be an adaptation to gripping slugs
and snails.

Members of the subfamily Dipsadinae,
from Central and South America, are all
highly specialized slug and snail eaters.
They have characteristically blunt snouts,
and long teeth at the front of the lower jaw,
which is more rigid than in other snakes.
Species in the genus *Dipsas* are further
modified by the absence of a groove along
the chin (mental groove). These adaptations
help the snakes to extract snails from their
shells. They brace the shell of the snail
against the roof of their mouth and thrust
the lower jaw between the shell and the
fleshy part of the snail. The long front teeth
are used to hook the body out of the shell,
with a twisting movement of the jaw. Using
this method, *Dipsas* and related species
can extract snails' bodies quicker than
snakes that have no such modifications:
Sanzima (1989)[4] timed the process at one to
six minutes (in *Dipsas indica*), and also
describes the way in which this species may

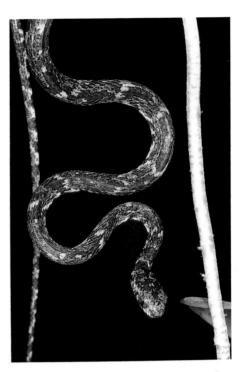

▲ *Sibon nebulata*, a tropical American species that
feeds exclusively on slugs and snails.

wedge the snail in its own coils. On the
other hand, the same species handled slugs
even more quickly (10 to 45 seconds) and
ate them by simply lifting them away from
the substrate and swallowing them, usually
tail first. Other authors have noted that,
in related species, slugs seem to be preferred
over snails, presumably because of the
reduced handling time.

African slug and snail eaters belong
to the genus *Duberria*, of which there are
two species. They live in damp situations
and hunt by following the slime trails
of the molluscs. Slugs are merely lifted off
the ground and eaten in exactly the same
way as they are by the *Dipsas* species. Snails
are reputed to be grasped by the body
and bashed against a hard surface until the
shell breaks, but there appears to be no
first-hand confirmation of this.

In Asia, the members of the subfamily
Pareatinae are the counterparts to the
American dipsadinine snakes; all feed exclusively on slugs and snails and have blunt
snouts and lower jaws that can be thrust
forward to a greater degree than most other
snakes. Their method of snail extraction is
unknown and may not have been observed.
A specimen of the monotypic *Aplopeltura boa*
that ate snails and slugs in captivity always
fed at night and the method of feeding was
not observed. This specimen was captured

▲ The African slug-eater, *Duberria lutrix*, feeds on slugs and snails, which it finds by following their slimy trails. The specimen illustrated is a rare colour mutant, lacking most of its pigment.

at night, foraging among damp vegetation on the fringes of rainforest.

Soft-bodied insects and their larvae are widely eaten by many small snakes. The North American green snakes, *Opheodryas*, feed largely upon them although they also eat other types of insects. The crowned snake, *Tantilla relicta*, eats mainly larval tenebrionid beetles, which may make up

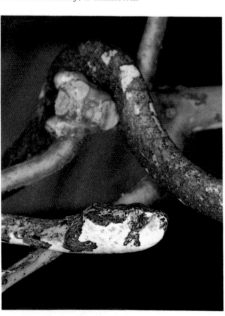

▼ *Aplopeltura boa* is an uncommon Asian slug-eating snake. Its method of hunting, like much of its natural history, is unknown.

as much as 90 per cent of its diet. Many other small, secretive snakes undoubtedly rely heavily on this source of food, although positive information is lacking. A rather surprising case of insect eating is that of the European meadow viper, *Vipera ursinii*. Luisella (1990)[5] found that captive adults ate a significant number of wingless orthopterans while in captivity, especially at certain times of the year. Furthermore, he found that young individuals, less than one year old, would only accept grass-hoppers of certain species and usually refused crickets.

Among the more unusual types of invertebrates eaten by snakes are aquatic crustaceans. The sea snake *Aipysurus laevis* will eat prawns and crabs that it finds in crevices in reefs. It also eats fish. The homalopsine colubrid, *Fordonia leucobalia*, lives on mud flats and is highly specialized, feeding exclusively on small crabs that it pins down with its body or constricts. The semi-aquatic Graham's water snake, *Regina grahami* from south-eastern North America eats only freshwater crayfish (crawfish) and, according to research carried out by Seigel (1992),[6] takes them only when they have recently moulted and their cuticle is soft, presumably to facilitate swallowing. Other species in this genus also eat crustaceans. The file snake *Acrochordus granulatus* also eats crabs on occasion as do the *Nerodia* species that are sometimes found in brackish habitats, although fish form the most important part of the diets of all these snakes.

Centipedes are eaten by the specialized *Aparallactus* species, aptly known as centipede eaters, from southern Africa. They are

burrowing snakes, sometimes associ[ated] with termite nests, which their ch[...] prey also inhabit. Centipedes may als[o] eaten by the American hook-nosed sna[ke] *Ficimia*, which are rear-fanged, altho[ugh] these species apparently prefer spiders.

Fish

Moving on to vertebrate prey, there [are] no groups that do not form part of the [diet] of snakes somewhere. Fish are the [main] prey of most aquatic and semi-aqu[atic] snakes (other than the specialized c[rus]tacean eaters mentioned above). With [few] exceptions, the sea snakes belongin[g to] the Elapidae (or Hydropheidae) eat [fish] often crevice-dwelling reef species w[hile] the snakes, with their narrow heads [and] necks, are well adapted to extricate [fish from] their hiding places. For the same rea[son] fish that live in burrows in mud are [also] hunted. As a rule, slow-moving fish [are] the favoured prey but some sea sn[akes] also look for more active fish while they [are] resting or sleeping at night. Some [sea] snakes specialize in particular types of [fish;] eels are popular, especially among mem[bers] of the genus *Hydrophis*, and small g[obies] and blennies form a large part of the di[et of] other species. An interesting case of reso[urce] sharing occurs in the brackish [lake] Te-Nngano in the Solomon Islands; [two] species of sea kraits, *Laticauda colu[brina]* and *L. crockeri* live here but, whereas [the] former eats only eels, the latter eats [only] sleeper gobies (*Eleotris*).

The two species of sea snakes belongin[g to] the genus *Emydocephalus* and a third spe[cies,] *Aipysurus eydouxii*, are extreme specia[lists;] they eat only fish eggs, which they [find] in crevices in coral reefs and in burrow[s in] sand. As a result, the venom apparatu[s of] all three species has degenerated. There [are] other sea snakes that eat fish eggs, suc[h as] some *Hydrophis* species and *Aipysurus la[evis]* but these also eat other prey.

Freshwater fish-eating snakes are num[er]ous and are especially common among [the] natricines, most of which inhabit ma[rshy] areas and the fringes of ponds and lakes. [The] homalopsine colubrids from south-east [Asia] are probably all fish eaters. Together w[ith] the sea snakes, these species are among [the] most aquatic of snakes and some spe[cies] rarely, if ever, leave the water. It is thou[ght] that most of them feed opportunistica[lly,] waiting in dense aquatic vegetation [and] ambushing their prey. The tentacled sn[ake,] *Erpeton tentaculatum*, which also belong[s to] this subfamily, was formerly thought to

two strange appendages on its snout
re fish within range. This theory has
been disproved and the structures are
ght to break up the outline of the snake,
ncing its camouflage.

l three species of file snakes, *Acro-
dus*, are aquatic and feed mostly on fish.
y are unusual in that they constrict their
before swallowing it, and it is assumed
the rough, warty skin of these species is
daptation that enables them to handle
ery prey.

mong the vipers, only the cottonmouth,
strodon piscivorus, is an important fish
r, although it also eats an astonishing
ety of other prey. A very interesting
rvation by Wharton (1969)[7] concerns
Florida cottonmouth, *A. p. conanti*, on
Horse Key where the snakes feed heavily
marine fish dropped by adult seabirds
rning with food for their chicks. Other
s of food, such as rats, squirrels, small
s and lizards, sustain the snakes when
birds are not nesting. A number of
d-dwelling lizards also make their living
cavenging around seabird colonies.

phibians

y of the species that eat fish also eat
phibians when they are present. Again,
diet tends to be available mainly to
atic and semi-aquatic snakes, especially
ies such as the American and Eurasian
er snakes, *Nerodia*, *Natrix* and so on.
re are snakes from drier habitats that
mphibians; these include the American
nose snakes, *Heterodon*, which have
ified snouts in the form of an upturned
ral scale that they use to root out toads
have burrowed into the soil, and the
can night adders, *Causus* species. Many
oreal snakes, including the young of
er species such as the green tree python,
dropython viridis*, eat tree frogs. Some
hese snakes are generalists, however,
g a wide variety of prey according to
lability.

s and toads

ies that eat frogs, either exclusively or
ially, tend to swallow them live. Few
s have defences, although some species,
bly members of the Dendrobatidae
son dart frogs) from South America,
luce highly toxic skin secretions that
e them immune to predation. Toads
nging to the genera *Bufo* and others
produce toxins and this may deter
es on occasion although they are most
itely eaten by certain species. The

▲ The cross-barred tree snake, *Dipsadoboa aulica*,
from southern Africa, feeds on geckos and small
frogs. Here it is eating a reed frog, *Hyperolius
tuberilinguis*.

European grass snake, *Natrix natrix*, for
instance, will eat them in areas where they
are the most abundant prey available
although in other areas they may avoid
them.

The South and Central American cat-
eyed snake *Leptodeira septentrionalis*, and
possibly other members of its genus, feed on
the eggs of frogs, among other items, a habit
that is only made possible by the large

number of arboreal frogs that lay their eggs
on leaves overhanging pools. (Perversely,
the breeding habits of the frogs are thought
to have arisen as a means of minimiz-
ing predation by fishes!) Other snakes, for

▲ A green tree snake, *Dendrelaphis punctulatus*, from south-east Australia, eating a ranid frog.

instance *Rhadinea bilineata* and *Liophis atraventer*, both from South America, are also known to eat frogs' eggs, usually those of the terrestrial breeding species belonging to the genus *Eleutherodactylus*.

Salamanders

Salamanders are absent from Australia and from much of Africa, but in areas where they are reasonably common they may be eaten by the same species that eat frogs and toads. Once again, a number of them produce defensive toxins from glands in their skin and they are sometimes brightly marked to give warning of the fact. The European fire salamander, *Salamandra salamandra*, which produces particularly strong toxins, appears not to be eaten by any snakes. Other species, such as the crested newt, *Triturus cristatus*, only gain partial protection by this means as some grass snakes will eat them. In North America, salamanders seem not to have evolved such powerful toxins, and are eaten by a variety of snakes, especially garter snakes and other small species that live in damp environments. Lind and Welsh (1990),[8] for instance, found that *Thamnophis couchii* in northern California ate adults and larvae of the Pacific giant salamander, *Dicampton ensatus*. In one instance a snake weighing 92 g (3.24 oz) ate a salamander weighing 80.9 g (2.85 oz), representing 88 per cent of the weight of the snake. Other snakes in the same study contained the tails of larval salamanders. All South American salamanders belong to the genus *Bolitoglossa*. As they are largely arboreal, and not very common, they would be unlikely to form an important part of the diet of any snake, although there is a record of *B. altamazonica* found in the stomach contents of *Liophis reginae*, a species that normally eats frogs, tadpoles and small fish.

A most unusual case is that of a rubber boa, *Charina bottae*, which disgorged an adult salamander belonging to the species *Ensatina eschscholtzi* together with 12 eggs of the same species. The adult had been eaten first, followed by the eggs (this salamander guards its eggs by coiling around them). Rubber boas usually eat nestling mammals.

Reptiles

Reptiles form the largest part of the diet of a huge number of snakes and at least half the species depend heavily or entirely on them.

Lizards

Small lizards such as geckos, skinks, small iguanids and lacertids can be very abundant in favourable habitats. For this reason they represent an enormous reservoir of food for a wide variety of predators, inc ing snakes. Furthermore, lizards are m defenceless and are easy prey to sna which can catch, overpower and swa them with little risk of injury.

Although there are lizard-eating sn from all parts of the world, two area particular are worthy of note. In Austr the number of small mammals is str limited due to the mostly dry and nature of the country. Reptiles, howe are numerous, especially small specie skinks and geckos. These are the main for a large variety of snakes, some of w eat nothing else. Even large species s as the whipsnakes, genus *Demansia*, wil small lizards here because there is a sh age of larger, more substantial prey, unlike other parts of the world, where la snakes tend to eat larger prey, there se to be little such correlation among Australian snakes that have been stu so far. The sole exceptions are the taip which appear to feed exclusively on wa blooded prey (see below).

A somewhat similar situation exists the West Indian islands, where the common vertebrates by far are the sle lizards belonging to the genus *Anolis*. T lizards are eaten by almost all West In snakes at some stage in their lives and s species eat almost nothing else. For insta one study revealed that over 60 per ce the food eaten by eight species of colub living on the large island of Hispaniola v *Anolis* lizards. In another study, Hende (1993)[9] found that on a number of V Indian islands, young tree boas, *Cor enhydris*, fed exclusively on *Anolis* liza Larger tree boas also ate the lizards but other types of prey as well. Overall, *A* formed about 66 per cent of the species' By contrast, on the South American m land, lizards constituted less than 5 per of the prey taken by the same species. worth remembering that these boas h highly efficient heat sensing facial pits, may be better equipped to detect and h warm-blooded prey than lizards (altho in the early evening, at least, the b temperatures of lizards will be above th their surroundings and can also be dete by the same means). The other group of V Indian boas, those belonging to the g *Epicrates*, seem not to have adapted to a of lizards (with the exception of two spe *E. gracilis* and *E. monensis*) and the reaso this is unclear at present.

A species of spiny-tailed iguana, *Ct saura similis*, seems to be a regular if seas

juvenile diamond python, *Morelia spilota
~ta*, eating a small skink. This species switches
~diet of small mammals and birds as it grows
~r.

~y to *Loxocemus bicolor* in Costa Rica,
~re the snakes have been seen catch-
~re hatchling lizards as they emerged from
~r nests, along with the young of green
~anas, *Iguana iguana*, which share the
~e nesting sites.

~lthough snakes are unable to dismember
~r prey, lizards sometimes dismember
~nselves by discarding their tails when
~y are captured. Lizard tails have been
~nd in the stomachs of a number of species
~nakes, and it seems likely that some
~ll snakes exploit the system by catching
~rds that would normally be too large
~wallow but which can be relied upon to
~ate their tails!

~he wolf snakes, *Lycophidion* species, from
~hern Africa, specialize in eating diurnal lizards,
~h are captured while asleep.

Amphisbaenians

Amphisbaenians (sometimes known as worm lizards) are closely related to the lizards and the snakes but are more limited in their distribution, being found in the tropical and subtropical parts of the Americas, and in North Africa, south-western Europe and the Middle East. All are burrowing reptiles, spending the greater part of their time out of sight beneath the surface. This does not eliminate them from the menu of snakes, however, and a number of burrowing snakes actually specialize in eating them. These include members of the coral snake genus *Micrurus*, which follow the amphisbaenians through their tunnels. *M. corallinus* feeds mainly on the amphisbaenian *Leptosternon microcephalum* in south-eastern Brazil and *M. laticollaris* eats *Bipes canaliculatus* in Mexico (Papenfuss, 1982).[10] In the latter survey, many *Bipes* were found with damaged tails, possible evidence of predation by snakes. The colubrid burrowing snakes of the genus *Elapomorphus* also seem to specialize in amphisbaenian prey, as does *Pseudoboa neuwiedii*, judging from its behaviour in captivity (Perez-Santos and Moreno, 1987).[11]

In Africa, the atractaspidid snake *Chlorhinophis gerardi*, is a confirmed eater of amphisbaenians although all members of the Atractaspididae are burrowing snakes that feed largely on other burrowing reptiles and there can be no doubt that these include worm lizards whenever they are encountered. The quill-snouted snakes, *Xenocalamus*, however, of which there are five species, are highly specialized and feed only on worm lizards, which they catch and swallow underground.

Turtles

Turtles must rate high on the list of indigestible food items, but are not totally overlooked. Among the species eaten by snakes are musk turtles, a snapping turtle, box turtle, two species of sliders and baby alligators found in the stomachs of cottonmouths, *Agkistrodon piscivorus*, and a hatchling hawksbill turtle, *Eretmochelys imbricata*, that was eaten by the Cuban ground snake *Alsophis cantherigerus*. Rather less surprisingly, freshwater turtles and caimans are eaten by anacondas, *Eunectes murinus*, and probably also by the smaller species *E. notaeus*, in South America.

Snakes

That snakes eat snakes is hardly surprising. After all, snakes are the ideal shape to fit inside other snakes! It is probably true to say that most of the species that eat lizards will also eat snakes given the chance. The few snake-eating specialists are known more through hearsay than through scientific endeavour and often concern snakes that eat venomous species. The North American kingsnakes, *Lampropeltis getulus*, of which a number of subspecies are recognized, are in this category as they will tackle rattlesnakes and have some degree of immunity from their venom. Other species of kingsnakes have little immunity, however, and probably prey on other snakes only very occasiona[l] None of the kingsnakes appears to h[ave] immunity to the venom of the Texas c[oral] snake, *Micrurus fulvius*, which is an ela[pid] On a smaller scale, western populati[ons] of ring-necked snakes, *Diadophis puncta[tus]* eat snakes among other prey, while [the] sharp-tailed snake, *Stilosoma extenua[tum]* appears to prey largely on the crowned sn[ake] *Tantilla relicta*, in peninsular Florida.

In Asia, several members of the Elapi[dae] prey mainly on smaller snakes. These incl[ude] the king cobra, *Ophiophagus hannah*, kraits, *Bungarus* species, and the Asian c[oral] snakes, *Maticora*. The members of [the] Atractaspididae, all but one of which [are] African, are equipped with specia[l] fangs that enable them to bite prey w[hile] in the enclosed space of a narrow burr[ow] although they eat a variety of prey, o[ther] burrowing snakes, especially the sle[nder] blind snakes, *Typhlops*, are probably im[por]tant components of their diet. The si[ngle] Middle Eastern species, *A. engaddensis*, eats snakes, including the little coll[ared] snake *Eirenis coronelloides*.

Two Australian pythons, the black-hea[ded] python, *Aspidites melanocephalus*, and [the] woma, *A. ramsayi*, specialize in repti[lian] prey, including other snakes (they will [also] take small mammals, etc.), while the Pap[uan] python, *Liasis papuanus*, has also been reco[rded] with a carpet python, *Morelia spilota*, i[n its] stomach.

These records are just a few exam[ples] it is probably true to say that the majo[rity] of snakes will eat other snakes, either hab[itu]ally or occasionally.

Cannibalism

Snakes that eat other species of snakes [are] numerous. Snakes that eat their own spe[cies] are not so common and, even where rec[ords] exist, they often involve captive anim[als] that may eat cage mates by accident, o[r] when both snakes begin swallowing a si[ngle] item of food from opposite ends. Polis [and] Myers (1985)[12] listed 19 species of snake[s in] which cannibalism had been reported. T[his] comprised 10 colubrids, three elapids, [one] atractaspidid and five vipers: at least se[ven] took place under captive conditions. Si[nce] then further species have been added to [the] list of incidents of cannibalism, but, ag[ain] they are concerned almost entirely w[ith] snakes in captivity.

One incident involved a ladder sn[ake] *Elaphe scalaris*, that ate its own eggs [and] several other cases of oophagy can be ad[ded] to this account: a Mexican hognose sna[ke]

▼ Many snakes include other snakes as all or part of their diet. This spotted harlequin snake, *Homoroselaps lacteus*, is eating a thread snake, *Leptotyphlops nigrescens*.

rodon nasicus kennerlyi, ate most of its clutch on two separate occasions, a *deira annulata* ate her entire clutch and *Oligodon taeniolatus* ate three of her eggs. Other cases involve snakes that eggs of their own species, but not necessarily their own. These include a male *ropeltis triangulum* that ate its cage 's eggs and two instances of scarlet es, *Cemophora coccinea*, eating eggs of own species: in one case the eggs were ost fully developed. Live-bearing snakes eat dead embryos or infertile egg ses; this is especially common among but has also been seen in a pit viper, *strodon bilineatus*.

phagy

about the most bizarre accounts of e feeding behaviour must be those of rat es, *Elaphe obsoleta*, eating themselves! individual, a captive, did this on two sions and died at the second attempt. other individual was wild and was d in a tight circle and had consumed it two-thirds of its body when it was vered.

s

s present snakes with two obvious prob-: how to catch them and how to obtain ood grip through the thick layer of ners and down. For this reason, they to be eaten by certain species, mainly real ones, that have developed special niques to deal with them. The tree , *Corallus*, and the tree python, *Chon-ython viridis*, for instance, have long, rved teeth that penetrate the feathers retain a firm grip on the bird. Their hod of hunting is to hang, head down, a bough and wait for a bird to pass w. Their strike is fast and accurate, g their ability to sense body heat ugh their facial pits, as well as their es of sight and smell. Other species of es prey on birds when they are helpless, when they are nestlings. Black rat es, *Elaphe obsoleta obsoleta*, for instance, on fledglings of a number of small birds, e of which nest on the ground and rs which nest in bushes and trees. The h American colubrid *Leptophis ahaetulla* also been seen eating feathered chicks tanager while the European ladder e, *Elaphe scalaris*, and Montpellier snake, olon monspessulanus*, have both been d in the nest burrows of European bee-rs, having gorged themselves on the ks. In addition, Eurasian vipers, *Vipera*

and *Macrovipera*, commonly eat nestling birds in the spring and early summer.

One of the best examples of extreme feeding specialization in snakes, concerns the population of tiger snakes, *Notechis ater serventyi*, on Chappell Island, in the Bass Straits, a subspecies that is significantly larger than other populations on the mainland or on other islands; these snakes feed almost entirely on the chicks of mutton birds, *Puffinus tenuirostris*, which nest on the island in high densities. The food is highly nourishing but seasonal, and the snakes gorge themselves for a few weeks in order to store enough energy to see them through until the following bird breeding season. The presence of small skinks on the island is important; these are the food of young tiger snakes, until they grow large enough to eat the mutton bird chicks, and so without them the population could not survive.

Generalist feeders will also eat birds but they are restricted largely to ground-nesting species or odd situations where birds come within range by chance. In three studies on the diet of rattlesnakes, for instance, birds made up 2–8 per cent of the total food. On the island of Guam, the brown tree snake, *Boiga irregularis*, which is a generalist, and which was introduced to the island accidentally, has apparently wiped out all the native forest bird species.

Arboreal snakes are not necessarily bird eaters, though. For instance, the Pacific tree boa, *Candoia bibroni*, though thoroughly arboreal, rarely if ever eats birds, and subsists largely on skinks, along with a few frogs and small mammals. Also when Luisella and Rugiero (1993)[13] compared the diets of arboreal Aesculapian snakes, *Elaphe longissima*, with that of the terrestrial asp viper, *Vipera aspis*, from the same region, they found that they were practically identical (both ate lacertid lizards and mice). We have to conclude from these observations that some arboreal snakes take to the trees for reasons other than finding food.

Mammals

Mammals of various types are eaten mainly by medium sized to large snakes. The size of mammals, and the risk of injuries from them, prevents many small snakes from using them as a staple diet, although nestling rodents, for instance, may be taken opportunistically, even by quite small species.

Australia is unusual in having no native rodents, although there are marsupial

counterparts. Nevertheless, there are few mammal specialists in Australia, except the two species of taipan, *Oxyuranus microlepidotus* and *O. scutellatus*, which eat small marsupials and introduced rodents. The larger pythons, such as the carpet and diamond pythons, *Morelia spilota*, also eat large numbers of mammals but their diets are not restricted to them. Juveniles, in particular, eat small lizards, especially skinks. This is thought to be a result of their activity patterns; juvenile pythons are diurnal, whereas the adults are more nocturnal in their habits, when there are likely to be more small mammals available.

On other continents, all the larger species of snakes take a large proportion of mammals and many species feed exclusively on them. Common names such as rat snake, applied to numerous snakes in North America, Europe and Asia, highlight the diet of the more common species.

Larger species of mammals, such as ground squirrels and rabbits, form the prey of larger species of snakes. For instance, in an Idaho population studied by Diller and Johnson (1988),[14] these two species made up the majority of prey species eaten by prairie rattlesnakes, *Crotalus viridis*. Furthermore, they estimated that the rattlesnakes accounted for 14 per cent of the population of ground squirrels each year and a further 5–11 per cent of the population of juvenile cottontail rabbits. Gopher snakes, *Pituophis melanoleucus*, by contrast, ate smaller quantities of ground squirrels (4 per cent of the total population) but more of the cottontails (22–43 per cent of the total population). These figures give a good idea of the efficiency with which snakes control the populations of rodents and related species under natural circumstances and this is well known in some communities where snakes are actively encouraged to take up residence in barns and other areas where grain is stored.

Although rodents are probably the main prey of snakes in the northern hemisphere, in the tropics and elsewhere other groups of mammals are sometimes more common, and therefore more important prey species. Marsupials have already been mentioned in the context of Australian snakes. The New World marsupials, opposums, are known to be eaten by several species including the mussurana, *Clelia clelia*, the neotropical tiger snake, *Spilotes pullatus*, and the rainbow boa, *Epicrates cenchria*.

Bats, though, are the most numerous form of mammal in many tropical regions and are

▶ Bats are the most common mammals in many parts of the world and are preyed on by several of the more agile species of snakes, such as Children's pythons, *Liasis childreni.*

potential prey to many arboreal and semi-arboreal snakes. Species that are known to eat bats in the natural course of events include several boas such as the rainbow boa, *Epicrates cenchria*, and related species such as *E. angulifer* and *Boa constrictor*, and it seems likely that the arboreal boas belonging to the genus *Corallus* also eat them sometimes. The Australian Children's python, *Liasis childreni*, eats bats on occasion while the cave racer, *Elaphe taeniura ridleyi*, which is a large Asiatic colubrid, apparently feeds almost exclusively on them. The American lyre snake, *Trimorphodon biscutatus*, has been seen plucking young bats from the roof of a culvert in Mexico: bats probably do not represent a common prey for this generalist species, however.

Larger prey species probably receive a disproportionately large amount of publicity. Although the giant boas and pythons undoubtedly tackle and eat large animals such as deer, antelope, domestic pigs and goats and even humans, it is likely that they usually subsist on more manageable items of food.

Eggs

Eggs are a useful (and defenceless) source of protein. It is no surprise, then, that snakes exploit this as a food supply. The rare cases of frogs' and amphibians' eggs as food have been listed above, as have the occasions when insects eggs are eaten by thread and worm snakes, but reptile and bird eggs are an important part of the diets of a number of snakes from different families and different parts of the world.

The most famous egg-eating species are, of course, the African egg eaters belonging to the genus *Dasypeltis*, of which there are six species. These snakes are highly specialized and the series of vertebrae running along the top of their throats have modified downward-pointing processes (the hypapophyses), with which they saw through the shells of birds' eggs, then swallow the contents and regurgitate the shell. Their capacity to swallow eggs that are several times the diameter of their heads is truly amazing. The very rare Indian egg-eating snake, *Elachistodon westermanni*, is said to have similar habits and also has modified vertebrae in the neck region. Unfortunately, it is rare and poorly known.

Other snakes that eat birds' eggs include members of the following genera: *Boiga*, *Conophis*, *Elaphe*, *Lampropeltis*, *Pseustes* and *Spilotes*. All these species are colubrids. A python, *Liasis fuscus*, eats goose eggs when 'in season' and a young yellow anaconda, *Eunectes notaeus*, has been found with eggs of the limpkin, a wading bird, in its stomach. The eggs were swallowed pointed end first. As far as is known, the *Dasypeltis* species are the only ones that reject the eggshell, the others swallow their eggs whole.

Many other snakes eat the eggs of reptiles. Some are specialists while others are opportunists and eat them only if they come across them by chance. As far as is known,

all of the snakes belonging to the large A genus *Oligodon* are specialists, altho they will also eat other kinds of prey. (man *et al.* (1993)[15] described the pro in *O. formosanus*. The snake used one enlarged teeth on the back of its upper to slash the eggshell. It repeatedly the tooth along the shell until it had ma slit. The slit was further enlarged by u the cutting edge of the same enlarged t until it was large enough for the snak push its head inside the shell and cons the contents. These snakes are comm known as kukri snakes, after the cerem knives that the enlarged rear teeth are to resemble.

...ke all the members of its genus, the brown egg
r, *Dasypeltis inornata*, feeds only on birds'
. The egg is first engulfed (left), then the shell is
...hed in the snake's throat (right).

Oligodon is paralleled in Australia by the
...ll elapids *Simoselaps semifasciatus, S.
...eri*, and possibly other closely related
...cies. These feed entirely on lizard and
...ke eggs and have a single enlarged tooth
...each of the lower jaws, in contrast to
...odon*, which have their modified teeth in
...upper jaw. It seems that these teeth slit
...shells of reptile eggs as they pass through
...mouth.
...n Africa, the shovel-snouted snakes,
...*symna*, also feed largely on reptile eggs.
...ey do not appear to have specialized denti-
...n but use the sharp teeth on the maxilla
...uncture the shells as they pass into the
...oat. The shell as well as its contents are
...llowed.
...A common factor in all the above species
...*godon, Simoselaps, Prosymna*) is an up-
...ned snout. This is thought to enable the
...kes to bring their sharp cutting teeth into
...y without the need to bite the eggs
...ich, in many cases, would probably be
...large to fit into their gapes). Significantly,
...species of *Simoselaps* that do not eat
...s do not have this feature. An upturned
...ut does not necessarily imply egg-eating

...he two-striped shovel-snouted snake,
...*symna bivittata*, and its relatives, from
...hern Africa, feed on reptile eggs. Unrelated
...kes with a similar diet often bear superficial
...mblances to them.

tendencies, though, as many burrowing
species have also evolved this characteristic
(see Chapter 4).

In America, the niche is filled by the
two species belonging to the genus *Phyllorhynchus*, known as leaf-nosed snakes.
These snakes eat lizards, especially the
banded gecko, *Coleonyx variegatus*, but are
thought to prey heavily on their eggs as
well. (*Coleonyx* are eublepharid geckos
and, as such, they lay soft-shelled eggs,
unlike the majority of gecko species, which
lay calcareous eggs.)

Species that feed exclusively on reptile
eggs must either live in parts of the world
where reptiles breed throughout much of
the year, that is, the tropical regions, or, if
they live in places where reptile breeding

is a seasonal event, they must be able to
feed heavily when eggs are available and
store enough fat to tide them over the rest
of the year.

In addition to the specialists, many generalists undoubtedly also eat reptile eggs. The
North American kingsnakes, for instance,
are known to eat reptile eggs occasionally
and there is at least one record of a kingsnake stealing the eggs from the nest of a
freshwater turtle. Another opportunist is
the Mexican *Loxocemus bicolor*, which eats
Ctenosaura and *Iguana* eggs in Costa Rica. At
certain times of the year, these eggs may
make up almost 100 per cent of the food of
this species.

Carrion

In the past, there was a widely held view that
snakes rarely if ever ate carrion. Problems
associated with establishing carrion as a
normal food source include the rare and
opportunistic nature of happening upon a
snake that is feeding on such prey, coupled
with the fact that, when stomach contents
of snakes are examined, there is no easy way
to distinguish prey items that have been
killed by the snake as opposed to those that
were already dead when eaten.

Recent observations have changed this
view to some extent. There are several
reported observations of snakes eating carrion. A large prairie rattlesnake was seen
eating a dead cottontail rabbit, for instance.
The rabbit had been dead for over one day
as maggots and carrion beetles were present
on the carcass and the snake took one-
and-a-half hours to swallow the rabbit, due

to *rigor mortis*. Other instances include a cottonmouth, *Agkistrodon piscivorus*, that ate a dead water snake, *Nerodia erythrogaster*, and another cottonmouth that was seen to scavenge around the nests of sea birds, searching for spilled fish. Venomous snakes may be more disposed to take dead prey than other snakes because their hunting method involves killing and releasing prey, after which they track it down and eat it some time later. The process of finding such prey may take several hours, by which time the body will be well and truly dead.

Non-venomous snakes may also take carrion. A specimen of the West Indian ground snake *Alsophis portoriciensis richardi*, from Congo Cay, Puerto Rico, was watched by Norton (1993)[16] as it found and ate dehydrated fish dropped by brown pelicans while feeding their chicks. The snake appeared to be actively searching in areas where spilled fish may have become lodged. Yet another example concerns a ribbon snake, *Thamnophis sauritus*, which was watched as it tried to peel a squashed toad from a tarmac road, while Bedford (1991)[17] watched an Australian colubrid, the keelback, *Tropidonophis mairii*, taking road-killed frogs from road surfaces on more than one occasion.

These casual observations seem to indicate that snakes are not averse to eating carrion when the opportunity arises. They are, of course, in competition with scavenging birds and mammals and are, by comparison, poorly equipped to find such prey first.

In captivity, most snakes can be encouraged to eat freshly killed prey animals. Many will also eat food that has been frozen and thawed out and a number seem to prefer food that has been left in their cage for several hours and has become 'high'. Observations on captive snakes should be regarded as suspicious but, nevertheless, they do demonstrate the flexibility of feeding behaviour.

Shifts in prey type
Snakes do not necessarily eat the same type of prey throughout their lives, nor do different populations of the same species always eat similar prey. Shifts in prey preference are related to size, the ability of young snakes to overpower and swallow their prey, and the availability of different sorts of prey in different places.

Young snakes are, by definition, smaller than adults of the same species. This places obvious constraints on the type of food they

can handle and, whereas the young of some species merely eat smaller versions of the adults' prey, others eat totally different items. Availability plays an important part; fish, for example, are usually available in a range of sizes and fish-eating snakes tend to eat them throughout their lives, tackling progressively larger fish as they grow. At the same time they may drop small fish from their diet altogether, as in most sea snakes, or they may eat all sizes. Foraging behaviour may play a role here because small fish are often found in shallower water than large fish so, as the snake grows, it may hunt in deeper water and so reduce, or eliminate, the possibility of finding small fish. This behaviour has been found to occur in some garter and ribbon snakes, *Thamnophis*.

Other semi-aquatic species, such as certain water snakes, *Nerodia*, start their lives as fish eaters and graduate to amphibians as they grow. Snakes belonging to the genus *Regina* eat crustaceans as adults but *R. alleni*, and probably the other three species as well, eat smaller species of crustaceans, such as shrimps as well as dragonfly larvae, when they are young.

A common switch is from lizards to mammals. Many mammal-eating snakes are too small at hatching to tackle adult rodents, etc. and, although they may eat nestling mice when the opportunity presents itself, most eat lizards which, due to their shape, are more easily swallowed. The European vipers, for instance, feed almost entirely on small lizards when they are young but gradually work up to small mammals as they grow. Switching does not take place suddenly but their diets change gradually; even the adults of small species continue to take lizards along with small mammals although the larger species may drop lizards from their diets altogether. A similar situation exists with many of the pit vipers in North, Central and South America. Numerous colubrids are known to eat lizards at hatching, then switch to small mammals as they grow: these include several of the king snakes, *Lampropeltis* species, especially the smaller montane species that hatch at a time when there is an abundance of small lizards within their habitat. Judging from their behaviour in captivity, many of the young of these species do not eat even newly born mice during the summer and autumn of their first year but will accept them the following spring after a period of hibernation, even though they may not have grown appreciably.

Where populations become isolated, an island or mountain range for instan their diets may need to change due to availability of prey types, which may di from those of the main population. Th has been little research into this area bu couple of examples can be mentioned.

The rattleless rattlesnake, *Crotalus ca nensis*, living on the island of Santa Catali in the Gulf of Mexico, is descended from, a closely related to, the red diamond rat snake, *C. ruber*. Whereas the mainland fe eats mainly small mammals, the island fe seems to have undergone a dietary sh probably because small mammals are r on the island. Instead, it appears to small birds and spiny lizards, which more common. To this end, it has beco partially arboreal and has evolved int more slender form than its relatives on mainland. In addition, its teeth are sig cantly longer. On another of the Gulf islar Isla Cerralvo, the rattlesnake *Crotalus e cerralvensis* also climbs into bushes, pr ably to feed on birds and lizards, altho no morphological adaptations have b noted; it is noteworthy that another viper, *Bothrops insularis*, from the islanc Queimada Grande, off the south-east cc of Brazil, may have undergone sim dietary shifts. Although its ecology is well known, it may also have beco arboreal or semi-arboreal. The length o fangs are not known, but it appears to h evolved an especially powerful and fa acting venom so that it can subdue b quickly.

In a study of the tree boa, *Corallus enhyc* on the mainland of South America anc the West Indies, Henderson (1993)[18] fou that different populations had differ diets, with the mainland snakes taki mainly mammals with some birds and a lizards, and the island populations taki mainly lizards with a few mammals a hardly any birds. This may reflect the re tive abundance of the different prey ty between habitats and, in particular, large number of arboreal lizards on Caribbean islands.

Another example involves the Nc American kingsnake, *Lampropeltis getu* which ranges over a large geograph area encompassing several different hab types. Eastern forms, such as the ch kingsnake, *L. g. getulus*, are small at hat ing and are reluctant to take mice althou they will readily accept lizards and sma snakes. On the other hand, western for such as the Mexican black kingsnake, *L*

Young Amazon tree boas, *Corallus enhydris*, living on West Indian islands, undergo a shift in their diets as they grow, from lizards to birds and mammals, whereas those living on the mainland are more likely to feed on birds and mammals from the time they are born.

...itus, are much larger at hatching and are prepared to take mice from the time they ...h. More subtle differences are seen in another form, the Californian kingsnake, *...californiae*, in which young from some ...s, e.g. the coastal region, take mice ...ily, whereas young from the desert ...1 prefer lizards. It can only be assumed ...prey availability, over a long period of ..., has shaped both the ability of the ...es to feed on different types of prey, and ...r behaviour.

...unt of food
...amount of food eaten by snakes has ...ived little attention. The two extremes ...represented, on the one hand, by the ...mple of a thread snake that contained ...0 food items (see page 96) and, on ...other hand, by snakes that contained ...ing in their stomach. The latter situa-...appears to be normal: of many surveys ...ied out by dissecting large numbers of ...erved museum specimens, the most ...mon state is for the stomach to be empty. ...e snakes take several days to digest ...food, an empty stomach indicates ...the snake has probably not fed for ...e time.

...e quantity of prey eaten will depend on ...ral factors. Temperature is important, ...akes will not hunt if it is too cold or too ...The type of prey is also of importance:

snakes that eat small items will need to feed more frequently than those that eat larger ones. Superimposed on this are the require- ments of the snakes. Active, diurnal species use up energy more quickly than sluggish species that ambush their prey, and so they will need to eat more often, all other things being equal.

Availability is another factor: many snakes probably do not feed as often as they would like. Lack of suitable food can occur for long periods of time. Some prey species are only seasonally available (the mutton bird chicks mentioned on page 103 are an extreme example) and the snakes concerned may need to feed heavily in order to lay down reserves for the rest of the year when there is little or no chance to feed. Female snakes may not feed when they are in advanced stages of pregnancy, presumably because the developing eggs or embryos take up all the available body space leaving insufficient room for a meal: live-bearing species may go without food for several months for this reason. Similarly, snakes fast voluntarily when they are about to shed their skin.

Size of prey
Snakes are capable of eating relatively large prey. Obviously, as they grow the range of prey open to them increases. Small snakes, then, are restricted to small prey, whereas large snakes could eat large *and* small prey. There are costs involved in eating small prey, however, and it may not always be in their interests to do so. For example, snakes that chase their prey are likely to expend as much energy in catching a small lizard as they do in catching a large lizard, although

the benefits will be much less. Snakes may also expose themselves to danger each time they hunt and eat their prey and so one would expect them to forego food items that are of little value. It is important that they optimize their hunting in such a way that the benefits outweigh the costs.

In view of the fact that snakes must swallow their food whole, they must have means of assessing the size of a prey animal before they launch an attack. Smell may play an important role as small species of rodents, for instance, may smell different from large species. Young animals may also smell different from adults. Snakes that kill their prey, either by constriction or by envenomation, often examine their prey closely before beginning to swallow it. This is normally interpreted as a search for the head, but it may also help the snake to decide whether or not the food will fit into its mouth.

The capacity to swallow large prey is not equal throughout the snake kingdom. The limitation of having rigid jaws in the case of many small burrowing snakes has already been mentioned but there are also differences between the more advanced species. On average, vipers are capable of swallowing proportionately larger prey than other types of snakes, over twice as large in some cases. The body shape of vipers obviously helps them to accommodate large prey, as do their lethargic habits. In addition, their sit-and-wait tactics may have forced them into taking larger prey since they must depend, to a large extent, on random meals passing by and cannot afford to reject too many feeding opportunities. Their wide heads may have evolved in response to this necessity.

In absolute terms it is the boas and pythons that eat the largest prey. This is not without its hazards, though, as there are several documented cases of them dying because the horns of their prey have pierced their bodies from inside the gut, and even more cases where bloated pythons and boas have been killed (by humans) because a recently eaten large meal has rendered them unable to escape.

Competition for food and resource partitioning
Within communities of snakes, it often appears that the different species avoid direct competition with each other by con- centrating on different types of food. Thus, different species of snakes in a given area may hunt for different types of prey, or they

may hunt at different times or in different places.

Although a brief look at the various species of snakes occurring in one area often leads, intuitively, to the conclusion that food partitioning is taking place, there have been very few thorough studies to confirm this. Many snake communities are very complex, especially in the tropics where there may be dozens of species living in the same area, including terrestrial, arboreal and burrowing species, large, medium-sized and small species and nocturnal and diurnal species, in addition to generalists and specialists. Several species may prey on some of the others. For these reasons, it is simpler to look at snake communities that contain only a few species.

In Britain, there are two common species of snakes that may occur together, the adder, *Vipera berus*, which eats lizards and rodents and the grass snake, *Natrix natrix*, which eats fish and amphibians. A third species, the smooth snake, *Coronella austriaca*, also eats lizards and rodents but may avoid competition with the adder by foraging in burrows and crevices. Communities of garter snakes in North America seem to have more subtle differences in their diet. Species occurring together eat worms, slugs, amphibians, fish and mammals, and, although there is some overlap, some species have preferences for one or more groups of prey. In south-western Australia, where there are a number of small terrestrial elapids, Shine (1984)[19] found

▼ Desert snakes, such as the horned adder, *Bitis caudalis*, may drink only rarely, if at all. Some desert species rely entirely on condensed fog for their water.

that closely related species sharing the same habitat often specialize in different prey: *Simoselaps bertholdi* and its allies eat only small lizards, *S. semifasciata* eats only reptile eggs, and so on. Several other related species are less specialized and eat lizards and reptile eggs.

Drinking

Most snakes drink. In order to do so, they submerge their snouts and, by pumping with their throats, draw water into their oesophagus. The tongue is not used to lap water.

Some groups of snakes drink rarely or not at all, because they live in habitats where fresh water is not freely available. These include sea snakes and species from deserts. The true sea snakes, belonging to the subfamily Hydropheinae, probably do not drink, but extract water from their food. The sea kraits, Laticaudinae, come ashore occasionally and have been observed drinking from rainwater pools along the sea shore and from overhanging vegetation. Desert snakes drink when they get the opportunity but their main strategy is to extract water from their food and retain it as effectively as possible. Techniques include scale rasping (and possibly rattling) instead of hissing, polishing the scales in order to reduce their permeability, and the production of solid uric acid as their metabolic waste.

It seems likely that some individuals hardly, if ever, drink throughout their lives, and in experimental situations several species, such as the carpet viper, *Echis coloratus*, have been successfully reared without access to water.

Snakes tend to be stereotyped in their hunting methods. That is, each species use particular method and, by and large, st to it. There may, however, be differen in hunting behaviour between adults juveniles and different populations of same species may also hunt in slig different ways (often depending on availability). When looking at hun methods, two main strategies can be rec nized: sit-and-wait predators that amb their prey, and active hunters that out their prey, chasing and running it de if necessary. These only represent the extremes of a continuum of strategies, h ever, and between them there are sev variations and modifications, evolved optimize the snake's success rate.

Hunting strategy obviously depends the type of prey a snake tends to eat. I area where small mammals are comm for instance, sitting and waiting may very cost effective method, but it is m less likely to succeed where the main pr birds' eggs or termites!

Active diurnal hunters

Active diurnal hunters are epitomize the fast-moving and agile diurnal colut such as the racers, whipsnakes, coachw and sand snakes, *Coluber*, *Masticophis Psammophis*, the Australian elapids *Dema* (also known as whipsnakes) and oth These species feed by using their sigh locate prey, stalking it carefully in orde get as close as possible, then taking it a rush. The method is not always succ ful – lizards, the most common prey of type of snake, are equally alert and agile many attacks, possibly most, fail. Cha teristics of active hunters are a slender b long tail, large eyes and a tendency search by raising the head slightly off ground as they progress. Many are mar with longitudinal stripes along their bo Active hunters may be found among ter trial, arboreal, aquatic and semi-aqu snakes.

Active foragers

Species that eat sedentary or slow-mov prey, such as molluscs and other inve brates, or bird and reptiles eggs, are obl to forage. Finding prey is their main – once found it is relatively easy to c and overpower it.

In warm parts of the world, where m snakes are nocturnal, a large propor are nocturnal foragers. These inc species that search for prey such as liz

Sonoran whipsnake, *Masticophis bilineatus*, ...shows many of the characteristics of an ..., diurnal hunter: slender body, long tail and ...eyes.

...e they are asleep. To this end they ...ent low bushes and shrubs, where ...es such as the West Indian *Anolis* roost, ...oke their heads into crevices in rocks ... trees where species such as small ...s, teiid and lacertid lizards sleep. ...d examples of these nocturnal foragers ...he arboreal neotropical *Imantodes*, the ...strial *Telescopus* from Europe and ...a, the American lyre snakes, *Trimor-* ...on, the Egyptian cobra, *Walterinnesia*

...timal foraging

...though snakes' food provides the ...ergy they need for other activities, ...thering it also incurs a cost. As long ... the energy derived from the food is ...eater than the energy used in ...thering it everything will be fine. ...ere comes a point, however, where ...all items of food do not give a good ...ough return to make them worth ...nting. In order to hunt and feed ...iciently, all animals need to take this ...o account and those that are most ...icient are the ones that are ...st likely to grow and reproduce ...ccessfully.

...Obviously, larger snakes eat larger ...ey, because they are able to, but the ...timal foraging theory, which predicts ...e ideal hunting strategy, goes one ...ge further. It suggests that large ...akes should drop small prey items ...m their diets, because they do not ...e a good return when compared to ...e energy used up in capturing them. ...is ideal system has been confirmed in ...me populations of rattlesnakes, for ...stance, in which young snakes of less ...an one year old eat only shrews but, ... they grow, gradually shift their ...eferences until, by the time they are ...ult, they feed on larger mammals ...d birds and rarely take small prey ...ms.

...Unfortunately, overall evidence for ...is type of shift in prey size is not conclusive. There are indications that some species of snakes are more selective when it comes to prey size than others, but there have been too few studies on this aspect of snake biology to draw any general conclusions. Furthermore, many of the feeding records published over the years fail to include the sort of information that is essential for this type of study (they often lump prey items together without giving an indication of size, or they give only the average size of prey).

Even where it has been shown that large snakes do drop small prey items from their diet, optimal foraging may not necessarily be the reason. Small prey sometimes becomes unavailable to large snakes, as in tree boas that hunt for sleeping *Anolis* lizards (because the small lizards sleep on thin branches that will not support large snakes). Fish-eating snakes are in a similar situation because small fish tend to be found in shallow margins of ponds and lakes whereas the larger ones are found in deeper water: once the snake has moved up to larger fish, it will rarely have the opportunity to catch small ones, even if it wanted to. Furthermore, small fish may also be more elusive to large snakes than big ones and therefore the energy spent in catching them may actually be *greater* than that spent in catching large ones. On the other hand, rodent-eating snakes may find nests containing litters of young – it would obviously be worth their while to eat these as, collectively, they constitute a sizeable meal as well as one which represents little risk.

Prey type is another important consideration. Snakes that feed on easily obtained prey, such as invertebrates, can afford to be less fussy about the size of individual items – they expand very little energy in catching and handling their prey anyway and even a small meal will be worthwhile. For the same reason, snakes that ambush their prey would also be expected to take any suitable food that passes within range; again, they expend little energy in hunting for their food once they have found a productive place in which to lie in wait. (Having said this, most snakes that ambush their prey are large-bodied species which are able to accommodate larger prey than active foragers, which tend to be more slender).

Species that have restricted diets are also less likely to be fussy. Australian snakes, for example, have few large prey available to them. They therefore tend to take any prey that comes along, predominantly skinks in many species, and large individuals eat the same sized skinks as small ones do.

▲ The lyre snake, *Trimorphodon biscutatus*, a nocturnal prowler, with a slender body, large eyes and vertical pupils. The flattened head is perhaps an adaptation that allows the snake to thrust it into nooks and crannies where sleeping lizards are often found.

aegyptia, and a number of small Australian elapids. As the sleeping lizards are cold and therefore comatose, catching and subduing them is a relatively easy task for these snakes once they have located them, although a short chase may be necessary. Other nocturnal foragers eat frogs which, though active and lively at night, are often preoccupied with calling and mating and are therefore easy prey.

There are also diurnal counterparts of these nocturnal foragers: diurnal snakes that look for resting frogs and other nocturnal creatures that sleep during the day. A position somewhere between hunters and foragers is taken by species such as garter snakes and water snakes, *Thamnophis*, *Nerodia* and *Natrix* species and their relatives. These snakes work their way through marginal vegetation, repeatedly thrusting their heads into it, hoping to flush small amphibians from their hiding places. Once this occurs they give chase, often catching their prey before it has covered more than a few inches. European whipsnakes, *Coluber*, have also been seen behaving in a similar fashion, poking their heads into the holes in old dry stone walls, where diurnal lizards often hide.

Aquatic species are normally active foragers, although some members of the Homalopsinae, such as the fishing snake,

Erpeton tentaculum, ambush their prey. file snakes, *Acrochordus*, forage over muddy bottoms of estuaries and sea b looking for crabs and fish. Other sea sn investigate nooks and crannies along reefs, in search of eels and gobies, or for eggs. Snakes such as the American *Ne* and the European *Natrix* species hunt in water and may try to catch fis swimming in a seemingly random ma with their mouths open. As they swim, swing their heads to and fro, gras any fish with which they come into con

Sit-and-wait predators

Many snakes do not hunt or forage merely install themselves in a likely and wait for their prey to come al Because their sense of smell is so acute, would expect snakes to be good at detec a well-frequented rodent run, for insta and to optimize their time by waiting favourable place. If they were unsucce for a long period of time, they coul expected to move to a better location. T appear to have been few studies that looked at this particular aspect of hur strategy in snakes.

Snakes that sit and wait for their food characterized by heavy bodies and l heads. They tend to be well camoufla usually having some kind of disrup coloration. Many boas, pythons and vi

Foraging in bushmasters: an object lesson in patience

Sit-and-wait predators seem to have a fairly simplistic approach to life: they find a productive place to wait and feed whenever they get the chance. Because they do not use much energy by moving around, they do not need to feed very often and, in addition, they reduce the chances of being spotted by a predator.

A radio-tracking experiment carried out on bushmasters by Harry Greene seems to confirm this picture (*American Zoologist*, 23:897).

The bushmaster, *Lachesis muta*, is the largest pit viper. It is quite rare and is found only in the rainforests of Central and South America. It is cryptically coloured and, like most vipers, it ambushes its prey.

Greene tracked three bushmasters for varying periods of time; one of them, a female measuring 90 cm (3 f in length, used only three sites over a 45-day period. During the day it reste beneath small plants but it was alert each night and obviously hoping that meal would materialize. On the 24th night its patience was rewarded: it at a rodent estimated to weigh at least 40 per cent of its own body weight. After eating, it was inactive for nine more nights before moving to a new site.

The hunting sites chosen by this an two other tracked bushmasters were always near *Weltia* palms, the seeds of which are eaten by the rodents that t snakes prey on.

rrestrial sit-and-wait predators, like this death
r, *Acanthophis* species, from New Guinea,
large stocky bodies to provide an anchor
t and small heads that they can throw forward
great speed. They are invariably well
ouflaged and sometimes have brightly coloured
o their tails, which serve to entice their prey a
closer.

rboreal sit-and-wait predators, such as the
n tree python, *Chondropython viridis*, are also
camouflaged but their body size is limited by
ize of the branches along which they climb or
vhich they rest. Their tails are often prehensile,
iding an alternative means of anchoring
iselves when they strike.

sit-and-wait predators: the blood python,
ion curtus, Gaboon viper, *Bitis gabonicus*,
the puff adder, *Bitis arietans*, are three
obvious examples but representatives of
ral other families also use this strategy.
Australian death adder, *Acanthophis*
rcticus, which, despite its name. is an
id, is another sit-and-wait predator.
rboreal snakes that are sit-and-wait
lators are not so heavy bodied as their
estrial counterparts but they are still
tically marked. They include the twig
tes, *Thelatornis*, and several boas and
ions, including the three species belong-
to the South and Central American
us *Corallus* and the Australasian *Chondro-
on viridis*. Aquatic snakes that ambush
r prey are also well camouflaged.

ng
umber of sit-and-wait species of snakes
ease their chances of success by using
r tails to lure prey within range. They
i to have cryptically coloured bodies and
is but brightly coloured tails. The
nique seems to have evolved separately
veral families and has been recorded for
ierous unrelated species from various
s of the world.
iring involves raising the tail above the
and twitching or waving it in an entic-
nanner in order to attract the attention

▲ Snakes with brightly coloured tips to their tails often use them as lures. Luring has been seen in snakes belonging to several families, and may be present only in juveniles (which eat smaller prey) or in all ages. This form of Cuban wood snake, *Tropidophis melanurus*, with a sulphur yellow tail, feeds on small frogs and lizards and would be a good candidate for luring, although this has not yet been definitely established.

► Several species of pit vipers, which are typical sit-and-wait predators, have coloured tips to their tails which they use as lures. Again, these are sometimes present only in juveniles, but may persist in adults as in the cantil, *Agkistrodon bilineatus*.

of possible prey animals and encourage them to investigate further by approaching the snake. Two types of luring have been noted for several species: slow, speculative luring when no prey has been detected and a more active luring when prey is present. Certain prey types seem to be more susceptible than others and luring tends to be more common among snakes that eat lizards and frogs. In most cases, juvenile snakes have the coloration to lure but lose it as they mature: this usually reflects a change in diet but may also be due to the inability of large snakes to carry out the deception effectively.

Among the pythons, young green tree pythons, *Chondropython viridis*, are bright yellow (sometimes brownish orange) but always have yellow coloured tails. Murphy, Carpenter and Gillingham (1976)[20] observed caudal luring in a group of captive-hatched juveniles when rodents were offered. Even more remarkably, *Anolis* lizards, which were loose in the laboratory, approached the cages in which the young snakes were housed and tried to attack the tails through the glass!

Among the Tropidophidae, some forms of the wood snake, *Tropidophis melanurus*, have a black tip to their tail while others have a

bright yellow tip. Although luring has been observed in this secretive species coloration suggests that it may oc Similarly, the closely related *Trach* species have bright orange tips to their when young. (Some species may brightly coloured tails to deflect attack a from their head, however, as discusse Chapter 6.)

In the Colubridae, luring has not b observed very many times, conside the large number of species in the fan Juveniles of the Brazilian species *Tro dryas striaticeps* are greenish grey or br in colour but the tips of their tails are whi to yellowish. They are also covered flared scales making them appear broa (juicier?) than they really are. Sazima Puorto (1993)[21] observed freshly cau captives luring in the presence of poter prey (frogs and lizards) and immedia after feeding. The African bark sn *Hemirhagerrhis nototaeniata*, is also cr cally marked but has a bright tip to its pink or orange in this case. It is arboreal feeds on geckos, small skinks and f and may use the tail to lure them, altho this has not been observed.

By contrast to the limited numbe records of caudal luring in colubrids, m vipers have been observed employing technique. Greene and Campbell (197 noted the behaviour in *Bothrops* (=*Bothrio bilineata*, while Sazima and Puorto (19 noted similar behaviour in the Brazi species *Bothrops jararaca* and *B. jararaci* Several other related species, such as common *B. atrox*, have brightly colo tips to their tails, at least when young, w the young of *B. asper* seem to be sexu dimorphic, with only the males ha bright tail tips: both sexes, however, b been seen using their tail to lure. Lu behaviour is probably quite widesp among the South American pit vipers.

Of the African vipers, *Atheris nitsch* slate grey with a white tip to its tail w born. Catherine Pook (1990)[23] noticed they would wriggle their tails in 'a mag like motion' when offered food or distur *Atheris chloroechis* also has a light colo tail tip when young and probably uses as a lure. Luring seems not to have recorded in other African vipers. Simil caudal luring has not been recorded in of the European and Middle Eastern vi belonging to the genus *Vipera*, even the several forms of the nose-horned v *V. ammodytes*, e.g. *V. a. gregorwallneri*, *ruffoi* and *V. a. transcaucasiana*, have or to their tails when young, while young *montandoni* have greenish tips to their , *V. xanthina* also has an orange tip to its

mong the Elapidae, only the death r, *Acanthophis antarcticus*, seems to use ail as a lure and its behaviour is well mented, by Carpenter *et al.* (1978).[24] species, which is a particularly bulky nd-wait predator, rests with its body round so that the tail is next to the . The tail is waved about slowly until is detected, when the movements are eased. Interestingly, luring was observed wo subspecies, one of which (*A. a. rcticus*) had a contrasting orange tail e the other (*A. a. laevis*) did not.

n unusual form of luring may be present ne African twig snake, *Thelotornis kirt- i*. This species is very slender and is tically marked, resembling a dead branch ne. It has been observed resting with its ht red tongue extended and is said to ce birds within range by this strategy.

Having found their prey, the next problem that snakes face is that of overpowering it. The difficulties involved will depend on the type of prey, and for snakes that eat defence-less prey such as eggs, slugs and snails the problem does not arise. Other species, however, may need to deal with prey that is slippery and hard to grip, prey that may discard part of its anatomy in order to make an escape, or prey that is capable of inflicting serious damage.

A number of methods are used by snakes to render their prey helpless. These methods are not always mutually exclusive. The same species, or even the same individual, may use several methods according to the type and size of prey it is tackling and there is strong evidence that snakes can distinguish between potentially harmful and harmless prey. Having said this, feeding behaviour tends to be stereotyped so that, in a given set of conditions, a predictable sequence of events will take place.

In its simplest form, catching, overpower-ing and swallowing become a more or less continuous process. The European grass snake, *Natrix natrix*, for instance, eats frogs by grasping them in its jaws and beginning to swallow immediately: it sometimes turns the frog around until it can be swallowed head first but often swallows it backwards. The same technique is used by many of the lizard-eating snakes and by snakes that enter rodent nests and take the young. There is plenty of evidence to show that snakes can identify their prey with regard to type and age, and act accordingly. Whereas nestling mice are swallowed alive, sub-adults and adults are invariably rendered helpless before swallowing commences. Identification is not always based on size, though, as the same snake will kill adult mice but swallow nestling rats of the same size and weight without killing them.

Subduing prey completely before swal-lowing is initiated occurs in snakes from most families, and takes two main forms: constriction and envenomation.

Constriction
There is no clear-cut distinction between swallowing without killing and constric-tion. A number of snakes grasp their prey and begin to swallow. If the prey struggles, the snake may then throw one or two loose coils around it or use its body to pin the prey down. Species that hunt in the burrows or chambers of rodents, for instance, rarely have enough room in which to constrict their prey effectively but may crush them

against the sides of the burrows. Other species are more inclined to constrict their prey as a matter of course. Large boas and pythons, for instance, will often constrict their prey for long periods of time, even when fed with dead food in captivity. This behaviour persists throughout their lives even though they may never be faced with the prospect of killing their own food.

Constriction, in its most extreme form, consists of grasping the body of the prey animal, throwing two or more coils of the body around it in the same instant and then exerting continuous pressure until it expires. Although small bones may be crushed during the process, the prey is killed by asphyxiation – each time it breathes out the coils are tightened until it is unable to breathe at all. The time taken varies with the type and the strength of the prey and can be many minutes in some cases. Constriction tends to be more effective on mammals and birds, which need to breathe frequently, than on lizards or snakes, which can survive long periods without breathing. Species that feed on lizards and snakes, then, may constrict their prey but often begin to swallow it before it is completely dead. Furthermore, many of the species that feed on these prey types are mildly venomous.

Envenomation
Venomous snakes are found in four families: the Colubridae, Atractaspididae, Elapidae and Viperidae. Their methods of produc-ing the venom are not exactly the same, however.

Rear-fanged colubrids
Many colubrid snakes, including rear-fanged venomous as well as non-venomous species have a Duvernoy's gland. This is a modified salivary gland, and is named after the French anatomist who discovered it in 1832. It is situated towards the back of the mouth, on both sides, and varies greatly in size. A duct carries the toxic saliva, or venom, to the posterior maxillary teeth and discharges it into the furrow between the lips of the snake and the sides of its teeth. A more detailed account of Duvernoy's gland is given in Chapter 2 (see page 46)

Well over 100 genera of colubrids, amounting to about one-third of all species, are known to have a Duvernoy's gland. While some of the species involved have normal dentition, a number have enlarged fangs near the point where the glands discharge. Although the enlarged fangs

▲ Constrictors subdue their prey by restraining it in one or more coils, preventing it from drawing breath and restricting the pumping action of the heart. Death ensues from one or other, or both, of these effects. The snake is a small python, *Liasis maculosus.*

usually consist of a single pair, some species have two or three adjacent pairs. The enlarged teeth may have grooves running from their bases to their tips in order to allow the venom to travel up them by capillary action once they are embedded in the prey. The venom apparatus is not, therefore, as efficient as that of the cobras and vipers and the snake has to chew before an appreciable amount finds its way into the prey. Wherever there are enlarged fangs there is a gap, known as the diastema, in front of them, the purpose of which is to allow the fangs to be sunk fully into the prey.

Once the fangs have been thrust into the prey, the chewing action begins. This is thought to fulfil the dual purpose of opening up the wound and improving the flow of the venom along the fangs. The prey is held well back in the mouth and the snake passes through bouts of chewing alternating with periods of resting. The intermittent chewing bouts, as well as helping to inject the venom, may also serve to stimulate

activity from the prey and so tell the snake whether or not the venom has taken effect.

Eventually the prey will die or become unconscious. Once the snake senses this, it moves the prey around in its mouth and swallows it, usually head first. Should the prey show signs of regaining consciousness, the snake will clamp its jaws on it once more and repeat the process, giving the venom more time to take effect.

The venoms produced by Duverr glands vary slightly between species. S are more potent than others and cer rear-fanged colubrids have been respon for human deaths.

▼ The brown tree snake, *Boiga irregularis,* a accidental interloper on the island of Guam, w it has thrived at the cost of native species of bir and lizards. It has fangs towards the rear of its mouth and a moderately potent venom with w it immobilises its prey.

t-fanged snakes

bers of the Elapidae and the Viperidae
ss specialized venom fangs at the front
eir mouths. They differ in their form,
e of the elapids being relatively short
fixed and those of the vipers being
ively long and hinged, so that they can
ded flat when not in use.

thods of using the venom probably
little between these two families,
ugh the vipers, especially the American
ipers, have been studied most. Small
innocuous prey are struck and held
e the venom takes effect. Birds, which
l fly long distances before succumbing,
which are unlikely to harm the snake
vay, are always held. Large prey is
ed differently. It is struck and then
sed. The snake then begins to track the
g prey, using it tongue, until it finds
arcass. Swallowing can now take place
out danger to the snake. It is interesting

ge vipers, such as the Gaboon viper, *Bitis*
ica, envenomate their prey before
wing it.

to compare the killing methods of different
snakes that eat different kinds of prey: the
Australian elapids provide a good example.
As has already been noted, the taipans
are the only species that eat large warm-
blooded prey and their technique is to strike
and then release their prey, so avoiding
possible injury from the struggling victim.
All other Australian elapids, which prey
predominantly on lizards but some of which
also occasionally eat small rodents, bite
and hold on to their prey.

The length of time taken for the prey to die
will obviously depend on many factors: its
size, the potency of the venom and the accuracy of the strike being the most important.
Some prey undoubtedly recover, especially if
the strike hits an extremity or if venom is
absorbed by fur or feathers. Most snakes,
though, strike very accurately: rattlesnakes,
for instance, have been shown to hit the
chest or lumbar region of rodents and small
rabbits in a high proportion of attacks.
Death often takes place in less than one
minute – sometimes in a few seconds – and
the stricken animals may only travel a few
feet before dying.

Apart from immobilizing the prey, the
venom has a secondary function, that of
starting the process of digestion. Snake
venoms originate from saliva and contain
many of the same components as human
saliva, for instance: mucus, fats and different
salts of calcium. ammonia and magnesium.
The proteins that are responsible for the
effects of envenomation are of several different types but basically consist of those
which attack the circulatory system and
the blood (haemotoxins) and those which
attack the nervous system (neurotoxins).
Haemotoxins lead to circulatory failure
either through anti-coagulation or clotting,
whereas neurotoxins affect the nerve centres
controlling movement and, more importantly, breathing. Venomous snakes have
mixtures, or 'cocktails' of venoms belonging
to both groups – death may be caused by
one type or the other, or by a combination
of both. Generally speaking, neurotoxins
produce a more rapid response than haemotoxins but are not necessarily more effective
in the long term.

As a very general rule, vipers' venom
contains mainly haemotoxins and elapid

SWALLOWING AND DIGESTION

venom contains mainly neurotoxins. The massive bruising and tissue degeneration associated with bites from dangerous vipers is due to the haemotoxic effects of their venom whereas bites from elapids cause paralysis. There are plenty of exceptions, though. The black-necked cobra, *Naja nigricollis*, produces only haemotoxic venom whereas two vipers, the berg adder, *Bitis atropos*, and the neotropical rattlesnake, *Crotalus durissus terrificus*, produce mainly neurotoxic venom, for example.

The venom of sea snakes acts mainly on muscles, and is classed as myotoxic. A few terrestrial elapids from Australia also produce myotoxic venom. Rear-fanged snakes produce mainly haemotoxic venoms.

It should also be noted that the composition of venoms may vary within species. These differences are sometimes due to age (i.e. venom composition changes during the life of the snake) or to differences between populations. The latter situation is best documented in the case of the Mojave rattlesnake, *Crotalus scutulatus*, in which two distinct types of venom have been identified, a largely neurotoxic one (Type A) that produces almost no pain or local tissue damage and a haemotoxic one (Type B) that is similar to that of the western diamondback rattlesnake, *C. atrox*, and produces typical viperine symptoms consisting of massive local haemorrhaging.

The adder, *Vipera berus*, is also known to produce different types of venom over its wide range as does the asp, *V. aspis*. Richard Clark recently described symptoms of a bite by this species in which there was little local reaction but severe systemic effects, more typical of neurotoxic envenomation.[25]

Differences in the strength of the venom and its effects may also be correlated with differences between sexes, or different times of the year, but this aspect has remained largely unresearched.

Swallowing of the prey is one of the more remarkable facets of snakes' feeding habits, especially to the uninitiated. Animals several times the diameter of the snake's head and neck are engulfed, seemingly with little effort and often in a remarkably short time.

Swallowing

Relatively small prey is often swallowed without regard to its orientation: large snakes may swallow small rodents head first, tail first or even from the middle, depending on how they are first grasped. Relatively large prey is almost always swallowed head first, however. This aids swallowing because the limbs of lizards and mammals, and the wings of birds and bats, fold more easily in this direction. With birds and mammals, it is likely that the snake finds the head by a combination of sensory and olfactory senses. Snakes may take a considerable time in 'deciding' which end to start swallowing, and sometimes make several false starts. The direction of the fur is important while the heads of animals probably have distinctive smells. Nestling rodents, in which there is no fur, are more likely to be swallowed the wrong way round. Similarly, rodents in which an incision is made towards the posterior part of the body also seem to confuse snakes. Captive snakes fed on previously frozen food are more likely to make wrong

decisions than those fed on live or fr[...] killed food, perhaps because it has lost [...] of its smell, or because it has picked up s[...] from other food items with which it [...] stored.

Once the head has been found, swa[...] ing begins. The successful consumpti[...] large prey depends on the flexibility o[...] snake's skull, the shape of its teeth, w[...] are curved backwards, and the elastic[...] its skin. The snake first opens its mou[...] grip as much of the head as possible. It [...] hooks the teeth on one side of its jaw int[...] prey and moves the opposite jaw forw[...] This jaw is then hooked into the prey[...] teeth on the other jaw are disengaged[...] that jaw is moved forward. By movin[...] jaws forward in turn, the food is pulle[...] the mouth. As the bulk of the prey p[...] into the mouth, the two halves of the [...] jaw are forced apart and the quadrate b[...] which link the posterior ends of the [...] jaw with the top of the skull, are sprea[...] this way, an enormous amount of diste[...] is possible.

At this point, the prey fills the m[...] completely and the snake would be in da[...] of choking were it not for a further m[...] cation. The forward portion of the [...] pipe (the glottis) is strongly muscula[...] is pushed forward and held open d[...] swallowing, in order to maintain a pa[...] for air.

When eating large prey, or if distu[...] the snake may take a short rest, bu[...] process is usually continuous. Once th[...]

▼ Swallowing large prey is made possible by partial dislocation of the jaws and by a high degree of elasticity in the skin around them.

NOTES

entered the throat, the snake may, by
cle action, speed up the swallowing
ess by muscular wave-like contrac-
. Once the whole of the prey is in the
at, these actions continue to force it
n into the stomach. After swallowing,
es often stretch and manipulate the jaw
s by 'yawning' in order to put them
into their normal positions.
vallowing large prey is not without
azards, however. A lyre snake, *Trimor-
on biscutatus* that ate a spiny-tailed
na, *Ctenosaura pectinata*, took an hour
three-quarters to consume its meal
then died twenty minutes later. The
d was rather large for the snake and its
y scales had punctured the snake's
phagus and stomach (Ramírez-Bautista
Uribe, 1992).[26] Similar 'accidents' have
recorded for large pythons that have
n antelopes whose horns have pierced
tomach.

stion

stion begins almost as the snake starts
wallowing process, because the saliva,
h covers the prey, contains strong
mes. As it reaches the stomach, further
mes are secreted and the digestion
inues. As this is a biochemical process,
peed with which it takes place is depen-
on temperature, as well as the surface
of the prey, and so snakes that have
tly fed will normally attempt to raise
body temperatures slightly in order
eed it up. Small snakes may bask by
ng their entire bodies on a warm
trate or in the sun, but large snakes
etimes warm only the portion of their
containing the prey, which is easily
tified by the bulge it makes. about one-
of the way down the body.
e time taken for complete digestion
nds on many factors but, in the case of
dium-sized snake, such as a rat snake,
e, which has eaten an average sized
, such as an adult mouse, it is usually
t four days. Should conditions be
vourable, such as a sudden drop in
erature, digestion may be prolonged
in exceptional circumstances, it stops
ether. When this happens, the snake
usually regurgitate its food. Naulleau
3),[27] for example, found that all Euro-
asps, *Vipera aspis*, would regurgitate
food if maintained at 10°C (50°F) after
ng, about half would regurgitate if they
kept at 15°C (59°F) but less than 10
ent regurgitated when they were kept
e 20°C (68°F).

1. Shine, R. and Webb, J. K. (1990), 'Natural history of Australian typhlopid snakes', *Journal of Herpetology*, 24(4):357–363.
2. White, L. R., Powell, R., Parmerlee, J. S., Lathrop, A., and Smith, D. (1992), 'Food habits of three syntopic reptiles from the Barahona Peninsula, Hispaniola', *Journal of Herpetology*, 26(4): 518–520.
3. Rossman, D. A, and Myer, P. A. (1990), 'Behavioural and morphological adaptions for snail extraction in the North American brown snakes (genus *Storeria*)', *Journal of Herpetology*, 24(4):434–438.
4. Sanzima, I. (1989), 'Feeding behaviour of the snail-eating snake, *Dipsas indica*', *Journal of Herpetology*, 23(4):464–468.
5. Luisella, L. M. (1990), 'Captive breeding of *Vipera ursinii ursinii*', *British Herpetological Society Bulletin*, 34:23–30.
6. Seigel, R. A. (1992), 'Ecology of a specialized predator: *Regina grahami* in Missouri', *Journal of Herpetology*, 26(1):32–37.
7. Wharton, C. H. (1969), 'The cottonmouth mocassin on Sea Horse Key, Florida', *Bull.Florida State Mus., Biol. Sci.*, 14:227–272.
8. Lind, A. J. and Welsh, H. H. (1990), 'Predation by *Thamnophis couchii* on *Dicampton ensatus*', *Journal of Herpetology*, 24(1):104–106.
9. Henderson, R. W. (1993), 'Foraging and diet in West Indian *Corallus enhydris*', *Journal of Herpetology*, 27(1):24–28.
10. Papenfuss, T. J. (1982), 'The ecology and systematics of the amphisbaenian genus *Bipes*', *Occ. Pap. California Acad. Sci.*, 136:1–42.
11. Perez-Santos, C. and Moreno, A. G. (1987), 'Feeding behaviour of a false coral snake, *Pseudoboa neuwiedii*', *Herp. Review*, 19(4):69.
12. Polis, G. A. and Myers, C. A. (1985), 'A survey of intraspecific behaviour among reptiles and amphibians', *Journal of Herpetology*, 19(1):99–107.
13. Luisella, L. and Rugiero, L. (1993), 'Food habits of the Aesculapian snake, *Elaphe longissima*, in central Italy: do arboreal snakes eat more birds than terrestrial ones?', *Journal of Herpetology*, 27(1):116–117.
14. Diller, L. V. and Johnson, D. R. (1988), 'Food habits, consumption rates and predation rates of western rattlesnakes and gopher snakes in southwestern Idaho', *Herpetologica*, 26(1):32–37.
15. Coleman, K., Rothfuss, L. A., Ota, H. and Kardong, K. V. (1993) 'Kinematics of egg-eating by the specialized Taiwan snake *Oligodon formosanus*', *Journal of Herpetology*, 27(3):320–327.
16. Norton, R. L. (1993), 'Life History Notes', *Herpetological Review*, 24(1):34.
17. Bedford. G. (1991), 'Record of road kill predation by the fresh water snake (*Tropidonophis mairii*)', *Herpetofauna*, 21(2):35–36.
18. Henderson. R. W. (1993), 'On the diets of some arboreal boids', *Herpetological Natural History*, 1(1):91–96.
19. Shine, R. (1984), 'Ecology of small fossorial Australian snakes of the genera *Neelaps* and *Simoselaps*', *Vertebrate Ecology and Systematics*, Univ. Kans. Mus. Nat. Hist. Spec. Publ. 10:173–184.
20. Murphy, J. B., Carpenter, C. C. and Gillingham, J. C. (1976), 'Caudal luring in the green tree python, *Chondropython viridis*', *Journal of Herpetology*, 12(1):117–119.
21. Sazima, I and Puorto, G. (1993), 'Feeding technique of juvenile *Tropidodryas striaticeps*: probable caudal luring in a colubrid snake', *Copeia*, 1993(1):222–226.
22. Greene, H. W. and Campbell, J. A. (1972), 'Notes on the use of caudal lures by arboreal pit vipers', *Herpetologica*, 28:32–34.
23 Pook, C. (1990), 'Notes on the genus *Atheris*', *British Herpetological Society Bulletin*, (23):31–36.
24. Carpenter, C. C., Murphy, J. B. and Carpenter, G. C. (1976), 'Tail luring in the death adder, *Acanthophis antarcticus*', *Journal of Herpetology*, 12(4):143–161.
25. Clark, R. (1993), 'Viper bite in France – a cautionary tale', *Herptile*, 18(4):159–164.
26. Ramírez-Bautista, A. and Uribe, Z. (1992), '*Trimorphodon biscutatus* (Lyre snake): predation fatality', Life History Notes, in *Herpetological Review*, 23(3):82.
27. Naulleau, G. (1983), 'The effects of temperature on digestion in *Vipera aspis*', *Journal of Herpetology*, 17(2):166–170.

6
Defence

Despite being predators themselves, snakes have many enemies. These are often other snakes, and Chapter 5 lists a small selection of species that feed on other snakes, or even on their own species. Other types of predators are dealt with here.

◀ The Californian kingsnake, *Lampropeltis getulus california*, is usually patterned with bold black and white bands which create an optical illusion when it moves quickly. This species also occurs in a striped form, an example of polymorphism which is thought to be related to another of its defensive strategies.

PREDATORS OF SNAKES

Apart from other snakes, significant predators include many birds of prey, such as eagles, hawks, buzzards, storks and hornbills and a few specialists, such as the roadrunner, *Geococcyx californianus*, the African secretary bird, *Sagittarius serpentarius*, and the serpent eagles belonging to the genus *Circaetus*. Other birds that are recorded as having eaten snakes include red-tailed hawks, *Buteo jamaicensis*, red-shouldered hawks, *Buteo lineatus*, bald eagles, *Haliaetus leucocephalus*, caracaras, *Polyborus plancus*, several owls, including the Mexican spotted owl, *Strix occidentalis*, and a number of corvids, including the raven, *Corvus corax*, and the blue jay, *Cyanocitta cristata*.

Among mammals, their predators range from omnivorous opportunists such as foxes, skunks, the European hedgehog and the North American racoon, to a number of specialists such as the various species of mongooses that are present in several parts of the world. Venomous as well as harmless snakes fall prey to these animals, and a number of predators have devised techniques that help them to avoid being bitten. Snakes in hibernation are particularly vulnerable and surveys have shown that a relatively high proportion are killed at this time, by predators as diverse as foxes, skunks and shrews.

Among the more unusual predators, though probably not significant in terms of the numbers taken, can be included various invertebrates, including spiders such as the large mygalomorphs and the black widow, or red-backed spider, *Lactorodectus mactans*, which was observed by Paul Orange (1990)[1] capturing an Australian elapid, the monk snake, *Rhinoplocephalus monachus*. The same author reported a large centipede that had fatally bitten a worm snake, *Ramphotyphlops australis*.[2] North American scorpions belonging to the genera *Diplocentrus*, *Hadrurus* and *Paruroctonus* also eat thread snakes, *Leptotyphlops humilis*, and also take larger snakes on occasion, including the night snake, *Hypsiglena torquata* (Hibbetts, 1992).[3] Also in North America, the vinegaroon, *Mastigoproctus giganteus*, is known to have eaten small snakes, while aquatic bugs (Belostomatidae) and diving

beetle larvae are also recorded predators of semi-aquatic species such as garter and ribbon snakes. Fish may also eat snakes when they get the chance, although the only documented record appears to be that of a brook trout eating a sharp-tailed snake, *Contia tenuis*.

Frogs and toads eat small snakes, perhaps mistaking them for worms. Toads are especially voracious, with Asian black-spined toads, *Bufo melanostictus*, having eaten more than one flowerpot snake, *Rampho-*

typhlops braminus, and the western t Bufo boreas*, eating a sharp-tailed sn *Contia tenuis*. A South American bull *Leptodactylus pentadactylus*, regurgitate specimen of the terrestrial colubrid *Atr zidoki*, while a more remarkable re involved a preserved specimen of the Afr bullfrog, *Pyxicephalus adspersus*, that consumed what appeared to have bee newborn litter of 16 rinkhals, *Haemach hemachatus*: mysteriously, the front ha an additional young cobra was also pres

► (top) Where they occur, crocodiles and alligators are among the predators of snakes, especially aquatic and semi-aquatic species.

► (bottom) Large monitor lizards such as *Varanus albigularis* frequently prey on snakes, including venomous species such as the puff adder, *Bitis arietans*.

der to avoid predation, snakes, in their
, have evolved defensive strategies.
e vary from species to species and a
rtoire of defensive behaviour may be
by the same species under different
umstances. Conversely, several defen-
strategies may be used in conjunction
one another, or one attempt to deter
nies may be followed by another, quite
rent, behavioural sequence.

ost snakes try to avoid confrontations
never possible and this they do by
realment, crypsis or by flight. All these
niques are amazingly effective. Just
effective they are, of course, is hard to
e, it being rather difficult to count the
ber of snakes that are not seen! A good
ration of population densities can be
etimes gleaned, however, when a road
t through a forested habitat or when
ng across a desert or swamp on a little-
road. Snakes often turn up in their
dreds in these situations even though
y hours of conventional searching will
been completely unproductive.

cealment

t snakes conceal themselves when they
not actively trying to raise their body
erature by basking, searching for food
earching for mates. Because of their
, slender shape, they are well suited to
ring small crevices in the ground, in
trunks or between rocks. Many snakes
found when old buildings are pulled
n or when rocks are moved during
vations, for instance. Very often, the
of the snake belies the apparent size of
chamber in which it was hiding and
e keepers are often amazed at the small
e that even bulky snakes can fit into
they are equally amazed at the small
ings through which they can escape).

most environments, then, there will
st always be an abundance of places in
h snakes may be hidden. Some places
habitually frequented by the same
e, as evidenced by the number of shed
s that may be found in them. Only when
snake outgrows its hideaway will it
e to another. Where there are no suit-
nooks and crannies for concealment, as
nd deserts, snakes conceal themselves
urrowing, either making permanent
els and chambers in which to live or by

shuffling or 'swimming' below the surface
as the necessity arises.

Crypsis

Snakes are ideally placed to exploit the
natural phenomenon of crypsis. In the first
place, they can change into an almost
infinite number of different shapes – a
predator with a search image of an out-
stretched snake may overlook a tightly
coiled one, and vice versa. There are, of
course, many intermediate shapes that each
snake can assume. Colour and markings
are frequently used cryptically. Crypsis
relies on the ability to blend into the background, to 'hide in full view'. This is best
achieved by a colour scheme that not only
matches the surroundings but which also
helps to break up the outline of the snake.

Few snakes are uniformly coloured for
the simple reason that few substrates are
uniformly coloured: a plain brown snake
resting on a substrate of dead leaves, for
instance, would be easily seen because its
outline would separate it visually from
the leaves. A mottled brown snake, or a
snake with markings comprising irregular
blotches of different shades of brown, would
blend into the background very well. There
are a few black snakes, however, in which
the coloration has almost certainly evolved
for purposes other than crypsis – there is a
trade-off here between the desire to remain

concealed and the necessity to absorb heat
as efficiently as possible, and the latter has
proved to be the most important factor,
especially in species from cool environments
(see Chapter 3, thermoregulation).

Green snakes tend to be arboreal, or they
may live in lush understory vegetation such
as reeds and grasses. Many green snakes are
countershaded – that is, they are lighter in
colour underneath so that, when seen from
the side, the shaded ventral surface appears
roughly the same shade of colour as the
dorsal surface. Aquatic snakes may also be
marked in this way for the same reason.
Other green snakes have some markings,
such as the white transverse bands found
along the dorsal surface of both the emerald
boa *Corallus caninus*, and the green tree
python, *Chondropython viridis*, in order to
break up their outlines. Other arboreal
species may be coloured in various shades
of green and some from humid rainforest
environments are beautifully patterned to
match the lichen and moss-covered twigs
and branches among which they rest.

Terrestrial snakes occur in a variety of
colours, many of which have evolved to
match the substrates on which they live.
Thus, desert snakes may be grey, yellow,
pale brown or even pinkish in colour, often
mottled or speckled to simulate light and
shadow playing on the sand and gravel on
which they rest. Where a species has a wide

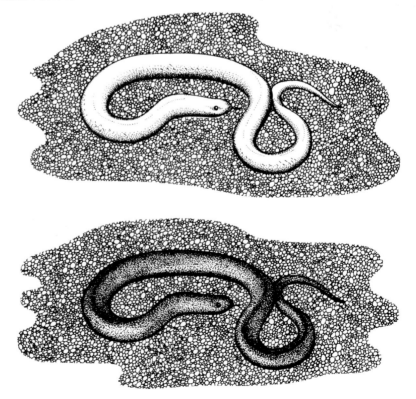

untershading helps to disguise the outline of
ke by compensating for the increased amount
ht falling on its upperside.

▲ The banded rock rattlesnake, *Crotalus lepi-
klauberi*, is well camouflaged when resting an
the grey rocks on which it lives.

◄ Many forest dwelling species, such as *Bothr
atrox*, are well camouflaged.

▼ Arboreal species tend to be well camouflage
sometimes with lichen-like coloration, as is
Bothriechis schlegelii.

The Gaboon viper, *Bitis gabonica*, despite its
seemingly gaudy coloration, is beautifully hidden
among forest debris.

range over an area with differing soil or
rock types, its colour will often vary from
place to place. Similarly, snakes that live in
rocky places usually closely match the rock
colour and they may be additionally marked
to suggest even the texture of the rock or, in
the case of the banded rock rattlesnake,
Crotalus lepidus klauberi, the lichens growing
on it.

In other snakes, the principle of breaking
up the outline, or disruptive coloration, has
become an end in itself. Some of these
species have patches of colours that do little
to match the snake's usual substrate but
which, because of the complexity with
which they are arranged, make the overall
snake very difficult to discern. The Gaboon
viper, *Bitis gabonica*, is the most obvious
and famous example but there are several
others, especially among the vipers and the
pit vipers. Disruptive coloration may be
used on the head of an otherwise striped,
banded or blotched snake. Dark lines often
pass through the eyes and the pigments
within the iris itself may form a continua-
tion of the pattern. This disguises the eye, an
organ that is easily discernible and which
may spoil an otherwise good camouflage.
The outline may also be disguised by
using appendages such as those of the fish-

ing snake, *Erpeton tentaculum*, an aquatic
species that has two fleshy 'tentacles' arising
from its snout. The species is also cryptically
marked and hangs motionless among
aquatic vegetation waiting for small fishes
to swim past. Other species have single nasal
appendages, those of the Madagascan twig
snakes, *Langaha*, being the most extreme:
males have simple tapered appendages but
those of females are lobed.

In order to enhance the effectiveness of
their colours and patterns, many cryptic

species 'freeze' when disturbed, relying
entirely on their camouflage for protection.
The twig snakes, *Thelotornis*, from Africa,
various vine snakes such as *Ahaetulla* from
Asia and *Oxybelis* from North America, as
well as the *Langaha* species mentioned above,
are well known for this behaviour and some
go so far as to protrude their tongues in order

▼ Slender arboreal snakes, many of which are
called vine snakes, often lie motionless in order to
avoid detection. *Chironius* species, from Ecuador.

to increase the effectiveness of the ruse. Other species, such as the Pacific ground boa, *Candoia carinata*, especially when young, may become quite rigid when handled and, if placed on the ground, sometimes remain motionless for several minutes. More commonly, however, cryptic species will resort to flight once detection seems imminent.

Polymorphism

Another type of defence through coloration is polymorphism. Many species exist in two or more basic colours or patterns. It is important to distinguish between regional variations, which may be adapted to different situations, and polymorphism.

Pattern polymorphism

A common type of pattern polymorphism is the co-existence of banded (or spotted) and striped individuals in the same population. The most often quoted example is that of the Californian kingsnake, *Lampropeltis getulus californiae*, which may have its black and white marking arranged as a series of bands or rings, or as longitudinal stripes.

▼ Polymorphism is relatively common among snakes. In its simplest form, snakes of the same species occur in spotted and striped forms, side by side, as in the European leopard snake, *Elaphe situla.*

There are many other examples, however, including the gopher snake, *Pituophis melanoleucus catenifer*, which is usually blotched but may be striped in parts of its range, the European leopard snake, *Elaphe situla*, and the Caicos boa, *Epicrates chrysogaster chrysogaster*, from the West Indies, which both have a striped and a spotted form.

Other species occur in a bewildering variety of colours and patterns. The sea snake, *Pelamis platurus*, for instance has longitudinal stripes of varying width and which may be black, yellow and brown (the most common combination), black and yellow or, in a few cases, plain yellow. The small ground snake, *Sonora episcopa*, may be plain coloured, barred with black or it may have longitudinal stripes running along its back. Similarly, *Vipera latifi*, from Iran, is

▲ Polymorphism can also involve the occurrence of the same species in a bewildering variety of colours and patterns. The Amazon tree boa, *Corallus enhydris*, is a good example, of which one colour form is shown here, while another is shown on page 199.

found in four distinct colour morphs. Male boomslangs, *Dispholidus typus*, are not only differently marked from females (see p. 163, Chapter 7) but are also highly variable themselves. These are but a few examples of snakes that show polymorphism of one kind or another.

The most feasible explanation for pattern polymorphism relies on the principle of 'search image'. It can be shown that many predators build up a mental picture of their prey. Animals that do not match this picture are often ignored, even though they

lly suitable as food. If a predator builds
a search-image of a striped snake, for
nce, spotted or banded individuals may
verlooked. As a rule, predators could be
cted to maintain a search image of the
common form and the less common
will benefit. After a while, *it* may find
to be the most common form, due to the
ection it received, and the population
redators may switch their attention
rdingly. In the long term, polymorphism
be maintained in the population and
forms can be expected to occur in
hly the same numbers, all other things
g equal. Polymorphism is controlled
enes, usually a simple Mendelian system
hich one phenotype is dominant over
ther.

ur polymorphism

ur polymorphism probably has similar
fits. Certain populations of snakes
differently coloured individuals and
species are so diverse that hardly
two are the same – the Amazon tree
Corallus enhydris, is a good example.
hermore, there are numerous species
vhich the young and the adults are
ured or marked differently – although
is a type of polymorphism, it relies not
he principle of search images but on the
ring habitats used by different ages of
snake.

t

overriding impulse for snakes that are
ght in the open is to escape. They may
his by fleeing, burrowing or retreating
small crevices. Anyone who has tried
hotograph snakes, for instance, will
w that the vast majority try repeatedly
cape, even when subjected to excessive
dling – only under severe duress do
become overtly aggressive. Even cryptic
ies will often resort to flight if they feel
their camouflage has been penetrated.
ough snakes cannot move very fast,
are able to move unhindered through
vegetation or over uneven ground.
y do not venture far from crevices
se location they seem to know and to
ch they return quickly.
number of species have coloration that
es it difficult for a predator to estimate
speed and even the direction in which
are travelling. Longitudinal stripes, for
nce, may appear to remain in the same
e even though the snake has started to
e away, so fooling a predator into
king it has more time to spare than it

▲ (top) A number of snakes have bold longitudinal
stripes: many of them are slender, fast-moving
species, such as the cave racer, *Elaphe taeniura
ridleyi*, from south-east Asia.

▲ (below) Other species have bold transverse
stripes, or bands, with black and white being a
favoured combination. This creates an optical
illusion when the snake is moving quickly, making
it hard for a predator to pinpoint its attack. This is
a Madagascan species, *Lycodryas betsileanus*,
which superficially resembles unrelated species in
several other parts of the world.

actually does. Transverse bands and saddles
can have an even more startling effect.
Once the snake is moving quite quickly, the
effect of these markings flickering past,
possibly glimpsed through a gap in the
vegetation, can have an almost hypnotic
effect. The speed of travel is hard to estimate

and, due to an optical illusion, it can even
look as though the snake is travelling in the
opposite direction. By the time the brain has
processed the information, the snake's tail
has disappeared from the spot and it is
well on the way to a safe place. Longitudinal stripes and bold transverse bands are
commonly seen in the markings of snakes
that are relatively fast moving.

Intimidation

When cornered, many snakes put up a
great show of aggression. This is often bluff
but its effect on predators can be significant.
Intimidation usually takes the form of puffing up the body to make it appear larger,
facing the enemy and raising or flattening
the head, hissing or making other warning
sounds and, as a last resort, striking, sometimes with the mouth closed. Temperament

varies greatly between the species. Some are invariably docile, even when first captured, whereas others are always aggressive.

Body enlargement

A common strategy among animals that are threatened is to make themselves appear larger than they are. This fulfils a dual function – predators may think twice before tackling them and, in the case of predators that swallow their prey whole, notably other snakes, a large size may cause them to reject an otherwise suitable meal. Enlargement may occur over the whole of the snake's surface or it may be concentrated in a particular area, usually the head and neck.

Puffing snakes

Numerous species inflate their bodies with air, puffing themselves up. Several of these are also 'hissers', exhaling the air forcibly to create a loud warning sound. Examples include the African *Bitis* species, especially *B. arietans*, which is commonly called the puff adder and the North American *Heterodon* species, which are also known in some areas by the local name of puffing 'adders'.

Spreading hoods

Many cobras raise the front part of their body and spread the ribs of their neck to form a hood. The hood may have bold markings on its back and the cobra may turn in order to display these. Species that use this behaviour as part of their defensive repertoire are those belonging to the genera *Naja*, including both African and Asian species, the monotypic *Ophiophagus hannah*

▲ (left) The bold marking on the back of the h of the spectacled cobra is used to warn enemies

▲ (right) The typical defensive posture of the monocled cobra, *Naja kaouthia.*

from Asia, both species of *Aspidelaps* the monotypic *Hemachatus haemachatus* from southern Africa and some specie black snakes, *Pseudechis*, from Austr This is purely a defensive action: co

---

Caterpillars that imitate snakes

Snakes have numerous ways of intimidating predators, mostly stereotyped behaviour patterns that make them look larger and more fierce than they really are. The signal they send may be real, as in venomous species, or false, as in harmless species that have similar displays to venomous ones. In either case, predators, including humans, frequently 'back off' to avoid further confrontation and possible risk to themselves.

Because the ploy works so well, it is hardly surprising that harmless animals in other groups have evolved displays that make them look superficially like snakes. Legless lizards are well placed to do this and some of the Australian flap-footed lizards belonging to the genus *Delma* appear to be convincing mimics of dangerous snakes whose habitat they share.

Perhaps the most remarkable mimics, though, are found among the insects. Whereas many adult butterflies and moths have large eyespots that are designed to imitate birds of prey, their larvae may imitate snakes. This behaviour is especially common among the caterpillars of the Sphingidae, or hawkmoths. Larvae of the elephant hawkmoth, for instance, have large eyespots on the upper part of their bodies and are frequently mistaken fo snakes by human observers.

The larvae belonging to the hawkmoth genus *Leucorampha*, which come from Central America and northern South America, have an eve more cunning trick. When disturbed, they detach the front part of their bod from the twig on which they were resting and hold it rigid. At the same time it is inflated to form a broad triangular 'head' and turned through 180° to expose the eyespots. Other small markings simulate scales and additional dark areas in front of the eyespots seem to be pits, just like thos of the arboreal pit vipers that they mimic. If further disturbed, the caterpillars 'strike' accurately at any object that touches it.

▼ A South American hawkmoth caterpillar mimicking an arboreal pit viper.

▲ Some species, such as the twig snake, *Thelotornis capensis*, inflate their throat, displaying the bold markings on their interstitial skin, normally hidden by their scales.

kes other than cobras also spread their
in an attempt to make themselves look
and more fierce than they are. The eastern
se snake, *Heterodon platyrhinos*, and its
es, are great bluffers.

ot rear or spread their hoods prior to
king prey.
art from the elapids, there are a num-
colubrids that have less well developed
s. These species may seek to imitate
s but the same behaviour can also be
in species outside their range. The
e Eastern species, *Malpolon moilensis*,
ample, flattens the front part of its body
raises it from the ground, possibly
cking cobras, which are found in the
region. The American hognose
es, *Heterodon*, flatten their heads and
s, often hissing angrily and making
strikes at the same time. These actions
bly serve simply as a means of intimi-
n, but there is also a possibility that
snakes mimic pit vipers. Even small
es may spread their necks: *Ninia sebae*,
Central America, for instance. Again,
cry may be involved but there is a
g possibility that spreading and raising
neck serves the simple function of
ng the snake appear larger and more
than it really is.
imilar form of behaviour can be seen in
a number of snakes that inflate
throats, often revealing brightly
red patches of interstitial skin or bold
rns. These include the boomslang,

Dispholidus typus, a dangerously venomous back-fanged colubrid, the closely related bird or twig snakes, *Thelotornis*, and a number of other tree snakes such as those belonging to the genus *Boiga*.

Finally, very many snakes flatten just their heads when threatened. This may serve to make them look bigger and more fierce, or it may make them resemble vipers, which have characteristically broad heads. In other species, such as the African herald snake, *Crotaphopeltis hotamboeia*, and the South American *Pseustes sulphurens* the labial scales are brightly coloured, red and yellow respectively in these two species, and by flattening the head these coloured scales are exposed.

Gaping

Intimidation can also take the form of opening the mouth widely, sometimes exposing brightly coloured interiors. The cottonmouth, *Agkistrodon piscivorus*, has a white mouth that contrasts strongly with its otherwise dark coloration and the parrot snakes, *Leptophis*, of Central and South America have blue areas inside their mouths. These displays are not entirely bluff – they act as preliminary warnings and are followed by striking if the warning is not heeded.

ere snakes have brightly coloured labial
such as this *Pseustes sulphureus*, spreading
ad or neck may help to display them more
nently.

► The South American parrot snake, *Leptophis ahaetulla*, has a stereotyped defensive behaviour, in which it gapes widely, displaying the inside of its mouth. If this fails, it bites.

▼ The cottonmouth, *Agkistrodon piscivorus*, is well named: its intimidation display consists of opening its mouth widely to show the white interior.

Warning sounds

Although snakes do not hear airb[...] sounds very well, most of their enemie[...] They make use of this fact by produci[...] variety of sounds in their defence. T[...] take the form of hissing, common t[...] snakes except the most primitive [...] rattling the tail, an option that is only [...] to two genera of specialized pit vipers, [...] rubbing the scales on the body togeth[...] produce a buzzing or rasping sound, an[...] less common strategy only performed [...] few species in Africa and the Middle Eas[...]

Hissing

With the exception of the primitive bur[...] ing species, most snakes can hiss. Very [...] hissing accompanies mock strikes or [...] taking up of a defensive posture and in s[...] species, notably the American gopher sn[...] *Pituophis*, the sound is amplified by the v[...] tion of a flap or membrane of skin i[...] glottis.

Rattling

Rattles are found only in two gener[...] snakes, *Crotalus* and *Sistrurus*. By vibra[...] their tails, which they do when they [...] alarmed, these snakes cause the segmer[...]

The snake that lost its rattle

The Santa Catalina rattlesnake, *Crotalus catalinensis*, is unique among members of its genus in lacking a rattle. This island form is most closely related to the red diamond rattlesnake, *C. ruber*, and probably reached Santa Catalina by rafting. During its residence on the island its rattle appears to have become progressively smaller until it disappeared altogether. Why should this species have lost its rattle?

The evolution of a rattle, to be used as a warning device, was probably possible only because most rattlesnakes ambush their prey: it could never have evolved if they actively hunted for their food because the need to drag such an unwieldy and noisy appendage behind them would be a severe handicap, one that would outweigh any advantage that the rattlesnake gained by alerting its enemies.

In the case of the Santa Catalina rattlesnake, two factors may be important. Firstly, because the island has no large predators nor any large hoofed mammals, both of which are threats to rattlesnakes on the mainland, the warning function of the rattle has become largely redundant. Secondly, the snake appears to have undergone a shift in its diet and its feeding habits: it preys largely on spiny lizards and sparrows, which it hunts at night while they are roosting in shrubs. The rattle, far from being an asset, would soon become a distinct liability for any snake trying to use stealth to stalk sleeping prey and it may also impede its progress through twigs and branches. There would therefore be a strong selective pressure favouring the individuals that had small or missing rattles.

Along with the loss of its rattle, natural selection seems to have favoured a more elongated body than related mainland forms, and significantly longer teeth: both of thes[...] characteristics are associated with snakes that hunt in trees and shrubs. Furthermore, the Santa Catalina rattlesnake does not bite and release i[...] prey in the usual rattlesnake fashion, [...] but holds it in its jaws until the venom[...] takes effect, thus avoiding the possibil[...] ity that its prey could drop or fly out o[...] reach before it succumbed.

Two other populations appear to be[...] in the process of losing their rattles an[...] both are confined to islands in the Gu[...] of California: these are a form of the re[...] diamond rattlesnake, *Crotalus ruber lorenzoensis*, from the island of San Lorenzo Sur, and the San Esteban forr[...] of the black-tailed rattlesnake, *Crotalu[...] molossus estebanensis*. The feeding habits of these two rattlesnake subspecies have not yet been studied.

ırning behaviour in desert vipers

ause snakes do not hear airborne
nds very well, they do not
ımunicate with each other by
nd and have not evolved the same
ge of vocalizations found in the
cts, birds and mammals. They may
sounds as warning, however, since
ny of their predators hear well:
se sounds are mostly limited to
sing, although the rattlesnakes have
lved an alternative method. The
-scaled viper, *Echis carinatus*, and
closely related horned desert vipers
onging to the genus *Cerastes*, have
lved a third method.
hese species produce a loud rasping
nd by rubbing together several rows
pecialized scales on their flanks. The
les involved are those of the third to
ninth scale rows on each side. Each
hese scales is heavily keeled as they
in many other snakes: in *Echis* and
istes, however, the scales, and
refore the keels, are arranged at an
que angle instead of being aligned
ıg the body. Furthermore, the keels
these specialized scales are serrated,
the teeth of a saw.
Vhen the snake is threatened, it
ns a characteristic U-shaped
insive coil, in which it folds its body
k on itself several times. The snake
v moves the coils against one

w-scaled viper, *Echis*.

▲ Scales of *Cerastes cerastes*.

another, so that the saw-toothed ridges
on adjacent parts of the body rub
together, producing a harsh, rasping
sound.

This unique structure and behaviour
may have evolved because the snakes
live in arid habitats, in parts of North
Africa, the Middle East, India and Sri
Lanka, where water is precious. If they
were to hiss, they would lose water, in

the form of vapour, as the air was
expelled through their mouth. By
rubbing their scales together instead,
they may avoid this.

In Africa, some of the harmless
egg-eating snakes, *Dasypeltis* species,
which have similar markings to the
vipers, also mimic their defensive
behaviour where their ranges overlap.

▼ Egg-eating snake, *Dusypeltis medici*, in
defence coil.

▲ Rattlesnakes rattle only when they feel threatened. They raise the tail to do so, and may form an S-shaped loop with the body, so that the head is raised off the ground. This species, *Crotalus atrox*, has a variable temperament but will often 'sound off' with little provocation.

their rattles to knock against one another, although the noise produced when rattlers 'sound off' is more of a buzz than a rattle, and often ends with a few tick-like clatters as the vibrations ease off. The structure of the rattle, and how it is formed, are described on page 32.

Contrary to the belief of some nineteenth-century naturalists, the rattlesnake does not use its rattle to serenade lady rattlesnakes, nor does it use it to warn other rattlesnakes of danger! There is no doubt that the rattle is only used when the snake finds itself in a potentially dangerous situation. The main function is therefore to warn enemies, a theory that is reinforced by the fact that rattlesnakes frequently take up a defensive posture when they are sounding off – the front part of their body is formed into an S-shaped coil and the head is held off the ground, facing the direction from which the threat is coming.

In addition, rattlesnakes may benefit by warning larger animals of their presence, so avoiding the risk of being trodden on – a great asset for snakes that are well camouflaged. With the coming of man, it could be

that the rattle is now a disadvantage because not only does it draw attention to the snake, which might otherwise be overlooked, but it also identifies it as public enemy number one!

The evolution of the rattle is something of a mystery. There are no snakes with any intermediate stages – they either have a rattle or they don't. Many other snakes, though, do vibrate their tails if they are disturbed and, if they happen to be resting among dead leaves or loose pebbles, a rustling or rattling sound is the result. The first step towards the evolution of a rattle could have been taken by a snake that vibrated its tail which had, by chance, a deformed tip, causing a build-up of shed epidermis.

'Popping'

A few snakes from North and Central America have been observed lifting their tails and emitting a bubbling or popping sound from their vents. Since they do this only when threatened it is assumed to be a defensive mechanism, although why it should be effective is hard to guess.

Warning coloration and mimicry

Animals that are able to inflict injury often perform ritualized behaviour patterns in order to avoid direct confrontation. Others are coloured in such a way that they warn of their ability to cause pain or death.

Venomous snakes are no exception. behaviour such as spreading of hoo rattling the tail, while primarily intenc intimidate their enemies, may also to identify the snake as a venomous Other species use distinctive patterr colour to identify themselves.

By far the most famous exampl warning coloration among snakes ar coral snakes, *Micrurus* and *Micruroi* North, Central and South America. Th or so species are all coloured with b bands or rings (annuli) around their be These bands are frequently black, whi yellow) and red. Some species have and one other colour but the majority a coloured. All these species are danger venomous.

Other members of the Elapidae, in dif parts of the world, also have bri coloured bodies. These include species Africa, such as *Aspidelaps lubricus*, also k as coral snakes, and garter snakes, *Elaps* species, others from Asia, including kraits, *Bungarus*, and the coral sn *Maticora*, and yet others from Aust especially the small species belonging t genera *Simoselaps* and *Vermicella*.

There has been a great deal of deba to the way in which warning color benefits the snakes. The simplistic th that predators learn to avoid such bri coloured species, is not without its lems, not least of which is the fact many of these species are deadly an animal attacking them would be un to live long enough for the lesson to benefit, either to itself or to the snake addition, most of the species involve secretive or burrowing snakes that r occur on the surface in daylight. Fu more, many snake predators, inclu mammals, are colour-blind.

▼ The tropical coral snake, *Micrurus lemnis* is widespread through Central and northern America.

(...ft) The brightly coloured Texas coral snake,
...*urus fulvius*, a small venomous snake related
...e cobras and mambas.

(...ght) Certain kingsnakes and milksnakes,
...h are harmless, are thought to mimic coral
...es and *Lampropeltis triangulum elapsoides*
...inly gives a good imitation of one.

...veral alternative theories have been
...osed. One of these is Mertensian mim-
... the deadly coral snakes are mimicking
...larly marked snakes that are only mildly
...mous. Although these do exist, in the
...n of the false coral snakes, *Erythro-*
...*rus*, for instance, they are restricted
...entral and parts of South America,
...reas the American coral snakes have a
...h wider range. Furthermore, this theory
...res the coral, and other boldly marked
...ies from other parts of the world.
...ther theory is that the bright coloration
...arisen purely by chance; since the coral
...es are secretive, there is no selective
...sure on them to be any particular
...ur. This theory is equally hard to accept
...use most other burrowing snakes, such
...e worm and thread snakes, tend to be
... in colour, probably because there is a
...siological cost involved in producing
...ent and this cost can be reduced if
...ent is sparse or lacking altogether.
...erhaps the most likely theory is that of
...ate aversion'. In a series of experiments,
...n Smith (1975)[4] showed that young
...ratory-reared birds avoided wooden
...painted with black, yellow and red rings
...did not avoid a series of rods painted in
...r colours and patterns. The implications
...that animals have an innate aversion
...rightly coloured animals and objects.
...ans use such colour patterns to warn of
...ger on roads, railways, and so on. Many
...steful insects are also brightly coloured.
...n colour-blind predators would be able
...istinguish the light and dark bands
...ayed by these snakes.

▲ (centre) The back-fanged snakes belonging to
the genus *Erythrolamprus* are found over much of
the range of coral snakes and there are some
suggestions of mimicry. Their similarity could
equally well be coincidental, however.

▲ (bottom) Many other brightly coloured 'false'
coral snakes, such as the Sonoran mountain
kingsnake, *Lampropeltis pyromelana*, do not
share the same habitat as coral snakes, nor are
they very convincing mimics.

◀ Defensive 'balling' behaviour in a tropidoph
snake, *Ungaliophis continentalis*. Balling is al
universal in this small family of secretive, harn
snakes and has also been noted in members of
several other families.

Calabaria reinhardtii, also uses the met
All tropidopheid snakes probably use
method of defence as it has been noted i
the more common species, and sin
behaviour patterns have been seen in m
species of colubrid snakes.

Attack deflection (mimetic behaviour)

Although all parts of a snake are import
some are more important than otl
Mimetic behaviour may occur whe
snake is prepared to sacrifice one part c
anatomy in favour of a less essential µ
The least important part of a sna
anatomy is its tail.

Some of the species that coil into balls «
their tails while hiding their heads – ru
boas and the Calabar burrowing pythor
all proponents of this technique, w
they are well suited for owing to their b
tails which have similar shapes to t
heads. Many adult specimens of these spe
have scarred and damaged tails, prc
ing good evidence of the effectiveness o
technique.

In certain cases, the tails of some spe
have markings that increase their rese
ance to the snake's head. One such exar
is the Asian sand boa, *Eryx tataricu*
which the tail markings consist of a s
horizontal line and a small black spot, re:
bling the mouth and eye. The atractası
snake, *Chilorhinophis gerardi*, has a sin
pattern: its head and the tip of its tail
black, while the rest of the tail is blue, w
single black spot. The burrowing pytl
Calabaria, goes one step further in ha
a shallow horizontal groove around th
of its tail, simulating its mouth. W
threatened, all these snakes will ofter
the tips of their tail and wave them arc
as though they were the head. In extr
cases, the false head makes simul
striking movements. The purpose of
behaviour is obviously to deflect the at
away from the real head by occupying
attacker with the false one.

There are several other example
snakes that use their tails in defence. N
of these have brightly coloured under:
to their tails: an attack results in the sı
raising its tail to expose the bright colc
Examples include the American ring
snake, *Diadophis punctatus*, which turr

It has been shown, in other contexts, that predators with plenty of time to examine potential food are far more choosy than those that have to make snap decisions. Because they are so secretive, the colours of the coral snakes need to send a very clear signal so that, if they are suddenly uncovered by the activities of a predator, they can be read instantaneously.

In addition to the true coral snakes (that is, venomous members of the Elapidae), there are any number of 'false' coral snakes among the Colubridae and other families. They are said to be the mimics whereas the true coral snakes are the models. To list just a small number of examples, they include the milksnakes, *Lampropeltis triangulum* (North and Central America); several king snakes including *Lampropeltis pyromelana* and *L. zonata*, and the shovel-nosed snakes, *Chionactis* (North America); the false coral snakes belonging to the genus *Erythrolamprus* and the pipe snake, *Anilius scytale* (Central and South America); the spotted harlequin snake, *Homoroselaps dorsalis* (Africa); and two whipsnakes, *Coluber elegantissimus* and *C. sinai* (Middle East).

Supporters of the learned-warning-coloration theory would argue that these species benefit because they look like coral snakes and predators would avoid them just as they have learned to avoid the models. The main flaw in this theory is that many of the mimics inhabit areas where there are no coral snakes. In addition, many of the 'false' coral snakes are not very good

mimics – although they have the same basic colours, their arrangements are different, significantly so in several cases. These objections are difficult to refute whereas the 'innate aversion' theory applies equally well to harmless as well as harmful snakes.

Bright, contrasting colours, especially when they are arranged in bands or rings, serve the additional function of disrupting the outline of the snake and, in some cases, of creating an optical illusion when the snake moves quickly. Additional benefits may include startle – the initial reaction of a predator uncovering a brightly coloured snake unexpectedly may be to hesitate, so giving the snake more time to escape.

With the combination of these three effects – innate aversion, disruptive coloration and startle – there is probably no need to look further for the evolutionary pressures that have resulted in many species of snakes with bright rings of colour around their bodies.

Balling

A common strategy that can be recognized in a number of snakes from different families has been called 'balling'. The snake forms its body into a tightly coiled mass, with its head towards the centre. The purpose appears to be to present the enemy with a shape that is difficult to deal with, while protecting the vulnerable head.

The royal python, *Python regius*, is also known as the ball python in reference to this behaviour. Another African python,

'corkscrew' display of the ringneck snake, *phis punctatus*, exposes the snake's brightly ed underside. At other times it is well flaged.

ver, and forms it into a tight corkscrew e. The underside of the tail is brilliant most forms of this species. The Asian snakes, *Cylindrophis*, are boldly marked ck and white underneath. When they isturbed, they flatten their body, raise tail off the ground and curl it over their , as though they were rearing their and neck. From the same part of the , the kukri snakes, *Oligodon*, have tail ays that involve raising and coiling the vhich is brightly coloured underneath. er annoyance is registered by using il to strike at the aggressor (Mori *et al.*,).[5]

final example is that of the African l-snouted snakes, *Prosymna*, which nd uncoil their tails rapidly and repeat-when disturbed. Their tails are not tly coloured, however, and it is the ment that is presumed to occupy ttention of the attacker.

here species have tails that end in a point, they may be pressed against flesh of a predator, presumably to ate a bite. This behaviour is common g snakes of the genus *Leptotyphlops* s also seen in the American mud and ow snakes, *Farancia abacura* and *F. ogramma*, (sometimes known locally as ing snakes' for this reason) and in the wing asp *Atractaspis engaddensis*.

al autotomy

al autotomy, or voluntary tail loss, is non among lizards of several species but e in snakes. Even among species that

occasionally lose their tails, the mechanism is not as well developed as it is in lizards. In the latter, several vertebrae towards the base of the tail have fracture planes across them and so, when the tail breaks, it is due to the parting of two halves of a vertebra. With two possible exceptions, snakes do not have this feature, and their tails break off at the point at which two vertebrae join. The two exceptions are the South American colubrids *Pliocercus elapoides* and *Scaphiodontophis venustissimus*, neither of which have common names. In these species, examination of the lower part of the tail reveals a slight groove running around the centre of each vertebra; this is circumstantial evidence that they may allow their tails to break off across the vertebrae but there is no definite proof that this is what happens. Furthermore, the broken tails of snakes do

not regenerate, other than forming a small conical scale over the wound, whereas those of lizards do. The result of this is that an individual lizard may use the technique several times during its lifetime, growing a new tail after each episode, whereas snakes are capable of escaping only once by this means.

For these reasons, it can be argued that tail breakage in snakes is not true autotomy because there is no nervous control over the operation, as there is in lizards. Snakes' tails break merely as a result of the application of mechanical tugging. Notwithstanding this, a number of species are found to have a greater proportion of individuals with broken tails than others. These include several colubrid genera such as *Coluber*. They may also develop behavioural traits that increase the chances of their tails breaking, so allowing them to make their escape. For instance, the African marsh snakes, *Natriciteres*, and the sand snakes, *Psammophis*, spin their bodies rapidly if they are picked up by the tail, so breaking it off. It has been suggested that this behaviour in *Natriciteres* has evolved in response to heavy predation by predatory fish or wading birds. Another colubrid, *Coniophanes fissidens*, from Central and South America, shows a high incidence of broken tails – up to 50 per cent in some areas – and may be the result of predation by coral snakes such as *Micrurus nigrocinctus*.

▼ The African marsh snakes, *Natriceteres*, may discard their tails if they are grasped by a predator. The species is N. *fulinoides*.

Odour

Most snakes have musk glands situated at the base of their tails, the primary function of which is probably to produce hormone trails used in chemical communication. When attacked, or roughly handled, many of them excrete quantities of these substances, many of which have an unpleasant smell, to say the least. The secretions are milky in appearance and are sometimes produced in copious quantities. Some species are especially adept at wrapping themselves around the hand and liberally smearing their captor. The European grass snake, mentioned above, is responsible for a particularly disgusting smell, often enough to persuade human predators to release them. (In my youth I was once evicted from a bus as a result of a particularly pungent grass snake that I had captured and was hoping to take home.) Members of the colubrid genera *Lampropeltis* and *Elaphe* also produce unpleasant substances and the fox snake, *Elaphe vulpina*, is named for the supposed resemblance of its particular potion to that of foxes.

Autohaemorrhagy

Autohaemorrhagy is the term given to the voluntary rupture of small blood vessels, allowing blood to ooze from various parts of the body. Although certainly a defensive reaction, the way in which it works is uncertain although in lizards which autohaemorrhage (horned lizards, *Phrynosoma*), there is some suggestion that the blood has an unpleasant taste, causing predators to drop them.

Autohaemorrhagy has often been observed in the dwarf boas, *Tropidophis* species, when they are handled. They first form tight balls then produce relatively large quantities of blood from their eyes and mouth. The

▲ Spitting cobras, such as *Naja mossambica,* a formidable method of defence. Their venom cause intense pain and temporary, sometimes permanent, blindness.

(a)

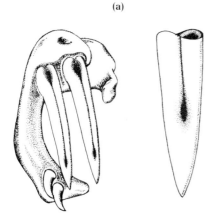

(b)

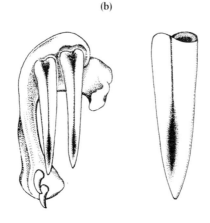

◄ The fangs of spitting cobras (a) have small aperatures than non-spitters (b) and they are located in the front rather than towards the t

es involved are six from the West Indies
 greenwayi, *T. haetianus*, *T. maculatus*,
lanurus, *T pardalis* and *T. semicinctus* –
two mainland species, *T. parkeri* and
cisquamis*: it seems probable that the
ining few species, some of which
oorly known, also use this method of
ce.

her than this genus, autohaemorrhagy
nly been noted, occasionally, in three
 species, all from North America.
e are: the long-nosed snake, *Rhino-
s lecontei*, which bleeds from its cloaca
less commonly, nostrils; the eastern
ose snake, *Heterodon platyrhinos*,
h bleeds from its cloaca, sometimes
 to feigning death; and the water
e, *Nerodia erythrogaster*, which bleeds
its gums. In these colubrids, bleeding
companied by wild thrashing and
be accounted for by increased blood
ure during extreme exertion, possibly
entally, whereas the dwarf boas appear
ve greater control over the bleeding.

ing venom

only snakes that can project their
m are the spitting cobras. Spitting
s to have arisen twice in this family, in
African spitting cobra, or rinkhals,
chatus haemachatus*, and in a group of
an and Asian species belonging to the
s *Naja*. The Asian spitting cobras were,
recently, classified as a single species,
naja*, but recent research has shown
there are at least nine species, of which
(N. naja* and *N. oxiana*) do not spit
he others do (or are thought to do so).
e African species, *N. mossambica* and
gricollis* are spitters.

itting is accomplished by forcing the
m through small apertures in the front
 fangs, causing it to be squirted out at
speed and in a fine spray. This involves
odification of the fangs, in which the
ture, normally fairly large and elon-
d, is reduced in size and rounded in
e. A strange situation occurs in *N.
pinensis*, where the fangs of males have
t openings whereas those of females
 long ones. This would suggest that
the males are able to spit but this has
een confirmed.

e venom may be sprayed several
es with a fair degree of accuracy. As the
as rear their heads prior to spitting, the
ker often receives the venom in its eyes,
e it causes instant and intense pain. If
reated, temporary or even permanent
ness may follow in humans.

Feigning death

Pretending to be dead may seem to be a
strange form of defensive behaviour as
many predators are more than happy to
eat carrion. It must be effective, however,
for it to have evolved in a number of species
of snakes. Foremost among these is the
European grass snake, *Natrix natrix*, which
may put up a convincing display by turning over and opening its mouth, allowing
the tongue to hang out. Not all specimens
perform, however, and individuals from
some populations never do it. The American
hognose snakes, *Heterodon*, and the African
spitting cobra, or rinkhals, *Hemachatus
haemachatus*, and the Egyptian cobra, *Naja
haje*, are also well known for the same
technique, but, like the grass snake, their
willingness to play dead varies from snake
to snake. It is noteworthy that, in all three
of these species, death feigning comes at
the end of a repertoire of other defensive
activities, including intimidation and odour
production. Death feigning has also been
noted, although rarely, in the two small
North American snakes belonging to
the genus *Storeria*, *S. dekayi* and *S. occipitomaculata*.

▼ Several snakes, including the European grass
snake, *Natrix natrix*, feign death if they are
threatened.

1. Orange, P. (1990), 'Predation on
   Rhinoplocephalus monachus by the redback spider
   Latrodectus mactans', *Herpetofauna*, 20(1):34.
2. Orange, P. (1989), 'Incidents of predation on
   reptiles by invertebrates', *Herpetofauna*,
   19(1):31–32.
3. Hibbetts, T. (1992), *in* Life history notes,
   Herpetological Review, 23(4):120.
4. Smith, Susan M. (1975), 'Innate recognition of
   coral snake pattern by a possible avian
   predator', *Science*, 4178:759–760.
5. Mori, A., Narumi, N. and Kardong, K. V. (1992),
   'Unusual putative defensive behavior in *Oligodon
   formosanus*: head-slashing and tail-striking',
   Journal of Herpetology, 26(2):213–216.

7
Reproduction

All animals have a basic urge to reproduce in order to pass their genes on to the next generation, and snakes are no exception. The more offspring they can produce, the more their genes will proliferate. All aspects of reproductive behaviour are directed towards this goal.

◄ Pythons make exemplary parents. This blood python, *Python curtus*, will brood her eggs, protecting them from predators and keeping them at the right temperature, until they hatch two months later.

The way in which snakes reproduce is potentially one of the most fascinating aspects of their biology and has attracted a lot of interest from researchers, especially in recent years. There are several reasons why this should be.

(1) Snakes may reproduce by laying eggs or by retaining the eggs inside their bodies until they are fully formed, thus giving birth to live young. This latter process should, strictly speaking, be termed ovo-viviparity, because (with one possible exception – see page 140) the young do not normally receive nourishment from their mother, via a placenta, as do the mammals and several groups of invertebrates, which are said to be viviparous in the true sense. Snakes that give birth to live young, however, are normally referred to as 'viviparous', despite this distinction.

(2) As well as variation in the reproductive method, snakes also vary in their reproductive output: clutch or litter size may be large or small in relation to the size of the species. The size of each offspring tends to vary in inverse proportion to the number of offspring, i.e. there is a trade-off between number of young and size of young.

(3) Snakes continue to grow throughout their lives, but reach sexual maturity when they are about half their potential maximum size. This is known as 'indeterminate growth' and results in a constantly increasing reproductive output, i.e. as females grow larger, they are able to channel more resources into their offspring. This is not seen in other animals, such as mammals and birds, which do not begin to breed until they have finished, or almost finished, growing. The way in which snakes use this extra output (i.e. into more young or bigger young) can be measured and assessed in terms of its evolutionary significance.

(4) The shape of snakes puts certain constraints on the size of young or eggs they can deliver. This varies with species and their life-style. Slow-moving, bulky snakes are less constrained in this respect than active, slender ones.

(5) Female snakes are unusual among animals in that they can separate the time of mating from the time the eggs are fertilized. They do this by storing the sperm in their bodies. Whether or not they delay fertilization in this way will depend on several factors, foremost of which is the necessity to lay eggs or give birth at a suitable time of the year.

In order to examine these options, it is first necessary to understand the reproductive biology of snakes, and their breeding habits. Their reproductive systems, that is the parts of their anatomy concerned with reproduction, are described in Chapter 2.

► The ovarian cycle in a female snake. Small egg follicles form in the ovaries and are released into the body cavity. They are collected from here by the funnel-like end of the oviduct and, assuming sperm is present, are fertilized and undergo development here.

Physiological reproductive cycles, i.e. t variation in the state of the reproducti system, are distinct from breeding season which refer to behavioural activities th take place at various times of the ye Annual reproductive cycles can usua be identified in male and female snak although their timing may differ betwe the sexes.

The male reproductive cycle

Most of what is known about males' rep ductive cycles relates to temperate speci i.e. those species that undergo a period inactivity in the winter. Males of this ty of snake produce sperm in their tes during the part of the year when they a most actively feeding, usually summer a autumn. In tropical species the situatio less clear; it seems likely that males of ma such species produce sperm through the year, even when there is a disti breeding season, but males of other spec may produce sperm at certain times of year only, often immediately prior to breeding season.

Whenever the sperm is produced, i stored in a bladder-like structure form from part of the ureter, where it stays u mating takes place. Each male produces stores enough sperm to mate several tin either with the same female or with number of different ones. Mating may

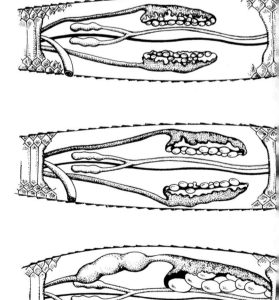

ur until the following spring in the case of
mperate species. Although mature males
often reproductively active throughout
year, with viable sperm present, mating
only take place when females are recep-
, usually at a well-defined time of the
r.

female reproductive cycle
e again, most of the information relating
emale reproductive cycles comes from
arch into temperate species. The timing
he female reproductive cycle tends to be
er defined than that in males and several
es can be recognized.

ovarian cycle
first stage is the formation of small,
cular eggs in the ovary. These eggs, or
, may mature slowly, even taking
ral years in the case of large, long-lived
ies, with only a proportion of them
uring each breeding season. Maturation
olves surrounding each egg with yolk,
ocess known as vitellogenesis. Vitello-
esis normally takes place immediately
re the breeding season, usually in the
ng in temperate species, but it may also
ur in the autumn, before hibernation.
kes appear to produce more yolked
cles than they will ever use to produce
e eggs. This may be a way of allowing
size of the clutch to be adjusted right up
e last minute: if there is plenty of food
ediately before mating they may be
to produce larger clutches than if food
ort. Follicular eggs that are not used are
sorbed by the female.

at cycle
production of yolk is dependent on an
uate store of fat and if the female has
fed well this may be lacking, in which
the follicular eggs do not develop
er but are reabsorbed. It has been
vn that fat reserves usually accumulate
e female's body until the time of egg
uration. By the time the eggs leave the
uct, they have grown considerably
the fat store is heavily depleted. The
le must feed well before another batch
able eggs can be produced. Fat cycles
well established in lizards and some
e snakes, such as the boas and pythons.
e appears to be a fat cycle in most, if not
emperate colubrids, elapids and vipers.
ical snakes, especially small species,
ever, may be in a position to form eggs
tly from their food intake, without
ng on stored fat.

The snake egg

The eggs of snakes, like those of all
reptiles, and birds, have large amounts
of yolk. The yolk contains the fats and
carbohydrates necessary for development of the embryo. The embryo starts
its development as a flat disc lying on
the surface of the yolk and, as it
develops, it lifts away from the yolk and
begins to form itself into a young
snake. The yolk nourishes it throughout development and, towards the final
stages, is drawn into the snake through
a slit in its underside, visible as a small
scar at the time of hatching.

The embryo is surrounded by two
sets of membranes. One set is formed in
the oviduct of the mother, and includes
an outer layer, the shell, containing
calcium salts. The other, much thinner
set of membranes, is produced by the
embryo, and comprises the amnion,
the chorion and the allantois. These
membranes usually develop after the
egg has been laid. All the membranes
help to conserve water and are one of
the fundamental differences between
amphibians' and reptiles' eggs, and
account for the reptiles' colonization of
the land.

In addition to the shell, embryo and
yolk, snake eggs contain a small
amount of albumin and an air bubble.

The albumin is composed of a solution
of proteins which, through osmosis,
attracts water into the egg while the air
bubble controls the exchange of oxygen
and carbon dioxide and also acts as a
pressure regulator.

Towards the end of incubation, some
of the calcium is extracted from the
shell by the embryo and is used to form
its skeleton: the shell becomes thinner
and more flexible around this time.
Oxygen passes through the shell more
readily and, for a while, this compensates for the embryo's increased oxygen
requirement. Eventually, though, it will
need to leave its shell to breathe.

▲ An Australian diamond python, *Morelia
spilota spilota*, with her eggs.

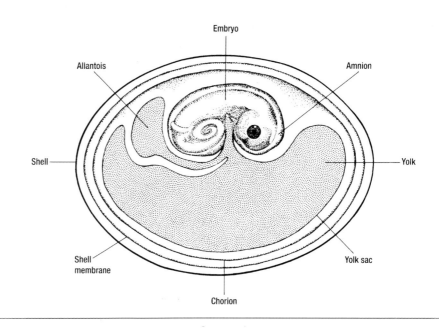

Ovulation

Once the eggs have been released from the ovary they move into the body cavity and are then 'caught' by a funnel-shaped opening, known as the infundibulum, at the upper end of the oviduct. At the time of ovulation, the infundibulum grows around the ovary in order to reduce the chances of eggs being lost; even so, some eggs do become lost within the body cavity and yet others are caught by the oviduct on the other side of the body, i.e. eggs released by the left ovary end up in the right oviduct and vice versa. This process of transferring the eggs from the ovaries to the oviducts is known as ovulation.

A stimulus may be required before ovulation occurs and this varies from species to species. In temperate snakes, it seems that increasing temperature provides the necessary stimulation whereas in some tropical species it is provided by cooler conditions, such as would occur at the beginning of the wet season. Females of species that have no distinct breeding season may be stimulated by the act of mating or the presence of one or more males in close proximity. Finally, there may be an interplay between environmental conditions, i.e. temperature, and additional stimulation by males.

Fertilization

Once the eggs have moved into the oviduct they may be fertilized, assuming sperm is present. In the absence of sperm, or if the sperm is not viable, the female will either lay infertile eggs or reabsorb them. Once the eggs have been fertilized, however, they cannot be reabsorbed.

Some snakes are able to store sperm for lengthy periods and so delay fertilization. This may be useful if males are only present early in the breeding season, before ovulation, when fertile matings can still take place, with the stored sperm fertilizing the ova at a later date. Many temperate vipers, for instance, ovulate in early June, irrespective of the time of mating, which may be several months earlier in some species. It is logical to assume that fertilization and subsequent development will be timed to coincide with warm weather, in order to accelerate the development of the young. Furthermore, the timing of the birth of the young is also important because they must often rely on seasonally available prey, such as young lizards or rodents.

In species that produce more than one clutch in a single breeding season, sperm storage may be used in fertilizing the second clutch. In other cases, sperm may be stored from one season to another, so that if the female is unable to find a mate she may still produce fertilized eggs, drawing on the surplus sperm from the previous season. Fertility from clutches produced from stored sperm is, however, usually lower than in clutches fertilized by fresh sperm.

Finally, sperm storage may be used by species that are widely scattered and have difficulty finding one another at a specific time of the year. These species may mate whenever the opportunity arises, with the females storing the sperm until they ovulate, perhaps as a result of environmental stimuli. The sperm is stored at the lower end of the oviduct in special chambers known as seminal receptacles.

Developing eggs are retained in the oviduct and, if the species is oviparous, each is provided with a parchment-like shell which is produced in a specialized area in the lower portion of the oviduct. Very occasionally, two developing ova are encased in a single shell, so that when the egg hatches two young emerge instead or one. (Although these are commonly known as twins, all the offspring from a single clutch of eggs are twins, or triplets, or whatever, and the emergence of two young from one egg is merely the result of a malfunction in the shell-producing process.) Live-bearing species do not produce a shell but each developing embryo is enclosed in a separate membrane.

It is important to note that the developing embryos, whether or not they are enclosed in a shell, are nourished by the yolk surrounding the egg, and there is no physiological connection between them and the gravid female. There may be a single exception, that of the Australian elapid *Pseudechis porphyriacus*. This species may be truly viviparous, as some studies have shown what appears to be the transfer of nutrients, in the form of electrolytes and amino acids, between the mother and her developing embryos.

BREEDING SEASONS

Most snakes have breeding seasons t[ ] are under the control of external fact[ ] such as temperature. Unlike lizards, ther[ ] no evidence at present that snakes' breed[ ] cycles are affected by daylength. This wo[ ] seem to be a logical result of their orig[ ] as burrowing animals, and their secret[ ] habits, where any differences in daylen[ ] would go largely unnoticed.

It seems that the reproductive behavi[ ] of very many snakes follows a fairly stand[ ] sequence and other systems can be c[ ] sidered as variations. Most of our knowle[ ] comes from studies on temperate sna[ ] especially North American and Europ[ ] species such as the kingsnakes, *Lamprope*[ ] rat snakes, *Elaphe*, water snakes, *Natrix a*[ ] *Nerodia*, garter snakes, *Thamnophis*, rat[ ] snakes, *Crotalus*, and vipers, *Vipera*, and[ ] these can be used as a starting point.

A typical cycle for these snakes wo[ ] be for mating to take place in the spri[ ] shortly after they emerge from hibernati[ ] for fertilization to occur shortly afterwa[ ] and for the young to be born, or to ha[ ] before the end of the summer. Species t[ ] come from places where there is no w[ ] defined winter, such as the tropics, may h[ ] similar cycles but they may be timed[ ] synchronize with wet and dry seasons. Ot[ ] species appear not to cycle at all and r[ ] be thought of as opportunists, breed[ ] whenever they are in a reproductively ac[ ] state, regardless of season.

Temperate species

Snakes from temperate regions usu[ ] hibernate or go through a period of redu[ ] activity during the time of year when a[ ] age temperatures are insufficient to al[ ] them to maintain a suitable body temp[ ] ture. Depending on their whereabouts, t[ ] may pass through a period of deep hi[ ] nation lasting many months, during wh[ ] time they are more or less comatose[ ] they may merely hide away for short[ ] periods. Either way, they seem to have l[ ] interest in reproduction until the wea[ ] warms up permanently in the spring[ ] this time males usually hunt actively[ ] females.

Courtship and mating may take p[ ] immediately after hibernation or a few w[ ] later; each species has its own system, w[ ] some species differing from populatio[ ] population. For example, chequered ga[ ] snakes, *Thamnophis marcianus*, in Ariz[ ] mate as soon as they have emerged [ ] hibernation, but in Texas mating takes p[ ] about twenty days after they have emer[ ]

The breeding cycle of the chequered garter
snake, *Thamnophis marcianus*, varies according
to where it lives.

Spring matings allow females to lay their
eggs at a time when the weather is still
warm enough to incubate them (or to allow
the young to develop in the oviduct if
they are of a live-bearing species) and to
ensure that when the young hatch or are
born, conditions are suitable for them
to freely to disperse and find food. In addition, hatching or birth often coincides with
a time when there is an abundance of
young lizards, amphibians and rodents, so
that the young can feed and grow quickly
before the coming winter.

The timing of mating and egg laying
may be shifted slightly, according to species.
The American Trans-Pecos rat snake,
Bogertophis subocularis, for example, mates
in late summer, several months after other
species from the same region, and its eggs
are not laid until the end of summer or the
beginning of autumn. Hatching takes place
in the winter. This schedule must have
been due to some aspect in the ecology
of the species which is, as yet, not fully
understood, although it is worth noting that
this species is found in southern Texas and
northern Mexico, where summers are hot
and dry and winters are mild.

Other species mate during one period of
activity and give birth, or lay eggs, during
the next. There are actually two systems
operating here. In its most simple form,

autumn mating seems to be an insurance
against not finding a mate in the spring
and therefore wasting a breeding season.
Females of these species enter hibernation
with a store of sperm in their reproductive
system. This sperm is still active in the
following spring and may be used to fertilize
the eggs that ovulate at this time. If she gets
the opportunity, however, the female will
mate again in the spring and so the autumn
mating is not always essential in order to
produce fertile eggs.

One such species is the crowned snake,
Tantilla coronata, from North America,
whose reproductive cycle was investigated
by Aldridge (1992).[1] Mating can apparently
take place in late summer and the sperm

is stored in receptacles in the lower part of
the oviduct. During the following spring,
mating may take place again but, whether
or not this is the case, females have viable
sperm in their oviduct, at the same time
as the eggs are maturing. The eggs are laid
at the beginning of summer and, by the end
of summer, the females have little or no
sperm in their oviducts or their storage
receptacles, perhaps because the eggs carry
unused sperm out of the body when they
are laid. The female must mate again to
replenish her store of sperm. Autumn
mating, in which the female stores sperm
over the winter, has also been recorded
in hognose snakes, *Heterodon*, another egg-
laying species. Again, this species also
mates in the spring.

Autumn matings also take place in the
pygmy rattlesnake, *Sistrurus miliarius*
(Montgomery and Schuett, 1989),[2] and the
massassauga, *S. catenatus*. The latter species
has also being observed to mate in the
spring. It seems most likely that these two
viviparous species store sperm over the
winter and ovulate in the following spring,
using either the stored sperm or sperm
from more recent matings to fertilize their
ova, just as the crowned snake does.

Other viviparous vipers, including some
populations of the prairie rattlesnake,
Crotalus viridis, and the ridge-nosed rattlesnake, *C. willardi*, mate in late summer
and store their sperm over the winter.
Ovulation and fertilization take place the
following spring and the young are born in

The Trans-Pecos rat snake, *Bogertophis
subocularis*, is unusual in breeding towards the
end of the summer: other colubrids from the same
area breed in the spring.

the following summer (Graves and Duvall, 1993[3] and Martin, 1976).[4] Spring matings have not been recorded for these species, however.

Biennial breeding cycles

Species or populations that live in cold places may not breed every year. Most of these species are live-bearers, for reasons that are discussed later. Females that are carrying young or eggs are often unable to feed, either because the burden of the young, and the amount of time they spend basking, prevents them from hunting, or because the developing young or eggs take up so much space in their bodies that they are unable to accommodate food. If the summer is short, as it is at higher latitudes, the females may be gravid for almost all of the active season. This being the case, they will not be in a position to regain their condition before hibernation and will emerge the following year with very little fat reserves. A 'fallow' year will then be necessary in order for them to build up enough reserves to produce eggs or young. There is even a possibility that snakes at very high latitudes, such as the adders in northern Scandinavia, breed only every third year, requiring two feeding seasons in order to become fit enough for one breeding season.

These biennial breeding cycles may or may not be fixed genetically in the snakes. Prevailing conditions, particularly the amount of food available during a particular year (itself sometimes dependent on rainfall), will control the frequency of breeding in populations that are borderline. Some species that normally breed every other

year, such as European adders, will breed every year in captivity if they are provided with plenty of food and a longer active season.

Conversely, a poor year, in terms of food availability, can lead to small numbers of females breeding during the following year, regardless of when they last bred. Where the food supply is unreliable, then, breeding is not regular but opportunistic and in any given year the proportion of females breeding can vary from a quarter to three-quarters or more. Other species seem more or less 'locked in' to biennial breeding, regardless of food supply and conditions, the Tasmanian tiger snake, *Notechis scutatus*, being an example of the latter type of species.

▲ Snake breeders have found that many speci such as the speckled kingsnake, *Lampropeltis getulus holbrooki*, will lay more than one clut during a single breeding season. It remains to seen whether this occurs among wild populati but it seems likely that it does occasionally.

There are also viviparous species have annual as well as biennial populat The northern Pacific rattlesnake, *Cro viridis oreganus*, may breed every even though related subspecies are bie breeders (Wallace and Diller, 1990).[5] I ing in mind that this species mates ir summer (see above), females feed thro out the spring and again in the autu after they have given birth, and ma fit enough to breed again the following

Multiple clutches

Cases of snakes that breed every other are well documented, but example species that breed more than once each are not as well known. Some species tainly have the potential to do so, bec in captivity they will often produce a se or even third clutch in the same bree season provided they are well fed in good condition. These may result separate matings or, in some cases, fem that have only been mated once, ir spring, will go on to lay another clutch in the year, even though the male ha been present after the first clutch. In ord do this, she must store sperm from the i mating and use it to fertilize the subseo clutch of eggs.

Because of the difficulty of monit individual snakes throughout the seas

---

Sperm storage in a small rattlesnake

The ridge-nosed, or Willard's, rattlesnake, *Crotalus willardi*, is a small species that is found only in a few isolated mountain ranges in southern Arizona, southern New Mexico and northern Mexico. It is specialized in its habitat preference and is only found at high altitudes, where it is subjected to extended periods of inactivity during the long, cold winters.

Mating takes place in the summer, with matings recorded in July and August. Development begins the following spring, after a long

hibernation, and the females give birth to small broods of offspring the following August or September. The period of time that elapses between mating and birth therefore totals about 14 months. This precludes the possibility of females breeding in successive years.

This, coupled with the small litters produced, and their exacting habitat requirements, has led to concern over their future survival, especially of the subspecies *C. w. obscurus*, the New Mexican form.

rd to say how often multiple clutches in wild snakes. It does seem likely that urs at least occasionally, if for no other n than that it is physiologically possi-f multiple clutching does occur, it will und in species that have long active ns.

ese variations in breeding seasons, all erning temperate species, serve as a der that each species of snake has ted its reproductive timetable to its rements and to the prevailing condi-. Although many species have similar ms, others will have evolved unusual ique systems if they happen to suit better.

cal species

though most snakes are tropical in , there has been less research into ontrolling factors of breeding seasons ese species. Like temperate species, may also respond to temperature but nal differences are likely to be more . The beginning of the wet season is ally accompanied by lower tempera-, at least during some part of the day. may stimulate the snakes to breed. On ther hand, they may mate at the end of wet season, when temperatures rise ly, so that the birth or hatching of young is timed to coincide with the wet season and therefore provide food and cover. The olive sand snake, mophis phillipsi, from northern Africa, s to fit into the latter category. Egg ation in this species begins around the of the rainy season and the eggs are zed and laid by the middle of the dry n. Hatching occurs at the onset of the rainy season (Butler, 1993).[6]

erall, the timing will depend on the h of the gestation coupled with the h of the wet and dry seasons. Both factors are variable. In parts of the s where wet and dry seasons are not ctable, female as well as male snakes be in more or less permanent readiness ed, perhaps as a response to increased supply or a sudden lowering of temper-during occasional downpours.

e of the problems with unravelling easonal breeding rhythms of tropical es is that, unlike temperate species, ropical species are kept and bred in vity. Of those that are, most are large and pythons but, as these species long gestation times, they may breed at ent times of the year from small species. eserved specimens are dissected it is

sometimes possible, by examining their reproductive tracts, to establish some seasonal patterns, and this has been carried out with some species. Results seem to vary, though, with some snakes showing distinct breeding seasons, others with less distinct, or extended seasons, and yet others in which no obvious pattern can be discerned. It seems likely that regional differences occur, even within the same species, especially with those that range widely and over areas that have different climatic conditions.

The Hispaniolan snake *Antillophis parvifrons protenus* is a case in point. Where it occurs on the main island there is a fairly consistent rainfall throughout the year and plenty of moist habitat; in these regions the reproductive season is extended and may even continue throughout the year. Where it occurs on two small satellite islands, however, there is seasonal variation in rainfall and on these islands the snakes' breeding seasons are timed to coincide with the rainy season (Powell *et al.*, 1991).[7]

Other examples are not so straight-forward. Solorzano and Cerdas (1989)[8] studied the pit viper *Bothrops asper*, which has a fairly extensive range in South America. The seasons vary throughout this species' range: in Costa Rica, for instance, it occurs on both sides of the Central mountain range, which divides the country into two different climatic zones. On the Pacific side, females mate from September to November and give birth from April to June, at the beginning of the rainy season. The newborn snakes eat frogs, which are plentiful at this time of the year. On the

▼ The timing of the reproductive cycle and the litter size of the pit viper, *Bothrops asper*, vary according to location: in some parts of Costa Rica, for instance, it is more prolific than in others.

Atlantic side of the country, the seasons are almost reversed, and mating takes place in March, at the end of the rainy season, when the temperature rises. The young are born from September to November, which is the beginning of the rainy season in *this* part of the country.

Females of both populations, then, give birth at the beginning of the rainy season. But, because the duration of the rainy seasons vary from one side of the country to the other, one group of snakes can time its mating to coincide with rising temperatures at the end of the previous rainy season whereas members of the other population have no such environmental trigger. They mate at a time when conditions are more or less constant, and there is no way of knowing what stimulates them. Another interesting difference between the populations, for which there is no explanation as yet, is that of litter size: females from the Pacific population have litters of five to 40 young (average 18.6) whereas females from the Atlantic population have larger litters, of 14 to 86 (average 41.1).

Biennial cycling in boas and pythons

Biennial cycling occurs in some of the larger boas and pythons, none of which comes from especially cool climates. These species carry their young for long periods of time, up to ten months in some cases, and often fast for most of this time. There simply would not be enough time to feed sufficiently during the remainder of the year. Under captive conditions, many of these species can be induced to breed every year by intensive feeding immediately after the birth and during the early part of pregnancy. On other occasions, however, they may mate every year but produce young only every second year.

MATING SYSTEMS

The animal mating systems that are applicable to snakes can be broadly divided into three types. One is where a male and a female stay together, either for life or for the duration of a breeding season, and all the offspring have the same mother and the same father (monogamy). A second is where males mate with several females (polygamy) and the third is where females mate with several males (polyandry).

All three systems can be found among snake populations. Lifelong monogamy has not been proved, because it is difficult to observe pairs of snakes from one year to the next, but there are several examples of species in which males and females stay together throughout the breeding season.

Polygamy and polyandry often go together. Whereas in monogamy, the presence of a male will limit the female's opportunity to mate with other males, with polygamous systems, once the male goes in search of additional mates, the female may be found and mated by a second, third or subsequent males and it has been shown that females may produce a batch of eggs or young that have been fertilized by more than one male. One way around this problem, from the male's point of view, is described below.

Mate finding
As with seasonality, the systems by which snakes find and court members of the opposite sex vary with species and the particular life-styles they lead. Where snakes congregate in large numbers to hibernate, such as in rattlesnake dens, mating usually takes place before the animals have dispersed, often within a few weeks of their emergence. Finding a mate in these situations is not a problem, although increased competition may mean that only a small proportion of males is fortunate enough to father a batch of young. Other species, including those that pass the winter in small groups individuals, must search for mates o larger area. This is made easier by production of pheromone trails, inv chemical tracks that are left by snak they move around. Males are ade homing in on females, especially when are in a state of reproductive receptivit

From a collector's standpoint, it will happen that some species are most found at the time of year in which ma take place, but invariably the sa contain more males than females. This cates that males go in search of fe rather than the other way round. Fe are able to remain near familiar terr and are less likely to be caught, by pred as well as by snake hunters.

Courtship and mating
When males and females meet, mating not necessarily take place immedi Although the ritual of courtship in sr is not in the same league as that of for example, males do need to stim females before they will mate with t Stimulation is usually tactile, alth odour probably plays an additional During courtship, it is usual for the m crawl along the back of the female, making regular jerking movements pythons and boas, the rudimentary are used to scratch or tickle the back female. When the female is ready to she allows the male to lift her tail wit and coil his tail around hers. As cloacae come into contact, the male e one of his hemipenes into the fem cloaca and copulation takes place. Co tion can last from a few minutes to se hours, depending on species.

Once the snakes are joined, they ar easily separated. If one of the pair de to move off, the other will be dragged too. Large females are often seen dra smaller males behind them, but some it is the male that takes the lead: Lilly (1985),[9] reported on a male black r *Coluber constrictor*, that he watched climbed into a tree, dragging the fe behind him to a height of 5 m (16 ft).

During the breeding season, males of species may remain with females for se days or even weeks. The purpose o may be to ensure that they are able to as soon as the female is receptive a copulate several times. Multiple copula ensure that the male's sperm outnu those of any other male that may have r with the female previously. Once the fe

---

Enforced chastity in garter snakes

Males of some species use a 'trick' in order to get the best of both worlds. This involves the use of copulatory plugs. Plugs are formed from fluid secretions, made in a specialized part of the male's kidney, and deposited into the lower part of the female's oviduct immediately after sperm is ejected. The fluid hardens after a few minutes, forming an effective barrier to further impregnation of the female by other males. The male is then free to search for more mates, secure in the knowledge that another male cannot replace or dilute his sperm. The plug, which was first discovered in a few species of garter snakes, *Thamnophis*, remains in place for two to four days, after which time it begins to break down and is ejected by the female. It is doubtful if the period of time during which the plug is in place is sufficient to prevent further fertile mating altogether, as female snakes may remain receptive for several weeks but, when mating aggregations take place, as they do among garter snakes, the most vulnerable time for additional matings probably occurs in the first few days of sexual activity, after which the adults begin to disperse.

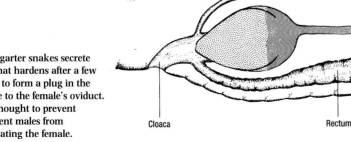

▶ Male garter snakes secrete a fluid that hardens after a few minutes to form a plug in the entrance to the female's oviduct. This is thought to prevent subsequent males from impregnating the female.

es to become recephtive, the male's chment to her ceases and they usually go separate ways.

to male combat

ng the time that a male is attending a otive female, rival males may approach. esident male will attempt to drive them y by ritualized combat dances in which male raises its head, neck and the fore of its body off the ground, entwines the r's body and tries to press him to the nd. These bouts last varying amounts e, depending on how well matched the rsaries are, and the combatants may rests between bouts. Eventually, one of nales, usually the smaller individual, edes defeat and crawls away. The rious male then returns to the female, normally remains nearby during these eedings, and mating may take place. male snakes rarely, if ever, do serious age to one another, although under artificial circumstances of captivity, e the submissive male is unable to e the scene, the dominant animal may nim savagely, sometimes inflicting deep nds. In boids, males sometimes use spurs to scratch at their rivals.

mbat of one form or another has been d in a wide array of species, including s, numerous colubrids, many vipers pit vipers, including rattlesnakes, and y elapids, particularly Australian es, such as blacksnakes, *Pseudechis*, snakes, *Demansia*, white-lipped snakes, dalia, brown snakes, *Pseudonaja*, taipans, ranus, swamp snakes, *Hemiaspis*, -eyed snakes, *Cryptophis*, tiger snakes, chis, and copperheads, *Austrelaps*.

cause larger males nearly always win bouts of combat, there will be strong itionary pressure for males to become r: large males mate more often than ones and so the genes for being large oe passed on. The males of species that ge in combats tend to be relatively r than males of the species that do not. ne significance of male to male combat at the female mates with the strongest and, thanks to his 'good' genes, their ring will have a better chance of sur-. On the other hand, small males may r win a combat and therefore would r get to mate. Sometimes, small males oe seen in the vicinity of mated pairs of es and there is a strong possibility that e are 'satellite' males that, given the fact they can never win a female through means, try to steal matings while the

▲ Copulation in some of the more arboreal snakes takes place while they are coiled around branches. Green tree pythons, *Chondropython viridis*, seen here, and emerald boas, *Corallus caninus*, for example, intertwine their tails to keep their cloacae adjacent to each other. Other snakes usually intertwine their tails while lying on the ground but the methods of courtship and mating in aquatic and burrowing species is unknown. Most of the observations on courtship and mating in snakes have involved captive individuals.

Three breeding systems compared: male–male competition, scramble competition and extended mate searching

Different breeding systems evolve in response to different circumstances: the best strategy for one species may not be equally good for another. Studies have also shown that, in addition to variations between species, different populations of the same species can also vary and there may even be slight differences from year to year. Although it can sometimes be hard to see exactly which system is at work, a few detailed studies have identified at least three distinct patterns of reproductive behaviour.

Male–male competition in the adder

One of the first species to be thoroughly studied was the European adder, *Vipera berus*, in southern England, by Ian Prestt (*J. Zool. London*, 164:373–418). He found that adders spend the winter in communal dens, containing large numbers of males and females. They emerge in the spring, with males emerging before females. The males move away from the den to nearby favoured basking sites, which they may use year after year. They remain at these sites for several weeks during which time they shed their skin but do not feed. When the females emerge from the den, receptive individuals tend to congregate in areas that could be termed mating sites, and the males gravitate towards these sites.

In many years, only a small proportion of females breed, with the result that there are often many more males than breeding females. The males then have to compete for mates, sometimes combating with each other to establish dominance in the spectacular and well-known 'combat dances'. The victorious males, which are usually the largest, drive the losers away from the vicinity of the females, and may immediately mate with the females. The losers, however, may return repeatedly in the hope of finding an unattended female and sneaking a mating.

In other years, the number of receptive females may be almost as high as that of males: in these years

▲ Adders, *Vipera berus*, typically congregate during the breeding season, with several males competing for the opportunity to mate with females. Here one male is mating with the larger female while another stays nearby in the hope of stealing a mating.

competition between males is less intense and most of them may find mates regardless of size. Each female frequently mates with more than one male.

The mating season lasts about four weeks, after which the males and females disperse into areas where they can find food. The females give birth towards the end of the summer and males, females and juveniles begin to congregate around hibernation sites again in the autumn.

Scramble competition in wandering garter snakes

Brent Graves and David Duvall studied two species, the wandering garter snake, *Thamnophis elegans vagrans*, and the prairie rattlesnake, *Crotalus viridis*, in Wyoming (*Journal of Herpetology*, 24(4):351–356). They found interesting differences in their respective mating systems, and both differed from that of the adder.

Wandering garter snakes spend the winter in communal hibernation dens. Males always emerge before females but remain in the vicinity of the den.

When the females emerge, the males not engage in combat with one anoth but scramble to mate with them; each male tries forcibly to dislodge other males in order to effect copulation, resulting in large 'mating balls'. Once all the females have been mated, both sexes disperse to begin feeding and th females give birth later in the summe

Mate searching in prairie rattlesnake

Prairie rattlesnakes also overwinter i communal dens but their subsequent behaviour is somewhat different from that of the garter snake. They emerge from their hibernation dens later, and males and females emerge at the sam time. There is no mating activity at th time and both sexes make their way immediately to feeding areas: this ma take them several kilometres (miles) away from the den site. Not until late in early summer, do the males begin look for mates, probably using pheromone trails to locate them. Because females are so widely dispersed, males find them singly, an combat is not thought to take place (although it does in many other speci of rattlesnakes). They mate after a fev days of courtship and the mating season is over by the end of August. Shortly afterwards, both sexes make their way back to the den in readines for hibernation. The young are born the following spring or early summer

inant male is otherwise occupied, such
hen he is defending his female from
r rivals.

ie activities described probably apply
any temperate snakes, although only
aall proportion of species have been
ed. In other species, as far as can be
olished, matings are more casual,
males tracking down and mating with
les, then departing immediately, pre-
ably to look for other females. This
s to the possibility that several males
find and mate with a single female and
her eggs may be fertilized with sperm
a number of them. Males of species
employ this mating system do not
ge in combat as they rarely meet
rivals. Competition between sperm,
vhich sperm reach the unfertilized ova
then becomes the significant factor
ntrolling which male fathers the most
ig, instead of competition between
iduals. This is an interesting area of
irch that has only recently begun to
ct attention from researchers.

is worth emphasizing that almost all
is known about mating and mating
ms in snakes is based on observations
e of the most common and most con-
ous species. There is still an enormous
unt that is not known and, in particular,
methods of mate finding, courtship and
ng in snakes belonging to some of
nore primitive families, particularly the
n and thread snakes, is virtually
iown.

Snakes without fathers

Parthenogenesis is the term given to a
method of reproducing without the
help of a member of the opposite sex;
that is, without males. A number of
invertebrates have evolved methods of
reproducing parthenogenetically, as
have some fish and a few lizard species
but, as far as is known, only one
species of snake is parthenogenetic.

This is the small worm snake
Ramphotyphlops braminus, sometimes
called the flowerpot snake. Although
nobody has yet succeeded in rearing
and breeding this species in captivity,
and thereby proving beyond doubt that
it is parthenogenetic, there is strong
circumstantial evidence. Firstly, all the
specimens that have ever been found
have turned out to be females: since it
is not a rare snake, one would expect to
find at least some males if they existed.
In addition, colonies of the species have
become established in many parts of
the tropical and subtropical world
through accidental human introduction: parthenogenetic species are
far more likely to establish themselves
in new places because only a single
individual is needed to found each new
colony.

Being parthenogenetic has costs as
well as benefits. Looking at the benefits
first, not having to find a mate is an
obvious advantage when it comes to
establishing new colonies – one solitary

individual, even an immature one, is
enough to get things started. Also,
populations of parthenogenetic species
tend to grow very quickly, because each
individual is female and therefore able
to produce young (i.e., the number of
individuals that can lay eggs is doubled).

There is a drawback, however. In
normal (sexual) reproduction, genes
from both parents mingle and express
themselves in various combinations in
their offspring. This causes an almost
infinite amount of variation within the
population. Variation is important if
conditions change because, in all
likelihood, some individuals will be
better able to adapt to the change than
others. (This is the basis of natural
selection and speciation.)

With parthenogenesis, however, all
individuals are identical (i.e., they are
clones of the female that bore them)
except in the rare cases of spontaneous
mutation. Being identical is fine for as
long as conditions remain unchanged
but, sooner or later, a need to adapt to
new conditions is likely to arise.
Without variation, the species cannot
respond to changing conditions and is
likely to die out.

Parthenogenesis, then, gives
short-term advantages and long-term
disadvantages.

▼ Flowerpot snake, *Ramphotyphlops braminus*.

GESTATION

The fact that snakes can store sperm creates problems when trying to estimate the length of gestation period – obviously, unless the exact time of fertilization is known, it is not possible to calculate the time from fertilization to egg laying or birth, and instances in which widely varying gestation periods have been recorded may well result from cases of sperm storage. Furthermore, many snakes mate several times over a long period of time – several weeks or even months in pythons and boas, for instance. Calculations are normally made using the latest date of observed mating but this method is prone to errors since eggs may have already been fertilized by this time, by sperm introduced at a previous mating.

The period of time from mating to egg laying or birth is also subject to variation for other reasons. Egg-laying species naturally have a shorter gestation than viviparous species but even egg layers may retain their eggs until they are partially developed. It is dangerous, therefore to generalize. Temperature also plays a role and cool weather may prolong the gestation period, despite attempts by the female to absorb as much heat as possible.

Having said this, there is plenty of reasonably sound information, based on snakes that have been allowed to mate only once. Gestation periods for many medium-sized colubrid snakes seems fairly constant at about 40 to 50 days. Elapids seem to have a similar gestation period. Pythons generally take longer, however, sometimes twice this length of time. This may be partly due to their larger size, although even the smaller species, such as the Australian Children's and spotted pythons, *Liasis childreni* and *L. maculosus*, take longer than colubrids of equivalent size.

Pregnancy in viviparous species also varies. Indeed, it is subject to even greater variation because of the greater likelihood of vagaries in the weather over this longer period. As has been noted, some species, such as the prairie rattlesnake, *Crotalus viridis*, and the ridge-nosed rattlesnake, *C. willardi*, mate one year and give birth the next, at least in some parts of their range. If the months when the snakes are hibernating is included in the calculations of gestation period, it will appear to be unusually long. Most temperate viviparous species, though, mate early in the spring and give birth to their young towards the end of the summer, with a gestation period of four to six months. Tropical viviparous species have similar gestation periods.

Females with developing eggs may need to maintain a high body temperature in order to speed up the development of their eggs. For tropical species this is not usually a problem but snakes from cool climates tend to bask for long periods when they are gravid. This increases the risk of predation, but is preferable to delaying development until the weather becomes even cooler. Females of a few species are darker in colour than males, and, in one or two species, such as the Madagascan tree boa, *Sanzinia madagascariensis*, there may be a colour change during pregnancy, so increasing heat absorption and speeding up development.

Many female pythons assume a peculiar posture when they are carrying eggs, coiling upside down to expose most or all of their ventral surface. Although there is no firm evidence, the assumption is that they are attempting to raise the temperature of their developing eggs, perhaps by moving them away from a cold substrate.

EGG LAYING AND BIRTH

As we have seen, egg laying and birth be timed in such a way that the ye snakes hatch, or are born, at a time v there is suitable food available. They also find themselves in an environ where they can get off to a good start. will normally be the same environme which the adults live but, where the b range does not contain any suitable females may move some distance in ord find places in which to lay the eggs.

Live-bearing species
The young of live-bearing species are in the thin membrane that was surroun them in the oviduct during their dev ment. They have to break free from before they disperse and this is achi simply by wriggling, usually within sec of birth.

The birth itself usually takes place secluded place, perhaps a retreat tha female has used for the late stages o pregnancy. It may consist of an u ground tunnel, a space beneath a roc log, or a cavity among the roots of a Sometimes, however, the young sr are born in the open, and live-be arboreal species may give birth amon; branches where they live. The memb surrounding their young may hel prevent them from falling by stickir foliage. Birth in completely aquatic spe such as the sea snakes, is rarely obse but always takes place in the water. S aquatic snakes, such as the garter ribbon snakes, *Thamnophis*, however, birth away from the water.

Females may eat any infertile egg-m that accompany the birth of the young they have also been known to eat young. This may merely be a way of cling waste material. There is no evider parental care in live-bearing snakes an female apparently takes little interest ii young once they are born. Litters of y« are occasionally found with females t seems most likely that, when they do together, it is by chance: if the weath cold, for instance, and neither the m« nor the young are active.

Egg-laying species
Oviparous snakes must also find a sui place in which to deposit their eggs, an« is more demanding because certain requirements must be met if the egg to develop to hatching. Snakes' eggs a water throughout their development especially during the early part of inc

The substrate in which they are laid
therefore be moist. The eggs also
re oxygen, however, and a substrate
is too wet will impede the oxygen
ange across the egg shell and the devel-
nt of the young will be adversely
ted. Since the incubation can last for
three months, the properties of site
en for laying the clutch must be very
tant. Finally, snakes' eggs are not pig-
ed to any great degree and therefore
e an easy target for predators, so they
be hidden or buried.

laying sites

happens, snakes are so good at hiding
eggs that nests are rarely found by
an observers, even in areas where
es are known to be numerous. Much of
is known about egg laying, clutch sizes
incubation periods comes either from
ction of preserved specimens, from the
viour of captive snakes or, more rarely,
lucky observations.

utches are probably secreted in safe,
ided places where they will be able to
lop and hatch without interference.
e sites are likely to be within the area
the female uses for her other activities
ugh females of some species need to

travel to separate areas in order to find sites
with the correct conditions. Rough green
snakes, *Opheodryas aestivus*, for instance,
have been observed leaving their usual
habitat, alongside a small lake, and moving
away from the shore in order to lay their
eggs in cavities in trees (Plummer, 1989).[10]
They probably use the same holes year
after year because the remains of previous
clutches were found in them. One individual

▲ Viviparous snakes, such as the Argentine
rainbow boa, *Epicrates cenchria alvarezi*, are
born inside a thin membrane, supplied with blood
vessels. The young snake usually frees itself as
soon as it is born, but it may remain inside the
membrane for up to 24 hours, while it absorbs its
yolk sac.

▼ A horned adder, *Bitis caudalis*, with part of her
brood of young.

▲ A female Baird's rat snake, *Elaphe bairdi*, in the process of laying her clutch of eggs.

tried repeatedly to gain access to a hole that was too small, presumably because the growth of the tree had reduced the size of the opening or because the female had grown slightly since her last visit.

The sea kraits, which are the only marine species to lay eggs, come ashore to lay them.

▼ A clutch of eggs, belonging to the golden-crowned snake, *Cacophis squamulosus*, discovered beneath a stone. Snakes hide their eggs so well that finding a clutch in nature is a rare event.

Tu *et al.* (1990)[11] found that on Orchid Island, off Taiwan, eggs of *Laticauda semifasciata* and *L. laticauda* were laid above sea level in tidal caves, where they would not be inundated with sea water. The correct moisture was maintained by fresh water dripping from the roof of the caves and this also served to dilute any sea water that entered during storms. The humidity within the caves was 100 per cent and the temperature was fairly constant at 23–26.8°C (73.4–80.2°F). The eggs took from four to five months to hatch. Several females of both species had used the same cave and broken egg shells, from previous clutches, were also present.

Communal egg laying

On the basis of other studies on egg laying, and on a number of chance observations as well, it is clear that, when egg-laying sites are in short supply, several females may all lay their eggs in especially suitable places, sometimes using them year after year.

In addition to the sea kraits mentioned above, communal nesting is also known in several other species, including the European grass snake, *Natrix natrix*. Females of this species choose piles of decaying vegetation in which to lay, in order to make

use of the additional heat produced by process of decomposition to accelerate de opment. Farmyard manure heaps, com heaps and piles of sawdust have been in addition to natural sites, especiall agricultural areas. They often become focal point for several females in the s area, which each lay their moderately clutches in them. The total number of may even exceed 1,000. As breeding is f well synchronized in this species, the egg tend to hatch over a short period of t causing a local population explosio young snakes.

Communal egg laying also occurs in species of the American green snakes, *O dryas*; large batches of eggs of the sm green snake, *O. vernalis*, have been fc together, despite an average clutch si about five to six, while Palmer and Bras (1976)[12] reported on a group of 74 eg the rough green snake, *O. aestivus*, in a p from an abandoned refrigerator, pa with insulating material. Since the sp also lays small clutches of five or six eggs. batch must have been produced by at ten females, probably more.

Communal nesting has also been reco in several other North American sn and in the Australian whipsnake, *Dem* nmophis. It may be more widespread these isolated cases indicate but, until naturally occurring nest sites are d, this cannot be confirmed.

urger and Zappalorti (1991)[13] studied ing behaviour in the northern pine ke *Pituophis melanoleucus melanoleucus.* y found that the female digs burrows andy soil, bending its neck to scoop the out of the burrow. It digs down until it a layer of soil in which the moisture tent is suitable, taking two to three s to excavate the tunnel. The tunnels isure about 1.5 m (5 ft) and slope down-ds at first but then rise slightly before ing in a chamber. The eggs are laid in chamber. It appears that females use same egg-laying site every year, but dig tunnels. Not every female digs her own nel, however, and several may use the e one. This cannot be accounted for by hortage of nest sites, so some females ear to specialize in using the tunnels dug thers in order to save time and energy.

gator nests as egg-laying sites

Florida, eggs of the mud snake, *Farancia cura*, have been found inside the nests of gators, *Alligator mississippiensis.* Alligator s consist of large piles of dead and rotting etation, situated in or near swamps. The ale attends the nest, guarding the eggs l they hatch. Both active and abandoned s have been used by the mud snakes (and by turtles).

he pile of damp and rotting vegetation st create a good environment for the ke eggs and, when the alligator is in resi-ce, they would also gain a highly effective y-sitter'.

and termite nests as egg-laying sites

ation should be made of another special-type of egg-laying site, used by a variety nainly tropical snakes. These species their eggs in ant and termite nests, ing use of the constant temperature humidity found inside them. The tem-atures of the inner chambers of these ctures have been found to be stable at 29°C (80.6–84.2°F) in relevant ant s despite fluctuations in the outside air perature. Termite nests can average 1°C (9–20°F) higher than outside perature because they are usually ori-d in such a way as to catch the rays of sun in the early morning and late ing, when air temperatures are low. er advantages of such sites may include a ree of protection from predators and also

from bacterial and fungal attack of the eggs, as ants and termites are meticulous in their attention to hygiene in their nests.

Eggs of at least 18 species of snakes have been found in this type of site, and were listed by Riley *et al.* (1985).[14] They include two species of blind snakes, both of which use termite nests, and one elapid, the coral snake *Micrurus frontalis*, which uses ant nests. All the other species are colubrids, including two species, *Liophis obtusus* and *Philodryas patagoniensis*, that between them accounted for 146 clutches of eggs found in 83 nests in Uruguay. Most colubrids use ant nests rather than those of termites, probably because hatchling snakes would have problems in finding their way out of the nests of termites, which construct nests of hard-baked clay and quickly repair any damage that occurs to their outer surface. Having said this, eggs of the colu-brid, *Adelphicos quadrivirgatus*, have been found in a termite nest that was situated 1–1.5 m (3–5 ft) from the ground in a tree (Pedrez-Hidareda and Smith, 1989).[15] This is a small species with a pointed snout and slender body, better adapted to finding its way in and out of termite nests than many other colubrids. Eggs of two species of *Boiga*, *B. drapiezii* and *B. jaspidea*, have also been found in termite nests in Java.

Although the eggs of at least one species (*Lamprophis fuliginosus*) have been found in a variety of sites, apart from termite nests, it seems that many species *only* lay in them. Most are West Indian or South American, where large nests of species such as leaf-

cutter ants, genera *Acromyrmex* and *Atta*, are a prominent feature of the rainforest floor, and most eggs have been found in the central fungus chamber, where the ants cultivate the fungus on which they feed.

One other snake that has a strong associ-ation with termite nests is the anthill python, *Liasis perthensis*, which preys heavily on a gecko, *Gehyra pilbara*, that also uses the nests as egg-laying sites. The eggs of *L. perthensis*, however, are unknown in the field.

Clutch size

Taking snakes as a whole, their clutch size (including litters of live young) ranges from one to over 100 but only a few species have ever been recorded with clutches or broods of more than 100. These include three pythons, the Indian, African and reticulated pythons, *Python molurus*, *P. sebae*, and *P. reticulatus*, and two vipers, the puff adder and the fer-de-lance, *Bitis arietans* and *Bothrops atrox*. The remaining four species are all colubrids: the mud snake, *Farancia abacura*, the green water snake, *Nerodia cyclopion*, the African mole snake, *Pseudaspis cana* and the common garter snake, *Thamnophis sirtalis*. The largest single brood appears to be that of a puff adder reported from the Dvur Kralove Zoo, in Czechoslovakia, which produced 157 living young. The snake measured 1.1 m (3 ft 7 in) in length.

▼ The mud snake, *Farancia abacura*, has truly enormous clutches of eggs, with over 100 having been recorded.

All of these records are exceptional, and clutches or broods of more than 50 are unusual for any snake but it is worth noting that, of the nine species listed above, three are very large pythons, two are large-bodied vipers and three are large-bodied colubrids. Only the garter snake could be considered of average, or below average build.

Very small snakes tend to lay very small clutches. Thus species in the families Typhlopidae and Leptotyphlopidae, as well as a number of small colubrids, lay clutches as small as one and may only average two to three eggs per clutch (although clutches of up to 34 eggs have been recorded for an Australian worm snake). These examples are extremes, however, and the vast majority of clutches number between three and 16. The average clutch size, taking all snakes into account, works out at about seven.

As females grow, so they can produce larger numbers of eggs or young. An average colubrid, such as a corn snake, *Elaphe guttata*, may produce about six eggs in her first season but steadily increases her

▼ Part of a clutch of eggs from a heavily built snake (a well grown female rat snake, *Elaphe bairdi*, and a clutch from a more slender snake (a young female milk snake, *Lampropeltis triangulum*). Because of its body size, the milk snake can only lay eggs with a small diameter: this means that they must be relatively elongated in order to be large enough to produce a viable hatchling. The rat snake, being thicker, can lay eggs with a greater diameter and therefore they are more rounded.

productivity until, when she is fully grown, her clutches will consist of about 20 eggs. Animals that produce exceptionally large numbers of offspring, like those listed above, were probably very old, large individuals.

Egg size and shape
Being cylindrical and slender is not the ideal shape for carrying large eggs around. Snakes therefore tend to lay relatively smaller eggs than their closest relatives, the lizards. Because each egg is smaller, they can afford to produce more of them, and this is probably why snakes lay, on average, a greater number of small eggs than lizards, which tend to lay a small number of relatively large eggs.

The size of snakes' eggs is obviously closely connected to the size of the species. As a very rough figure, the total reproductive output of a female (the weight of her whole clutch or brood), accounts for about 20 per cent of her own body weight. This figure is sometimes known as the relative clutch mass, or simply the RCM. So, if the snake produces an average-size clutch of, say, seven eggs, each egg will weigh about 3 per cent of the weight of the female.

Snakes of similar size, therefore, tend to produce eggs of similar size. There is some variability, though. Within closely related species of snakes, different strategies can sometimes be recognized. Females of two different species may 'decide' (in an evolutionary sense) to share out their reproductive output in different ways, one laying a

few large eggs and the other a lot of sm eggs. Even within the same species, memb of some populations or subspecies may larger or smaller eggs than others. The No American gopher and pine snakes, *Pituo melanoleucus*, give us a good example this: many of the western subspecies clutches of six to 10 moderate-sized eggs the rare Louisiana pine snake, *Pituophi ruthveni*, lays two to four exceptionally la eggs.

Leaving aside variations such as this looking at snakes as a whole, small sna and very slender snakes, always seem to clutches consisting of a few large eggs: clutches are smaller, and each egg is lar relative to the size of the female, than other snakes. The European leopard sna *Elaphe situla*, for instance, which is one of smallest species in its genus, lays clut of between three and six large, elonga eggs, whereas other members of the ge lay much larger clutches, over 20 egg some cases.

Why do small snakes have relatively la young when compared with large sna Perhaps there is a lower size limit be which young snakes cannot survive. T may have trouble finding food, avoid predators or just maintaining a suita body temperature if they fall below lower limit.

This means that small species of sna need to produce relatively large young, e at the cost of producing fewer of them. Si as we have already seen, slender anim and large eggs do not go together very w they must find a way around the probl The solution is to lay eggs that are l and slender, sausage-shaped, and wh therefore fit into the body of the snake m easily; small snakes, and slender tree sna then, lay elongated eggs, larger snakes more rounded eggs. Somewhere around borderline are those species that be breeding when they are small and carry growing until they are large. Very often, eggs of these species are elongated wh they begin to breed and become mo rounded in later years, as they grow.

⸨e eggs develop only if they have the ⸨conditions. These include some degree ⸨oisture in the substrate, as mentioned ⸨e, and a suitable temperature. The ideal ⸨erature seems to be about 28°C (82°F) ⸨mperate species, a few degrees higher ⸨tropical species, including pythons. ⸨perate species will continue to develop ⸨nuch lower temperatures, although ⸨lopment slows down and hatching is ⸨ved. Also, eggs incubated at signifi- ⸨ly higher or lower temperatures than ⸨deal, produce young that are smaller ⸨ average and which are weaker. As ⸨cted, tropical snakes have less tolerance ⸨is respect than temperate species do.

⸨iring incubation, snake eggs swell, ⸨cially in the days immediately following ⸨g. The biggest increase is in their width ⸨r than their length and, by the time ⸨hatch, their weight will have increased ⸨out 50 per cent. This is largely due to ⸨influx of water, which passes through ⸨semi-permeable eggshell and is used ⸨ie developing embryo. If the moisture ⸨ent of the substrate is too low, water ⸨low in the other direction, i.e. from the ⸨e to the outside of the shell, and the ⸨ryo will dehydrate.

⸨ntal care

⸨ntal care is, apparently, very rare in ⸨es. When it does occur it invariably ⸨lves only the female. In addition, it is ⸨ned to egg-laying species: as far as we ⸨w, live-bearing species show no interest ⸨eir offspring after they are born.

⸨ding in pythons

⸨ough parental care of eggs is found in ⸨es from several families, nowhere is it as ⸨agly developed as in pythons. Female ⸨ons gather their eggs together as they ⸨aid, manipulating them into a pyramid- ⸨ed pile and surrounding them with their ⸨. Brooding may have evolved originally ⸨ means of protecting the eggs against ⸨ation – pythons tend to be large, power- ⸨pecies that are well able to drive away ⸨ of the small predatory animals that ⸨attempt to steal their eggs. At some ⸨t in the evolution of brooding behaviour, ⸨ever, temperature control became an ⸨rtant factor.

⸨males of at least one python species are ⸨to produce a small amount of metabolic ⸨ from their own bodies: this is the only ⸨sion on which any snake becomes ⸨thermic. External signs of the process ⸨pasmodic contractions of the muscles

▲ Even small species of python, such as this Children's python, *Liasis childreni*, brood their eggs, coiling around them during incubation to protect them from predators and, in some cases at least, helping to regulate their temperature.

along the body. Brooding pythons appear to shiver at regular intervals: the time between bouts of shivering varies with the temperature – the lower the temperature, the more often they shiver. Female Indian pythons, *Python molurus*, maintain a temperature of 32–33°C (90–91°F) within their pile of eggs, as much as 7°C (13°F) above that of the surrounding air. Although all species of pythons brood their eggs, and shivering has been observed in several of them, it is debatable whether or not they raise their temperature. In most cases, it has not been possible to show temperature rises within the pile of eggs, although the brooding behaviour may help to prevent heat loss. In addition, the dark colour of the female may allow her to absorb radiant heat and transfer it to the pale-coloured eggs by conduction. It is significant that the temperature at which python eggs develop is much more critical than it is in other snakes and relatively slight drops in temperature can result in poorly developed, abnormally pigmented or deformed young. At 23°C (73°F) they fail to develop altogether.

Egg guarding in other snakes

Other snakes coil around their eggs purely in order to guard them; there is no evidence that temperature control is within their capabilities. Species in which this type of behaviour has been seen include the king cobra, *Ophiophagus hannah*, which is also

unusual in constructing its own nest by using its coils to pull together a pile of dead vegetation. It then coils around the eggs until they hatch. Other Asian species of cobras, *Naja*, may also remain with their eggs throughout at least part of their incubation. Egg guarding is also found in the spotted skaapsteker, *Psammophylax rhombeatus*, from southern Africa, which lays its eggs in a hole in the ground then coils around them. Similar behaviour has been observed in the related *P. variabilis* in areas where it is oviparous: this species can also be viviparous (see page 157). The Chinese colubrid *Sinonatrix percarinata* also guards its eggs: like *Psammophylax rhombeatus*, this species is part of a genus in which viviparity has evolved in other species.

Other species in which some degree of guarding has been seen include some members of the genus *Elaphe*, the North American mud snake, *Farancia abacura*, the same species that sometimes uses alligator nests in which to lay its eggs, and the Texas thread snake, *Leptotyphlops dulcis*. A final example is found among the Viperidae, where one of the few oviparous species, the Malaysian pit viper, *Calloselasma rhodostoma*, lays clutches of about 20 eggs and coils around them for the duration of their incubation, which normally takes about 40 days.

Egg guarding, though a rarity among snakes, is found in at least five families: the Leptotyphlopidae, Boidae, Colubridae, Elapidae and Viperidae. This is almost half of a possible 11 families, some families being exclusively viviparous. Considering the huge proportion of species about which little is known, especially the colubrids, it may be more widespread than we realize.

HATCHING

Hatching takes place when the young snake is fully developed and when the yolk has been absorbed. Because the shell consists of a parchment-like material, and is not heavily calcified, it must be slit rather than broken. Escape from the egg is helped by a small thorn-like growth on the snout of the young snake, popularly known as the egg-tooth. The events that stimulate the young snake to begin slashing at the inside of its shell have not been studied in snakes but are likely to be similar to those that take place inside the shell of turtles and birds.

As the embryo develops inside the egg its requirement for oxygen goes up. At first, this requirement is met by oxygen passing through the permeable shell but, eventually, the young animal requires more oxygen than can be supplied in this way. It begins to become restless, twisting and turning inside its shell and pushing at the inner surface with its snout. There is a tiny egg-tooth on the end of the snout and this cuts through the material. Several long slits are usually made. It seems that snakes may slit their eggshell at any time of the night or day – since the eggs are normally buried or hidden in cavities, the time would be immaterial in any case.

After their initial breakthrough, the hatchlings usually rest. They will often poke their head through one of the slits they have made, but seem reluctant to leave their shell. If they are disturbed they will draw back their heads and disappear again, sometimes for several hours. It may be two or more days after first slitting the shell that they finally leave it altogether. They disperse within a few days of hatching but they may stay in their nest until they have shed their skins, usually within the first week. There is no information about subsequent contact with their siblings and it is not known whether or not they are able to discriminate between related and unrelated snakes at a later date.

▶ Two corn snakes, *Elaphe guttata*, emerge from their eggs. Hatching is surprisingly synchronous in most clutches.

◄ A young hognose snake, *Heterodon nasicus*, emerges from the egg in which it has been developing for several weeks.

ipans, *Oxyuranus scutellatus*, hatching.

ron's blind snake, *Typhlops bibronii*, lays walled eggs that hatch in a matter of days.

The rate at which snakes grow is largely under the control of genetic programming and several factors are involved – how large they are at hatching, how efficiently they assimilate their food, and their eventual adult size. Environmental factors, including the amount of food they find, the climatic conditions under which they live (especially the length of their active season) and their susceptibility to parasites and diseases, also play their part. Because of the great amount of variation within all these categories, generalizations about the growth rate of snakes are not very useful.

Sexual maturity is always a good landmark in the life of animals, and is especially useful for snakes because they continue growing after they have reached sexual maturity. Therefore, 'adult' snakes are considered to be those that have reached breeding size, regardless of their eventual maximum size. As a very rough guide, snakes begin to breed when they are about half their potential maximum size. Some individuals, of course, never reach their adult size, owing to predation and disease, whereas others may live a long time but still not reach the same size as other members of the same species. This may be due simply to different amounts of food eaten by different individuals, or different kinds of food, or differences between the sexes. Sexual dimorphism in size is dealt with below.

The age at which snakes mature seems to range from less than one year to four or five years. In most of the species that have been studied, males mature earlier, and at a smaller size than females, even though they may eventually become the larger of the two sexes. Sometimes, both sexes mature at about the same age but there are no species in which females mature earlier than males. The reason for this is that larger females can produce more young, whereas the number of young a male can produce is not linked to his size. It is therefore in the interests of females to wait until they are a reasonable size before they start to breed: males have no need to wait. Reproduction also involves a greater cost to the female in terms of energy lost, mainly through the amount of energy she puts into the developing young, but also because she often will not feed during the times she is gravid. If she breeds too soon, she may not be able to recover and her future chances of breeding may be less.

Other patterns that emerge are that small species tend to mature earlier than

REPRODUCTIVE STRATEGIES

large ones living under similar climatic conditions, and that live-bearing species mature later than egg-laying species, all other things being equal.

Combining all these factors, the longest period for maturation should be found in females of large, live-bearing species from cool regions. This appears to be so. Females of several species of bulky vipers from high latitudes, for instance, mature at four years or more of age, males slightly earlier. Conversely, the species that reach maturity quickest should be small, egg-laying tropical species. Again, this appears to be so and, although there is not much information to go on, some species in this category mature at less than one year of age.

In captivity, abundant food, reduced disease and parasites and a long active season can combine to accelerate maturity. Most frequently kept colubrids, such as kingsnakes, *Lampropeltis*, and rat snakes, *Elaphe*, for instance, can be made to mature at less than two years of age, i.e. they breed in their second summer, even though the same species may require three, four, or perhaps even more years to reach maturity in the wild. Even large species, such as common boas, *Boa constrictor*, and Indian pythons, *Python molurus*, are known to have reached breeding size in less than two years, yet other species in this family are less flexible: they seem reluctant to breed until they are at least three or four years of age, regardless of how well they are fed or how quickly they grow.

▲·The European smooth snake, *Coronella austriaca*, is live-bearing, whereas the other two members of its genus lay eggs. This is an adaptation to the cooler regions where this species lives.

We have looked at the ways male and female snakes get together and what happens when they do. This section is directed more towards the evolutionary aspects of reproduction, and, in particular, attempts to explain why some of the variations that are seen have evolved.

There are many facets to the problem of how best to optimize reproductive effort. Each individual tries to produce as many viable young as possible and any advantage that it gains, through a change in its physiology or behaviour, is likely to spread through the population as its genes become more numerous through its comparative success. The best reproductive strategy, then, is the one that will enable the snake to produce the maximum number of offspring, but a strategy that works well for one species may not do so for another because its circumstances may be different.

It should be made clear that terms like 'decisions', 'choices' and 'trade-offs' are used for convenience, not because they are made by individual snakes. A female viper does not 'decide' whether to lay eggs or give birth to live young. That decision has already been made for her, by the process of trial and error, in other words, by natural selection. If her ancestors had made the 'wrong' decision they would have left no offspring. Because they did leave offspring, we can assume that they made the 'right' decision.

Egg laying versus live bearing

Of the four orders of reptiles (the crocodilians, chelonians, tuatara and squamata) only the latter have evolved viviparity. F[...] so, the more primitive snakes lay eggs [...] so the ability to give birth to live young [...] be regarded as a system that evo[...] through selective pressures. The evolu[...] towards viviparity begins with egg re[...]tion. Females of some species retain [...] inside their bodies until the embryos [...] well developed and the incubation peri[...] very short. The smooth green sn[...] *Opheodryas vernalis*, for example, lays [...] that are partially developed; in the south[...] part of its range, in the Chicago region, [...] need about 30 days to hatch but fur[...] north, in northern Michigan, they so[...]times hatch after just four days. Indeed, [...] possible that, under certain conditi[...] they hatch before they are laid. Altho[...] they are normally regarded as ovipar[...] species of this kind can be thought o[...] intermediate in their reproductive met[...] they are some way along the evolution[...] route to viviparity.

The line between oviparity and vivip[...]

t clearly defined, therefore, and closely
d species may differ in their repro-
ve modes. A good example of this repro-
ve flexibility can be seen in the African
s *Psammophylax*. Two of the three
es, *P. tritaeniatus* and *P. rhombeatus*, lay
while the third, *P. variabilis*, lives up to
ame: the subspecies *P. v. multisquamis*
ggs but the other subspecies, *P. v. vari-*
, gives birth to live young. One of the
aying species, *P. rhombeatus*, guards its
A second example concerns the two
es of smooth snakes *Coronella*, from
e: *C. girondica* lays eggs whereas *C.*
aca is viviparous. The third species in
nus, *C. brachyura*, comes from Asia and
parous. Finally, the South American
rid *Helicops angulatus* may be oviparous
viparous, depending on where it lives.
members of its genus are oviparous.
ether a snake should give birth or lay
s an ecological 'decision', with advant-
and disadvantages that must be care-
weighed up. The reasons for the
tion of viviparity, and therefore the
in which this system is advantageous
rtain cases, has several explanations,
of which may be superimposed on the
s. In other words, there is a 'trade-off'
een the costs and benefits. The reasons
e evolution of viviparity can be divided
several categories. These categories –
te, life-style, habitat and ancestry – are
interrelated and may act together.
se of this, it can sometimes be difficult
e exactly which is the deciding factor or
s.

te

nost important factor is probably tem-
ure. Snakes that live in cold climates,
because of high latitudes or high
des, tend to be viviparous. The reasons
his are not difficult to understand.
evelopment of reptile eggs is entirely
dent on outside sources of heat, and
opment rates vary, with eggs at cool
eratures developing much more slowly
those at warm temperatures. At very
temperatures (the exact level may
d on the species) development stops
ether and the embryo dies.
nales that lay eggs, then, must rely
e weather. Where this is constantly
, the eggs will develop normally, hatch
reasonable time and the young will
ge to a suitable environment to feed and
. Where the weather is cold, or where
edictable cold periods are possible, the
may fail to develop, or they may develop

so slowly that the young hatch at a time
when temperatures are not suitable for their
continued activity. Under these circumstances, it is advantageous for the female to
retain her eggs inside her body so that she
can optimize temperatures by alternately
basking and seeking refuge from the cold.
She may then lay the eggs when they are
part of the way through their development
or, more commonly, wait until they have
hatched and give birth to live young.

Of the examples listed above, where some
members within a genus lay eggs while
others give birth to live young (*Psammophylax*, *Coronella* and *Helicops*), in every case
the live-bearing species live in cooler regions
than the egg-laying species, and there are
several other examples that bear out this
theory.

Frequency of reproduction may also play
a part but is firmly linked with climatic
effects. If a species has the potential to breed
more than once each year, because of a
suitable climate, we would expect it to lay
eggs because the female would be able to
breed again sooner than if she were to carry
her young for the whole of their development. Species that could only breed once
every year (because the active season
was short, for instance) would not benefit
to the same degree. Since multiple breeding
is probably restricted to tropical and subtropical species anyway, it is difficult to
assess the importance of this particular
factor.

Life-style

Other factors involved in the evolution of
viviparity include methods of defence and
hunting. When female snakes retain their
eggs, they place an extra burden on their
ability to move rapidly. This is more of a
limitation in some species than in others.
For example, large, inactive snakes, such as
several of the vipers, rely heavily on camouflage, both for defence and for catching their
prey, which they ambush. The extra burden
of a clutch of developing young would not
be such a strong disadvantage in this type of
species as it would in slimmer, more agile
species that rely more heavily on speed and
agility to escape from predators and to catch
their prey. All of the fast-moving diurnal
hunters listed in Chapter 5, page 108, for
instance, (*Coluber*, *Demansia*, *Masticophis*
and *Psammophis*) are oviparous.

Using the same argument, we would also
expect burrowing snakes, which are out of
sight most of the time and do not need to
worry quite so much about predation, to be
viviparous. Unfortunately, the picture is not
clear here because many of them belong to

▼ Active, slender snakes, such as coachwhips,
Masticophis flagellum, tend to lay eggs because
they rely heavily on speed and must eat regularly:
they cannot afford to carry developing embryos
around with them. Heavy-bodied snakes, most of
which are sedentary, sit-and-wait predators, are
more likely to be live-bearers: the extra burden of
developing young has little effect on their activities.

primitive families such as the Typhlopidae and the Leptotyphlopidae in which viviparity seems not to have evolved: they don't have the option of giving birth to live young. In addition, most burrowing snakes are tropical in origin, and so the benefits of egg laying may outweigh the benefits of live bearing. Some families of burrowing snakes, however, such as the shield-tails and their relatives, Uropeltidae, *are* viviparous.

Habitat

Certain groups of snakes may evolve viviparity because of the habitat they live in: this consideration may be more important than other factors, such as climate. They are the species that have thoroughly adapted to environments that have no suitable sites for laying their eggs, and include totally aquatic snakes. Laying eggs would involve, for these species, leaving the environment to which they are best adapted and becoming vulnerable to predation. Most aquatic species are therefore viviparous, regardless of their distribution, the only notable exception being that of the sea kraits, belonging to the subfamily Laticaudinae, which must leave the sea to lay their eggs ashore.

Some tree snakes find themselves in a similar situation. If they are only semi-arboreal, egg laying may be most advantageous to them, remembering that most tree snakes are long and slender and would therefore want to unload their eggs at the earliest possible opportunity. If they are so highly adapted that they never come down to the ground, however, live bearing is the best option. Species in this category include the long-nosed tree snakes, *Ahaetulla*, of Asia.

Ancestry

Finally, viviparity may be a legacy of snakes' ancestry. The strength of the selective pressure will determine the degree to which a particular species deviates from its close relatives, but some lineages of snakes seem to be more flexible than others when it comes to taking up the viviparous option.

The three families of primitive, burrowing snakes, Anomalepididae, Typhlopidae and Leptotyphlopidae, are all oviparous, as far as is known (although the method of reproduction in many species has not been established).

Of the Boidae, all the pythons are oviparous, and are therefore probably more primitive than the boas, which are all viviparous, regardless of size and habitat, including arboreal species. (Here we are disregarding the possibility that *Calabaria*

▲ Boas are viviparous. Livebearing in this subfamily seems well and truly established because even relatively slender species such as *Candoia carinata* give birth to live young whereas many terrestrial other snakes of similar build are egg-layers.

may be a boa, as noted in Chapter 10, page 202.) All these species therefore appear to have little flexibility in their breeding methods and it is especially interesting to note that ecological counterparts still maintain the ancestral trend; the emerald boa from South America is viviparous whereas the green tree python, from south-east Asia, is oviparous, despite their similarity in every other aspect of their appearance and life-styles.

The pythons are an especially interesting case because they appear to go against the argument that large, heavy-bodied snakes tend to be viviparous; many pythons fall into this category but viviparity has not evolved. What seems to have happened is that pythons use their size in another way. Female pythons brood their eggs for the duration of their incubation. Brooding is, in a way, similar to viviparity, in that the developing embryos remain with the female, who protects them and has some control over their environment. Brooding may have evolved as an alternative to viviparity.

The colubrids consist of such an assorted assemblage of species, some of which are known from only a few specimens and

many whose relationships are not c that reproductive patterns are difficu pick out. Some subfamilies are reason consistent: the Homalopsinae, for exar are all aquatic and all give birth to young, as expected. The Natricinae tend to be aquatic or semi-aquatic viviparity is common in this subfa although some species lay eggs. Other families are more variable and, as already been mentioned, species in the genus, or even individuals within a sp may differ in their reproductive n Where variations occur, the vivipa species, subspecies or populations tend found in cooler regions than their ovipa counterparts.

Among the elapids, oviparity seen be the rule, particularly among Africar Asian species; most are slender snakes actively hunt for their prey and rely on rather than camouflage for defence, they are mainly tropical in their dist tion. Exceptions include the African sp cobra, or rinkhals, *Hemachatus haemacl* which is oviparous, perhaps becau inhabits cooler regions than most co and several of the Australian elapids, no those occurring towards the south o continent. The death adder is an intere case because, although it is an elapid, i moved into the niche that vipers norr occupy when they are present. It has be short and stocky, well camouflaged,

ashes its prey. Viviparity is an extension
s parallelism.

pers have a strong tendency to be vivi-
us, perhaps because they are mostly
and heavy bodied species that ambush
prey: in addition, many species come
cold climates. Even so, there are plenty
ceptions. The Eurasian species *Macro-
a lebetina*, *M. schweizeri* and *Vipera
ina* are oviparous in parts of their
e. These are more southern forms than
y other members of their genus.
arly, the North African horned viper,
tes cerastes, is oviparous; here, the
alized method of locomotion may have
enced the breeding system although it,
has a counterpart, in the form of
North American sidewinder, *Crotalus*

w vipers, such as the West African night
Causus maculatus, lay eggs.

e most of the more advanced vipers, the
bush viper, *Atheris chloroechis*, from
al Africa is a livebearing species.

▲ Like most vipers, the American copperhead, *Agkistrodon contortrix*, gives birth to live young.

▶ Live-bearing and egg-laying species are found among the Asian genus *Trimeresurus*. Arboreal kinds, such as *T. flavomaculatus*, are live-bearers.

cerastes, which has retained the viviparous mode of reproduction. The other species of *Cerastes*, *C. vipera*, may also be viviparous although this has not been confirmed.

The African and Asian genus *Echis* is variable, with one 'species' *E. carinatus* (probably consisting of more than one species) being oviparous or viviparous depending on its locality – in North Africa and Turkey it is oviparous but in India and Pakistan it is viviparous. The African vipers belonging to the genus *Bitis* are all viviparous.

The pit vipers are found in North and South America, and in Asia. Asian species are variable, with *Trimeresurus* species being equally divided between viviparity and oviparity: terrestrial species tend to lay eggs while arboreal species are viviparous. The other large Asian genus is *Agkistrodon*, members of which are viviparous as far as is known. Two related genera, *Deinagkistrodon*

Calloselasma, which have only one ...ber each, are oviparous. The American ...ipers, including the rattlesnakes, are ...ominantly viviparous, but the Central ... South American bushmaster is ...arous. The reasons for this are unclear.

...ntal effort

...ntal effort is the term given to the ...unt of effort that parents put into pro- ...ng young. It covers every stage of ...oduction, including the amount of food ... is diverted into the production of sperm ...va, the amount of energy spent search- ...for a mate and in courtship, and the ...unt of time devoted to producing and ...ng young.

...rental effort in female snakes is easier ...easure than in many other groups of ...als because parental care of the young ...most non-existent: the few exceptions ...dealt with later in this section. Males put ...effort into the production of the sex cells ...m) than females, which produce rela- ...y large eggs. The major contribution to ...next generation, therefore, in terms of ...gy, comes from females. This can be ...idered a disadvantage to females, but ...g a male snake also has drawbacks.

...hereas every female in a population of ...es is almost bound to reproduce, at ... at some stage of its life, it seems likely ... some males never breed. Other males, ...gh, may father many offspring by mat- ...with many females each breeding sea- ... This is due to sexual selection, in which ...inant males, or males that are espe- ...y good at finding mates, get to mate ... more females than subordinate ones. ...inance, where it exists, is achieved ...ugh male to male combat, and appears ...e present in some boids, colubrids, ...ds and vipers, though not in all species ...nging to these families. Sexual selection ...in the other families of snakes has not ... established one way or the other.

...rental effort in males is difficult to ...sure. It would be necessary to look at ...amount of energy each male spends in ...ng and defending a mate, and in the ...unt of food it gives up during these ...ities. Searching for a mate may also ...e it more vulnerable to predation and, ...as already been mentioned, males that ... to range over a large area in order to ...females are more likely to come to the ...tion of predators than are females of ...ame species.

...male reproductive effort can be mea- ...ᵈ in part by measuring the proportion

of her body weight that each female contributes towards her batch of eggs or young. This is usually referred to as her 'relative clutch mass'. As female snakes grow, they have more resources to divert towards reproductive effort. They can use these extra resources in two ways: they can either produce more offspring, or each off-spring can be larger. This is another example of a trade-off, where the factors that need to be balanced are: is it better to produce a lot of small babies, or a few large ones?

Relative clutch mass among most snakes is somewhere around 20 per cent – a female snake that weighs 1 kg (2 lb) will produce a clutch of eggs or a litter of young weighing, on average, a total of 200 g (7 oz), for exam-ple. Females of some species, however, put more or less effort into their reproduction. Why should this be so?

Mode of reproduction plays a part: vivipa-rous snakes have, on average, a lower relative clutch mass than oviparous species. This suggests that the other costs of repro-duction (leaving aside weight) are higher in viviparous species, perhaps because they carry their young for a longer period of time and would therefore be more prone to predation.

Sea snakes, which are viviparous, have even lower relative clutch masses than other viviparous snakes, probably because their body is partially filled with an organ that reg-ulates their buoyancy, and so they have less room for developing embryos.

In general, small snakes have higher relative clutch masses than large ones. This is difficult to explain but may be related to life expectancy. Large snakes tend to live longer. Their reproductive effort in any one year must be weighed against their chances of surviving until the next year. If they put too much effort into reproducing, they may not survive. Small snakes, on the other hand, are more likely to die or to be killed before they get another chance to breed and so it may be in their interests to produce more young while they have the chance.

More young or bigger young?

This is another 'decision' that must be made. Given that a female has only a limited amount of energy to devote to reproduction, how should it be shared out. As she grows, she may produce more young, or the same number of bigger young, or a compromise – slightly more young, each of which is slightly bigger. In most species that have been studied, it seems that females tend to compromise.

Differences between species are much more complicated. Closely related species of about the same size may use different strate-gies: one will lay a large number of small eggs and the other a few large eggs. Dif-ferences may arise because of the feeding habits of the young. Where a species eats prey that is available in a range of sizes, such as frogs, it may be able to produce small young that have a good chance of surviving. It may pay the female to lay a lot of small eggs. If the available prey comes in large 'packages', such as mammals, young that are too small will not be able to find enough food and will all die. In this case the best strategy is to lay a few large eggs.

Sexual dimorphism

Just as male and female snakes behave differently, or rather, *because* they behave differently, these differences may be reflected in their appearances. Where males and females show differences in design, they are said to be sexually dimorphic.

Internal differences, which are not visible in the living animal, usually involve the reproductive organs (see below) and are referred to as primary sex characteristics. Secondary sex characteristics are those not directly concerned with the reproductive system, although some of them may also play a part in reproductive behaviour.

Snakes do not usually show the same degree of sexual dimorphism found in many other animals, such as lizards and birds, for instance. This is largely due to the lack of visual displays in snakes' interactions with one another. There are, however, various more subtle differences between the sexes, although these are not found generally across all species or families.

Differences in size

There are two factors that significantly affect the size of snakes. Females can produce more offspring if they are larger, whereas this is not an important factor in males, which do not carry eggs or young. But in species in which males fight one another, large males tend to be more successful than small ones. Males may still be smaller than females even in this scenario, however, because the benefits of being larger may be more important to females than males. Bearing these two points in mind, we would expect males to be relatively larger (compared to females) in those species that fight than in those species that do not fight.

By looking at comparative sizes of males and females within a species, it should be possible to pick out those species in which fighting takes place. This does seem to be generally true, despite some problems associated with how sizes are compared (because snakes grow throughout their lives). In some species that fight, males ultimately reach larger sizes than females – in rattle-snakes, Australian whipsnakes, *Demansia*, and in some populations of Australian tiger snakes, *Notechis scutatus*, for instance, even though they may start breeding when they are smaller. In species in which combat almost definitely does not take place, blind snakes, for instance, females are larger than males.

Differences in shape

Female snakes are often more heavy-bodied than males of the same species and similar size. This is apparent in many vipers, includ-ing pit vipers, and also in some boids, such as *Boa constrictor*. Greater girth is beneficial to females in allowing more room for devel-oping eggs and young. The relative length of the tails usually differs significantly between male and female snakes, with those of males being longer. This is due to the presence of the hemipenes in males, which must be accommodated in the base of the tail when retracted.

▲ The green water snake, *Nerodia cyclopion*, a species in which males do not combat and in which they are often noticeably smaller than females.

▼ The differences between male (below) and female (above) *Langaha nasuta* are plain to see, but the reason for their strange appendages is unknown.

Less easily explained is the fact females often have relatively larger h than males, or the shape of their h may differ. The differences have been especially in semi-aquatic natricine sn including *Nerodia* and *Thamnophis* North America and *Natrix tessellata* Turkey, but also occur in other species. difference may be apparent right from

ent of hatching or birth and in some
s it may be associated with differences
ey between the sexes of young snakes.

her differences in head shape involve
various ornamentations that some
es carry, as in the strange protuber-
s on the snouts of the Madagascan
es belonging to the genus *Langaha*,
h are more elaborate in females. Some
tree snakes, including *Ahaetulla picta*
Bothrops moojeni, have larger eyes
females, and, in at least two species
nging to the South American genus
todes*, males have longer tongues!

cobras belonging to the genus *Naja*,
ales of *Naja naja*, *N. samarensis* and *N.
a* have longer fangs than females. Two
ese species spit venom, but *N. naja* does
In another species, *N. philippinensis*,
ales have short orifices in their fangs,
eeping with species that spit, whereas
females have long ones; although the
es is known to spit, it is not known if
sexes do so.

inor differences are found in the body
s of some species, and these concern two
ps of scales. In some species, including
ral North American water snakes,
dia and garter snakes, *Thamnophis*,
s have small warty tubercles on the
. This may serve to stimulate the female
ng courtship, when the male rubs his
along the length of the female. In these
e species, but also in several others that
ot closely related, males have a group of
ily keeled scales in the region of their
. These may assist in helping the male to
te the vent of the female during mating
ey may help him to retain a better grip
ng copulation. Similar scales, but not so
lized, have been found in some species of
snakes, where their function is also
rtain.

boas and pythons, males have vestigial
s in the form of spurs on either side of
vent. These are used to stimulate the
le during courtship and, sometimes,
amage other males during combat.
ales may also have spurs, although
e are often smaller. In some species, or
ertain populations, spurs are lacking
gether in females. In the tropidophids,
es have spurs but they are completely
ing in females. Indeed, female *Ungali-
continentalis* and *U. panamensis* have
all traces of their hind limb girdles.

ration

rences between the coloration of males
females are not widespread among

snakes and, when they do occur, they tend
to be rather subtle. In several European
vipers, *Vipera*, males are more brightly
marked than females, usually as a result of
a lighter background colour. It has been
suggested recently (Shine and Madsen,
1994)[16] that the reason for this difference
lies in the fact that males move more rapidly
than females, especially in the spring when
they are defending females, and that under
these circumstances their markings may
help to fool predators by 'flickering' as the
snakes move. Females are more sedentary
and rely heavily on camouflage and so their
markings will have evolved in a different
way.

In some populations of the boomslang,
Dispholidus typhus, males are also more
brightly coloured than females, and show
great variation, being bright green, red or
pinkish, yellow, or even blue, sometimes
with black-edged scales or speckles, while
others are uniformly coloured. Females, on
the other hand, are usually plain brown or
olive. The banded rock rattlesnake, *Crotalus
lepidus klauberi*, shows dimorphism in some
areas, where males may have a greenish hue
but the females are grey. In other populations, both sexes are identically coloured. In
Bothrops asper, juvenile males have brightly
coloured tips to the tail whereas females do
not. Both sexes apparently use their tails to
lure prey but it is not known if the preferred
prey of both sexes is the same.

1. Aldridge, R. D. (1992), 'Oviductal anatomy and seasonal sperm storage in the southeastern crowned snake (*Tantilla coronatum*)', *Copeia*, 1992(4):1103–1106.
2. Montgomery, W. B. and Schuett, G. W. (1989), 'Autumnal mating with subsequent production of offspring in the rattlesnake *Sistrurus miliarius streckeri*', *Bull. Chi. Herp. Soc.*, 24(11):205–207.
3. Graves, B. M. and Duvall, D. (1993), 'Reproduction, rookery use and thermoregulation in free-ranging, pregnant prairie rattlesnakes, *Crotalus v. viridis*', *Journal of Herpetology*, 27(1):33–41.
4. Martin, B. E. (1976), 'A reproductive record for the New Mexican ridge-nosed rattlesnake (*Crotalus willardi obscurus*)', *Bulletin Maryland Herpetological Society*, 12(4):126–128.
5. Wallace. R. L. and Diller, L. V. (1990), 'Feeding ecology of the rattlesnake, *Crotalus viridis oreganus*, in northern Idaho', *Journal of Herpetology*, 24(3):246–253.
6. Butler, J. A. (1993), 'Seasonal reproduction in the African olive grass snake, *Psammophis phillipsi*', *Journal of Herpetology*, 27(2):144–148.
7. Powell, R., Maxey, S. A.. Parmerlee, J. S. and Smith, D. D. (1991), 'Notes on the reproductive biology of a montane population of *Antillophis parvifrons protenus* from the Dominican Republic', *Journal of Herpetology*, 25(1): 121–122.
8. Solorzano, A. and Cerdas, L. (1989), 'Reproductive biology and distribution of the terciopelo, *Bothrops asper*, in Costa Rica', *Herpetologica*, 45(4):444–450.
9. Lillywhite, H. B. (1985), 'Trailing movements and sexual behaviour in *Coluber constrictor*', *Journal of Herpetology*, 19(2):306–308.
10. Plummer, M. V. (1989), 'Observations on the nesting ecology of green snakes (*Opheodryas aestivus*)', *Herp. Review*, 20(4): 87–89.
11. Tu, M. C., Fong, S. C. and Lue, K. Y. (1990), 'Reproductive biology of the sea snake, *Laticauda semifasciata*, in Taiwan', *Journal of Herpetology*, 24(2):119–126.
12. Palmer, W. M. and Braswell, A. L. (1976), 'Communal egg-laying and hatchlings of the rough green snake, *Opheodryas aestivus*', *Journal of Herpetology*, 10(3): 257–259.
13. Burger, J. and Zappalorti, R. T. (1991), 'Nesting behaviour of pine snakes (*Pituophis m. melanoleucus*) in the New Jersey Pine Barrens', *Journal of Herpetology*, 25(2):152–160.
14. Riley, J., Stimson, A. F. and Winch, J. M. (1985), 'A review of squamata ovipositing in ant and termite nests', *Herp. Review*, 16(2):38–43.
15. Pedrez-Hidareda, G. and Smith, H. M. (1989), 'Termite nest incubation of the Mexican colubrid snake *Adelphicos quadrivirgatus*', *Herp. Review*, 20(1):5–6.
16. Shine, R and Madsen, T. (1994), 'Sexual dichromatism in snakes of the genus *Vipera*: a review and a new evolutionary hypothesis', *Journal of Herpetology*, 28(1):114–117.

8
Snakes
and Humans

People's interactions with snakes down through the ages form an interesting study. Much of it is within the realms of anthropology, however, and has only a limited place in a book about snakes. For this reason, only a very brief overview is given here.

◀ The corn snake, *Elaphe guttata guttata*, is deservedly among the most popular snakes in captivity, being attractive, docile and easy to breed.

SNAKE MYTHS AND SNAKE WORSHIP

Snakes have been objects of fascination, fear and worship in many cultures throughout the world – almost wherever they are found, in fact.

Snakes in ancient cultures

The earliest evidence of man's interest in snakes comes from cave paintings in southern Europe, some of which date from at least twenty to thirty thousand years ago. Additional scratchings and engravings have been found on fragments of bone and wood from the same era.

From more recent times, rock and cave paintings depicting snakes can be found in regions inhabited by tribal peoples whose life-styles have changed little until recently. These include bushman paintings in southern Africa and aboriginal paintings in many parts of Australia. Aborigines also decorated their own bodies in the form of stylized snakes in certain of their ceremonies.

Although little can be deduced about the motivation of prehistoric snake images, the stories behind the aboriginal paintings are well known because many of the painters still practise their art. Snakes play a number of different roles in the mythology of these people. Their importance as food is obviously relevant as is the regularity with which they appear from seemingly sterile habitats during rainy periods. The various rites and ceremonies associated with them may therefore serve to increase the fertility of snakes, thereby ensuring a good supply of food, or to ensure that the rains come. The rainbow serpents are among the most dramatic manifestations of snakes in their mythology. They live deep in permanent waterholes during the dry season but leave them and take to the skies, where they appear as rainbows, during the rainy season. The importance of such a custodian of natural water supplies is obvious when one considers the arid nature of the Australian interior, and the paintings of them are carefully restored at the approach of each rainy season.

The worship of snakes, as part of religious activities, is also widespread. It was common in Africa, where the python was singled out for special attention, and African slaves later carried snake worship to Haiti where it took the form of the voodoo cult, still apparently practised to the present day.

▲ The staff of Aesculapius, incorporating an entwined snake, is commonly used throughou world as a symbol of the medical profession.

▲ The aesculapian snake, *Elaphe longissima*, named for the Roman god Aesculapius.

▼ An Australian aboriginal painting, depicting a snake along with other animals and symbols.

In India the cobra has been widely worshipped since ancient times. Snake gods, in the form of Nagas and their wives, Naginis, are associated with everyday village life and may be good or bad depending on their mood; in former times, human sacrifices were made to them as a form of appeasement.

In China, the dragon takes the place of the Indian Nagas. Although it has legs, it owes it origin to snake worship and was also thought to have control of several natural phenomena such as rain making.

The ancient Egyptians are thought to have maintained 'asps' in their homes and temples. Judging from their painting and inscriptions, these were probably cobras, even though the modern day asp is a viper (*Vipera aspis*), which is not found in North Africa. As in many other cultures, the Egyptians associated snakes with rain, and therefore fertility. There are also associa-tions with the river Nile, which brou fertility, and therefore wealth, to their la A rearing cobra, with hood extended, the symbol of one of their goddesses, Ejo, a similar symbol was incorporated into headdress of the Pharaoh.

Snakes were also sacred to the Greeks, Romans and the Minoans. Many of t gods appeared as snakes or with th although Hercules, the Greek hero, famed as a slayer of serpents. The or serpent, Gaea, was defeated in a fight Apollo but its wisdom continued to be of through the oracle at Delphi, the 'nave the earth', while the generic name of sand boas, *Eryx*, commemorates a m spear, thrown on to the flanks of Mo Olympus, whereupon it promptly tur into a snake.

ere are many other legends and myths
erning snakes, and their associations
the gods, one of which has persisted
the present time. It concerns the wide-
d belief that snakes are immortal,
lly attributed to their habit of shed-
their skin periodically, looked upon
ncient times as a type of rebirth. For
reason, the Greek god Asklepios (later
porated into Roman mythology as
ulapius) is portrayed as a man with a
e as a staff. The emblem of two
ined snakes is still widely used as
emblem of the medical profession. The
es most often identified with Aescu-
s is the European colubrid *Elaphe*
ssima, which is commonly known as
Aesculapian snake. It has a disjunct
lation throughout parts of Europe
this is thought to be due to its having
introduced to sites of Roman baths and
in various parts of the Roman empire.
the New World, as in the Old, snakes
associated with rain. North American
ns held snakes in high esteem for this
n and in some of the more arid parts
orth America rain dances involved
se of living snakes, those of the Hopi
ns being the best documented because
were continued until very recently.
parading with the snakes, they were
sed into crevices in the ground in the
that they would carry the Indians'
ers to the rain gods. The snakes, then,
not worshipped as gods but acted as
engers. It is not hard to see how snakes
live in underground chambers, and
ge only when conditions are favour-
can be linked with the underworld
the forces of nature.

Central America the Aztecs and
ans decorated their temples and monu-
ts with gigantic carvings of stylized
es, often in gruesome attitudes. Although
ot known what part they played in their
re or religion it is most obvious that
s an important one. Furthermore, many
heir important deities were depicted
serpents entwined around them in
orm of cloaks, skirts or belts and some of
carry staffs in the shape of snakes.
e Christian religion may have done
e harm to the way in which we view
es than any other. The snake, being
bolic of so many heathen cults and
res, was an obvious scapegoat. It
me synonymous with evil, an attitude
ed by the episode in the Garden of
, and even today some communities,
cially in the Mediterranean region,

still regard snakes as fundamentally evil
and persecute them mercilessly, whether
venomous or harmless.

Legends and superstitions

Several of the ancient beliefs and prejudices
surrounding snakes live on into the twentieth century, often modified as 'old wives'
tales'. There are hundreds, if not thousands,
of these stories throughout the world, most
of them without any scientific basis whatsoever but they are none the less important
to the people whose daily lives often bring
them into contact with wild snakes.

Throughout the ages, humans have
assumed that other animals were placed on
earth because they were of some potential
use to them. The trick was to find out what
that use was. Snakes, with their potent

symbolic and actual properties, have been
thoroughly investigated by medicine men,
herbalists, quack doctors and bona fide
medical practitioners in almost every part of
the world.

Some traditional remedies call for various
parts of snakes' anatomy, including their
shed skins. Ailments that they are said
to cure include rheumatism, sore throats,
headaches and backaches. Snake skins
were sometimes used to ease childbirth and
snakes' gall bladders have also been used
for the same purpose. The flesh of snakes
has been used to improve the complexion,
while snake fat was thought to be a cure
for premature baldness. The Chinese ate
snake flesh for the prevention of tuberculosis
and sea snakes were thought to be effective
against malaria and epilepsy.

The snake festival of Cocullo

Dominic de Guzman, a Spaniard and
founder of the Dominican Order, lived
from about AD 1170 to 1221. In 1215
he travelled throughout the Abruzzese
Mountains in central Italy, preaching
to the heretical Albigenses, who
deviated from the Roman Catholic faith.
The Albigenses were represented by
snakes, to whose venom he was
supposedly immune; thus his snake
association.

In the village of Cocullo he is still
honoured with an annual procession,
in which his effigy, draped with snakes,
is paraded through the streets. The
festival of San Domenico, 'Il rito die
serpari', takes place early in May.
During the morning a mass is held
in his honour then, at midday, the
church doors are swung open and the
statue is carried out into the village
square. It is placed in front of the
church and local people approach the
statue and place live snakes around the
head and body, where they stay for the
duration of the ceremony. The species
used is the four-lined snake, *Elaphe
quatuorlineata*, a large and impressive
colubrid that is found in the region.
Each snake is marked with a spot of
paint on the top of its head.

The litter containing the statue is

then lifted and the procession begins.
The priest and the mayor of the village
walk ahead, followed by young girls
dressed in local costume. The litter is
carried by local men and is flanked by
policemen dressed in their ceremonial
finery and wearing cocked hats topped
with black and red feathers. The
procession wends its way round the
village, accompanied by local people
and tourists. Afterwards, the snakes
are released or sold to tourists.

CURRENT ATTITUDES

Rattlesnake oil, of course, was widely sold in travelling medicine shows in North America, mainly as a cure for backache and stiffness but also for use in cases of toothache, deafness, sties, ringworm and mosquito bite. Medicines made from various snake preparations have also been claimed effective against the black death, measles, smallpox and leprosy, among other diseases. The list is almost endless!

Snake venom has always been held in high regard by the medical profession and is credited with many special properties and its use in medicine is under current investigation in a number of fields. Some of the claims are obviously fanciful but dried Russell's viper venom acts as a blood coagulant and was used in cases of haemorrhage and haemophilia until recently. Cobra venom may act as a pain reliever under certain circumstances and its use also continued until recently.

Snake bite has always been a hazard to people living in areas where venomous species are common. Although their fears were mostly justified, there were, and still are in some parts, superstitions surrounding the power of poisonous snakes. According to some cultures, snakes are able to spit their venom for great distances and one mythological serpent, the basilisk, could apparently kill with a single glance from its fiery red eyes. Snakes were also thought to sting with their tails, a myth that may have arisen because a number of species have sharp pointed tails that they press into the skin if they are restrained. Several species, especially burrowing snakes, have blunt tails that could be mistaken for their heads, although none of them are venomous.

In order to protect against snake bite, spells and charms were widely used, many of them using parts of snakes, such as teeth and skin. Quite recently, ropes of hair were used in North America to encircle camps in the belief that snakes would not crawl over them. Plants such as the ash tree were also thought to repel snakes, as were the ashes and extracts of numerous plants. Even human saliva was thought to be effective.

Immunity to snake bite was claimed by a number of clans of native peoples and many acted as Shamans, to cure snake bite in others. Cleopatra was apparently attended by Shamans from two tribes in an attempt to save her life after her self-imposed asp bite. Many cures involve the use of parts of the culprit, such as wine in which the head of an asp has been pickled or a broth made from the snake. These cures were held in high regard in Europe until the eighteenth century. The most universally used cure was suction, no doubt as a result of the natural reaction of humans to suck any small injury. Suction can be beneficial, as snake venoms are relatively harmless when swallowed. Various devices were used to help draw out the venom, including porous stones, pieces of burnt bone and poultices made from a variety of generally disgusting natural products.

Cauterization has been widely used to prevent the effects of snake venom spreading, as have the applications of ligatures and, more drastic, summary amputation. As only a small proportion of snake bites are potentially lethal, one is left to ponder to what degree these mutilations were actually necessary.

More recently, alcohol was thought to counteract the effects of the venom and this proved to be a most popular cure, for obvious reasons. The patient was given enough to make him or her well and truly drunk and there are many stories of fictitious bites and prophylactic treatments. Only a few years ago, an Australian character, interviewed on television, maintained that a shot of whisky was the best cure for snake bite, adding that it was most effective if taken before the bite! As it happens, alcohol may increase the effects of a bite by speeding up the circulation, and the enormous doses recommended by some may kill the patient before the venom has had time to work.

Current attitudes towards snakes greatly. While there is greater awarene the western world of the value of wildli a whole, there is still an underlying dist of snakes. This obviously stems in from the fact that many species are cap of causing rapid and spectacular death is also fuelled by an irrational revulsion

Prejudices

Snakes rank higher than spiders, c roaches or rats as the most disliked typ animal. The majority of people who c to be afraid of them will never have se wild snake. Even less will they have l bitten by one. Events in the Garden of l have undoubtedly done a great dea engender this attitude. Many popular ings, such as 'snake in the grass' 'speaking with a forked tongue', perpet the belief that snakes are dangerous, ev just 'not nice'.

A healthy respect for snakes is no thing, especially where venomous spe are known to occur, but there is little rea to loathe them nor is there any ex to persecute them. Interestingly, yc children are rarely afraid of snakes and perfectly happy to handle them; as grow, their dislike and mistrust of the encouraged, mostly by their parents.

Snake bite

Snake bite is a serious problem in only a parts of the world, mainly rural tro areas. Several factors contribute to Firstly, venomous snakes are more com in tropical areas. In addition, many r workers in tropical countries make th selves more vulnerable by wearing adequate or no protection on their fee lower legs. Finally, many of these coun have poor medical facilities and people r in any case, be reluctant to use th preferring instead to rely on traditi 'cures'.

The carpet, or saw-scaled, viper, *I carinata*, is usually regarded as the wo most dangerous species. This is due to wide distribution over much of Africa Asia, where it is often extremely commo relies heavily on camouflage, making i too easy to be trodden on, and has aggressive nature, never hesitating to b it feels it is in danger. Other danger species include Russell's viper, *V russelli*, in Asia, the puff adder, *Bitis arie* in Africa, the Malayan pit viper, *C selasma rhodostoma*, in Asia and the fe lance, *Bothrops atrox*, in Central and Sc

erica. It is notable that many of the more
orious venomous snakes – the mambas,
ras, taipans, rattlesnakes and the bush-
ter – are absent from this list; although
se species may cause a substantial
ber of fatalities, they are not regarded
ignificant as is popularly believed. This
 be because they are relatively rare (the
hmaster and the taipans, for example) or
use they live in regions where people
 well protected (the rattlesnakes and,
in, the taipans). Other venomous species
shy and reluctant to bite except under
eme provocation and this applies to
ny of the less dangerous species as well,
uding the European vipers, many small
lesnakes, coral snakes and cobras.
he effects of snake bite on man vary
rding to the species. Many bites are
l and their effects are insignificant, any
ptoms being slight and clearing up with-
treatment after a few days or hours. On
other hand, serious bites often produce
most alarming symptoms. These may
ocalized, as in bites from species that
luce haemotoxic venom (mainly vipers
back-fanged colubrids), or systemic, as
in bites from species that produce neurotoxic venom (mainly cobras).

Bites from haemotoxic species produce
local pain that may be immediate and severe.
Swelling and discoloration often follows
within a few minutes and may spread up the
limbs and on to the trunk. Internal haemorrhage is caused through the breakdown of
blood vessels and may be exacerbated by
damage to the clotting agents in the blood.
In other cases, clotting is caused, leading
to thrombosis. In extreme cases, irreversible
tissue damage may occur, leading to gan-
grene or even death. Death usually results
from damage to internal organs or low blood
pressure.

Bites from neurotoxic species produce
little or no local effects. Muscles become
weak, leading to drooping eyelids in the early
stages. Paralysis follows and breathing may
become difficult. In extreme cases, death
can result from asphyxiation. In serious
cases, where the bite penetrates a major
blood vessel, death can occur in a matter of
minutes.

Sea snakes rarely bite people, and their
venom apparatus is not adapted for giving a
deep bite. Fishermen may be vulnerable in
some parts of the world as the snakes often
become entangled in nets. They are usually
reluctant to bite, however, and are often
handled casually. Their venom affects the
muscles and symptoms include swelling,
muscular pain and stiffness. The muscle cells
are destroyed, releasing potassium ions into
the system. This may lead to death through
cardiac arrest. On other occasions, death is
caused by respiratory failure due to paralysis
of the muscles responsible for breathing.

The rear-fanged colubrids are not normally regarded as especially dangerous.
At least three species have caused fatalities,
however: these are the boomslang, *Dispholidus typus*, the twig snake, *Thelotornis
capensis*, and the Asian tiger snake or yamak-
agashi, *Rhabdophis tigrinus*. These species
produce symptoms similar to those of vipers,
with local tissue damage, bleeding, bruising
and reduced blood clotting. Death from
boomslang bite usually occurs within 24
hours due to respiratory failure but in the
case of the other two species it may occur
several days, or even weeks, after the bite,
due to kidney failure.

nake bite

ake bite statistics are notoriously
ficult to obtain. In many countries,
here medical facilities in rural areas
e primitive or non-existent, many
ses must go unrecorded. Confusion
ay also exist over the species that was
sponsible for the bite.

A fairly recent estimate gives a figure
about 25,000 deaths per year from
ake bite. More than half of these are
ought to occur in India and Burma,
here rural populations are dense,
edical facilities are often less than
eal and several potentially lethal
ecies are fairly common. It is thought
at Russell's viper is responsible for at
st 10,000 bites and 1,000 deaths in
irma alone. Other significant species
the region include the carpet viper
d several species of pit vipers,
bras and kraits.

Figures for South America are
tremely difficult to estimate due to
e high number of rural Indians who
ve little contact with the outside
world. Among the Waorani tribe of
Ecuador, it has been estimated that
almost 5 per cent of deaths are caused
by snake bite, and that nearly 80 per
cent of the population is bitten at least
once during their lifetime. A variety of
species will be responsible for these
statistics, with terrestrial pit vipers
making up by far the largest
proportion. In other parts of South
America about 0.5 per cent of the
population is bitten per year, but only a
small fraction of these are fatal. Figures
for parts of tropical Africa point to a
similar incidence.

Snake bite fatalities in westernized
societies are far less frequent. Snakes
have all but disappeared from many
urban and agricultural areas, the
population is usually better informed
and protected, and medical facilities are
of a high standard. In Australia, for
example, which has the distinction of
having more venomous species than
non-venomous ones, deaths number
less than 10 per year on average while
in North America, with a fair
sprinkling of potentially lethal rattlesnakes, about 15 people become
victims each year. A similar figure is
often quoted for the whole of Europe,
where most of the more dangerous
species of vipers live in the south and
east. Of these deaths, a number can be
put down to casual handling by snake
keepers and unnecessary heroics.

Western diamondback rattlesnake, *Crotalus
atrox,* **the species responsible for most of the
serious snake-bites in North America.**

Treating snake bite

The most effective treatment for serious snake bite involves the use of antivenom. The first stage in manufacturing antivenom is obtaining pure venom by 'milking' the snake: its fangs are hooked over the lip of a glass vessel and its venom gland massaged until the venom is ejected through the apertures in the fangs. After processing, small quantities of the venom are injected into animals, usually horses but sometimes cattle, sheep or goats, at regular intervals until they have built up an immunity. Blood taken from the animal is then separated so that the serum containing the antibodies can be isolated and used in the treatment of snake bite.

Antivenom is made in laboratories throughout the world, some of which produce antivenom against common local species and some of which produce a range of antivenoms for sale and distribution in other countries or for use in zoos, etc. Most antivenoms are expensive, due to the difficulty involved in producing it, ranging in price from US$25 to US$1,000 per ampoule, depending on species. In severe bites, the use of several ampoules may be necessary. They also have limited shelf-lives, often only two or three years: in countries where snake bite is frequent, such as Papua New Guinea, the purchase of antivenom can absorb a significant proportion of the annual health budget.

Antivenoms may be polyvalent (i.e. effective against a range of species) or specific (i.e. effective against a single species or a group of closely related species). Polyvalent antivenoms are useful in regions where there is a number of venomous snakes, and where the species involved cannot always be positively identified. The range of species against which they are effective may be limited to snakes that produce broadly similar venoms, such as polyvalent *Crotalus* (which is

effective against bites of a number of dangerous rattlesnake species), polyvalent coral snake (effective against bites from a number of *Micrurus* species) and so on. Others contain antivenom of two or more species; they are mixtures that are designed to target the most dangerous species from the same region, regardless of which type of venom they produce, e.g. Indian cobra and Russell's viper (produced by Central Hills Research, Kasauli, India), or Indian cobra, Indian krait, Russell's viper and carpet viper (produced by the Serum Institute of India).

Specific antivenoms, e.g. anti-bushmaster, black snake antivenom, mamushi antivenom (against *Agkistrodon halys*), etc., are intended to be used where the species has been positively identified, although they may also be effective against bites from similar snakes.

Because they can have harmful side effects, however, antivenoms should only be used by qualified medical staff. In particular, some people are allergic to horse serum, and the anaphylactic shock it produces can be even more dangerous than the bite. Also, since the venom must be given intravenously, there are the additional dangers of infection and injury associated with inexpert administration.

In practice, antivenom is not normally necessary except in cases of a serious bite. In an information sheet produced by the Liverpool School of Tropical Medicine, 30 per cent of viper bites, 50 per cent of elapid bites and 80 per cent of sea snake bites are reckoned to produce no clinical symptoms whatsoever: the snakes often produce 'dry' bites. Local symptoms are produced as a result of 80 per cent of effective viper bites and 50 per cent of bites from spitting cobras; systemic symptoms, including bleeding gums, shock, respiratory and cardiac problems, occur in 40 per cent of viper bites, 20 per cent of elapid bites and 20 per cent of sea snake bites. Not all the bites that produce symptoms are lethal of course, and natural recovery is likely in the majority of cases. The death rate in the absence of treatment, is thought to be somewhere in the region of 1 per cent for viper bites, 5 per cent for elapid bites and 10 per cent for sea snake bites. These are generalized estimates and in certain parts of the world, where some of the more dangerous species are found, the death rate is likely to be higher than average.

In the event of snake bite, medical help should always be sought. First-aid treatment should be confined to reassuring the patient and keeping him or her calm. Avoid movement, especially of the bitten limb, so that the venom is not carried around the body any faster than is necessary. Tourniquets are no longer recommended, nor is opening the wound or sucking out the venom. The most effective interim measure is to apply a firm crepe or elasticated bandage to the entire limb. This will slow down the circulation of lymph and delay symptoms for several hours, by which time expert medical attention should be possible. Given proper care, full recovery is highly likely.

...es as a whole have little commercial ...e compared with other groups of ...als. The various ways in which they are ...oited tend to be limited to specific regions ...a few species.

...es are eaten, though not as much as ...ormer times, by a number of native ...les. They are easily caught and killed ...although they often yield only a small ...unt of flesh, their occurrence in areas ...re other animals are scarce or hard ...atch must have made them an impor- ...addition to the diet in times of need. ...ralian aborigines, for instance, eat all ...ties of snakes and relish pythons in ...icular. In parts of tropical Africa the ...python is held in high esteem and ...ondas and common boas are eaten in ...h America.

...Asia, snakes are widely eaten, even ...he urban population. Sea snakes are ...cially prized and huge numbers are ...umed. A wide range of other species is ...n, however, including cobras and kraits. ...long Kong, snakes' gall bladders are ...ght to be a tonic and are often removed ...the living snake and swallowed whole. ...r parts of snakes are sold and eaten as ...odisiacs and cures for various ailments. ...e-eating in China is commonplace in ...Canton region where certain species, ...cially the python, fetch very high prices ...arkets.

...North America rattlesnakes were eaten ...arly settlers but only in times of hard- ...– prejudice came to the snake's aid in ...instance. On the other hand, tinned ...esnake is still available, often originat- ...from animals killed during rattlesnake ...d-ups.

...es in entertainment

...entertainment value of snakes has not ...overlooked. Revulsion often goes hand ...and with fascination and snake charm- ...snake dancers and side-shows play on ...quirk of human nature.

...ake charmers are found in North ...ca, the Middle East and India. Their ...ns are thought to go back to ancient ...tian times, where power over snakes ...regarded as a divine gift. The mystique ...ounding snake charming can be put ...n to an intimate knowledge of snake ...viour. Accomplished charmers use ...ct' highly venomous species and ...accidents are not unheard of. Less ...ipled performers remove the fangs of

venomous species, sew up their mouths, milk the venom regularly or use non-venomous species. The snakes most used by snake charmers are, of course, the cobras, whose hooded stance makes them instantly recognizable for what they are. Where it occurs, the king cobra is the most favoured species. Other species are used, however, including pythons and vipers.

Other snake shows include exotic dancers and various types of cabaret act in which snakes figure. Large pythons are the obvious choice for these performers as they are spectacular and quite easily handled. The American snake side-shows, previously to

be seen at roadside petrol stations and restaurants, are less of an attraction than they used to be.

A more specific case is that of the snake temple in Penang, Malaysia, where pit vipers, *Tropidolaemus wagleri*, are draped around ornaments throughout the temple and are used as 'props' with which tourists may be photographed for a fee. The snakes are normally sluggish during the day and may also be stupefied by the atmosphere inside the temple. These snakes are not maintained in a healthy state and casualties must be continually replaced with fresh stock taken from the wild.

Rattlesnake round-ups

Rattlesnake round-ups, or rattlesnake 'bees' as they used to be known, have a history dating back to at least 1680, when men were employed at two shillings a day to kill rattlesnakes in Massachusetts. This programme of extermination developed until, by 1740, a day was set aside each year for a general snake hunt, during which men would gather at rattlesnake dens to kill as many of the snakes as possible. These early rattlesnake hunts were carried out with the purpose of eliminating rattlesnakes in areas where settlers were attempting to make their land safe for themselves, their children and their livestock.

As communities grew, the rattlesnake hunts became progressively more competitive, with prizes awarded to the participants who killed the greatest number of snakes; one account, of a hunt in Iowa which took place in 1849, describes how two men killed 90 rattlesnakes each in one hour and a half, and the total killed in the year was 3,750.

Rattlesnake round-ups became popular 'sport' in many areas, including those where rattlesnakes presented little or no threat to human life or livestock. The hunt developed into a carnival, where local spectators would take picnics along to watch the proceedings. Civic authorities and charities often sponsored the events

to raise money and to provide entertainment; they included exhibitions of rattlesnake handling, after which the snakes were killed and the skins and flesh sold.

Incredibly rattlesnake round-ups are still carried out in several states, the most notorious being that of Sweetwater, Texas, where 70,773 snakes were reported to have been killed over a 16-year period. Other figures include 751 timber rattlesnakes, *Crotalus h. horridus*, killed over a nine-year period at the Morris snake hunt, Pennsylvania and 3,205 in 17 years at the Keystone Reptile Club, also in Pennsylvania. Other States where rattlesnake round-ups still take place are Alabama, Florida, Georgia and Oklahoma.

In the early years, rattlesnakes were caught in the open and round-ups were timed to coincide with the most productive time, just after they had emerged from the hibernation dens but before they had dispersed. Later developments included dynamiting the dens. At present, a common method is to pour gasoline into the dens and into gopher tortoise burrows, with the aim of driving out the snakes; this method is particularly insidious because the rattlesnakes often remain in the burrows and die, along with harmless snakes and other wildlife that may be sheltering there.

Where do all the snakes go?

Exploitation and persecution of snakes takes many forms. Often, it is difficult or impossible to quantify the effects on their populations – for instance, the numbers of snakes killed through habitat destruction, consumed as food or medicine, out of prejudice and on the roads are incalculable. When snakes enter commercial trade, however, we have some measure of numbers involved, through the licensing system operated by CITES. Even these figures need to be viewed with caution, however, because certain species are exempt from CITES control and some countries are not party to CITES. Furthermore, the movement of snakes and snake products around the world are difficult to keep track of and, whereas some items may not be counted at all, others are counted more than once. Then again, a number of snakeskin products may be made from a single skin.

In Britain, trade in snakes is controlled by the Department of the Environment. Since the relaxation of licensing regulations in 1993 (due to the free trade agreement within the European Community) these figures are less complete. The figures for previous years, however, may be considered useful indicators of the extent of trade, and the uses to which snakes and snake products are put.

They show that in 1992 the total imports of snakes, snake skin and snake products totalled almost 350,000 items. Of these, about 230,000 were imported as skins, 112,000 were imported as products (mostly shoes, boots and handbags) and the remaining 3,500 or so were imported live, presumably for the pet trade and for exhibit in zoos, and use in laboratories.

Of this total, the greatest numbers consisted of Asian species, including

▶ An Asian rat snake, *Ptyas mucosus*, a species that is heavily exploited in the skin trade.

Ptyas mucosus, which accounted for roughly 133,500, of which most (125,000) were imported as skins, *Python reticulatus* (about 64,500 of which over 58,000 were skins), *Elaphe carinata* (53,500 of which over 48,000 were snakeskin products) and *Zaochys dhumades* (nearly 42,000 of which over 27,500 were snakeskin products). In addition, almost 16,500 skins of the Java file snake, *Acrochordus javanicus* were imported and there were nearly 38,000 importations of other species, as snakeskin products (22,000), skins (12,000) or alive (3,500). The 'other species' comprised a wide range of snakes, some of which were imported in small numbers (often one or two) and some of which were bred in captivity.

During the same period, nearly 40,000 skins or snakeskin products were re-exported to other parts of the world.

As may be expected from the species concerned, the main exporting countries were Asian, especially Indonesia, Hong Kong and Singapore. Many of the skins and products exported from the latter two countries originated in China.

From figures such as these, bearing in mind that they represent trade passing through only one country, it is difficult to see how snake populations can continue to sustain trade of this magnitude.

Snakes as pets

The trade in living snakes destined for pet trade is growing. Tens, if not hundr of thousands of snakes change hands e year for the enjoyment of amateur enth asts. Smaller, but significant, numbers collected for display in zoos and snake pa Fortunately, the trend is moving away trade in wild-caught specimens tow captive-bred ones. Several commercial br ing operations have been set up in N America and Europe to supply the dem producing many thousands of yo snakes each year. Countless more part-breeders produce varying quantities supplement these. There is still a trad wild snakes, however, either because tain species are not easily bred in suffic quantities or because the cost of produ them often exceeds the paltry amounts which they can be purchased from na collectors.

Regulation of the trade in wild anima controlled by the Convention on Inte tional Trade in Endangered Species of Fauna and Flora (CITES), which came force on 1 July 1975. Member coun issue permits for the import and expo snakes, among other animals, only w they feel that trade is not likely to enda the survival of that species. Several snakes are subject to severe restriction CITES and the numbers of many others carefully monitored.

Overall, collecting for the pet trade pr bly has little serious effect on the populat of most species, although there has little or no research into wild populat that are regularly 'harvested' in this Desirable species are obviously at more than others although, again, many of t are widely bred in captivity. Accurate n bers reflecting the trade in wild snakes very difficult to obtain. Since the settin of CITES, data have become more e obtainable.

Snake skins

The colours and patterns of snake skin well as their curiosity value, have creat demand for them in the fashion indu Figures are even harder to estimate those pertaining to the trade in live sn Certain species are more useful than ot The main markets for these products North America, Europe and Japan the species mostly exploited are two o large pythons, *Python reticulatus* an *molurus*, two species of anacondas and common boa. These species alone repre

...akeskin products on sale in Madagascar.

...industry generating several million ...rs annually in the United States. Other ...ies, such as the file snakes, *Acrochordus*, ...the Indian rat snake, *Ptyas mucosus*, ...e been equally heavily exploited. The ...r species has shown a marked decline in ...ral areas where they were formerly ...mon. Trade figures measure exports of ...ies such as this in pounds (kilograms), ...er than individual numbers. Recently, ...e countries, including India and Sri ...ka, have become concerned about the ...ts of the skin trade and have banned ...rtations.

...kes in research

...scientific community must take respon- ...ity for the exploitation of snakes in the ... Museums and universities through- ...the Western world are often crammed ...preserved specimens, including many ...have never been properly studied or ...classified. Nineteenth-century zoo- ...ts collected huge numbers of animals ...shipment back to their sponsors in ...ope and North America, often without ...rd to the effects on local populations ...sometimes without the collection data ...would have made them more useful to ...re workers. Taxonomists and anatomists ...d to co-operate with one another and ...nany collections were duplicated un- ...ssarily. Even quite recently, published ...rs have reported the killing of large ...bers of individuals for the sake of ...arch, sometimes to confirm facts that ...already well known, such as the ...of various species. More responsible ...archers, however, have used the store of ...erved material already in collections ...ave developed methods of research that ...ot involve killing the subjects.

Snakes may become rare or endangered as a result of several factors. Several of these are listed above under the heading of exploitation. Other threats include habitat destruction, far and away the most serious, and pollution, either killing the snakes directly or indirectly, by affecting their food supply.

Most biologists would agree that many species of snakes are in need of protection but, where the general public is concerned, snake conservation has a low priority. This is largely due to prejudice and a 'what use are they' factor. Where species are afforded some degree of protection, it is usually through chance – they happen to live in a region where other, more appealing species are found and become protected incidentally, along with their habitat. In National Parks and National Monuments, for instance, all species of plants and animals are protected and there are many such areas, especially in North America and Europe, and also, increasingly, in other parts of the world.

Local protection

Laws and regulations designed to protect snakes are rarely specific, although numerous species are technically protected in Europe and North America. These laws are often designed to prevent collectors from taking certain species identified as rare or endangered, although habitat destruction and wanton slaughter on the roads, for example, still take place, largely unhindered. Token protection is given, for instance, to all Australian species, which may not be legally exported from the country, and similar restrictions apply to a number of countries in other parts of the world. Restrictions of this kind do little to protect snakes, however, because collection for the pet trade is insignificant, in most cases, compared with other causes of decline.

Specific protection *per se* is afforded to a few species, as opposed to protection acquired through blanket restrictions on all wildlife in a country or region. The albino rat snakes, *Elaphe climacophora*, living in the city of Iwakumi, Yamaguchi Prefecture, Japan, are protected as a national monument. In China, Pallas' pit vipers are protected on Snake Island, 40 km (25 miles) south of Lushun on the Liaoning peninsula. These snakes occur in high densities, with a total population of about 13,000 on the small island. The island has been declared a nature protection zone and measures have been taken to safeguard the snakes.

A notable U-turn was taken by the Greek government who, in 1977, protected the endemic viper *Macrovipera schweizeri* (formerly regarded as *Vipera lebetina schweizeri*) on Milos and a few neighbouring islands in the Cyclades group, having previously placed a bounty of 10 drachma on each snake.

Three snakes are federally protected in the United States. These are the San Francisco garter snake, *Thamnophis sirtalis tetrataenia*, the eastern indigo snake, *Drymarchon corais couperi* and the New Mexico ridge-nosed rattlesnake, *Crotalus willardi obscurus*. Many other species are protected in certain parts of their range. Similarly in Europe, species that are common elsewhere may be protected in certain countries where they are rare, often because they include the edge of the species' range.

International protection

The International Union for the Conservation of Nature and Natural Resources (IUCN) lists five full species and a further subspecies, the San Francisco garter snake, as endangered. These comprise three boids (one of which is probably extinct), one colubrid, a cobra and a viper. A further five species are listed as vulnerable. This gives absolutely no indication of the scale of the problem, however. Snakes are becoming rare in many of the places where they were formerly common. Other snakes have been exterminated, some before they have been scientifically described. Three species are thought to have become extinct on the island of Mauritius in the last hundred years, for example, although one of these is still found (just) on Round Island.

▼ The San Francisco garter snake, *Thamnophis sirtalis tetrataenia*, is an endangered subspecies that is federally protected in the United States and listed on Appendix 1 of CITES.

Dodd (1987)[1] identifies a total of 186 species as in need of conservation. Some of these may not be rare, but are rarely collected owing either to their secretive natures or a remote and little-studied distribution. Others may always have been naturally scarce and are destined to remain so. There are undoubtedly many other endangered species not listed, however, which would more than compensate for these.

Conservation of snakes could take place through several pathways. Prohibiting commercial collecting is an obvious method and may help to stem the flood of certain species that reach the pet trade in huge numbers. Collection for the skin trade is another area that could be similarly controlled. Regulations such as these are in force already, although they probably do not go far enough. Even with tighter restrictions, however, they can only protect individual snakes from individual collectors. Habitat protection is far more effective and logical. This, in effect, means the setting up of reserves where rare species are known to live. The reserves must be large enough to be effective although, in the short term, even small reserves may sustain some populations.

Captive breeding

Many species of snakes are bred in large numbers in captivity. The purpose of this is often to make the species available to other snake keepers and, while it may reduce the drain on natural populations, it does little to conserve species in the true sense of the word. Captive breeding programmes may be useful where certain species' habitats are seriously degraded or have disappeared entirely. There should, however, be ultimate goal of restoring the species t natural habitat at some time in the fu and, if this is to be achieved, its ger integrity should be carefully managed crosses between subspecies, or even betw animals from different populations, sh be avoided.

There is little evidence so far reintroductions have been a significant cess in preserving snakes. The African python, *Python sebae*, has apparently successfully reintroduced to the East (region of South Africa, where it had extinct since 1927. This impressive sr is considered useful by farmers becau feeds largely on cane rats, a pest species. eastern indigo snake, *Drymarchon c couperi*, has been reintroduced into par the south-eastern United States by 'l

Death on the roads

In many parts of the world snakes suffer greatly at the hands of motorists: their elongated bodies make them easy targets, whether intentional or accidental, and they are relatively slow moving. In addition, many linger on the warm tarmac surfaces during their nocturnal wanderings. The corpses of dead snakes often litter roads passing through good habitat. Drivers frequently go out of their way to hit snakes, sometimes swerving on to the shoulder or even across to the wrong side of the road; several accidents have been caused in the process. Other studies have shown that drivers will often stop and reverse over snakes, sometimes several times, in order to make sure they are dead.

Two recent studies have highlighted the problem. Bush, Browne-Cooper and Maryan counted dead snakes along sections of the Great Northern Highway and the North West Coastal Highway, Western Australia (*Herpetofauna* 21(2):23–24). In several places, the road passes through small reserves, intended to provide a haven for flora and fauna that would otherwise be eliminated due to increased agricultural activities in the region. In under 9,000 km (5,600 miles) of driving they found a total of 396 dead reptiles, of which 109 were snakes, belonging to 12 species (four species of pythons and eight species of elapids).

In a separate study, Philip Rosen and Charles Lowe surveyed US Highways

▼ A rare Milos viper, *Macrovipera schweizeri*, crushed by traffic.

85 and 86, which pass through the Organ Pipe Cactus National Monument, in southern Arizona (*Biological Conservation* 68:143–148). This area is well known for its rich herpetofauna, including one species and one subspecies of snake that are not found elsewhere in the United States (*Chionactis palarostris* and *Lichanura trivirgata trivirgata*). Several other rare species, such as the saddled leaf-nosed snake, *Phyllorhynchus browni*, also have their strongholds in the region. In 15,585 km (9,740 mile of driving they recorded 368 snakes belonging to 20 species on the road: over two-thirds were dead.

Allowing for the number of snakes that were overlooked, especially smal species, and those taken away by scavenging animals before they could be recorded, it is not difficult to see that, over an extended period of time, heavily used roads throughout the world must account for many hundreds of thousands of snakes annually Furthermore, roads often cross reserv and other protected areas, as in the tv studies above, creating a conflict of interests between road users and wildlife.

The Aruba Island rattlesnake, *Crotalus* *olor*, is the subject of a captive breeding **ramme** with the eventual aim of repopulating **sland** where it has been almost exterminated.

ting' juveniles, that is by raising them in tivity until they are of a less vulnerable , a technique pioneered by sea turtle servationists. At the present time it is too early to say whether this has been cessful.

imited success has also been achieved 1 the Aruba Island rattlesnake, *Crotalus* *olor*. This species is the subject of pecies survival plan operated by the erican Association of Zoological Parks Aquariums (AAZPA) in which several itutions co-operate in planning effective ding programmes to increase numbers reatened species. The only other snake resent involved in these programmes is neril's boa, *Acrantophis dumerili*, from agascar, although stud books are also g compiled for other species, including Madagascan ground boa, *Acrantophis* *gascariensis*, the Louisiana gopher snake, *ophis melanoleucus ruthveni* (of which about 20 individuals have ever been d), the king cobra, *Ophiophagus hannah*, the bushmaster, *Lachesis muta*. ture projects that are being considered ide breeding programmes for the annu- boa, *Corallus annulatus*, the Madagascan

tree boa, *Sanzinia madagascariensis*, and the San Francisco garter snake, *Thamnophis sirtalis tetrataenia*. All these species breed readily in captivity. Plans to improve their chances of survival through captive breeding must concentrate on breeding programmes that avoid inbreeding, and the possibilities of eventual reintroduction.

A number of species come from habitats that are so severely damaged that re-introduction is unlikely to be possible in the foreseeable future. Foremost among these is the Round Island boa, which is bred by the Jersey Wildlife Preservation Trust.

Education

Perhaps the most effective means of conserving snakes, at least in the long term, is education. A predominantly urban population is unlikely to seriously consider setting aside large areas of land for snakes while current attitudes and prejudices prevail. In this respect, zoos and snake parks have an important role to play and there has been a noticeable change in attitudes towards this aim in recent years. Amateur herpetological societies also have a contribution to make, through putting on responsible demonstrations and displays to the general public and, in particular, by encouraging young members. The British Herpetological Society, for example, formed the Young Herpetologists Club in 1980, with its own education officer. Its purpose is to encourage an interest in reptiles among young people and involve them in practical conservation projects.

▼ Dumeril's boa, *Acrantophis dumerili*, an endangered species from Madagascar, which is widely bred in zoological institutes and private collections.

STUDYING SNAKES

The study of snakes is a branch of the science of herpetology. The term comes from two Greek words, *herpeton*, meaning crawling thing and *logos*, meaning knowledge or reason. Herpetology, then, is the study of crawling things, although its current meaning has become narrower, the study of reptiles and amphibians.

The history of herpetology

In 1989 the Society for the Study of Amphibians and Reptiles published *Contributions to the History of Herpetology*, edited by Kraig Adler.[2] This book is essential reading for anyone interested in a detailed account of the main players in herpetological research or in classic herpetological literature. Much of the following information has been summarized from this publication.

Snakes have been seriously studied for several centuries. The earliest studies, such as those by Aristotle, were more concerned with classifying animals, and snakes were placed within the reptiles by him. In 1587 Gessner's *Serpentium Natura*, an account of snakes and scorpions, was published posthumously. The Italian Francesco Redi was the first to establish the nature of viper venom through experiments performed in the 1660s. Several other books included snakes in the late seventeenth and early eighteenth centuries, many of them crossing the boundaries between fact and fiction and often written from a herbalist's point of view.

Carl Linnaeus, one of the most famous names in the study of biology, published various editions of his *Systema Natura* from 1735 to 1766, in which the reptiles are classified within the order 'Amphibia', along with the cartilaginous fish. Linnaeus's most important contribution, however, was in his development of the binomial system by which all plants and animals are now named, often referred to as the Linnaean system. Linnaeus described many species of snakes, including the common boa, anaconda and several other large South American snakes, and established the genus *Coluber*. His name for the common boa, *Boa constrictor*, still stands, although many of his other species have since been reclassified.

With the discovery of new worlds and the travels of explorer–naturalists over the next century, numerous new species were discovered and described and Linnaeus's original classification began to become chaotic. This was corrected by the Frenchman Constant Duméril when he published his *Erpétologie Générale ou Histoire Naturelle Complète des Reptiles* between 1834 and 1854. In this work he organized the genera of reptiles into natural groups and described 1,393 species, of which many are illustrated. His work was continued after his death by his son, who succeeded him at the Natural History Museum of Paris.

There was now an explosion of literature on reptiles, including snakes, with new species being added at an ever increasing rate. Great herpetologists of the time included John Edwards Holbrook, Louis Agassiz, Spenser Fullerton Baird and Edward Drinker Cope in North America, and John Edward Gray, Thomas Bell and George A. Boulenger in England. Some of these men were amazingly prolific writers. Cope, for instance, published almost 1,400 titles, most of them on fossil reptiles and amphibians, but many on new species from North America and Mexico. As well as naming and describing new species, he also studied the anatomy of reptiles, establishing some of the principles that are used in snake classification today, such as the arrangement of the lungs and the anatomy of snake hemipenes. In Europe, Boulenger published a series of catalogues of reptiles and amphibians, a monumental task in which 8,469 species are covered. The snakes were dealt with in three volumes published between 1893 and 1896.

Alexander Strauch was the first serious Russian herpetologist and the rich herpetofauna of Australia was first thoroughly studied by Gerard Krefft, who was born in Germany and later emigrated, first to the United States, and then to Australia. His *Snakes of Australia* was first published in 1869 and reprinted as recently as 1984. Snakes of other countries were often studied by ex-patriots stationed abroad. Foremost among these was Frank Wall, an English medical officer who lived in various parts of India, Burma and Sri Lanka. He published several important articles in the *Journal of the Bombay Natural History Society* and wrote a number of books, including *The Poisonous Snakes of our British Indian Dominions* in 1907 and *Ophidia Tapronica or the Snakes of Ceylon* in 1921. This work is characterized by accurate and astute observations of the natural history of the species he describes, making it as useful today as it was when first written.

Most of the early books on snakes are scientific treatises, intended for serious students of the subject and often written in styles that the layperson would have difficulty in understanding. From the turn of the nineteenth century, however, more popular books on snakes began to app of interest to the amateur naturalist the general public. This tradition be in North America, with books such as *Reptile Book* in 1907 (later revised reissued in 1936 as *The Reptiles of N America*) and *Snakes of the World* in 19 both by Raymond L. Ditmars, Assist Curator of reptiles at the Bronx Zoo. Europe, George Boulenger found time write *The Snakes of Europe*, a pop account of European snakes, in 1913.

Books such as these popularized herpe ogy and spawned a new generation of k amateur and professional herpetolog By the latter half of the twentieth cent herpetology had come of age, with a la number of students working in the m areas of research, including the taxono anatomy, physiology and ecology of rept

Research areas

Although early herpetologists concentr largely on the taxonomy and classifica of snakes, so laying the foundations for t further investigation, more recent tre have seen the diversification of herpetol into specialized disciplines. Taxonomy is continuing, of course, and serves the important dual purpose of firstly labe species so that other workers can comm cate their findings accurately and, secon of organizing the various species, ge and families into natural groupings assemblages in an attempt to establish t inter-relationships.

Although taxonomy takes place main museums, many taxonomists are also workers, searching for new species subspecies in areas that have previo been little explored. Regrettably, there few such areas left nowadays but m regions have only been superficially sam and new species are still turning up, so times unexpectedly, even in countries are usually regarded as well known a herpetological standpoint. The discove a huge python, *Morelia oenpelliensis* northern Australia as recently as 1977 good example.

Other parts of the world are virtually go' areas for various reasons and there almost certainly interesting discoveries to be made. These areas include muc tropical Africa, parts of the Middle East remote regions in South America.

Other new species are established by ing more closely at series of specir formerly classified as one but which tran to have minor but significant differe

e Oenpelli python, *Morelia oenpelliensis*, a
snake overlooked in a remote part of
ern Australia until 1977.

een them and this is the way in which
new species have been 'discovered' in
it years. Countering this, species that
formerly thought to be distinct are
times shown to be identical to others
they are suppressed. Taxonomy often
ists, therefore, of 'lumping' and 'split-
species, genera and families, much to
lismay of amateur herpetologists who
neither the time nor the inclination
ep abreast of recent developments.
e anatomy of snakes has been fairly
oughly established on a general scale,
unique organs such as Jacobson's
n, the heat-sensitive pits of some boas
pythons and the pit vipers, and the
ipenes of male snakes having been
isively studied. Minor anatomical dif-
ices, especially in the structure of the
and the arrangement and structure of
cales are other useful tools in classifying
es.

Biochemists have long been fascinated by
the composition and effects of snake venom
due to its medical importance but, again,·
biochemical differences in venom and blood
have become useful tools that can be used in
classification. The physiology of snakes has
been studied mostly from the standpoint of
thermoregulation, but reproductive biology
is also an important field.

Studies on the behaviour and ecology of
snakes has historically been the most
neglected aspect of their biology. This stems
from the difficulty with which they can
be observed, because they remain hidden
for a large amount of the time and are easily
disturbed by the observers, leading to the
cessation of natural behaviour. Much of
what we know about snake behaviour relies
on anecdotal evidence – chance encounters
with snakes doing something interesting
such as eating or mating. Using this method,
it would take an infinite amount of time
to compile a reasonably comprehensive
picture of snake behaviour. Similarly, studies
on captive snakes, though useful, are difficult to back up with parallel studies on
free-ranging, wild snakes.

One method is to catch and mark snakes,
usually by clipping a number of ventral
scales in a unique pattern so that the snake
can be identified if it is caught again, even if
several years have elapsed. By this means,
growth rates, movement and breeding
behaviour can be established. A lot is left to
chance, though, as it must be possible
to find the same animals again at a later
date, and so it is only really effective for
species that occur in fairly high densities in
a specific place.

The availability of sophisticated electronic
equipment for monitoring the movement
of snakes that are out of sight has revolu-
tionized this type of research. Snakes are
first caught and then implanted with a
small electronic transmitter. This generates
a signal that is used to locate the snake
again at a later date and it may be possible
to obtain additional information such as
the snake's body temperature. A number
of species have been studied in this way,
especially in Australia and North America,
where snakes are reasonably numerous,
and some interesting results have been
obtained.

Radio-tracking snakes

In the past, one of the biggest obstacles to snake research has been the difficulty of observing them going about their activities in a natural and undisturbed situation: much of the information that is available has had to come from anecdotal evidence or from observations made in captivity.

The development of miniaturized electronic systems has had a great impact in this area. Small transmitters can be located on the snake and its subsequent movements can then be tracked over the following months or even years. The transmitter contains a battery which provides enough power for a regular signal to be transmitted every few seconds. Additional information, such as the temperature of the transmitter (and therefore the snake) can also be relayed if necessary although this depletes the battery more quickly. Similarly, the range of the equipment can be altered but long-range transmitters are also heavy on battery power. Larger batteries, of course, can be incorporated but this may only be possible in large snakes.

A typical system consists of a battery and transmitter capsule about 3–4 cm (1½ in) long with a diameter of 1 cm (⅜ in) or less. For a medium-sized snake this represents a 'payload' of less than an average meal. The capsule can be force-fed to the snake, in which case it will only be operational for the length of time that food normally stays in the system, 4 to 12 days on average.

▲ Implanting a transmitter.

Alternatively, it can be inserted surgically, by making a short incision and positioning the capsule between the skin and the body wall. The antenna is then threaded along the body of the snake, also between the skin and the body wall. After the incision has been sealed and the snake has recovered from the anaesthetic, it is released at the site of capture.

Subsequently, the snake can be located by tuning a receiver to the correct wavelength. An antenna is held aloft and will pick up a signal from the transmitter, in the form of a series of 'bleeps', which become louder if the antenna is orientated towards the snake. Different designs of antenna may be used, one to locate the snake's whereabouts at long distance, and another to pinpoint its position with more accuracy.

Results obtained from these studies can provide much information which

would otherwise not be available. Da and annual activity patterns can be established, for instance. Preferred habitats can be identified at different times of the year and snakes can ever be located during hibernation. Activi patterns of males can be compared to those of females and juveniles. In the long term, growth rates and reproductive rates can be investigated

Information from these studies can be used to find out more about the private lives of snakes. They can also a powerful tool in snake conservation

▼ Tracking a radio-tagged snake.

Although much of the research is directed towards finding out more about snakes *per se*, sometimes more far-reaching biological principles can be investigated. Evolutionary ecology is the term that describes the study of various aspects of animal behaviour in which predictions of how animals should react to various situations can be tested. Birds and insects are widely used in this field because they are relatively easily studied but snakes have certain qualities that make them equally useful in some cases. By

using them as biological models, aspects of thermoregulation, feeding strategies and reproductive strategies can help us to understand how the behaviour of animals has evolved.

The role of the amateur

Traditionally, the study of animals, especially those which had little or no commercial value, was almost exclusively the bailiwick of the amateur. Early naturalists were frequently well-heeled persons who financed

their own travels and studies and often for the publication of their own observat Charles Darwin epitomizes the 'gentle naturalist' of the time and, although h not work specifically in the field of he tology, his voyage on the *Beagle* prod many new species of reptiles and amp ians, including snakes.

More recently, the great Amer amateur herpetologist, Laurence M. Klau an electrical engineer by training, not discovered about 50 new species and

ies of reptiles but published extensively
he natural history of many of the snakes
d in the south-western United States.
leveloped several statistical methods of
ysing large quantities of data, accumu-
d a collection of over 35,000 preserved
imens and was the first to see the poten-
of driving a car along desert roads in
r to find and capture snakes, a technique
is still regarded as the best method
mpling large areas. His speciality was
esnakes and he published many papers
heir natural history and distribution,
inating in his two-volume *Rattle-
es*, published in 1956, possibly one of the
t monographs ever produced on a single
p of animals, and including many facts
it the folklore, superstitions and bite of
esnake.

nce Klauber's day no amateur has matched
ledication in pursuit of knowledge about
es, nor his output of literature, but a
army of amateur snake fanciers contin-
o make useful and original observations
it the natural history, distribution,
oduction and feeding habits of snakes,
r by keeping them in captivity or by
ing regular field trips, often squeezed in
reen professional and personal commit-
ts and invariably self-financed.

lthough their resources are usually
ewhat limited compared to those of
essional herpetologists, there are plenty
reas where even basic information is
ing about snakes. Observations by ama-
s are regularly published in society
sletters and bulletins and even the more
itific journals are pleased to accept and
ish papers by amateurs provided they
well written, original and thoroughly
arched.

Brusher Mills

Henry 'Brusher' Mills was born in 1838 in the New Forest in Hampshire, England. He became a well-known character in the area, where for most of his life he pursued the occupation of snake catcher. He reputedly caught between five and six thousand snakes, supplying most of them to zoos, where they were used to feed other, exotic, species of snakes. Other specimens went to collectors or scientific laboratories where their venom was extracted, or were used in the preparation of snake fat, which was supposed to possess medicinal properties.

Although no records were kept, most of the snakes he caught would certainly have been adders, *Vipera berus*, which is the most common species in the area. These he caught using the traditional forked 'snake-stick' although he was also known to handle them freely without getting bitten. Along with the stick, he carried with him a sailcloth sack and a tin, in which to carry his catch.

Brusher Mills became a famous attraction with the visitors that began to visit the New Forest around the turn of the century; he was then able to supplement his income by exhibiting his snakes and his snake catching techniques to day trippers. He was also known to surreptitiously release a snake in a crowded street and then catch it again after it had caused widespread panic, so earning gratitude, and a handsome tip.

For 20 years Brusher Mills lived in a small hut, similar to those used by the charcoal burners of the day. When he was not catching snakes, he followed the game of cricket, making it his responsibility to sweep the pitch at Lyndhurst between innings, and it was this occupation that led to his nickname of Brusher.

He died in 1905, shortly after he had been evicted from his squatter's hut by the local authorities, and is buried in the village churchyard at Brockenhurst. His local public house, the Railway Inn, was renamed The Snake Catcher in 1993.

▼ **An old postcard showing Brusher Mills in the New Forest.**

SNAKES IN CAPTIVITY

▲ Kingsnakes, *Lampropeltis*, are widely bred i[n] captivity, both in their natural form and in a variety of colour variants, such as this albino example of the speckled kingsnake, *Lamprope[ltis] getulus holbrooki*.

People keep snakes in captivity for a variety of reasons: for public exhibition in zoos, etc., for research purposes, for commercial breeding purposes or just because they like them. Techniques for keeping snakes healthy have improved greatly over the last 20 or so years and many now breed regularly under controlled conditions.

There are several excellent books that deal in detail with keeping and breeding snakes in captivity and so this section is intended to give an overview, without specific reference to any single species. Additional brief notes are given in the final chapter where applicable.

An understanding of the biology of snakes is important. As they are not domesticated animals, their habits and behaviour are still under the control of natural instincts. Placing them in a totally artificial situation, where they cannot behave normally, will lead to stress, resulting in poor health and, in extreme cases, death. This does not mean that their cages should represent exact replicas of the habitats from which they come, but that certain physical features, namely heat, light, security as well as a natural diet, should be carefully considered. Furthermore, snakes are not 'pets' in the true sense of the word. Some of them may give the appearance of enjoying being handled but it is likely that this is due to the warmth of the human hand rather than the warmth of the human spirit.

Although snakes do not respond to affection they do respond to other stimuli, and amateur snake keepers may be in a better position to make original observations than full-time professional herpetologists who have restricted time. For this reason, accurate records should be kept, especially of unusual behaviour and, even more especially, if rare species are being kept. Interesting observations should be written up and submitted to one of the herpetological journals or newsletters.

Obtaining snakes

Snakes can be obtained from a variety of sources. Foremost among them, and the starting point for most snake keepers, [are] other hobbyists who have surplus ani[mals] to sell or exchange due to a successful br[eed]ing programme. Obtaining snakes in [this] way has several advantages, including [a] greater likelihood that the snake will be [free] from diseases or parasites, and will ada[pt to] captivity better than a similar indivi[dual] plucked from the wild. Advice on its care [and] breeding will be freely available from [the] breeder at the time of purchase.

Alternatively, snakes can be obta[ined] from the wild, either by personal collec[tion] or by purchase through an animal impo[rter] or dealer. The pitfalls of this method ca[n be] inferred from the above comments. On [the] other hand, if your interest is in species [that] are not widely bred in captivity, then t[here] is little alternative. Collecting your [own]

es is usually preferable to obtaining
through the animal trade, where they
have been kept under poor conditions
everal weeks or even months before
hase and where they may have been
d with species from other parts of the
d and picked up diseases and parasites
hich they have little or no resistance.

aware, however, that there are often
ictions on the capture of wild snakes,
ially of rare species or in National
s, and that there may also be restric-
on importing animals collected abroad.
country has its own set of rules and
lations; the onus is on the collector to
re that he or she keeps within the law
that any necessary paperwork is in
.

ce of species

he 2,500 or so species of snakes
ibed, only a very small proportion
ese is suitable for captivity. Many are
mall, too large, too dangerous or too
to be considered. Some have specialized
that cannot be satisfied in captivity
others are so secretive, or dull in colour,
oth, that keeping them in captivity is
ig, to say the least, unless they are the
cts of a particular study.

e most popular snakes are found
ng the boas, pythons and colubrids.
e boas and pythons suffer from the prob-
of size: when buying a young snake
e sure that you will still be able to
mmodate it when it reaches its full size
years later. Other species in this family
are or endangered and should only be
idered by responsible and experienced
alists who stand a good chance of
ding from them. A few are aggressive,
would not normally be considered
mateurs wanting a snake that can be
led without fear of injury.

the colubrids, by far the best choices
ig to genera such as the rat snakes,
ie, the kingsnakes, *Lampropeltis*, and
opher snakes, *Pituophis*. All the species
ese genera eat rodents and adapt well to
vity. They occur in a variety of colours,
often there are a number of distinct
s even within the same species so an
esting and varied collection can be built
All species are widely bred in captivity
there should be no need to encourage
rade in wild snakes by buying imported
als. There are plenty of other colu-
that are worth considering, the main
irements being that they eat food that
adily available (mice and rats being

the obvious choice for most people), that
they adapt well to captivity and are not
endangered or otherwise restricted species.

It is possible to keep snakes from other
families but many have their drawbacks.
The primitive snakes are not freely available
and, being mainly burrowing kinds, they
have specialized requirements (and are
rarely seen). Their dietary habits are also
somewhat inconvenient unless an inex-
haustible supply of termites and similar
small invertebrates is to hand. Members of
the small families – Acrochordidae, Loxocemidae, Xenopeltidae, Aniliidae, Uropeltidae – are not easily obtained. *Loxocemus*
and *Xenopeltis*, though, often do quite well in
captivity. Potentially dangerous rear-fanged
colubrids, elapids and vipers should not
even be considered by amateur hobbyists
that have had limited experience of keeping
snakes. In addition, there are often legal
restrictions on keeping dangerous snakes
and licences are only granted to persons who
can demonstrate that they have adequate
facilities and knowledge to keep them in such

a way that they will not become a danger to
themselves and to members of the public.

Housing

Snakes do not necessarily require large
cages. Many species normally spend the
greater part of their lives coiled in a cavity
beneath a rock or within a log and venture
out only when the pangs of hunger or the
mating instinct is upon them. If these
species are provided with all their needs,
they will normally be content to live in a
cage that measures less than their body
length. More active species, especially if
they are nervous or aggressive, will be
stressed if they hit the sides of the cage each
time they try to move quickly, and they
require much larger accommodation. In
practice, many of the diurnal hunting
species do not make good captives for this
very reason.

The possible designs for snake cages
are numerous and varied. A simple cage is
often based on a glass aquarium, with a
modified lid to make it escape-proof and to

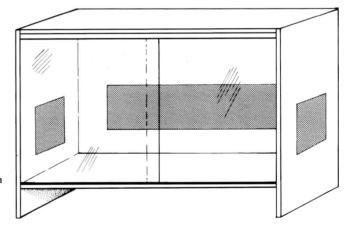

▶ A simple but effective
snake cage, with ventilation
panels in the back and
sides, and a sliding glass
front.

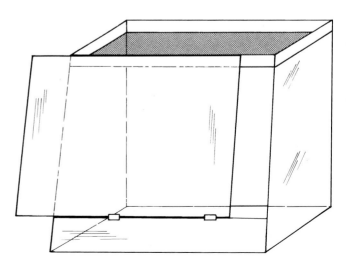

▶ A snake cage made
entirely of glass, with a
removable front.

▲ The twin-spotted ratsnake, *Elaphe bimaculata*, is sometimes imported in vast numbers for sale through the pet trade. Many die at the hands of inexperienced keepers and dealers.

provide adequate ventilation. These cages can be bought ready-made, together with a vivarium-type lid, in a variety of sizes, or they can be made. If they are home-made, the shape and size can, to a certain extent, be tailored to accommodate the animals or to fit a specific space in the home. Security is especially important when venomous or aggressive snakes are concerned and a design that can be locked should be seriously considered.

A rather better design consists of a glass or wooden cage with sliding glass doors. As well as being easier to service, cages of this type have the distinct advantage that ventilation can be incorporated at a lower level, and therefore a better rate of air exchange can be expected. In addition, they can be stacked on top of one another if necessary. Again, the dimensions of this type of cage can be tailored to suit its use, within reason, and it is often easier to fix heating and lighting equipment, etc. to a cage that has at least part of its structure made from wood or plastic. The glass doors can be wedged, or even locked, in order to prevent the escape of the snakes and care

should be taken to see that the doors are fully closed after the cage has been serviced – failure to do this often results in the snake working away at the opening until it either damages its snout or enlarges the opening and escapes.

If tall cages are required for arboreal snakes, sliding glass fronts do not work too well and some other arrangement will be necessary. Sometimes a removable front is most convenient and the cage can be designed so that it slopes backwards slightly, helping to hold it in place (although clips should also be used). In large cages, the front can be made of transparent plastic, rather than glass, for safety reasons.

For large collections, or where the snakes are required solely for experimental purposes or for commercial breeding, large plastic containers may be used. These are easily cleaned and a large number can be stacked in a system of racking with heating built into it. Such cages are also useful for housing young snakes temporarily, and for newly acquired snakes that are in quarantine.

Heating and lighting

Because snakes are not able to generate their own body heat, they are entirely dependent on heat sources outside their bodies. In captivity, this means an electrical heater of

some description. Temperature contr one of the most important aspects of s keeping. Different species of snakes have different temperature requirem however, and even the same individual prefer to be at different temperature certain times of the day or season. As t is no way of knowing exactly what tem ture to keep every snake every minu every day, the answer is to give the choice. This is very easily arrange installing all heating equipment toward end of the cage. This provides a tempera gradient and the snake can move about it finds the temperature that best it. Upper temperatures, i.e. in the war part of the cage, should be about 30°C (8 and temperatures in the coolest part o cage should be about 20°C (68°F). range will suit most tropical and tempe species under normal conditions. It wil matter if the overall temperature falls sli at night – indeed, it may be beneficial.

The preferred means of providing hea most types of snake is the undercage mat or heat pad. These low-power units be placed under the cage, obviating need for electrical supply to enter the itself. They give out a continuous, g heat and, if only part of the cage is pl over them, they will warm one end v allowing the other end to remain cool. (

e is no need for a thermostat, although
manufacturer's instructions should
arefully studied. Alternative methods
ude the installation of radiant light
ces in the lid of the cage, either in the
of an incandescent light bulb or an
-red heater. Both methods are more
ble for larger snakes in larger cages.
bulbs have an obvious drawback
ey are only effective when they are
ched on, and the snakes must either be
ed at night or they must be subject to
etual light. If light bulbs are used with
ermostat, the situation is worsened
light will flash on and off throughout
day and night. Dull infra-red emitters
e in several forms, including power-
ceramic heaters designed mainly for
agricultural industry, as well as less
erful units designed specifically for rep-
keeping. Before buying and installing
pment, it is as well to investigate all
possibilities and to use the equipment
seems best suited to each particular
tion.

ghting is probably not strictly nec-
ry for snakes unless they are kept in a
n with no daylight. There is no evidence
uggest that day length has any great
ence on snakes' feeding or breeding
nes, and temperature, coupled to their
ilt biological rhythm, is by far the most
ortant factor. Lighting may be applied
akes that are on public display in order
nhance the appearance of the cages,
it must be said that most of the species
are normally kept shun intense light-
and will usually hide themselves away
eir cage is too bright. A few diurnal
es, however, may display themselves
by basking in the heat of a spotlight in
h the same way that diurnal lizards do.

ling

e species are chosen wisely, feeding
ld not present a problem. Most of the
e popular snakes eat rodents at all
es of their lives, although the size of the
items will obviously vary according to
age. Rodents such as mice and rats can
red for the purpose of providing snake
. This is not usually a favourite task
most snake keepers due to the time and
e required but has the advantage of
ring a reliable and cheap food supply
perhaps more importantly, offering a
e of sizes so that a mixed collection of
es can be fed with suitable prey. Small
ctions of snakes, however, are more
y maintained on a diet of frozen

rodents, which can be purchased in bulk,
stored in the freezer and thawed as required.

Species that require prey other than
rodents are not so easily kept. The American
garter, ribbon and water snakes, *Thamnophis*
and *Nerodia*, and European water snakes,
Natrix, can sometimes be persuaded to
accept strips of raw fish, whole, small frozen
fish or alternative foods such as earthworms
(for garter snakes) or rodents. Some of these
diets are more satisfactory than others, and
some experimentation with vitamin and
mineral supplements, with special regard to
Vitamin D and calcium, may be necessary.

It may be possible to obtain a regular
supply of small lizards, amphibians or fish for
other species, depending on your locality.
Catching large numbers of these items from
the wild may be frowned on, however, and
may also introduce parasites into the snake
collection. Frozen lizards and frogs are sometimes available through reptile importers,

who often suffer large losses when trading
in these animals. Each individual must
examine his or her own conscience when
deciding whether or not to use this food
source.

Snakes that eat invertebrates have
attracted little attention from amateur or
professional herpetologists and there is some
scope here to make interesting contributions
to the natural history of some of these little-
known species. A fair amount of success has
been had with keeping species such as the
American shovel-nosed snakes, *Chionactis*,
ground snakes, *Sonora*, ring-necked snakes,
Diadophis, and green snakes, *Opheodryas*, but
none of these are widely kept or bred and
captive-bred specimens are rarely available.

▼ Few insectivorous snakes enter the pet trade. An
exception is the rough green snake, *Opheodryas
aestivus*, which, unfortunately, is not widely bred
in captivity.

Apart from the fish-eating species mentioned above, vitamin and mineral supplements are not normally required for any of the rodent or lizard-eating species that are fed on natural diets.

Breeding

Encouraging captive snakes to breed is a worthy aim for a number of reasons. Most obviously, by breeding desirable species in captivity, the strain on natural populations is relieved. Some species are protected and would not otherwise be available to others. Captive breeding can provide useful information of a type that is often difficult to obtain from free-living snakes and, although such data must be used cautiously, information on clutch size, incubation periods, frequency of breeding and so on, has traditionally been provided by amateur or professional snake keepers. Captive breeding also indicates that the conditions under which the snakes are kept are suitable for the species concerned. Snakes will not breed if they are in poor health or if their environment is less than satisfactory.

Captive breeding also provides an opportunity for selective breeding experiments. These may involve naturally occurring variations in colour or pattern and are often the only way in which the genetic mechanisms controlling these variations can be thoroughly investigated. Alternatively, selective breeding may serve to increase the numbers of a particular colour

◀ Of the larger snakes, the Burmese python, *Python molurus bivittatus*, is the most commonly available species, and may be obtained in several colour variations, all of which have been produced by selectively breeding from mutants. The most common form is the albino or 'golden' python.

form originating from a chance mutation and some of the more popular species of snakes, notably the corn snake, *Elaphe guttata guttata*, and the Burmese python, *Python molurus bivittatus*, occur in a plethora of colour and pattern forms, some of which are more attractive than others.

The practical aspects of breeding snakes are not difficult to master, being a natural progression from keeping them properly. If they are in good condition, and a male and female are available, they should breed. Whereas some species require some environmental manipulation, others will breed under almost any conditions.

It is important to know the natural breeding season, if there is one, for the species you intend to breed. As described in Chapter 7, snakes may be seasonal or aseasonal in their reproductive habits. Seasonal species may breed in the spring or summer (most colubrids from temperate and subtropical regions, for example) or in winter (most tropical boas and pythons).

Sex determination

Although some species show a certain degree of sexual dimorphism in the form of different colours or markings, this is not the most reliable way in which to determine the sexes for the majority of species. Usually, adult males can be recognized by their longer tails and greater number of subcaudal scales. In addition, the base of the tail of male snakes is often noticeably swollen when compared with that of a female of a similar species and size. This swelling is due to the presence of the hemipenes, which lie inverted in a pair of pockets opening into the cloaca. For a more reliable diagnosis, the hemipenes can be

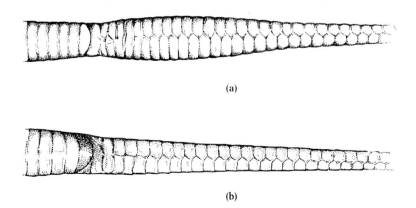

(a)

(b)

▲ The retracted hemipenes of male snakes may create a bulge at the base of their tail (a), which may also be longer than that of females (b).

▼ The retracted hemipenes of male snakes can be located by careful probing with a smooth instrument of appropriate size. The probe will typically enter to a depth of more than five subcaudal scales in males (a) but only to two or three scales in females (b).

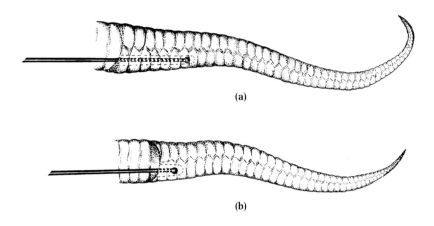

(a)

(b)

probed internally with an appropriately sized rod of metal or plastic, when it will be found that the probe will pass into the base of the tail for a considerable distance in the case of males but hardly at all in females. The probe should be lubricated with water, liquid paraffin or petroleum jelly, and eased very gently back into one of the openings. It sometimes helps if the probe is slowly twirled between the thumb and forefinger as it is inserted, and only minimal pressure should be used. If the probe can only be inserted to the depth of two or three subcaudal scales, the snake is probably a female. The other side should now be probed in confirmation. Should the probe pass into the tail for a depth of six or more subcaudals, the snake is almost certainly a male. There is no need to continue probing to the bottom of the pocket as damage can be inflicted if the snake suddenly twists or twitches. This method is very reliable once it has been mastered, although a few species are difficult if the male has short hemipenes; females have musk glands at the base of the tail into which the probe can also pass and there may be little difference in the depth to which the probe can be inserted.

Probing small hatchling snakes is not recommended, except as a last resort, as the size of the probe must be such that it would be all too easy to injure the snake. A better, and equally reliable, method is to evert the male's hemipenes by applying pressure at the base of the tail (often known as 'popping'). The base of the tail is grasped and the thumb is used to push the hemipenes gently out of the cloaca. Males are very obvious once their hemipenes have been everted, females often evert their musk glands, which are shorter than the male's hemipenes, and at the bottom there is a very small red spot. This method requires practice and some operators are better than others. Once mastered, though, it can be used with a high degree of accuracy and probing need only be used where results are inconclusive.

Once snakes have been sexed with a fair degree of confidence they should be identified in some way so that probing or popping does not need to be done any more than is necessary, normally only once in the snake's lifetime. Identification can take the form of noting or sketching some unique marking or scale arrangement on the snake's record.

Conditioning

Snakes will not breed unless they are in good condition. They should be well fed, though not overfed, and free of diseases or parasites. Seasonal breeders should be introduced at the correct time of the year. Note that snakes from the opposite hemisphere will have their biological rhythms reversed. Winter in the south is summer in the north and vice versa. Winter breeders from South Africa, for instance, will be programmed to breed in the northern summer. It may be necessary to reverse the local temperate regime by cooling them in the summer and warming them in the winter. Captive-bred snakes seem to adapt to local conditions at the first generation and such inconvenient manipulations are then rarely necessary.

Species that breed in the spring may require a period of cooling. How essential this is will depend on their origin: snakes from Canada or northern Europe are likely to need a longer and more severe cool period than those from Florida or Mediterranean region. Heat can be remo from hardy species as long as they in good condition but feeding should c at least 10 days beforehand so that digestive system is empty. Some individ stop feeding in the late summer or ea autumn anyway, and these should cooled once this has occurred, other they will lose body weight during the r ing period. During the cooling-off per snakes should have access to drink water; some species remain quite activ this time and even go through the s shedding process, probably because they not cooled to the same degree that t would experience in the wild. No harm come to them, however.

Mating

Serious snake breeders usually keep sexes separately when they are expected to breed, introducing them to another when they are considered 'r Other people prefer to leave the sna permanently together as pairs or br ing groups and allow the courtship mating process to occur spontaneously.

Snakes that have been cooled off sho be warmed up for a few days before they introduced. Some breeders like to give t sexes two or three meals before mat them, and others wait until they h undergone their spring shed. All sort variations have been tried and they all s to be equally successful as long as snakes are in good condition and are the opposite sex. Where males and fem are paired just for breeding purposes, t often mate immediately. It is still advis to leave them together for a while, o separate them and reintroduce them a days later in order that mating can t place several times. Fertility is likely t higher if this is done and it is especi important with boas and pythons. Once female begins to swell with eggs the pair be separated until the next matin required. The male may be used to m with another female if necessary.

Egg laying or birth

There is now some deviation in the pr dure, depending on the reproductive ha of the species concerned. Viviparous spe can be left to their own devices and b will take place without any assistance. only precaution to take is to ensure the cage is escape-proof as the young

ously be much smaller than their
her. Some species also seem to benefit
ey are given a hide box with a layer of
p moss in which to give birth, although
is by no means essential in every case.

gg-laying species will require a suitable
laying site, otherwise they may retain
r eggs or lay them in an unsuitable
e, such as the water bowl, where they
perish. Colubrid snakes give some
ning that egg laying is imminent by
lding their skin six to 12 days before
ng. A suitable container should be par-
y filled with a damp substrate, such as
s or peat, and placed inside the cage at
time. The female will begin to frequent
and, if all goes well, will lay her clutch
.

bation and hatching

ales often remain with their clutches,
ast for a few days. Pythons coil around
r eggs and may remain with them for
duration of incubation if given the
ortunity, and you may decide to allow
female to incubate her own eggs.
erwise, they should be removed at the
est opportunity and placed in a clean
strate in an incubator set at the correct
perature. Vermiculite is the most
monly used medium as it will hold a
siderable amount of water over a long
od of time and, being non-organic, will
encourage bacteria or moulds. A fairly
se grade of vermiculite works best and it
ld first be thoroughly soaked with clean
er and then gently squeezed until all the
lus has drained off. A layer of 5–10 cm
in) of moistened vermiculite should be
ed in a clean plastic container. The depth
nportant as it will ensure that any
aining water does not come into contact
a the eggs, which must have an adequate
of oxygen around them. Python eggs
ire a somewhat drier mix than colubrids.
e parts water in four parts vermiculite,
weight, usually works well, although
e experimentation may be necessary
use vermiculite from different sources
vary in its moisture content.

he eggs are placed in shallow depressions
e vermiculite, but not buried. If the eggs
e adhered to one another, no attempt
ld be made to separate them and the
p should be arranged in such a way that
greatest number of eggs is in contact with
medium: it may be necessary to draw it
round the clump slightly. The container
vhich the eggs are placed should be
ilated with a few small holes. Too much

ventilation will allow the incubating medium
to dry out too quickly, and too little will lead
to oxygen starvation resulting in dead or
poorly developed hatchlings.

An incubation temperature of 28°C (82°F)
is recommended for colubrid eggs. Python
eggs require a rather higher temperature
and 30–32°C (86–89.6°F) usually gives
good results. The incubation period varies
with species. Most of the commonly bred
colubrids hatch after 60–90 days but some
take less time. Pythons usually hatch in
about 60 days or slightly less. Hatching is
usually synchronous among a clutch of
eggs, provided they have all been kept at the
same temperature. If part of the clutch
hatches but some eggs are still not slit, it may
be advantageous to cut into them carefully
in order to help the young snakes to emerge.
Often these stragglers are dead or weak but
occasionally they can be saved in this way.

The hatchlings should be removed from
the container and housed individually. Most
breeders use small plastic boxes for initial
housing, and a clean substrate of paper
towels. A water bowl is essential and some
species benefit from a small box into which
they can crawl and hide. Most young
snakes shed their skins about one week after
hatching, and begin to feed afterwards.
Hatchling pythons and new-born boas, on
the other hand, may go several weeks before
this initial shed and may begin to feed before
it takes place.

▼ Snake eggs are usually incubated artificially
in an absorbent and inert material such as
vermiculite.

1. Dodd, C. K. (1987), 'Status, conservation and
   management', in *Snakes: Ecology and
   Evolutionary Ecology* (edited by R. A. Seigel,
   J. T. Collins and S. S. Novak), Macmillan
   Publishing Company, New York.
2. Adler, K., *Contributions to the History of
   Herpetology*, Society for the Study of Amphibians
   and Reptiles, Oxford, Ohio, 1989.

9
Taxonomy

There is probably no area of biology that causes as much frustration, especially among amateur naturalists, as taxonomy. And yet, taxonomy is of great value, not only in allowing the communication of information between interested parties, but also in helping us to understand the relationships between different animals: once a group of animals begins to be studied, some method of arranging them into groups, and naming them, becomes essential.

▶ What's in a name? As species' relationships with each other become better understood, name changes are inevitable. The red diamond rattlesnake is called *Crotalus ruber* at present but a name change, to *Crotalus exsul*, seems likely to take place soon.

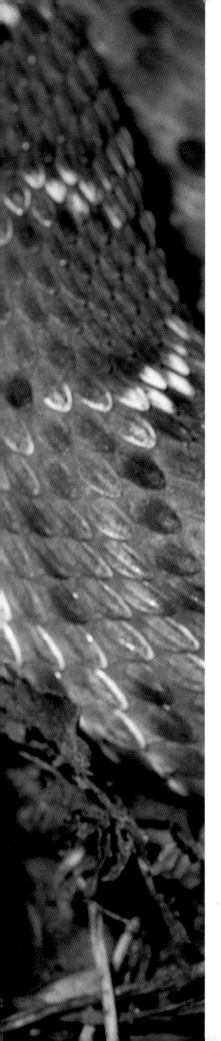

Taxonomy, or systematics, consists of two disciplines: *classification* and *nomenclature*. Classification is the process of establishing relationships between animals and arranging them into taxonomic groups. The groups that are produced are known as *taxa* (singular *taxon*). Nomenclature is the allocation of names to these groups.

Classification must be carried out first, so that the groups can be identified. Only when the taxonomist is sure that he has achieved the best possible arrangement, based on the evidence at his disposal, can the groups be named: classification precedes nomenclature.

In Chapter 1 we looked at the way in which snakes evolved from their early ancestors. At various points during their evolutionary history, groups of species broke away from the main stock and began to evolve and radiate into the side branches that we call families. Families are one level within the system of classification. The other important levels are: Order, Class and Phylum, all higher than the family level, and Genus and Species, both at a lower level. Between these levels, others are sometimes inserted: suborder, subfamily, subspecies, etc. Taxonomists may work at any of these levels.

The level with which most people are familiar is that of the species. The concept of species is not easily understood as there is no universally accepted definition of it (which is why taxonomists spend much of their time arguing over whether a certain animal belongs to this species or that). A common way of regarding species is to think of them as populations, or groups of populations, that can interbreed to produce fertile offspring. Animals of different species do not, as a rule, interbreed. If they do, their offspring are known as hybrids and may be infertile. Although there are numerous exceptions to this definition, including some snakes, it is probably the best we have at present.

Animals of the same species tend to look alike, although there may be differences between the sexes and between adults and juveniles. When a species is distributed over a large area, local differences in colour and pattern may arise and these are sometimes regarded as subspecies. Different subspecies may interbreed but would not naturally be able to because they live in different places. In areas where the range of one subspecies merges into the range of another, the animals may show characteristics intermediate between both subspecies, and are known as intergrades. Other subspecies, though, are physically separated (by a mountain range for instance) and so they have no opportunity to intergrade. If they are isolated for long enough they may evolve in different ways from one another and eventually become full species. But at what point does a subspecies become a full species? There are no hard and fast rules and so this can be another cause of dispute.

If two species are only slightly different from one another, perhaps because they have not been isolated for very long, they may be placed together in the same genus (plural genera). Genera that are not too different may be placed in the same family, and so on.

This produces a logical hierarchy of groupings which serves two purposes. Most importantly, the various levels within the hierarchy reflect different degrees of evolutionary divergence. It also serves as an aid to memory. Taxonomic hierarchy can be thought of as a series of boxes that fit inside one another. The biggest box, the one that contains all the others is, in our case, the suborder of snakes. Inside this box are the 15 smaller boxes representing the 15 families of snakes. Within each of these boxes are more boxes, representing the genera that are assigned to each family, and so on, down through species, then subspecies and, finally, individual snakes.

Taxonomists, then, decide which boxes to put inside which. So far, so good. The problems arise when individual snakes do not fit readily into any of the boxes. Or when the boxes containing genera do not obviously belong in any particular box representing a family.

CLASSIFICATION

The problem with higher classification is that the characters used must not be subject to the losses and gains that go with adaptation. Species from many different ancestral lines may evolve to look similar to one another if they lead similar life-styles. Several examples of this convergence have been cited. On the other hand, species that are from the same line may grow to be very different from each other if they radiate into different ecological niches.

Thus, boas may be long and slender if they are arboreal or short and stout if they are burrowers. How then can we tell that they are both boas? Or vipers, or whatever? Herpetologists hoping to classify snakes at levels higher than species must find characters that are less subject to evolutionary pressures than shape, size, colour and so on. Furthermore, the characters they use should not be immediately connected to a particular life-style. This invariably involves delving beneath the surface to look for features such as pelvic girdles, coronoid bones, hypapophyses, various muscles, various internal organs and, more recently, proteins and chromosomes.

None of these are much use in identifying a live snake in the hand, even less useful if it is seen rapidly gliding away through the vegetation. Identification normally takes place at the species level. Most parts of the world have some type of field guide or key to species that can be used to name the snakes found there, or at least the common ones. Problematical species may require close examination, even dissection in the case of blind snakes, *Typhlops*, and thread snakes, *Leptotyphlops*, for instance. Usually, though, identifying snakes is fairly straightforward. Having identified our snake, how do we know which family or subfamily it belongs to? And does it matter anyway? To the general field naturalist it probably doesn't matter too much. To the amateur or professional herpetologist, however, and to the student of evolution, higher classification is important because it attempts to link species in a way that reflects their relationships with one another. Thus, if two species are very closely related they will be placed in the same genus. We know that if two species have the same generic name, *Elaphe* for instance, they will have evolved from a common ancestor not too long ago (on a geological timescale, anyway) and that they will share certain characteristics.

So far, the criteria for placing snakes in the same genera or families have been rather vaguely presented. This is because evolution does not proceed in jumps but as a continuum. Variation within a population may be so great that specimens taken from either extreme look very different but all the intermediate stages between them are present. In this case they do not represent separate species but merely a single, highly variable species. But if populations at either end of the continuum become physically separated from the rest, they can evolve in different directions and become distinct.

Often, when specimens of snakes are first collected, preserved and deposited in museums, it is not always possible to know if there are intermediate forms. At a later date, intermediates may be collected and early opinions may have to be revised. Then again, the degree of difference required to constitute a species varies according to the researcher concerned: some would like to see more species with less variability whereas others prefer fewer species, taking in a much wider range of variation.

The same argument exists at higher levels. Are the pythons and boas different enough from one another to constitute separate families or are they merely subfamilies? In other words, are the differences between the *genera* greater than the differences between the *families*?

Every time new evidence becomes available, the classification system may need to be brought up to date. This may involve name changes. If all this seems confusing, it is worth remembering that the names we give to genera, species, subspecies and so on are for our convenience. Nature does not adhere to rules made by people and any difficulties we experience in this field are due to the inherent drawbacks in the system we use.

There is probably no field of biology in which the higher classification presents greater problems than in that of snakes. Problems that seem to be solved by one generation of classifiers rear their heads again when a later generation starts to use a more sophisticated technique. At the end of the day, though, academic arguments that centre on the relative importance of an obscure characteristic are of little concern to the average herpetologist. All that is required is a fairly stable system that is understood, if not totally accepted, by everyone.

NOMENCLATURE
How snakes are named

Classifying snakes into a logical syst would be of little use if they were nan in a haphazard way. Nomenclature is discipline of deciding how they are name

Names given to snakes are of two ty common names and scientific nan Common names are useful for everyday but have drawbacks. They may vary fr one part of the species' range to another some species have several common nan Red rat snake, corn snake, Great Pla rat snake and rosy rat snake all refer the same species, for instance. (The red snake is another name for the corn sn but the other two names refer to subspec one of which is no longer accepted valid!) Then again, many common nan are not international: in many parts of La America the bushmaster, for instance called *barba amarilla*, meaning 'yell beard', a descriptive name but one tha quite useless to workers elsewhere. Scien names are less variable. *Elaphe guttata* Lachesis muta* are understood by her tologists throughout the world.

This system of nomenclature, in wh each species is given a latinized name, first used by Carl Linnaeus in 1753 wher published his *Species Plantarum*. Additio publications followed in an attempt to na all living organisms, including sna Owing to the limited horizons of the natu history of the day, and to a basic lacl understanding of evolution (Darwin's Or *of Species* was not published until 1854, hundred years later), Linnaeus's efforts with only limited success but the systen nomenclature he proposed gained w acceptance and is the one in use today.

Basically, each species is given names, or a 'binomial' comprising genus followed by the species. Sometim third name is added, in the case of s species (in which case the name is a 'tri mial') but the species is the basic uni classification. The first, or generic, nam always written with a capital letter but second, or specific, name is not (even commemorates someone's name or name of a place). If a third name is add this also begins with a small letter. Spe names may repeat generic names, as *Natrix natrix*, and, where subspecies are ognized, one of them must be the nomin subspecies (i.e. the one on which the spe was based) and its subspecific name n repeat its specific name. The nominate s species of grass snake then becomes *Na natrix natrix* and the nominate form of American rat snake becomes *Elaphe obsc*

eta. Where there are no recognized
species, it is incorrect to use a trinomial
e.

he whole name is normally written in
cs. Finally, the full name is often written
the name of its 'author' (the person
first described the species) after the
ized name, written in normal type. This
ten abbreviated and may be in brackets.

brackets indicate that, although the
ies was first described by the stated
or, the species has since been removed
the genus he or she originally placed it
nd put in another. For example, the
mon boa was named *Boa constrictor*
innaeus in 1758. The name remains
today and may be written in full: *Boa
trictor* Linnaeus. The Indian python
also named originally by Linnaeus but
laced it in the genus *Coluber*. Once it
been reclassified into another genus its
name became *Python molurus* (Linnaeus).
e species are renamed many times,
the name of the original author is still
ed in the brackets. Obsolete names are
wn as synonyms.

ribing new species

n new species are discovered they must
rmally described in the scientific litera-
and at this time they are given a name
he person describing them. There are
erous rules governing the naming of
species in order to avoid confusion and
ication. The new names must also be
matically correct. Different authors
ur different ways of describing new
ies. The names may be descriptive of
animal, e.g. *scalaris*, meaning ladder,
referring to a ladder-like marking along
back of *Elaphe scalaris*, or descriptive
s life-style, e.g. *Natrix*, meaning 'the
mmer'. Then again they may be named
the place where the original specimen
found, e.g. *Arizona elegans*, or in recog-
n of the original collector, as in Fea's
r, *Azemiops feae*, after the European
orer M. L. Fea, who first collected the
e in China, or to honour a prominent
archer in the field, e.g. *Crotalus lepidus
beri*, the rock rattlesnake, named after
rence Klauber, who did much original
k on rattlesnakes, and Russell's viper,
ra russelli, named in honour of Dr
ick Russell, who pioneered work on
es and their venom in India in the
teenth century.

veral snake names may contain the
e stem, especially if they are derived
classical languages. Very many snake

names, for instance, contain the word *ophis*
which is derived from the ancient Greek
word 'οφιζ', meaning snake. Thus, we have
Cylindrophis meaning 'cylindrical snake'
and *Tropidophis*, meaning 'keeled snake'.
(The same stem crops up in some lizard
names, as in *Ophisaurus*, meaning 'snake-
lizard' and *Ophiops*, meaning 'snake-eyed'.)
Other snakes are named after mythical
creatures, such as *Python*, the fabled monster
of Greek mythology, killed by Apollo in the
Pythian Vale near Mount Parnassus.

Each species has to be assigned to a family.
If a new species does not fit into any of the
existing families, a new one must be formed,
although this occurs very rarely. Family
names begin with capital letters and have
the suffix -idae. Some families are divided
into subfamilies. The names of these also
begin with a capital, but they are suffixed
-inae.

'Types'

Another aspect of nomenclature that sometimes causes problems is that of 'type' and it
is worth noting some of the different ways in
which type can be used.

Type specimen

The type specimen refers to the original
specimen from which a species or subspecies
is described and named. If the specimen was
collected by the author of the description it is
known as the holotype. Types and holotypes
are deposited in major museum collections
where they can be referred to by future
researchers.

Type locality

The type locality is the place where the type
specimen was collected.

Type species

The type species is used in conjunction with
genera and is the species that was first
placed in that genus. *Boa constrictor* is the
type species of the genus *Boa*, for instance
(in fact, it is the only member), and *Coluber
gemonensis* is the type species of the genus
Coluber.

Type genus

The type genus is the genus chosen as the
standard reference for a family. For
instance, the type genus of the Colubridae
is *Coluber*. Problems sometimes arise when
the type genus is moved to another family.
This occurred in the case of the genus *Elaps*,
which was the type genus for the cobras
and their allies, the Elapidae. When the

genus was moved into the Atractaspididae
its name was changed to *Homoroselaps* in
order to avoid having to change the name of
the family, which would have caused no
end of confusion (although the genus has
since been moved back into the Elapidae).

The general rule is that, once a species has
been named, its specific name cannot be
changed. (The only exception to this rule is
where the name given has already been used
for another animal.) This sometimes causes
confusion if the given name is inappropriate
or incorrectly spelled. *Lampropeltis getulus*,
for example, is named for a tribe of people
inhabiting North Africa, even though it is
found in North America.

10
The Classification of Snakes

THE FAMILIES OF SNAKES – A QUICK REFERENCE

Family	Number of genera	Approx. number of species	Page
Anomalepididae	4	19	194
Typhlopidae	3	200	194
Leptotyphlopididae	2	80	195
Tropidopheidae	4	21	196
Bolyeriidae	2	2	197
Boidae	17	61	198
Acrochordidae	1	3	205
Loxocemidae	1	1	206
Xenopeltidae	1	2	207
Aniliidae	1	1	207
Uropeltidae	10	51	208
Colubridae	287	1500	209
Atractaspididae	8	55	231
Elapidae	65	290	232
Viperidae	25	214	241

ANOMALEPIDIDAE

Members of the Anomalepididae (sometimes called Anomalepidae) are among the most primitive snakes. Although they lack pelvic girdles, they are clearly closely related to the blind snakes and thread snakes. All are very small snakes with cylindrical bodies, smooth, glossy scales and a short tail. They have long, narrow lower jawbones, which are hinged and typically bear a single small tooth each, or none at all. They are mostly brown or black and some species have white or yellow heads and tails.

They are a burrowing species that are rarely seen on the surface and which feed on termites and, possibly, other soft-bodied invertebrates. Almost nothing is known about their natural history although they are presumed to lay eggs. Four genera are recognized and the family is restricted to Central and South America.

Anomalepis Three species found in Central America and northern South America. They have a single tooth in each side of their lower jaw.

Helminthophis Three species from Central America and northern South America. There are no teeth in their lower jaw.

Liotyphlophis About 12 species found in Central America and northern and eastern South America. There is a single tooth in the lower jaw.

Typhlophis A monotypic genus containing only *T. squamosus* from north-eastern South America. There are no teeth in the lower jaw.

TYPHLOPIDAE Blind snakes

A relatively large family with almost 200 species found over most of the tropical and subtropical world, also found throughout Australia and on several groups of islands. They are very small to small snakes with smooth shiny scales and rudimentary eyes that are covered over by scales. They have cylindrical bodies and short tails. Most species are very slender, but there are a few larger, more robust species. They have a pelvic girdle and a single oviduct. The left lung is vestigial or absent altogether but there is a tracheal lung. They have teeth on the upper jaw, attached to the maxilla, but no teeth on the premaxilla. The lower jaw has no teeth and is rigid. Most species are pale in colour, often pinkish, but others are brown, black or grey.

They are exclusively burrowing snakes, which eat ants and termites and their larvae and, possibly, other soft-bodied invertebrates. Despite the large geographical range of the family, only three genera are recognized at present, although more are due to be described shortly, including one from Madagascar.

Ramphotyphlops About 40 species, formerly placed in the genus *Typhlina*, which is now suppressed. This genus is naturally confined to the Old World and is found from India, through south-east Asia, on many South Pacific Islands, New Guinea and into Australia. One species, the Brahminy blind snake, *R. braminus*, is parthenogenetic and has been introduced to many parts of the world outside its natural range. These include Australia, South Africa, Central America and Florida. It is commonly known as the flowerpot snake because of the [fre]quency with which it has been acciden[tally] transported around the world along [with] potted plants. Several other species [are] known from only one or two specimens[.]

Description of the *Ramphotyphlops* sp[ecies] is as in the family description. Males of [this] genus are unique in having a solid por[tion] to their protrusible copulatory organ[, as] opposed to the soft tube-like structure fo[und] in other snakes. Some species are [quite] colourful, especially where they occu[r in] areas where the soil is red or yello[w. A] number are associated with termite mou[nds] where they move about through a netw[ork] of burrows and probably feed on the in[sects] and their larvae. As far as is kno[wn] all species lay small clutches of elong[ate] eggs.

Rhinotyphlops About 25 species, u[nder] revision at present. The genus is not re[cog]nized by some authorities, who cons[ider] that its members should be placed in [the] genus *Typhlops*. Otherwise, they are s[epa]rated from them by having a horizo[ntal] edge to their rostral shield. Most specie[s are] found in Africa south of the Sahara, but [one] comes from the Middle East (*R. simoni*) [and] there are two species in Asia. Their ha[bits] are similar to other typhlopids: they fee[d on] termites and other soft-bodied inverteb[rates] and lay clutches of tiny eggs.

Typhlops About 100 species foun[d in] Central and South America, the who[le of] Africa south of the Sahara Desert, the M[iddle] East, and south Asia. A single specie[s, *T.*] *vermicularis*, reaches Europe in the Ba[lkans]

Distribution of
Anomalepididae.

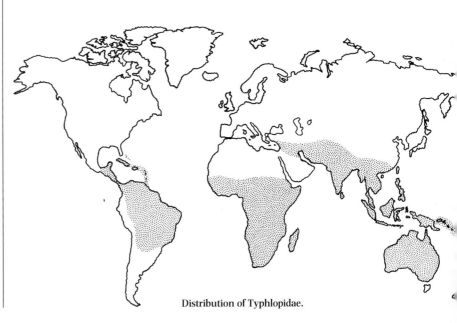

Distribution of Typhlopidae.

on. They are very small or small (excep-
ally, medium-sized) burrowing snakes,
lly grey, brownish or pinkish in colour,
resembling earthworms. Some species
black markings on pale grey or pink
grounds. They probably feed largely
ermites, ants and their larvae. As far as
own, all species lay eggs, with clutches
p to 60 in exceptional cases (e.g. *T.
gelii*) but more usually less than 10.
eggs may be retained by the female
they are well developed, however, as in
on's blind snake, *T. bibronii*, and they
h after five or six days. *T. diardi*, from
am, is said to retain the eggs until they
lly developed.

The thread snakes comprise about 80
species found in the southern parts of North
America (Texas and California) Central and
South America, the whole of Africa except
the Sahara Desert, the Arabian peninsula
and parts of the Middle East. They are small,
slender snakes with smooth, shiny scales.
They have a well-developed pelvic girdle
and some species have vestigial hind limbs
in the form of spurs. There are no teeth in
their upper jaw, which is rigid, and the
lower jaw is short and hinged about half

way along the skull. There is no left lung
and no left oviduct. Their eyes are small and
are covered by a scale rather than a brille.
Most are silvery pink in colour, but there are
a few more heavily pigmented species.

All species are burrowing snakes, seen on
the surface only occasionally at night or
when washed from their burrows by heavy
rain. They eat only termites and their larvae
and produce pheromones that prevent
the soldier termites from attacking them.
Because of their small mouths, the soft

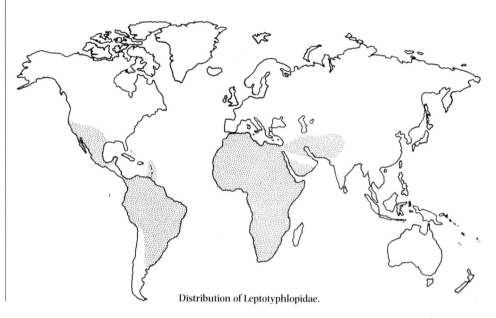

Distribution of Leptotyphlopidae.

ow big and how small?

es of snakes, though interesting to
ost people, are difficult to state.
aximum sizes, often quoted in field
ides, may refer to extra large 'freak'
dividuals and bear no relation to the
e of the average specimens that the
der is likely to come across. Then
ain, some snakes are poorly known
d it is difficult to know if larger or
aller individuals are waiting to be
und. In extreme cases, where only
e specimen is recorded, the maxi-
m size will also be the minimum
e!
Because of this, I have decided to give
proximations. In the following
criptions of genera, the terms 'very
all', 'small', 'medium-sized', 'large'
d 'very large' are used to describe the
es of the members of each genus.

These sizes are equivalent, roughly, to
the following measurements:

Very small	less than 30 cm (12 in)
Small	30–75 cm (12–30 in)
Medium-sized	76–150 cm (30–60 in)
Large	150–300 cm (60–120 in)
Very large	Over 300 cm (over 120 in)

In large genera, there may be species
of different lengths, and here it has been
necessary to give a range of sizes,
e.g. small to medium sized, etc.

Length is not the only measure of
size, of course, and some attempt has
also been made to give an impression of
the relative bulk of the various snakes
by describing the overall body form, e.g.
heavily built, slender, etc., giving a
reasonably good impression of the
snakes in question.

abdomens of large insects are grasped and
the contents squeezed out. Two genera are
recognized.

Leptotyphlops This is the largest genus,
containing all the species in the family except
one. The range of the genus is as for the
family. Found in a variety of habitats including semi-arid regions. They are usually
found in the nests of the termites on which
they feed. They lay small clutches of tiny
eggs, as small as grains of rice in some
species, and one species at least, the Texas
thread snake, *L. dulcis*, coils around its eggs.

Rhinoleptus A monotypic genus, containing
only *R. koniagui*, from West Africa. It is
distinguished by a hook-like rostral scale
and its large size (for a thread snake) of 50 cm
(1 ft 8 in). Its biology is poorly known.

TROPIDOPHEIDAE Wood snakes or West Indian boas

Members of this family were formerly placed in the Boidae, hence one of their common names. At other times they have been allied with the Round Island boas. They are distinguished mainly by the presence of a well-developed tracheal lung, a condition that is absent in the true boas and the Round Island boas. The left lung is greatly reduced and females of some species lack a pelvic girdle. Their eyes have vertically elliptical pupils. They are secretive, nocturnal snakes that are usually found among forest debris, under rotting logs, etc. All species are viviparous. The family comprises 21 species in four genera and has a restricted range in Central and South America and the West Indies. They are divided into two subfamilies, on the basis of their hemipenal morphology. Each subfamily has two genera.

TROPIDOPHEINAE

Species in this subfamily have prehensile, though short, tails. The body is thickset and roughly cylindrical and the scales may be smooth or keeled.

Trachyboa Two species are known, *T. boulengeri* and *T. gularis*. They are known as eyelash boas because of small protruding scales above their eyes. They are found only in lowland rainforests of southern Central America and northern South America, as far south as Ecuador. They have rough scales and dull coloration and appear to be terrestrial in habits. Rarely seen snakes about which little is known, but captives have produced litters of six and seven young.

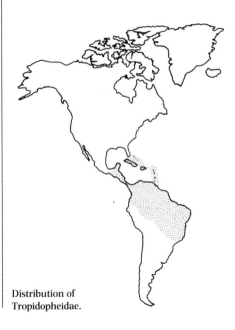

Distribution of
Tropidopheidae.

Tropidophis Sixteen species, 13 of which are found on various West Indian islands, including eight that are endemic to Cuba. The other three occur on the South American mainland, ranging as far south as Peru (*T. taczanowskyi*), Ecuador (*T. battersbyi*) and São Paulo Province, Brazil (*T. paucisquamis*). Small to medium-sized snakes, ranging in size from about 30 cm–1 m (1–3 ft). All species are opportunistic nocturnal hunters, taking frogs, lizards and small rodents. Some species force blood from their eyes and mouth when under stress: this unusual defensive behaviour may be unique among snakes. Some have brightly coloured tips to their tails: they may use these as lures. Many species and subspecies have very restricted ranges, often only one small island, and several are rare, having only been collected on a few occasions.

■ *Captivity* They are rarely kept in captivity, although *T. melanurus* is kept and bred on a limited scale. They prefer a cage with a substrate into which they can burrow or plenty of small holes into which they can crawl. Moderate humidity should be provided. Mating takes place in the early spring and the young are born about six to nine months later. They require small lizards or frogs at first but are also said to accept small fish. Later on they will take nestling mice, which they constrict.

UNGALIOPHEINAE

Only three species, in two genera, are placed in this subfamily.

Exiliboa A monotypic genus that contains only the Oaxaca boa, *E. placata*, from southern

▲ Haitian wood snake, *Tropidophis haitianus*

Mexico. It is a rare and little-known sr found only in cool montane cloud fores is uniform glossy black in colour with a small, light facial marking. Nothin known of its diet, behaviour or reproduc

Ungaliophis The genus contains two spe *U. continentalis* and *U. panamensis*, Central America. They are somet called banana boas because they have I accidentally transported in shipment bananas. They differ from the other mem of the family by having a large, conspicu internasal scale. Small to medium-snakes, rarely reaching 1 m (3 ft) in ler which appear to be largely arboreal nocturnal. Their natural prey is prob small lizards and frogs. *U. continentalis* given birth to small numbers of live yo under captive conditions.

■ *Captivity* One species, *Ungaliophis cont talis*, is occasionally kept. Its requirem are straightforward, although it is secr and must be given somewhere to I Adults will accept small mice but feedin; small young is sometimes problematica

small family contains only two species, ned to the diminutive Round Island, e Indian Ocean. They are often grouped the Boidae, but sometimes with the idopheidae, with which they have y similarities. They should probably be d in a family of their own, however, ly because of the form of the maxilla, h is jointed, and the absence of pelvic es, present in all other boid groups. In ion, the left lung is greatly reduced ugh there is no tracheal lung.

eria A monotypic genus containing *B. icarinata*, the Round Island burrowing Probably extinct; the last individual recorded in 1975. Apparently, this is a rial species, despite its long tapering Little more is known of it. It is not even n if it is live-bearing or whether it lays like its partner.

rea A monotypic genus containing ssumieri*, the Round Island keel-scaled This species has strongly keeled s and a narrow head. It appears to feed sively on the two lizard species that its island. Although commonly known 'boa' it lays eggs, clutches of three to aving been noted in captivity.

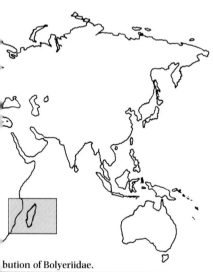

bution of Bolyeriidae.

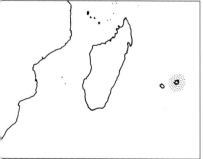

The boas of Round Island

Round Island is a small volcanic island off the north coast of Mauritius, in the Indian Ocean. Although its area is only 151 hectares (less than one square mile) it forms the total range of two boa-like snakes that are the only members of the family Bolyeriidae. (The Bolyeriidae is sometimes included in the Boidae or the Tropidopheidae.) The two species are *Bolyeria multicarinata*, the Round Island burrowing boa, and *Casarea dussumieri*, the Round Island keel-scaled boa.

Owing to habitat destruction, by goats and rabbits introduced during the nineteenth century, all the Round Island flora and fauna were brought to the brink of extinction. Apart from the boas, there are two other endemic reptiles on the island, a gecko, *Phelsuma guentheri* and a skink, *Leiolopisma telfairi*, and several endemic plant species.

Remedial action was instigated in 1976, with a programme to eradicate the goats. Extermination of the rabbits followed during the next decade. Regeneration of the endemic trees and understorey plants was encouraged by the absence of these two browsers and most of the reptile fauna began to recover slowly. Unfortunately, the action may have been too late for *Bolyeria*. The last live specimen was

▲ Aerial view of Round Island.

caught on the island in 1975 and no signs of it have been seen since. This species is especially vulnerable because it is (or was) a burrowing snake. The loss of the trees on the island led to rapid erosion of what little soil had collected over the island's rocky core. If *Bolyeria* has indeed survived it will be in one of the small fissures where a small amount of leaf-litter and soil may have been retained.

Casarea dussumieri, however, has responded favourably to the help it has been given by conservationists. Its numbers have increased significantly due, on the one hand, to the regeneration of the vegetation among which it lives and forages and, on the other, to a knock-on increase in the numbers of the small geckos and skinks which form its main prey. In addition, this species is being bred successfully at Jersey Zoo.

▼ The Round Island boa, *Casarea dussumieri*.

BOIDAE Boas and pythons

Taxonomically, this is a very problematical group of snakes. The boas and pythons are usually regarded as belonging to a single family, the Boidae, divided into at least three subfamilies consisting of 'boas' (two subfamilies) and the 'pythons'. Several other arrangements have also been proposed. The following arrangement, in which the two groups are dealt with separately, is used mainly because it helps to make the relationships between species, genera and subfamilies easier to understand. The various arguments for different systems of classification are put forward in the following important articles:

Kluge, A. (1991), *Boine snake phylogeny and research cycles*, Misc. Publ. Mus. Zool. Univ. Michigan, 178:iv+58 pages.

Kluge, A. (1993), 'Calabaria and the phylogeny of erycine snakes', *Zool. Journal of the Linnean Society*, 107:293–357.

McDowell, S. M. (1987), 'Systematics', in *Snakes, Ecology and Evolutionary Biology*, pp. 3–50, edited by R. A. Seigel, J. T. Collins and S. S. Novak, Macmillan Publishing Company, New York.

Underwood, G. (1976), 'A systematic analysis of boid snakes', in *Morphology and Biology of Reptiles*, pp. 151–175, edited by A. d'A. Bellairs and C. B. Cox, Linnean Society Symp. Series 3, Academic Press, London.

BOAS

In addition to the pythons, the Boidae formerly included the West Indian boas and the Round Island boas, but the latter two groups are now regarded as separate from the Boidae and from one another and are dealt with as the Tropidopheidae and the Bolyeriidae

This group now comprises 39 species in 12 genera and two subfamilies (but see the note regarding *Calabaria* on page 202). They are found in North, Central and South America, Africa, Madagascar and Asia, but are absent from Australia. A single species is found, on the edge of its range, in southeastern Europe. All members of the group, as understood here, give birth to live young.

The family is usually divided into two subfamilies, the 'true' boas, Boinae, and the dwarf boas, Erycinae.

Boinae

Eight genera are included in the Boinae. Heat-sensitive pits are present in some members of this subfamily and, when present, they are situated between the labial scales, not within the scales as in the pythons.

Acrantophis The two species forming this genus are restricted to Madagascar. They have no heat-sensitive pits. *A. madagascariensis* is the Madagascan ground boa and *A. dumerilii* is Dumeril's ground boa. They are heavy-bodied species, superficially similar to the common boa, but more intricately marked. Dumeril's boa grows to moderate sizes, 2 m (6½ ft) at most, whereas the Madagascan boa is larger, to almost 3 m (10 ft). Both species feed on birds and small mammals and both favour humid habitats and are therefore most commonly found near rivers and streams. Dumeril's boa is restricted to the south and south-west of the island whereas *A. madagascariensis* is found in the north and east. Both species have been placed on Appendix I by CITES.

■ *Captivity* Both species fare very well in captivity under a typical tropical regime and with a diet of rodents. *A. madagascariensis*, however, is not seen as often as its congener. This may be because it has proved to be the more difficult of the two to breed under artificial conditions and because it has smaller broods: a maximum of 8 as opposed to a maximum of 20. *Note:* It has recently been proposed that these two species should be placed in the genus *Boa*.

Boa This is a monotypic genus containing only the common boa, *Boa constrictor*. There are no heat-sensitive pits and the species seems to be more closely related to the Madagascan *Acrantophis*, despite their geographical separation, than any other genus of boas. This species is so well known

that a description appears superflu_ although there is much confusion _ geographical forms and subspecies. No fe_ than nine forms have been given subspe_ recognition at various times but the di_ ences between them are difficult, or im_ sible, to quantify. The Argentinian fo_ *B. c. occidentalis*, is the most distinct of_ mainland forms. The proliferation of na_ such as 'Colombian red-tailed boa', use_ snake-keeping hobbyists to describe par_ lar colour forms and slight variations _ add to the confusion as individuals _ many parts of the range can have re_ reddish coloured tails and this charact_ of no value in ascribing a particular sna_ a subspecies.

This snake has a truly enormous ra_ from Argentina in the south to as far n_ as Guaymas on the north-west coas_ Mexico (*Boa constrictor 'imperator'*). _ primarily a rainforest species, inhabi_ clearings and forest fringes, although it _ be found in semi-arid thorn scrub in par_ Sonora and in dry tropical forests in p_ of Central America. It is also found on sev_ islands including those of Trinidad, Tob_ Dominica (subspecies *nebulosus*) and_ Lucia (subspecies *orophias*) in the West In_ as well as a number of smaller off-s_ islands along the coast of Honduras. _ *sabogae* comes from Saboga Island an_ dwarf, nameless form, possibly extinct i_ wild, from Cayos Cochinos off the Carib_ coast of Honduras (commonly know_ Hog Island boas).

The common boa may grow to a m_ mum length of about 4 m (13 ft): _ specimens are appreciably less than th_

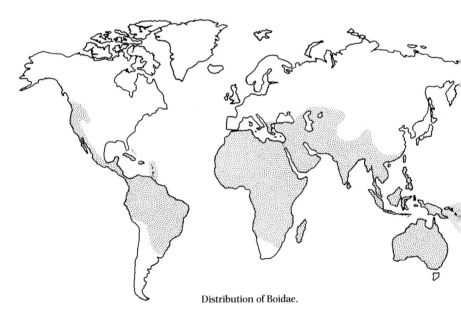

Distribution of Boidae.

generalist, feeding on mammals and
s, and may be arboreal in areas where
e trees grow. It is equally at home on the
ind, however, and is often encountered
g rivers, either in the water or lying out
he banks. It is also commonly found in
vicinity of human settlements.

iptivity Common boas are among the
st popular and undemanding of all
e snakes. They require accommodation
eeping with their size but, this apart,
rarely present any serious problems.
tive-bred animals are less inclined to be
ressive and adapt better than wild ones.
mon boas nearly always feed well on
l rodents, although a few seem to favour
s. This applies especially to some of the
ll island races although captive-bred off-
ng from the original collected animals
usually as easy to feed and raise as any of
other forms. Where the temperature is
constant throughout the year, they
mate at any time. Otherwise mating
ally takes place in the winter months in
onse to cooler conditions. Up to 50 live
ng are born after a gestation period that
es from five to eight months, depending
emperature.

doia This genus contains three well
ned species from New Guinea and neigh-
ring islands. The scales on the body of
se species are heavily keeled and the head
overed with numerous small scales.
ne of the species has heat-sensitive pits.
racteristic of the genus is a flat, angled
ral scale that gives the snout an oblique
ile. There is great variation in size and
ration within the species. Some of this is
to their distribution, scattered as they
among many oceanic islands, but even
nin groups from the same locality many
rent colours and patterns can be recog-
d. In *C. carinata*, 'long-tailed' and 'short-
d' populations can also be recognized
there is some correlation between tail
th and distribution. The three species
rly come from a common ancestor and
onstrate adaptive radiation: *C. aspera*,
smallest species, is short and stocky
i a prehensile but very short tail. It is a
estrial or semi-fossorial species. *C. bibroni*
ng and slender with a highly prehensile
and is totally arboreal in its habits.
arinata* is intermediate in form and may
ound in either habitat although it climbs
than *C. bibroni*.

iptivity All species are quite easily cared
but require a dark, secluded cage with
ng places. Adults usually feed readily

▲ Amazon tree boa, *Corallus enhydris*.

but young specimens sometimes refuse to
eat rodents. *C. carinata* gives birth to very
large litters of live young: almost 100 in
some cases. The other two species also have
relatively large litters and the newborn
young are very small in every case.

Corallus Three or four species are recognized (see note under *Xenoboa*), all South
American and slender arboreal boas. There
are very large, vertically arranged heat-
sensitive pits in the labial and rostral scales.
C. canina, the emerald boa is the most familiar. It is highly arboreal and closely parallels
the Asian *Chondropython viridis*, both in
appearance and in behaviour. It grows to
2 m (6½ ft). It is bright green when adult but
newly born juveniles are brick red or dull
orange and begin to turn green after a few
months. The species is greatly flattened
laterally. It probably feeds mainly on birds,
and possibly bats, and has long, recurved
teeth to prevent its prey from escaping once
it has been grasped. Unlike the green tree
python, it gives birth to live young.

 C. enhydris, the Amazon tree boa, may
grow to the same length as the emerald boa
but is a smaller species, being more slender in
build. Its markings are highly variable, even
within populations. It is found throughout
the Amazon Basin (subspecies *C. e. enhydris*)
and in northern South America and on
several West Indian Islands (subspecies *C. e.
cooki*). The annulated boa, *C. annulatus*, is the
least common and has a more restricted
range than the other two species. There

are three isolated populations, in southern
Central America (subspecies *C. a. annulatus*),
Colombia (subspecies *C. a. colombianus*) and
Ecuador (subspecies *C. a. blombergi*).

■ *Captivity* The emerald boa is far and away
the most widely kept of the three species,
followed by the Amazon tree boa and then
the annulated boa, which is hardly ever
available. All species are tropical and
require constant high temperatures or
around 25–30°C (77–86°F). Because they
are arboreal, they require tall cages so that
they can coil on a branch well above
ground level. This is especially important in
the case of the emerald tree boa because it
has great difficulty in feeding unless it can
hang downwards while it swallows its prey.
Breeding may take place at any time of
the year, although it is most commonly
recorded in the winter. The gestation period
lasts approximately six months and litters
of up to 20 have been recorded. Care of
the other species is similar, and *C. enhydris*
has been bred in captivity on numerous
occasions with litters of up to 15 young.
Some difficulty may be experienced in
getting the young to accept small rodents,
although they will often take lizards.

Epicrates Ten species, distributed throughout the West Indies (nine species) and
the South American mainland (*E. cenchria*,
of which up to nine subspecies are recognized). Some species, e.g. *E. cenchria*, have

heat-sensitive pits in the lower labial scales and also in the upper labials towards the snout. In others, e.g. *E. angulifer*, they are very shallow while *E. gracilis* and *E. exsul*, for instance, lack pits altogether. There is probably a correlation with prey types, those species with pits being the larger ones, which eat endothermic animals (birds, bats and other mammals) whereas the smaller species, which have no pits, eat mainly lizards and, possibly, frogs. Two forms, *E. m. monensis* and *E. gracilis*, appear to eat only reptiles, especially lizards.

Epicrates is the largest genus of boas, mainly because it is distributed throughout the West Indian islands, where a high degree of speciation has taken place. Many species are endemic to small islands, where their future is bleak. Of the 10 species, several have been divided into two or more subspecies. *E. cenchria*, the only species found on the mainland of South America (and on the offshore islands of Trinidad and Tobago), has a very large range, from Columbia (subspecies *maurus*) in the north to Argentina (subspecies *alvarezi*) in the south, and from the Pacific to the Atlantic coasts. Up to nine subspecies are recognized. This species reaches 2 m (6½ ft) in parts of its range and, like the other five larger species, has a rather generalized life-style. Four of the West Indian species, *E. angulifer*, *E. inornatus*, *E. striatus* and *E. subflavus*, are also quite large, exceptionally growing to 4 m (13 ft) in the case of *E. angulifer*, and about 2 m (6½ ft) in the others. They are also generalists. The five small species, *E. chrysogaster*, *E. exsul*, *E. fordi*, *E. gracilis* and *E. monensis*, are smaller, growing to about 1 m (3 ft 4 in). These tend to be more arboreal and are rather slender in build, although none of them shows the same degree of adaptation as *Corallus* species, for instance. The Puerto Rican boa, *E. inornatus*, is listed as endangered by the IUCN and the Jamaican species, *E. subflavus*, as vulnerable. Both are included on Appendix I by CITES, as is the Mona Island boa, *E. m. monensis*. The Bimini boa, *E. striatus fosteri*, is also in grave danger of extinction, while the Virgin Islands boa, *E. m. granti*, is known from several small islands but is nowhere common.

■ *Captivity* The rainbow boa, *Epicrates cenchria*, is by far the most commonly kept species, especially the Brazilian, Colombian and Argentinian subspecies (*E. c. cenchria*, *E. c. maurus* and *E. c. alvarezi* respectively). All these species are easily cared for and will breed under fairly simple conditions and will eat rodents readily. The Argentinian

subspecies probably requires cooler conditions than the others, which are more or less tropical in origin, and it may require a significant period of lower temperatures to induce it to breed. In all these subspecies, mating usually takes place during the cooler months of winter and the young are born about six months later, the exact period depending on temperature. Litters may number up to 30 in exceptional cases, although the Argentinian subspecies has significantly smaller broods of relatively large young. The young of most forms are noticeably brighter than the adults – this is especially so in the case of *E. c. maurus*, the young of which are often indistinguishable from those of *E. c. cenchria*, even though, as adults, they will fade to a fairly uniform brown coloration. *E. c. alvarezi* are again an exception, as the juveniles and adults are identically marked.

Of the other species, *Epicrates striatus*, are occasionally kept, and pose no special problems, while the rare Jamaican boa, *E. subflavus*, and the Mona Island boa, *E. monensis*, are subjects of captive breeding programmes in an attempt to increase stocks. The small species are difficult, however, as they feed primarily on lizards, at least when they are young.

Eunectes This is a South American genus, consisting of two to four species. The green anaconda, *E. murinus*, and the yellow anaconda, *E. notaeus*, are well known. The other two, *E. deschauenseei* and *E. barbouri*, are

sometimes recognized, but their existenc[e] shrouded in confusion. Both 'species' w[ere] described from Marajo Island, in the mo[uth] of the Amazon but their status is dubio[us.] There are no heat-sensitive pits on the la[bial] scales of any members of the genus.

Eunectes murinus is the world's larg[est] snake, growing to at least 9 m (29½ ft[) in] length. Its length may just be exceeded [by] that of the reticulated python but t[his] species is far more slender in build. It ha[s a] large range over much of tropical So[uth] America, including the island of Trinidad[. It] is a semi-aquatic species that is stron[gly] associated with swamps and slow mov[ing] rivers and is rarely found far from water. T[his] species has even been known to give bi[rth] under water in captivity. Its prey inclu[des] freshwater turtles and even small So[uth] American alligators (caiman), as well [as] mammals and birds. Anacondas are agg[re]sive and dangerous snakes and undoubte[dly] overpower and eat humans occasionally[.]

The yellow anaconda, *Eunectes notaeu*[s, is] a much smaller animal, growing to less t[han] half the length of it congener (and there[fore] only a small proportion of its weight). It, [too,] is highly aquatic but it has a more restric[ted] range, occurring in the southern parts [of] the Amazon basin.

■ *Captivity* The larger of the two specie[s is] rarely kept, owing to its enormous size a[nd]

▼ Yellow anaconda, *Eunectes notaeus*, from So[uth] America.

ntially vicious disposition. The yellow
...onda is kept and bred on a limited scale.
...ly rarely becomes tame but will usually
...rodents readily. Mating takes place
...ng the cooler months and the gestation
...d is six months or more, depending
...emperature. Litters of up to 20 young
...orn.

...inia A monotypic genus containing
the Madagascan tree boa, *S. mada-*
...riensis. This arboreal species has
...picuous heat-sensitive pits in its upper
...lower labial scales. Its coloration is
...ible but most are some shade of green or
...ish green. A larger, brown and yellow
... also occurs in parts of the island.
... boas are amongst the most common
...es on Madagascar but deforestation
...severely reduced suitable habitat. The
...es is placed on Appendix I of CITES.
...ptivity Although rare, the species is
...ly prized for its attractive coloration
... usually calm temperament. It feeds
...ily on rodents and has been bred on
...erous occasions. Four to 16 young
...orn after a gestation period lasting six
...ight months. The young are red and
...nge to the adult greenish coloration
...in their first year.

...oboa A monotypic genus containing
X. cropanii, which is found in the region
...o Paulo, Brazil. It is the least known of
...family, and only two additional speci-
...s having been found since its original
...ription in 1954.

...ccording to Kluge (1991), this species
...ld be moved to the genus *Corallus*,
...ough it is distinct from the other
...bers of that genus in having a very
...h smaller number of scale rows (29–32,
...pared with over 50 in *C. enhydris* and
...nulatus and over 60 in *C. caninus*).

...inae

Erycinae consists of four genera, three
...hem monotypic and the third, *Eryx*,
...aining about 10 species. All erycine
... are small fossorial or semi-fossorial
...es, with many of the adaptations
...cal of burrowing snakes, such as a cylin-
...al body, smooth scales, broad head
...h the eyes directed upwards in some
...ies) and short tail. The tail may be used
...eflect attention away from the head
...n the snake is under threat.

...rina A monotypic genus containing
... the rubber boa, *C. bottae*, of western
...th America (but see the note on page

202). This species grows to only about
75 cm. It is found from British Columbia,
Canada, in the north (and is therefore the
most northerly occurring boid) to southern
California in the south. In places it may
be found at altitudes of more than 3,000 m
(about 10,000 ft) and prefers cool,
humid conditions. Three subspecies are
recognized, two of them with very restricted
ranges. Although primarily a burrowing
snake, the rubber boa has been found in low
vegetation and on the top of stumps. It feeds
mainly on small nestling mammals and
birds but also takes amphibians and smaller
snakes. Litters of three to eight young
are born after a gestation period of three to
four months. There is some evidence that
females only reproduce every two or three
years.

■ *Captivity* Not often seen in captivity
because of its rarity (it is protected in parts
of its range). It requires conditions that are
not too hot and a substrate into which it
can burrow. Occasional light spraying of
the substrate appears to be beneficial.
The species rarely feeds during the winter,
irrespective of the temperature at which it is
kept.

Eryx (sand boas) Ten species, including
E. conicus, which is sometimes placed in a
separate genus, *Gongylophis*. It is exclusively
Old World in its distribution but its members
are found from East Africa, throughout the
Middle East and well into central Asia and
the Indian subcontinent, including Sri
Lanka. *Eryx jaculus* is the only boid to be
found in Europe, where it is restricted to the
extreme south-east. Members of the genus
are typically small, burrowing snakes that

▲ Rosy boa, *Lichanura trivirgata saslowi*, a
diminutive boa from Mexico.

live in arid conditions. They have stout,
cylindrical bodies with short tails. Their
heads are the same width as their bodies and
their small eyes are placed towards the top of
their heads. The largest species, *E. johnii*,
grows to about 1 m (3 ft 4 in) in length but
several species, e.g. *E. miliaris*, *E. tataricus*,
are less than half this size. Most are cryptically coloured in shades of brown, yellow,
orange or reddish, depending on the soil
type in which they occur. All species eat
small mammals, especially rodents, and
most will probably accept other prey such as
birds and lizards given the opportunity.
Several species, such as *E. elegans*, *E. muelleri*
and *E. somalicus*, are known from very few
specimens.

■ *Captivity* All available species fare well in
captivity under a variety of conditions. They
should be given a suitable substrate for
burrowing in, although this need not be
sand. All species take rodents of appropriate
size although a dwarf form of *E. jaculus*
turcicus from several Greek islands appears
to eat only small lizards. Breeding takes place
in the spring and the young are born about
four to six months later. Litters may number
up to 30 or more young (in *E. tataricus*) but
more commonly consist of around 10.

Lichanura A monotypic genus containing
only the rosy boa, *L. trivirgata*, of which four
or five subspecies are recognized (but see
Stebbins, 1985).[1] The rosy boa is North
American and is found in the more arid
parts of south-western United States and
north-western Mexico. Although a desert

species, it is also associated with rocks and is rarely found far from the rocky outcrops characteristic of the region. In all its forms this is a longitudinally striped snake although the clarity and colour of the stripes vary with locality and subspecies. The rosy boa grows to just over 1 m (3 ft 4 in) and feeds largely on rodents. It gives birth to four or five young although much larger litters, up to 12, are on record.

Note: In a recent paper, Kluge (1993) proposed that the genus *Lichanura* should be suppressed and its sole member, the rosy boa, included in the genus *Charina*. Even more surprisingly, he proposes that the African burrowing 'python' *Calabaria reinhardtii*, should also be placed in this genus, making it the only egg-laying boa.

■ *Captivity* The rosy boa is a popular species and usually fares well under captive conditions. Captive-bred specimens feed well and grow rapidly. As this is a temperate species it should not be subjected to constant heat. A thermal gradient, with heat applied at one end of the cage only, is recommended and heat can be withdrawn altogether during the winter provided the temperature does not fall below about 10°C (50°F). Breeding takes place in the spring and the young are born about five months after mating. Litters normally comprise three to five young although Stebbins (1985)[1] gives three to 12. Newborn rosy boas sometimes refuse to feed. If this behaviour persists it is best to take their heat away and allow them to remain cool until the following spring, when they will usually begin feeding voluntarily.

PYTHONS

As noted previously (page 201), the pythons are usually placed within the family Boidae, along with the boas. They differ from them mainly in the arrangement of bones in their skull and also in their distribution and their breeding habits.

Pythons are restricted to the Old World, but are not found on Madagascar. Their centres of evolution appear to be Africa and Australasia. All species lay eggs and a number are known to brood them throughout the incubation period. Many species are well known and they include four of the six so-called 'giant' snakes. Other species, however, are more moderate in size. Pythons feed on a variety of warm-blooded prey, amphibians or other reptiles. Some species have heat-sensitive pits situated within the scales bordering their mouth. The presence or absence of these pits, the size and arrange-

ment of the scales covering the top of their heads and the presence or absence of teeth on the pre-maxilla are the characters that have been most used in their classification.

Taxonomically, the family is in a state of complete chaos where the Australasian species are concerned. A minimum of five genera are recognized but some authorities consider that this should be expanded to at least seven. A conservative approach has been adopted here, using the six most widely accepted genera: short notes outline some of the other proposals.

Aspidites A clearly defined genus consisting of two medium sized pythons, endemic to Australia and characterized by the absence of heat-sensitive pits, large symmetrical scales on the top of the head and lack of teeth on the premaxilla. The species are the black-headed python, *A. melanocephalus* and the woma, *A. ramsayi*. Both are restricted to Australia and grow to approximately the same size, 2.5 m (8½ ft), although they average rather less than this, about 1.5 m (5 ft). The species are rather similar in appearance, and their most obvious difference is the black head and neck of *A. melanocephalus*. The latter is more northerly in its distribution and is found along the north coast of Australia and ranges south into the more arid regions of the interior. The woma, on the other hand, is confined to the desert regions of central Australia. Both species eat reptiles, including other snakes, in addition to a wide range of bird and mammal prey.

■ *Captivity* These pythons are rarely [s]… outside Australia. There are no obv[ious] problems, however, and both species h[ave] been bred under captive conditions. T[hey] mate mainly in the winter, Decembe[r to] May inclusive in the Northern hemisph[ere]. Although they will accept rodents in c[apti]vity, *Aspidites* also feed on snakes and th[ere] is a tendency towards cannibalism. [This] would indicate that they are best ho[used] separately except for breeding.

Calabaria This is a monotypic genus [con]taining only the Calabar ground pyth[on,] *Calabaria reinhardtii*, from West Af[rica]. A recent proposal, to place this in the ge[nus] *Charina*, is the subject of a short note on [this] page. It is a small, cylindrical burrow[ing] species, with a short tail, smooth scales [and] small eyes. It is variable in colour, usu[ally] being brown or reddish with a suffusio[n of] irregular black mottling. The tail is e[spe]cially blunt and rounded and is used a[s a] false head if the python is threatened. L[ittle] is known about its natural history and [its] relationships with the other pythons [are] rather obscured by characters that s[eem] to have evolved (or regressed) as a resu[lt of] its burrowing habits.

■ *Captivity* Difficult. Imported animals o[ften] fail to adapt to captive conditions and th[ere] is no supply of captive-bred young. [The] best results have been obtained by hou[sing] the animals in cages with a deep laye[r of]

▼ Calabar ground python, *Calabaria reinhard[tii]* from West Africa.

s into which they can burrow, or by
iding a dark retreat, such as an up-
ed clay plant pot. They feed on rodents.
y lay small clutches consisting of one to
large eggs.

ndropython This is a monotypic genus
taining only the green tree python, *C.
lis* (placed in the genus *Morelia* by Kluge,
3). The species is found on the island of
Guinea, where it is relatively common,
in the rainforests of north-eastern
tralia, where it is rare. There are heat-
sitive pits in some of the labial scales,
top of the head is covered with small
gular scales and there are no teeth on
premaxilla. It is highly arboreal in its
ts, rarely leaving the trees except to
its eggs. The young are bright yellow
netimes orange) in colour but gradually
nge to the typical green colour of the
lt during the first year of their life. Some
viduals are uniform in colour but others
e a series of white markings along the
ebral line. Tree pythons feed on birds
small mammals, including bats. The
ies is remarkable for its superficial and
avioural similarities to the South American
rald boa, *Corallus caninus*.

ptivity This species is among the most
ular pythons. It requires a tall cage
a perch near the top so that it can coil
fortably and hang down in ambush for
rey. It eats rodents and birds although
chlings sometimes require manipulation
re they start to feed. Most specimens are
derately aggressive and cannot be han-
easily. Breeding has been achieved on
ny occasions, with most matings taking
e during the winter, mainly from
tember to December inclusive. The eggs
nber from 4 to 20. They sometimes fail
atch and it appears beneficial to incu-
them in such a way that air can circu-
freely around them.

sis An Australasian genus, the 11 mem-
s of which have been the subject of much
sion and taxonomic confusion in recent
rs. As understood here, the genus
tains four small brown pythons from
tralia, *L. childreni, maculosus, perthensis*
stimsoni (recently placed in the genus
aresia* by Kluge, 1993) as well as six
derate to large species found in Australia
New Guinea. The larger species are:
ringed python, *L. boa* (sometimes placed
ne genus *Bothrochilus*), D'Alberti's python,
bertisii, Macklot's python, *L. mackloti* and
Papuan python, *L. papuanus*, all from
Guinea and surrounding islands, and

▲ D'Alberti's python, *Liasis albertisii*, a slender,
elegant species from Papua New Guinea.

the water python, *L. fuscus*, and the olive
python, *L. olivaceus*, from Australia. In addition, certain members of the genus here
regarded as *Morelia* are also included in
Liasis by some authors (see below).

The small species have much the same
life-style as medium-sized colubrids do in
other parts of the world, and are mainly
nocturnal. *L. perthensis* is known as the
anthill python as it is most often found in
termite nests. The larger species are more
variable in their habits. Some, such as *L.
fuscus*, are semi-aquatic and feed on water
birds and their eggs as well as on mammals.
Others, like *L. albertisii*, live in tropical
forests, while *L. boeleni*, comes from cool
montane rainforests in New Guinea. A very
small form of *L. mackloti*, *L. m. savuensis*, is
found only on the isolated Indonesian island
of Savu, one of the Lesser Sunda group.

■ *Captivity* The suitability and the finer
points of husbandry obviously vary somewhat between the species, especially as
there is quite a wide variation in size and
preferred habitat, but there are no major
problems associated with these species as
long as healthy stock has been acquired in
the first place. They should be kept in cages
appropriate to their size, but are not especially active snakes. An opportunity to hide
must be made available, and a range of

temperatures should be provided. All the
species will eat rodents, although at least
two of the small ones, *L. childreni* and *L.
perthensis*, can be quite small at hatching
and may require smaller prey at first, such
as lizards. All species appear to have more or
less seasonal breeding habits, mating most
commonly during the cooler months of the
year.

Captive-bred animals are available for
most species although some are not yet
widely available. Wild-caught animals are
invariably from Indonesia (there are no
legally exported animals originating in
Australia) and are often heavily parasitized.
As a result, these fare very badly in captivity
except in the hands of experts. Many captive-
bred dwarf pythons are hybrids between
L. childreni and *L. maculosus*: the distinction
between these species was not recognized
until 1985, by which time many stocks had
already been interbred.

Morelia An almost exclusively Australian
genus, and one that has been the subject
of much revision and counter-revision
recently. At one time it contained only the
carpet python and its variants, *M. spilota*
subspecies. At other times this species has
been placed in the genus *Python*. At present,
the genus contains a total of five species,
the amethystine python, *M. amethistina*,
Boelen's python, *M. boeleni*, the Oenpelli
python, *M. oenpelliensis*, and the rare and
newly described rough-scaled python, *M.*

▲ Boelen's python, *Morelia boeleni*, from highland regions of New Guinea.

carinata, in addition to the carpet python. An additional species, *M. bredli*, was described from central Australia in 1981 but is sometimes regarded as a subspecies of *M. spilota*. Only the amethystine python and the carpet python are found outside Australia, with ranges that extend into Papua New Guinea. Boelen's python is found only in New Guinea. Species in this genus have heat-sensitive pits in their labial and rostral scales. Their heads may be covered with small irregular scales (*M. spilota* and *M. carinata*) or with larger, more regularly arranged scales (*M. amethistina* and *M. oenpelliensis*). The scales on the body are smooth or slightly keeled, with the notable exception of *M. carinata*, in which they are heavily keeled. They are medium sized to large, the largest species, *M. amethistina*, averaging about 3.5 m (11½ ft) in length but often exceeding 4 m (13 ft).

Collectively, they are found in a wide variety of habitats, including desert, scrub and rainforest. Some forms of the carpet python are partially arboreal, whereas others are terrestrial. It is sometimes found, in one or other of its forms, in the vicinity of towns and villages. All the snakes in this genus are attractively marked, although there is great variation, especially in the carpet python. Typical markings are of saddles or reticulations of dark brown, dark grey or black on a paler background, which may be cream, yellow, buff or even pinkish.

■ *Captivity* The carpet python is by far the species of most interest to collectors. It occurs in numerous regional colour variations, some of which have been recognized, rightly or wrongly, as subspecies. The forms from Queensland and from central Australia are especially distinctive and sought-after. Care of this species is quite straightforward. It can be aggressive but usually settles down quickly in captivity and is quite undemanding with regard to temperature, etc. It eats small rodents and some individuals may develop preferences for a particular species of prey, e.g. rats or mice. It is widely bred in Australia and elsewhere and fully grown females lay clutches of about 20 eggs. Of the other species, only *M. amethistina* is kept to any extent, outside Australia at least. This species is not so popular as it grows large and has an unpredictable temperament. It is not difficult keep, however, and has been bred on m than one occasion.

Python A well-known (and stable) ge with seven members in Africa, south and south-east Asia. The reticulated pyth and the Indian python, *P. reticulatus* *P. molurus*, are the two largest snakes Asia, while the African python, *P. sebae* the largest snake in Africa. There are als number of small, stout-bodied species s as the royal python or ball python, *P. reg* and the Angolan python, *P. anchietae*, fr Africa, and the blood python, *P. cur* from south-east Asia. All members of genus have heat-sensitive pits in the la and rostral scales. The Timor python, *timoriensis*, is intermediate in size and is least known species. It is restricted to island of Timor and appears to form a l both geographically and morphologica between the pythons from northern A tralia, such as *Morelia amethistina*, those from south-east Asia, such as *Pyt reticulatus*.

■ *Captivity* Pythons of this genus are am the most popular captives. The royal pyth was, until recently, frequently availa at low cost, but it is often a poor cho especially for beginners, since it may f only sporadically if at all. The very la species require special arrangements

▼ Blood python, *Python curtus*, from south-eas Asia, with prey.

recommended only for those collectors
●ared to accommodate them.

●sides the size problem, and with the
●ible exception of *P. regius*, members of
● genus are hardy and trouble-free in
●ivity. The Burmese python is widely
● in captivity and a number of mutant
●ations, such as an albino form, are avail-
●. This species lays clutches of about 30
●0 eggs and captive females often make
● mothers, coiling around the clutch
● brooding it throughout development.
●*ticulatus* and *P. sebae* tend to have a less
●ictive temperament and are not as
●ly kept or bred. The blood python is
●y accommodated but wild-caught
●imens are invariably heavily infested
● a remarkable selection of parasites
● are best avoided; this species is being
● in fair numbers now and the captive-
● offspring are infinitely easier to cater
●This species is quite variable and the
●imens with a red or reddish wash are
●most desirable. The Timor species is only
●ly seen in captivity and the Angolan
●●on almost never.

▲ Small file snake, *Acrochordus javanicus*.

The wart snakes are set apart from other families of snakes by a combination of unique features. They are highly specialized for aquatic life and occur only in tropical freshwater, estuarine and seawater environments. They are practically helpless on land and appear never to leave the water voluntarily. They have a single lung but the tracheal lung is large and well developed. There are no traces of a pelvic girdle and the lower jaw is flexible, as in the colubrids. When the snakes submerge themselves, the nostrils can be closed by means of a flap in the roof of the mouth, while the lingual fossa (the notch in the upper jaw through which the tongue is protruded) can also be closed, by a pad on the lower jaw. The skin is loose and hangs in folds, especially when the snakes are removed from the water. The scales are unlike those of any other snakes and are small, granular and do not overlap one another – their common names are derived from the superficial appearance of the scales. Furthermore, the skin has microscopic hair-like bristles, the function of which is uncertain. The family contains a single genus.

Acrochordus (**wart or file snakes**) Three species are recognized. *A. granulatus* was formerly placed in the monotypic genus *Chersydrus* but this arrangement has been shown to be invalid. The distribution of the family is quite large, ranging from India, through Indo-China and south-east Asia to the South Pacific region and northern Australia. *A. javanicus* is found in fresh waters of Asia and Indonesia, and is replaced in New Guinea and Australia by *A. arafurae*, the Arafura wart snake. *A. granulatus* may be found in fresh water but also occurs in mangrove forests, estuaries and coastal marine waters throughout the area. The wart snakes are medium sized to large snakes, with the largest species, *A. javanicus*, sometimes reaching 2.5 m (8 ft). Two of the species are brown or greyish above and dirty white below, but *A. javanicus* is boldly banded in black and white. All species feed on fish, and give birth to live young.

■ *Captivity* File snakes are very rarely kept in captivity because of their specialized requirements. They would require very large heated aquaria and a steady supply of live fish. Captive breeding has not been achieved.

Distribution of Acrochordidae.

LOXOCEMIDAE Mexican burrowing snake

The Mexican burrowing snake comprises a family of one. It was formerly placed within the Boidae, and is sometimes called the Mexican burrowing python. A pelvic girdle is present, and consists of two bones. The left lung is about half the size of the right one.

Loxocemus A monotypic genus containing only the Mexican burrowing snake, *L. bicolor*. The species is found in Mexico and adjacent parts of Central America. It is a medium-sized snake with a stout, muscular body and large scales on the top of its head. The scales on its body are smooth and slightly iridescent and there are often irregular patches of white scales: these occasionally cover extensive areas. Otherwise, the upper side of the body is brown, the lower parts white. A semi-burrowing species that is active mainly at night. Its behaviour in the wild is poorly known. It is known to eat the eggs and young of turtles and iguanid lizards, but, judging from its behaviour in captivity, it probably takes a variety of vertebrate prey. It is oviparous.

■ *Captivity* Easily cared for in a vivarium containing a deep layer of peat or moss into which it can burrow. Alternatively, it should be given a hide-box containing similar material. It feeds readily on small rodents and is docile and easily handled. Captive breeding is, mysteriously, hardly ever achieved. It seems that a period of substantial cooling may be required.

Distribution of Loxocemidae.

▼ Mexican burrowing snake, *Loxocemus bicolor*, which comprises the family Loxocemidae.

family Xenopeltidae contains but two
ies, the sunbeam snake, *Xenopeltis uni-*
* and *X. hainanensis*. These species, and
efore the family, are restricted to south-
Asia and southern China. They have no
ic girdle or spurs, and their left lung is
developed, being about half the size of
ight one.

opeltis Natural history information
ing to the Chinese species, *X. hainanen-*
described in 1972, is largely lacking
ts habits are thought to resemble those
e sunbeam snake, *X. unicolor*, which is
r known. This is a burrowing species
is rarely seen on the surface. It is found
range of habitats including lightly
ted areas but also among the suburbs of
s on waste ground. It is a medium-sized
e with a cylindrical body, dark above
white or creamish below. Its scales are
oth and highly polished, and are more
scent that those of any other snake. The
and snout are flattened and shovel-
ed and the eyes are small. It is mainly
urnal, and feeds on small mammals,
hibians and reptiles, including other
es. It is oviparous.

ptivity The Chinese species, *Xenopeltis*
anensis, is unknown in captivity. *Xeno-*
s unicolor is a rather specialized snake,
commonly offered for sale. Wild individ-
may be in poor condition but, once
are acclimatized, they fare well and are
y accommodated. They should be given
ghtly humid vivarium with a deep layer
at or moss covering the base. They will
d most of their time below the surface,
ing out at night to take small rodents.
ive breeding has taken place on a few
sions. Clutches of up to 10 eggs are laid.
young are small and may require force
ng at first, although some will take
born mice. Once they begin to feed they
v quickly and are trouble-free.

The Aniliidae comprises only a single
species. It has a pelvic girdle and vestigial
hind limbs. The eyes of this species are small
and are not covered by a brille, but by a
large transparent scale. The ventral scales
are hardly larger than the dorsal ones
and the body is cylindrical in shape. The
skull is not very flexible, with only a limited
amount of articulation in the lower jaw and
none at all in the upper jaw. The left lung is
vestigial, as in more advanced snakes. This
snake therefore combines features of the
primitive snakes (Typhlopidae, etc.) with
some of those of the more advanced families
(Colubridae, etc.).

▲ The South American pipe snake, *Anilius
scytale*, is the sole member of the family Aniliidae.

Anilius A monotypic genus containing only
the South American pipe snake, *A. scytale*,
found in the Amazon Basin. It is a medium-
sized snake with a bold coloration of black
and red rings and is sometimes regarded
as a 'false' coral snake. It is a burrowing
species, usually found in moist habitats
including rainforests and more lightly
forested areas. It is most active at night
and is thought to feed on small vertebrates,
including smaller snakes. It is thought to be
viviparous but details are lacking.

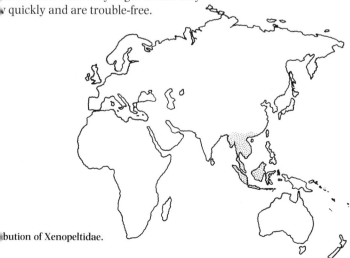

bution of Xenopeltidae.

Distribution of Aniliidae.

UROPELTIDAE Shield-tails and pipe snakes

A family of small burrowing snakes restricted to the Indian subcontinent and south-east Asia. Pelvic girdles are present in some species but not others. The left lung is either very small or absent altogether. Unlike the South American pipe snake, *Anilius*, the eye is covered by a brille. The family is divided into two subfamilies, the Cylindropheinae and the Uropeltinae. Some authorities regard these as separate families, sometimes combining the Cylindropheinae with *Anilius*, i.e. placing them together in the family Aniliidae. To add further to the confusion, the anatomy and biology of the sole member of the genus *Anomochilus* is virtually unknown.

CYLINDROPHEINAE (Asian pipe snakes)

As mentioned above, the Asian pipe snakes are sometimes placed with *Anilus* in the Aniliidae. They differ from that species in possessing a brille and in having no teeth on the premaxilla, both regarded as advanced features. Pelvic girdles are present in the species in this subfamily.

Anomochilus A monotypic genus containing only *A. weberi*, a very rare and little-known species from western Sumatra. A very small snake with a cylindrical body and a small head. It appears to live in rainforests and is probably a burrowing species. Apparently oviparous, in which case it is unique among the Uropeltidae.

Cylindrophis (pipe snakes) Eight species found from Sri Lanka, India, Burma, into Indo-China and to parts of Indonesia. Small to medium-sized snakes with cylindrical bodies but conspicuously flattened tails.

Their heads are small and flattened and their eyes are also small. Mostly burrowing snakes from moist or damp habitats. When threatened they may raise their tails, exposing bright coloration beneath. At the same time, they hide their heads among their coils. Little is known about their natural history or diet although some species at least feed mainly on other burrowing snakes. Viviparous, giving birth to up to 15 young.

UROPELTINAE (shield-tailed snakes)

The shield-tailed snakes are distinguished from the pipe snakes in not having pelvic girdles. They are specialized burrowing snakes that have a rigid skull and jaws. The eye is covered by a large polygonal scale rather than a brille. The teeth are absent from the premaxilla. The left lung is very small. The most notable feature of the members of this family concerns the tail. Its tip consists either of an enlarged rough scale with two points, or it ends in an oblique circular area covered with spines or tubercles. There is a bony plate immediately beneath this area. The head is narrow and pointed and is used to drive a burrow through the soil. Through modifications to the first few vertebrae, the neck can be twisted to a very sharp angle and this presumably allows the snake to use its head to enlarge the burrow by ramming the soil to one side or the other. The specialized locomotion of snakes of this subfamily is described elsewhere. The eight genera are restricted to Sri Lanka and southern India.

Brachyophidium A monotypic genus containing only *B. rhodogaster*, from southern

India. A very small snake in which tail ends in a spine rather than a sh Presumed to be viviparous, otherwise poorly known.

Melanophidium Three species from south India. Rare, medium-sized snakes foun forested montane regions about w almost nothing is known. Viviparous.

Platyplectrurus Two species, *P. triline* which is endemic to southern India *P. madurensis*, from southern India an Lanka. Small snakes in which the tails in a spine. Viviparous.

Plecturus Four species from southern In Small snakes in which the tail ends in a of spines. Poorly known. Viviparous.

Pseudotyphlops A monotypic genus taining only *P. philippinus*, from Sri La (the specific name was given in er A small species in which the tail ends circular, roughened plate, armed wi ring of spines around its rim. Foun wet or damp soil, especially in agricult areas. It apparently feeds on earthwo Viviparous.

Rhinophis Ten species found in south India and Sri Lanka. Small snakes large tail shields covered with tuber They live in a variety of habitats, inclu under decaying vegetation and logs in silted up drainage ditches. They are c found in small colonies and appear to mainly on earthworms. Viviparous.

Teretrurus A monotypic genus contai only *T. sanguineus* from southern Indi very small snake about which almost n ing is known. Presumed to be viviparou

Uropeltis About 20 species, three of w are found in Sri Lanka, the remainde southern India. Very small to small sn with small tail shields ending in a pa spines. Thought to feed on earthwo Viviparous.

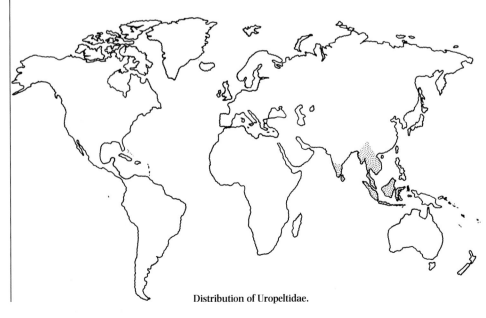

Distribution of Uropeltidae.

...ost parts of the world, colubrid snakes ...he species that most readers will be ...iar with. All colubrids lack a pelvic ...e, a functional left lung and a coronoid ...(a small bone in the lower jaw that ...nd in primitive snakes but which has ...lost in the more advanced families). ...heads are covered with large sym...cal scales and the vertebrae lack ...pophyses (downward-projecting spines) ...t in a few specialized species such as ...with aquatic habits and the egg-eating ...es, in which the pointed hypapophyses ...e oesophagus are used to saw through ...ells of eggs.

...er than these characters, or rather the ...of them, colubrids may be almost any ...e, size and colour. They have radiated ...y to fill almost every ecological niche ...ble, with the exception of the ocean ...ough some members of the Homalop-...., and certain races of *Nerodia fasciata*, ...made a brief flirtation with the marine ...onment and are found in coastal and ...rine waters around south-east Asia ...he Gulf of Mexico respectively). They ...an almost cosmopolitan distribution ...re the dominant family in most places, ...ugh they are poorly represented in ...ralia.

...ny of the morphological characteristics ...e various species of colubrids, such as ...shape, type of scales and coloration, ...e accounted for by their specializations. ...tion in reproductive biology – some ...es are oviparous whereas others are ...arous – can likewise often be correlated ...distribution and habitat. These adap-...eatures have caused many problems

for systematists over the years because convergent evolution has brought about groups of species that look very similar even though they are not closely related, while related species may be superficially distinct from one another merely because they occupy very different niches.

The family Colubridae, as traditionally understood, contains just over 1,500 species, divided into about 300 genera. In other words, three-fifths of all snakes are contained in this one huge, widespread family. It is highly unlikely that the family has a single ancestral line but it has become one of the great herpetological repositories – species that do not obviously belong in any of the other families are placed here and there is little doubt that the family will eventually be split into a number of smaller ones. Some authorities, such as Garth Underwood,[2] already recognize up to four families – Dipsadidae, Homolopsidae, Natricidae and Colubridae – within this assemblage of genera and species. Several of these are further subdivided into a number of subfamilies. Several other schemes have been proposed recently.

Until there is a reasonable consensus of opinion, it seems that there is no useful purpose to be served by trying to follow one or other of these schemes. Nor is there any point in listing the various arrangements, all of which are subject to change. In the absence of any generally agreed classification, then, the best option seems to be to continue to consider all the 'colubrids' together, bearing in mind that several of the subfamilies are likely to be promoted to full family status at some time in the future.

The Colubridae, as considered here, can be divided into a number of subfamilies: up to 28 have been recognized at various times[3] but it is more common to reduce these to fewer, but larger, subfamilies. McDowell's important paper of 1987, for example,[4] lists nine and he recognizes one other, the Psammophiinae. Although some subfamilies are well defined, for instance the Homalopsinae, other subfamilies consist at present of a 'core' of species that can be assigned to each, leaving a large number of species that cannot easily be slotted in. Unsatisfactory though this system is, it appears to be the best that can be followed at present. The following subfamilies may be recognized.

COLUBRINAE

'Typical' snakes, with large eyes at the sides of the head, nostrils at the sides of the snout. They actively search for their prey, and strike accurately. Some species have rear fangs, e.g. *Thelotornis* and *Dispholidus*, and a number of them, including these two, are dangerous to man. Some systems of classification place these back-fanged species in a separate subfamily, the Boiginae. Examples of genera in this subfamily include many of the familiar North American, European and Asian genera, such as the whipsnakes, *Coluber*, coachwhips, *Masticophis*, smooth snakes, *Coronella*, egg-eating snakes, *Dasypeltis*, rat snakes, *Elaphe*, kingsnakes, *Lampropeltis*, and gopher snakes, *Pituophis*.

HOMALOPSINAE

Aquatic snakes (freshwater and estuarine) that feed on fish, amphibians and crustaceans. Distributed throughout south-east Asia and northern Australasia. They have valved nostrils on top of the head and their eyes are small and directed upwards. They

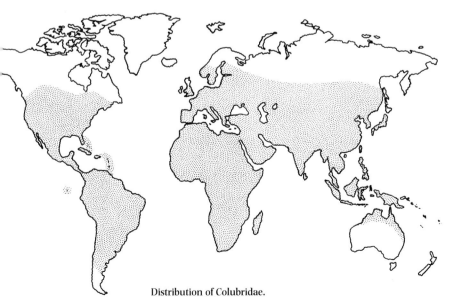

Distribution of Colubridae.

1. Stebbins, R. C. (1985), *A Field Guide to the Western Reptiles and Amphibians*. Houghton Mifflin, Boston.
2. Underwood, G. (1966) *A Contribution to the Classification of Snakes*. British Museum (Natural History), London.
3. Smith, H. M., Smith, R. B. and Sawin, H. L. (1977), 'A summary of snake classification', *Journal of Herpetology* 11(2):115–121.
4. McDowell, S. B. (1987), 'Systematics', in *Snakes: Ecology and Evolutionary Biology*, edited by R. A. Seigel, J. T. Collins and S. S. Novak, Macmillan Publishing Company, New York.

tend to grope for their prey or ambush it. The tracheal lung is large. All have rear fangs but are regarded as harmless to man. The best known species in the subfamily is probably the fishing snake, *Erpeton tentaculatum*. This subfamily is well defined and includes ten genera: *Bitia*, *Cantoria*, *Cerberus*, *Enhydris*, *Erpeton*, *Fordonia*, *Gerarda*, *Heurnia*, *Homalopsis* and *Myron*.

XENODERMINAE

Primitive colubrids with tuberculate scales, most of which are poorly known. Only a few genera are included in this subfamily and a number of them are monotypic. They are found in south-east Asia and include *Achalinus* and *Fimbrios*.

CALAMARIINAE

A small subfamily containing mostly small burrowing snakes. They are distributed in eastern Asia, including the Philippines, and apparently feed mostly on earthworms and other soft-bodied invertebrates. The natural history of snakes in this subfamily is poorly known and the genera include *Calamaria* and *Macrocalamus*.

PAREATINAE

Two genera of specialized slug- and snail-eating snakes from south-east Asia. Small, slender, nocturnal snakes. This subfamily contains only two genera, *Aplopeltura*, which is monotypic, and *Pareas*.

LAMPROPHINAE (sometimes known as the Boodontinae)

African and Madagascan colubrids, including fangless and rear-fanged species. A fairly large but ill-defined subfamily that includes specialized and generalist species. Genera placed in this subfamily include the house snakes, *Lamprophis*, the African wolf snakes, *Lycophidion*, and a large number of Madagascan snakes.

PSEUDOXENODONTINAE

A small subfamily containing only two genera of poorly known south-east Asian snakes, *Pseudoxenodon* and *Plagiopholis*.

NATRICINAE

The natricine colubrids are well-known snakes from North America, Europe and Asia. They are absent from South America and Australia. Many species are semi-aquatic and some are back-fanged. They include the North American garter snakes and water snakes, *Thamnophis* and *Nerodia*, the European water snakes, *Natrix*, as well as very many genera from south-east Asia, such as *Sinonatrix*.

XENODONTINAE

American genera with a range of forms and life-styles. Members of several genera have enlarged rear fangs and may produce mild effects of envenomation but none is dangerous to humans. Examples include the mussuranas, *Clelia*, ringnecked snakes, *Diadophis*, and hognose snakes, *Heterodon*, slug- and snail-eating snakes, *Sibon* and *Dipsas* (sometimes placed in a separate subfamily, the Dipsadinae) as well as a number of lesser-known South American genera.

PSAMMOPHIINAE

Mostly African but with some Asian and one European members. Characterized by greatly reduced hemipenes. Mostly active, fast moving diurnal hunters, with slender bodies and narrow heads. Rear-fanged snakes, some of which produce a fairly potent venom that can have some effects on humans. Examples of snakes in this subfamily include the sand snakes, *Psammophis*, skaapstekers, *Psammophylax*, and the Montpellier snake, *Malpolon*.

*   *   *

The following genera, which constitute the family Colubridae, are listed alphabetically and are not separated into subfamily groups.

Achalinus Eight or more species of small secretive snakes from China and south-east Asia. Nocturnal, hiding beneath logs, etc. during the day. Thought to feed on earthworms and slugs. Oviparous.

Adelophis Two species, *A. copei* and *A. foxi*, from western Mexico. Small snakes, closely related to *Tropidoclonion*, living in damp meadows and feeding on earthworms. Viviparous, giving birth to small litters of young.

Adelphicos Five species found in Central America. Small snakes from tropical forest habitats. Their natural history is poorly known.

Aeluroglena A monotypic genus containing only *A. cucullata*, from North Africa. Related to *Coluber* but poorly known.

Afronatrix A monotypic genus containing only *A. anoscopus*, from Africa. A medium-sized snake that lives in a variety of habitats from rainforest to savannah, but usually close to water. It eats frogs and, probably fish. Reproduction unknown.

Ahaetulla (**Asian vine snakes or snakes**) Eight species found in India, Sri Lanka, China and south-east Asia including the Indo-Australian archipelago. Formerly known as *Dryophis*. Medium-sized, slender snakes that are thoroughly arboreal. Diurnal hunters that specialize in eating diurnal lizards. Their heads are elongated and pointed and their eyes are almost unique in having horizontally slit, or hole-shaped, pupils, giving them a degree of binocular vision. Rear-fanged but probably of little or no danger to humans. Viviparous.

Alluadina Two species, *A. bellyi* and *A. quardi*, from Madagascar. Small snakes are poorly known.

Alsophis Ten species in the West Indies and several more on the South American mainland and the Galapagos Islands. species (*A. ater* and *A. sancticrucis*) be extinct. Small snakes with cylindrical bodies and smooth scales. Terrestrial and diurnal, feeding mainly on lizards. Rear-fanged but unlikely to be dangerous to humans. Probably oviparous, but biology poorly known.

Amastridium A monotypic genus containing only *A. veliferum* from Central America. It is a small species apparently confined to tropical rain forests.

Amphiesma About 20 species (formerly larger but many species have been removed to the genus *Tropidonophis*). Small to medium-sized snakes found throughout much of India, Sri Lanka, China, Indo-China and south-east Asia. Semi-aquatic, feeding on amphibians and fish. Oviparous.

Amphiesmoides A monotypic genus containing only *A. ornaticeps* from China and south-east Asia. Thought to be oviparous.

Amplorhinus A monotypic genus containing only *A. multimaculatus* from south Africa. It is a small snake that lives in damp places, feeding on frogs and lizards. Rear-fanged but not dangerous to man. Viviparous, giving birth to four to 12 young.

lohydrus A monotypic genus contain-
nly *A. aemulans* from Sumatra. A small
e that is thought to be nocturnal and
strial, but poorly known.

lophis Two species, *A. andreai* from
and *A. parvifrons* from Haiti and neigh-
ng islands. Slender, diurnal snakes
are active foragers, eating mainly
s lizards and also some *Eleuthero-*
lus frogs. Probably oviparous.

peltura A monotypic genus containing
the Asian snail-eating snake, *A. boa.*
d throughout much of south-east
including the Philippines. A medium
snake with a very slender, laterally
pressed body and a wide, angular head.
eyes are large and the snout is blunt.
ly arboreal, this species may also
und on the ground in rainforests. It
octurnal and feeds only on snails.
ably oviparous.

colepis Twelve species from South
rica. Small, fossorial snakes with blunt
ts. Rarely seen. Thought to feed on
tebrates, small lizards and snakes.
arous.

rogena A monotypic genus containing
A. fasciolatus from India. Closely related
luber. A medium-sized, slender species
is active by day. Thought to feed
ly on lizards but its natural history is
y known.

na A monotypic genus containing only
glossy snake, *A. elegans*, with a wide
e over much of southern North America.
amber of subspecies are recognized.
um-sized to large with smooth scales
a slender head. It may burrow to avoid
me conditions but is otherwise terres-
feeding on rodents, lizards and other
es. Oviparous, sometimes laying over
ggs in a clutch.
tivity Most feed readily on rodents and
e good captives. They have a calm
sition and hardly ever bite, even when
captured. Breeding appears to be rela-
 rare in captivity, probably through
of interest. The hatchlings are rather
l and may be difficult to feed.

yton Twelve species found in the West
s, mainly Cuba (eight species) and
ica (three species). Small to medium-
, secretive snakes that have Duvernoy's
ds and enlarged rear fangs. *A. exiguum*
on frogs, frogs' eggs (*Eleutherodactylus*
es) and lizards, including geckos and
s. Large prey is held until the venom

takes effect. Other species probably have
similar habits but are poorly known.

Aspidura Six species from Sri Lanka. Very
small to small snakes that are fossorial in
habit, being found mainly in leaf-litter and
beneath forest debris. Nocturnal, feeding
mainly on earthworms. Oviparous, laying
up to 20 eggs.

Atractus A large genus of more than 80
species, found throughout most of Central
and South America. Some species are
described from only single specimens and
there is a high degree of endemism, with
many species having very limited ranges.
Very small to small snakes that are found in
forest environments, often under leaves and
in rotting logs. They are thought to feed
mainly on invertebrates. Oviparous, laying
small clutches of about three eggs.

Atretium Two species found in southern
India and Sri Lanka (*A. schistosum*) and
south-western China (*A. yunnanensis*).
The Indian species is aquatic and lives in
paddy fields, ponds, streams and rivers,
feeding on fish and frogs. Oviparous. The
Chinese species is apparently found in moist
situations, up to altitudes of 1,500 m (5,000
ft) but is otherwise poorly known.

Balanophis A monotypic genus containing
only *B. ceylonensis*, found only in Sri Lanka.
A small terrestrial species that lives in moist
forests. It feeds mainly on frogs and is
oviparous.

Bitia A monotypic genus containing only
B. hydroides, from Burma, Thailand and the
Malayan peninsula, where it inhabits the
mouths of rivers and coastal waters. It is a
small snake with a narrow head and forebody, narrow ventral and subcaudal scales
and a compressed tail, and is thoroughly
aquatic, probably feeding largely on fish.
Viviparous.

Blythia A monotypic genus containing only
B. reticulata from Assam (India), Tibet,
Burma and southern China. A small, dark
coloured snake that is probably nocturnal
and semi-fossorial. Poorly known.

Bogertophis (rat snakes) Two species from
North America, formerly placed in *Elaphe*.
The Trans-Pecos rat snake, *B. subocularis*,
is found in southern Texas and adjacent
parts of northern Mexico, and the Rosalia
rat snake, *B. rosaliae*, is endemic to Baja
California. Both live in arid habitats but are
associated with rocky gullies and arroyos
where moisture may be retained locally.
Medium-sized, slender but muscular snakes

with keeled scales. Their heads are distinct
from their necks and the eyes are large.
Their scales are keeled. Very graceful in
their movements. Mainly nocturnal, feeding
on lizards, birds and small mammals.
Oviparous, laying clutches of up to ten eggs.
■ *Captivity* Very popular snakes with private
collectors, although the Trans-Pecos rat
snake is much more commonly seen than
the Rosalia species. They thrive under a
wide variety of conditions and will eat small
rodents readily, although hatchling Rosalia
rat snakes are sometimes difficult to feed at
first. Breeding takes place regularly. The
Trans-Pecos rat snake is unusual in mating
in summer rather than the spring: the eggs
hatch in the autumn or early winter.

Boiga About 20 species found in Africa,
India, Sri Lanka, southern China, throughout south-east Asia, including many island
groups, and into northern Australia. They
are medium-sized to large snakes with rear
fangs, one of which, the mangrove snake, *B.
dendrophila*, is considered slightly dangerous
to man. All species apart from one are
arboreal and mainly nocturnal, feeding
on lizards, including nocturnal geckos and
sleeping diurnal species and small mammals, including bats. The most widespread
species, the brown tree snake, *Boiga irregularis*, has been accidentally introduced to
the island of Guam, where, in the absence
of competition, it has caused damage to
the native fauna, especially small songbirds.
All the species are apparently oviparous.
■ *Captivity* A few species are occasionally
kept in captivity, but there is little interest in
most of them. They require tall cages and an
opportunity to climb. Rodents are normally
accepted. They rarely calm down sufficiently
to be handled easily, however, and the
keeping of the most attractive species, *Boiga
dendrophila*, may be subject to restrictions
on account of its venomous bite.

Bothrolycus A monotypic genus containing
only *B. ater* from central Africa. A small
snake about which almost nothing appears
to be known.

Bothrophthalmus A monotypic genus containing only *B. lineatus*, from West and
central Africa. A medium-sized snake that
lives in moist montane forests. Natural
history poorly known.

Brachyophis A monotypic genus containing
only *B. revoilii*, from Kenya and Somalia.
It may be related to *Aparallactus* and is placed
in the Atractaspididae by Underwood and
Kochva, 1993. Biology poorly known.

Brachyorrhos A monotypic genus containing only *B. alba*, from the Indonesian archipelago. A medium-sized snake, but very poorly known.

Calamaria (reed snakes or worm snakes) A large genus numbering just over 50 species, several of which are known from only a handful of specimens. Found from India and Burma, through southern and southwestern China into Indo-China and southeast Asia (19 species are known from Borneo.) Small, secretive snakes that live in underground burrows and feed on earthworms and other soft-bodied invertebrates. Most are dark in colour, with smooth scales. Oviparous.

Calamodontophis A monotypic genus containing only *C. paucidens*, from southern Brazil. A small rear-fanged snake. Assumed to be viviparous but poorly known.

Calamorhabdium Two species from the Celebes. Very small snakes with a spine at the tip of their tails. Poorly known.

Cantoria Two species of homalopsine snakes, *C. violacea* from coastal regions of the Malayan peninsula, the Andaman Islands, the Indonesian archipelago and from India, where it is very rare, and *C. annulata* from Prins Hendrick Island, New Guinea. Small to medium-sized snakes that are semi-aquatic and feed mainly on fish. Viviparous.

Carphophis A monotypic genus containing only the worm snake, *C. amoenus*. This very small snake is found throughout much of eastern North America, mainly in damp situations under logs, etc. It has a small head and a barely discernible neck, and smooth shiny scales. It feeds mainly on earthworms and other soft-bodied invertebrates. Oviparous, laying 1 to 8 eggs. The hatchlings measure only a few inches.
■ *Captivity* Not popular but easily maintained in a small vivarium containing a deep layer of moist soil or leaf-litter and given a regular supply of small earthworms. Captive breeding unknown.

Cemophora A monotypic genus containing only the scarlet snake, *C. coccinea*. This small species is found in south-eastern North America and is a brightly marked 'false coral' snake. A semi-burrowing species that may also be found under bark, etc. It feeds on small lizards and snakes. Reptile eggs are also eaten. Oviparous, laying up to six elongated eggs.
■ *Captivity* A poor captive on account of its dietary habits and small size. It requires a

cage with a loose substrate in which to burrow and a regular supply of small lizards to eat. Captive breeding is unknown.

Cerberus Three species found along the coasts of India and south-east Asia, including the Philippines, Indonesian archipelago, New Guinea and northern Australia. Medium sized snakes, completely restricted to tropical estuaries, mudflats and coastal mangrove forests, where they feed on fish and crustaceans. Rear-fanged but apparently harmless to man. Viviparous.

Cercaspis A monotypic genus containing only *C. carinatus*, from Sri Lanka. A medium-sized snake with a slender body, small head and distinctive coloration of white bands on a black background, closely mimicking the venomous krait, *Bungarus ceylonicus*, with which it shares its range. It prefers moist situations and eats lizards and snakes. Oviparous.

Cercophis Closely related to *Chrysopelea*, of which it is usually regarded as a subgenus.

Chamaelycus Two species, *C. fasciatus* and *C. parkeri* from West and central Africa. Small, burrowing snakes that are poorly known.

Chersodromus A small genus of two species from Mexico. Small snakes which are very poorly known.

Chilomeniscus (sand snakes) At present, four species of small burrowing snakes found in the Sonoran Desert of south-western North America. There is some confusion regarding the status of two species from islands in the Gulf of California (*C. punctatissimus* and *C. savagei*). Similar to *Chionactis* but even more highly adapted to 'sand-swimming'. Sometimes found on the surface at night. They feed on invertebrates, including scorpions. Oviparous.
■ *Captivity* Easily maintained in small containers. A layer of fine, free-running sand is required. Frequent spraying is essential as these snakes will not drink from a bowl and will quickly dehydrate. They require a diet of insects and their larvae. Captive breeding unknown.

Chilorhinophis Three species from central Africa. Small burrowing snakes with venom fangs near the front of the upper jaw. Thought to feed on amphisbaenians and other burrowing reptiles and possibly invertebrates.

Chionactis (shovel-nosed snakes) Two species found in arid regions of south-western

North America. Small, burrowing sn[akes] that 'swim' through loose sand or fine gr[avel] in search of insect larvae and other inv[erte]brates. Both species are brightly colo[ured] 'false coral' snakes. Oviparous.
■ *Captivity* Not widely available but e[asily] kept alive by housing in a cage contai[ning] a few centimetres (a couple of inche[s) of] natural sand or fine rounded pebble[s) in] which the snakes will spend most of [their] time. Cultured insects such as cricket[s and] waxworms are taken readily. The [cage] should be heavily sprayed occasional[ly as] these snakes seem unable to find wa[ter if] it is only available in a bowl. Breeding [un]known, although both species lay tw[o or] three small eggs.

Chironius Sixteen species from Ce[ntral] America and northern South Ame[rica.] Medium-sized to large species with sle[nder] bodies and very large eyes. Juveniles te[nd to] be marked differently from adults. Ma[inly] terrestrial but climbing occasionally, fo[und] in tropical forests. Fast-moving sna[kes,] largely diurnal, feeding mainly on ro[dents] and small birds. Oviparous.

Chrysopelea Five species found in India, [Sri] Lanka, Burma, southern China, Indo-Ch[ina,] the Malay peninsula, Indonesian islands [and] the Philippines. Medium-sized species [with] slender bodies and narrow, elegant he[ads.] The eyes are relatively large. All are arbo[real] and are mostly green, or green with b[lack] and red markings. They have long pre[hen]sile tails and smooth scales. These diu[rnal] tree snakes are sometimes known as 'fly[ing]' snakes owing to their habit of launc[hing] themselves from high boughs. They b[reak] their fall by making their under-su[rface] concave. They eat lizards, birds and s[mall] mammals. Rear-fanged but not regarde[d as] dangerous to man. Oviparous.
■ *Captivity* Adults do quite well in capti[vity.] They require tall cages and plenty of bran[ches] to climb and roost among. Food, consis[ting] of small rodents, should be offered on for[ceps. Their temperament is unpredict[able,] however, and they are inclined to [bite.] Breeding is not regularly achieved.

Clelia (mussuranas) Six species [from] Central and South America. Large sn[akes] with cylindrical bodies, smooth shiny s[cales] and small eyes. Found in moist fo[rest] habitats and active by night and day. [They] feed mainly on snakes, including m[any] venomous pit vipers to whose venom [they] appear to be immune, and rodents. [They] constrict their prey. Oviparous.

aptivity Occasionally kept and bred. lts are easily fed, on rodents, but the eniles require small reptiles.

nophis A monotypic genus containing *C. kirtlandi*, Kirtland's water snake, North America. Closely related to *odia*, in which genus it was previously ed. A small species with heavily keeled al scales. Found in moist places, inably near water. It feeds on worms and s. Viviparous.

orhabdium A monotypic genus containonly *C. williamsoni*, from the Malaysian insula (Cameron Highlands). Similar to, probably related to, the reed snakes, *maria*. Only a few specimens have been ected and its natural history is poorly wn.

uber (**whipsnakes and racers**) A large us, at present containing about 30 species. k on the genus is currently under way will undoubtedly result in regrouping species into several genera. One such, *ophis*, has already been proposed. One e-ranging and highly variable species is d in North America. The remainder distributed throughout Europe, North ca, West Africa, the Middle East and into ral Asia and Indo-China. Medium-sized rge, diurnal snakes. All are slender, agile xes with narrow heads and large eyes. n uniformly coloured although juveniles uently differ from the adults. They feed nly on other reptiles, which they run n, but also on birds and small mammals. arous.

ptivity Not frequently kept in captivity ccount of their nervousness and their lency to bite. Some individuals settle n and may accept a diet of small nts. Not frequently bred in captivity.

apsophis A monotypic genus containing *C. albiventris* from Madagascar. A very ll snake that may be fossorial but which rdly known.

iophanes Twelve species found from as, through Central America and into th America as far south as eastern Peru. nd in a variety of habitats from dry -desert regions to moist tropical forests. ll to medium-sized snakes with smooth, y scales and longitudinal stripes along r bodies. Terrestrial, diurnal snakes, ing on a variety of small vertebrates. r-fanged but producing a venom that little or no apparent effect on humans. arous.

Conophis Three species of medium sized snakes from Central America, found in arid and moist habitats. Terrestrial, feeding mainly on lizards. Apparently oviparous.

Conopsis Two species from Mexico. Small, semi-burrowing snakes with stout, cylindrical bodies and smooth scales. They are found in cool montane environments but are rarely collected and little known. Viviparous.

Contia A monotypic genus containing only the sharp-tailed snake, *C. tenuis*, found along part of the west coast of North America. A small, secretive, diurnal species that favours damp situations. It apparently feeds mainly on slugs. Oviparous, with small clutches of eggs.

Coronella (**smooth snakes**) Three species, two from Europe, North Africa and the near East and a third, *C. brachyura*, from India. Small to medium-sized snakes that have smooth scales, cylindrical bodies and a narrow head. They feed mainly on lizards, which they constrict. *C. austriaca* is viviparous, producing two to 15 young, whereas *C. girondica* and *C. brachyura* are oviparous.

Crisantophis A monotypic genus containing only *C. nevermanni*, previously included in the genus *Conophis*. A medium-sized snake with smooth scales. Found in lowland dry forests of Mexico. Biology poorly known, probably oviparous.

Crotaphopeltis Six species from Africa south of the Sahara, commonly called herald snakes. Medium-sized, rear-fanged species that are not dangerous to man. They live in marshy areas and feed on amphibians. Oviparous.

Cryophis A monotypic genus containing only *C. hallbergi*, from Mexico. Medium-sized with heavily keeled scales and large eyes. Otherwise, poorly known.

Cryptolycus A monotypic genus containing only *C. nanus*, the dwarf wolf snake from Mozambique. A small species, growing to less than 30 cm (12 in), it feeds on amphisbaenids. It lays two elongated eggs.

Cyclocorus Two species, *C lineatus* and *C. nuchalis*, from the Philippines. Small snakes with cylindrical bodies and small eyes. Apparently fossorial species, found mainly under logs and rotting vegetation. Said to eat other snakes but poorly known.

Cyclophiops Eight species from northern India and Burma, southern China and

▲ African egg-eating snake, *Dasypeltis scabra*. The snake is spreading its jaws as a defensive ploy, probably in imitation of a viper.

Indo-China, formerly included in the North American genus *Opheodryas* and sometimes referred to *Entechinus* or *Eurypholis*. Medium sized snakes found mainly in damp situations. Green in colour. Terrestrial or semi-arboreal. Oviparous.

Darlingtonia A monotypic genus containing only *D. haetiana* from Haiti. A small terrestrial snake that appears to feed almost exclusively on the small frogs of the genus *Eleutherodactylus*. Otherwise its biology is poorly known.

Dasypeltis (**egg-eating snakes**) A small genus of six highly specialized snakes found throughout most of Africa. They have modified vertebrae, used for sawing through egg shells, and only rudimentary teeth. Various species are mimics of the saw-scaled viper, night adders, etc., but they are harmless. Oviparous.
■ *Captivity* Adults are among the easiest snakes to keep in captivity as they will accept the eggs of hens, pigeons, etc. Obtaining small eggs for juveniles can be a problem but they can be fed small quantities of hens egg by means of a syringe and tubing.

Dendrelaphis About 15 species found in India, Sri Lanka, Burma, southern China, through Indo-China and south-east Asia into northern Australia. Often known as bronze-backed snakes. Medium-sized to large, slender-bodied, arboreal snakes with large prominent eyes. They are fast-moving, diurnal species that feed mainly on lizards but may also take amphibians and even fish. May be found swimming in large lakes and rivers. Oviparous, laying clutches of up to 15 eggs.

Dendrolychus A monotypic genus containing only *D. elapoides* from West Africa. A small, arboreal snake that is thought to feed mainly on frogs. Poorly known.

Dendrophidion Eight species (plus one undescribed at present) found from Mexico to northern South America. Medium-sized snakes with extremely slender bodies and long tails. Terrestrial and arboreal species that inhabit tropical forests and feed mainly on rodents and frogs. Oviparous.

Diadophis A monotypic genus containing only the widespread and highly variable species, *D. punctatus*. This species is found throughout much of North America, including parts of Mexico. It is a small, secretive species found in moist situations, where it feeds on earthworms, slugs and other invertebrates as well as small amphibians and reptiles, including other snakes. Oviparous, laying one to 10 eggs per clutch.
■ *Captivity* Not especially popular but an interesting captive if given a damp substrate with places to hide. The eastern forms will live indefinitely on earthworms although the larger, western forms may require a more substantial diet. Captive breeding not known and probably not attempted seriously.

Diaphorolepis Two species from Panama, Colombia and Ecuador. Medium-sized snakes with a pair of keels on each of their dorsal scales. *D. wagneri* is terrestrial, and oviparous. Poorly known.

Dinodon Eight species from Burma, southern China, northern Indo-China and Japan. Small to medium-sized snakes with thick bodies and broad heads. Found in moist forest habitats, rarely far from water. Thought to feed mainly on amphibians and fish.

Dipsadoboa Seven species from Africa. Small, moderately slender snakes with wide heads and vertical pupils. Arboreal, nocturnal snakes that eat geckos and frogs. Rear-fanged but not dangerous to man. Oviparous.

Dipsas Thirty-one species from Mexico, through Central America as far south as Brazil and Bolivia. Also Trinidad and Tobago. Their taxonomy is rather confused at present. Medium-sized snakes with slender, laterally compressed bodies and wide, rather square heads with blunt snouts. The eyes are large and have vertical pupils. Several species are boldly marked with rings or saddles contrasting with their back-ground colour. Nocturnal, arboreal snakes living in moist tropical forests and feeding exclusively on snails and slugs. Oviparous.
■ *Captivity* Rarely available but interesting species that fare quite well in tall vivaria with a humid atmosphere. They require a constant supply of land snails. Captive breeding unknown and probably not achieved.

Dipsina A monotypic genus containing the dwarf beaked snake, *D. multimaculata*, from southern and south-western Africa. A small snake that feeds on small lizards and lays two to four eggs.

Dispholidus A monotypic genus containing the boomslang, *D. typus*, found throughout much of Africa south of the Sahara. The boomslang grows to 2 m (6½ ft) in length and is notorious as one of the more dangerous rear-fanged colubrid snakes, producing a highly potent venom that can be fatal to man. Diurnal hunters of lizards, birds and mammals, with large eyes. Oviparous, laying clutches of up to 25 eggs.

Ditaxodon A monotypic genus containing only *D. taeniatus*, from Brazil. Virtually unknown.

Ditypophis A monotypic genus containing only *D. vivax* from Socotra Islands. Its relationships and biology are poorly known.

Drepanoides A monotypic genus containing only *D. anomalus*, from South America. A small, brightly coloured snake that is terrestrial and semi-fossorial. Biology unknown.

Dromicodryas Two species, *D. bernieri* D. quadrilineatus, from Madagascar. Medi sized snakes whose natural history is po known.

Dromophis Two species of which *D. pra natus* is found in West Africa and *D. line* has a large range covering most of trop Africa. Slender, elongated snakes that h small mammals and frogs by day. Ovipar

Dryadophis At least two species, someti included in the genus *Mastigodryas*. Medi sized snakes, with slender bodies and la eyes. Terrestrial, diurnal hunters, sin to, and closely related to, the more fam *Coluber* and *Masticophis* species. They on frogs and lizards and are found i variety of tropical forest habitats. Ovipar

Drymarchon A monotypic genus cont ing only the indigo snake, or cribo, *D. co* This large and impressive snake rar from Florida and Texas down into So America as far as Argentina. A numbe subspecies are recognized, of which the black Florida form, *D. corais couperi*, i known. The body is slightly triangula cross section and the scales are la smooth and shiny. A diurnal snake wl likes to bask. It feeds on a wide variet vertebrate prey including birds, mamm fish, amphibians and other reptiles, inc ing venomous snakes. Oviparous, la clutches of up to 12 eggs.

▼ *Drepanoides anomalus*, a secretive species a the only member of its genus, from central Sou America.

otivity The indigo snake has long been a *lar* species with snake fanciers. The *da* race is now rare due to habitat *ruction*, and is therefore protected, *captive-bred* specimens are sometimes *lable*. They make beautiful vivarium *ects* although they require a large *unt* of space and plenty of food. Breed-*is* not straightforward although it is *eved* on a fairly regular basis.

mobius (racers) Four species found from *hern* North America down into South *rica*. Medium-sized, slender, cylindrical *es* with a long tail. All have large eyes *ciated* with active diurnal hunting and *feed* largely on amphibians. Occurring *variety* of habitats from semi-arid scrub *opical* moist forests. Oviparous.

moluber Three species from tropical *h* America. Medium-sized snakes that *errestrial* or arboreal, diurnal and feed *ly* on lizards. Oviparous.

ocalamus Five species found in India, Sri *ca*, south-east Asia and the Philippines. *ll* to medium-sized arboreal snakes that *ctive* by night. Thought to eat inverte-*es*, frogs and lizards but diet, habitats *reproduction* poorly known.

Duberria (slug-eating snakes) Two species, one, *D. variegata*, restricted to southern Africa and the other, *D. lutrix*, extending as far north as Ethiopia. They are small, secretive snakes which feed exclusively on slugs and snails. Viviparous, with up to 20 young per litter.

Eirenis About 13 species found from North Africa, throughout the Middle East and into north-western India. Small, secretive snakes that feed mainly on invertebrates. The species are difficult to separate superficially and their natural history is poorly known. Apparently all oviparous.

Elachistodon A monotypic genus containing only the Indian egg-eating snake, *E. westermanni*. This species eats only birds' eggs and closely parallels the African *Dasypeltis* species. It is rare and poorly known.

Elaphe (rat snakes) A large genus containing at present 30 species found in North and Central America (five species), Europe (four or five species), central, southern and south-east Asia, China and Japan. This arrangement is undoubtedly artificial, containing groups of species from separate lineages. Some have recently been split away into several distinct genera, for instance,

▲ Four-lined snake, *Elaphe quatuorlineata*, from south-eastern Europe and parts of western and central Asia.

Bogertophis and *Senticolis*, but there is still plenty to do. Small, medium-sized and large snakes are included. They are slender, agile species, nocturnal or diurnal according to their distribution. Some are arboreal but most are terrestrial and they are powerful constrictors of small rodents and birds, although amphibians and lizards are also eaten, especially by juveniles. Although variable, many species are brightly coloured: several species are blotched or saddled as juveniles but become more uniform, or longitudinally striped, as they mature. All are of great interest to amateur naturalists and snake keepers on account of their beauty and the ease with which they adapt to captivity. Oviparous apart from the semi-aquatic *E. rufodorsata*, from China, which gives birth to live young: this species is only distantly related to the other members of the genus.

■ *Captivity* Among the most popular species in captivity, especially the corn snake, *E. guttata*, which is bred in large numbers by amateur and commercial snake keepers. A variety of colour forms, including selectively

▶ *Elaphe porphyraceae*, an Asian representative of the widespread rat snake tribe.

bred mutants, are available in this and some other species. In general, all rat snakes are very easily accommodated and bred, although some of the Asian species are not good choices unless captive-bred stock is available – wild animals frequently carry large parasite burdens and die after a short period of confinement. North American and European species are seasonal breeders, mating in the spring, but some of the tropical species may breed at virtually any time of the year. Although individuals of some species remain nervous and rather aggressive, they generally calm down well in captivity and are widely rated as among the best choices for both the beginner and advanced hobbyist alike.

▼ Fox snake, *Elaphe vulpina*, from North America eating a vole.

oidis A monotypic genus, containing *E. fuscus*, from Sumatra and Java. A [...]ll, dark brown, burrowing snake that is [...]ally found at high altitudes, where it [...] be very common in suitable habitats.

omorphus About eight species from [...]h America. Small, cylindrical snakes [...] smooth, shiny scales. Burrowing species [...] probably feed largely on invertebrates.

otinus A monotypic genus containing *E. picteti*, from tropical Africa. Its rela-[...]ships with other snakes are unclear: it [...] be related to *Aparallactus* (sometimes [...]ed in the Atractaspididae) but very [...]ly known.

nochliophis A monotypic genus con-[...]ing only *E. fugleri* from Ecuador. Only a [...]le specimen is known, from a humid [...]ronment. Its biology is unknown.

ydris Twenty-two species found from [...]a, China, south-east Asia, New Guinea [...]orthern Australia. Small to medium-[...]d, specialized freshwater aquatic species [...] rarely leave the water. They have [...]ndrical bodies, smooth shiny scales and [...]r eyes are directed upwards. Their diet [...]des fish and amphibians. Viviparous, [...]g birth to live young underwater.
ptivity Almost unobtainable nowadays [...] interesting if somewhat demanding [...]es. They must be kept in an aquarium [...]ch should be heated and well covered. [...]re should be a good growth of aquatic [...]tation in which the snakes will hide, [...]g in wait for their prey. They require a [...] of small fish.

lius Three species from Central America [...]orthern South America. Small, slender [...]es with long tails. The rostral scale is [...]rged as an adaptation for burrowing. [...]ly known.

iphas A monotypic genus containing [...] the Baja California night snake, *E. [...]ni*. A medium-sized nocturnal species [...] has a restricted range in north-western [...]ico. It appears to feed mainly on noc-[...]al lizards, snakes and amphibians. It is [...]-fanged but harmless to man. Ovipa-[...], laying a small clutch of elongated [...].

ton A monotypic genus containing [...] the tentacled snake, *Erpeton tentacu-[...]n*, from Thailand and Indo-China. A [...]ium-sized snake with several unusual [...]racteristics in addition to the pair of [...]nge appendages on its snout. Its body

is almost rectangular in cross-section and its ventral scales are greatly reduced. It is thoroughly aquatic and can be found in freshwater ponds and slow-moving waters. It feeds on fish and is viviparous, producing litters of up to 15 young.
■ *Captivity* Imported specimens are usually in poor condition and, if damaged, are susceptible to fungus infections. They require a densely planted aquarium heated to about 25°C (77°F), and a diet of small fish. Captive breeding has probably not been achieved.

Erythrolamprus (false coral snakes) Six species from Central and South America. Small to medium-sized snakes with cylindrical bodies and smooth scales. All species are brightly marked with red, black and white rings and are often claimed to mimic the coral snakes, *Micrurus* species, with whose range they overlap. Mainly diurnal, but secretive. Rear-fanged species that feed mainly on other reptiles, including venomous snakes. Not regarded as dangerous to man. Oviparous.

Etheridgeum A monotypic genus containing only *E. pulchra* from Sumatra. Biology virtually unknown.

Farancia Two species, *F. abacura* and *F. erytrogramma*, found only in the southeastern corner of North America. They are large species with smooth, glossy scales

and their eyes are situated on the top of their head. *F. abacura* has a sharp pointed scale at the tip of its tail. Both species are almost totally aquatic in their habits. They feed on eels and eel-like salamanders (*Amphiuma*). Oviparous, laying large clutches of eggs in underground chambers. There is some evidence that the females coil around the eggs until they hatch.
■ *Captivity* Apparently they fare quite well in captivity but the problem of obtaining sufficient food of the right type would be insurmountable to most people.

Ficimia Seven species, known as hook-nosed snakes. North, Central America and northern South America. Two species are known from a single specimen only. Small, secretive, back-fanged species with an upturned rostral scale. They apparently feed largely on spiders and centipedes. Oviparous.

Fimbrios A monotypic genus containing only *F. klossi*, from Indo-China. A small snake with spinose scales on its lower jaw, the function of which is not known. Terrestrial and nocturnal in habits but otherwise poorly known.

Fordonia A monotypic genus containing only the white-bellied water snake, *F. leucobalia*. It is found wherever there is suitable habitat throughout south-east Asia,

▼ *Erythrolamprus aesculapii*, one of several 'false coral' snakes from Central and South America.

including the Philippines and New Guinea, and along the north coast of Australia. This medium-sized snake inhabits coastal mudflats, especially those associated with mangroves. It is a highly specialized snake, feeding on small crabs, which may be constricted before being eaten piecemeal. Viviparous, with three to 13 young.

Geagras A monotypic genus containing only *G. redimitus* from Mexico. A very small burrowing snake with a modified rostral scale. It probably feeds on invertebrates but is generally poorly known.

Geodipsas Six species from Africa and Madagascar. Small snakes that feed on frogs. Poorly known.

Geophis A large genus containing up to 40 species, including a number of new species described in the last 10 years. Found throughout Central and northern South America, in dry and moist habitats. Small, slender snakes with pointed snouts. Terrestrial species, active mainly at night. Otherwise poorly known.

Gerarda A monotypic genus containing *G. prevostiana*, which lives along the coasts of India, Burma, Sri Lanka, Perak and Thailand. Aquatic, in mangrove swamps bordering tidal rivers and estuaries. Lethargic on land. Viviparous.

Gomesophis A monotypic genus containing only *G. brasiliensis*, from Brazil. Medium-sized. Poorly known.

Gongylosoma Three species from Asia. Poorly known.

Gonionotophis Four species from West Africa. Small snakes found in rainforests. Nocturnal, probably feeding on frogs and lizards.

Gonyophis A monotypic genus containing only *G. margeritatus*, from the Malaysian peninsula and Borneo. Found mainly in hill forests. Closely related to *Chrysopelea* and, like members of that genus, arboreal. Rare, and poorly known.

Gonyosoma Three species from south-east Asia, formerly included in the genus *Elaphe* (rat snakes). Medium-sized to large snakes with slender, muscular bodies and narrow, elegant heads. Usually green in colour, and highly arboreal. They feed on frogs, lizards and small mammals. Oviparous.
■ *Captivity* The red-tailed racer, *Gonyosoma oxycephala* is moderately popular. This colourful snake requires a large cage with

plenty of branches on which to climb and rest. Captive-bred animals adapt far better than wild-caught ones and usually settle down well in captivity. Not aggressive, but nervous. Adults eat small rodents without problems but the young can be difficult to feed at first. Captive breeding has occurred on several occasions but is not a regular event.

Grayia Four species from tropical West and central Africa. Medium-sized to large snakes that have aquatic tendencies. Thought to eat fish. *G. smythii* is oviparous but reproduction in the other species is unknown.

Gyalopion Two species, *G. canum* and *G. quadrangularis*, from southern North America and Mexico. The latter is brightly coloured and could be a coral snake mimic. Closely related to the *Ficimia* species, with which they share the common name of hooknosed snakes. Small, nocturnal, back-fanged species that feed on invertebrates, especially spiders. Oviparous.

Haplocercus A monotypic genus containing only *H. ceylonensis* from Sri Lanka. A small species with a brightly coloured underside which it displays if alarmed. Semi-fossorial and nocturnal, usually found under rotting logs, etc.

Hapsidophrys Two species, *H. lineata* and *H. smaragdina* from West, Central and East Africa. Medium-sized snakes with very slender bodies and green coloration. Highly arboreal, feeding on frogs and lizards.

Helicops Fifteen species of small to medium-sized snakes from South America. Aquatic or semi-aquatic, with eyes and nostrils

▲ Western hognose snake, *Heterodon nasicus* from North America.

positioned near the top of their heads, heavily keeled scales. Diurnal and thoug feed on fish and amphibians. Breeding ha may vary. Most species are viviparous, *H. angulatus* appears to use either met of reproduction, depending on its loca it may lay well-developed eggs that h after about 16 days, or the young ma born live.

Helophis A monotypic genus contai only *H. schoutedeni*, from Zaire. Its relat ships and biology are poorly known.

Hemirhagerrhis (bark snakes) Two spe *H. kelleri* and *H. nototaenia* found in cer and East Africa. Small, arboreal snakes hide beneath loose bark by day and l lizards at night. Oviparous.

Heterodon (hognose snakes) Three spe found only in North America, inclu northern Mexico. Short, stocky sn with short tails, heavily keeled scales a prominent upturned rostral scale. May l flatten their necks and make mock str if disturbed, or feign death. Speci feeders on toads, which they root out o ground with their plough-like rostral s although other prey may be taken. T have enlarged fangs towards the bac their mouths and there is some suspi that they produce a venom that has a v ing, but noticeable, effect on humans. normally considered dangerous, howe Oviparous, with clutches of up to 20 eg
■ *Captivity* Good vivarium subjects as l as they will accept rodents: most will

the western hognose, *H. nasicus*, usually
and is by far the best choice. Breeding
species is quite easy and the females
lay more than one clutch of eggs each

roliodon
monotypic genus containing only *H. oitalis* from Madagascar. A small snake ut which there is little known.

rnia A monotypic genus containing *H. ventromaculata*, from New Guinea. nedium-sized snake closely related to *ydris*. Semi-aquatic, feeding mostly on Viviparous.

rophis A genus containing at least seven ries formerly placed in *Coluber*. For ils see that genus.

ogerrhum A monotypic genus contain-only *H. philippinum*. Endemic to the nd of Luzon, Philippines. A small snake a cylindrical body and smooth scales. ear-fanged species which is harmless nan on account of its small size. Biology ost unknown.

nalopsis A monotypic genus containing *H. buccata*, from India, Burma, Indo-na and south-east Asia including Indonesian archipelago. A medium-d snake with a stout, cylindrical body. atic, found in fresh and brackish water feeding mainly on fish. Viviparous.

monotus A monotypic genus contain-only *H. modestus* from West and central ca. A medium-sized snake that is poorly wn.

rablabes Two species, *H. periops* and *H. frontalis*, from Borneo. Small, burrow-species about which little appears to be wn.

raethiops A monotypic genus contain-only *H. melanogaster*, from central Africa. mi-aquatic snake, related to *Afronatrix*.

drodynastes Two species from South erica, including the false water cobra, *H. s*, formerly placed in the genus *Cyclagras*, w defunct) and *H. bicinctus*. Large, heavy-ed snakes with smooth scales. *H. gigas* ens its neck when disturbed, forming ood. Young may be brightly banded these markings are often obscured as snake grows. Both species are found r water and have semi-aquatic life-styles, ing largely on frogs and toads but also ng other vertebrates, including small nmals. Oviparous, laying moderately e clutches (up to 42 eggs).

■ *Captivity* One species, *Hydrodynastes gigas*, is sometimes kept in captivity (usually under its old name of *Cyclagras*) especially in large collections in zoological gardens, etc. It settles down well and will usually adapt to a diet of rodents. It requires a large aquatic area but the cage substrate should be kept dry. Breeding has been achieved many times, and can take place at any time of the year. The young are easily reared.

Hydromorphus One to three species of semi-aquatic snakes found from Honduras to Panama in Central America. Their tax-onomy is uncertain at present. Small to medium-sized species with small eyes and dull coloration. *H. concolor* is oviparous, laying clutches of about seven eggs. Biology poorly known.

Hydrops Two species, *H. marti* and *H. trian-gularis*, found in northern South America, east of the Andes. Medium-sized snakes that have smooth scales and cylindrical bodies. They are brightly marked, resembling coral snakes. Highly aquatic, and active at night and by day. They feed on amphibians and fish, especially false eels, *Synbranchus*. Repro-duction not known, but they are probably oviparous.

Hypoptophis A monotypic genus contain-ing only *H. wilsoni*, from central Africa. A small snake about which little is known.

Hypsiglena (night snakes) Two or three species from North and Central America (*H. torquata* and *ochroryncha* may be forms of the same species). The other species is *H. tanzeri*. Small snakes with prominent eyes and vertical pupils. Found in arid, rocky habitats. Nocturnal, feeding on lizards, small snakes and small mammals. Oviparous.

Hypsirhynchus A monotypic genus con-taining only *H. ferox*, from Haiti. A medium-sized, heavy-bodied snake. Terrestrial, feeding on *Anolis* lizards. Otherwise poorly known.

Ialtris Three species from Hispaniola in the West Indies. Medium-sized snakes that have rear fangs but are otherwise poorly known.

Iguanognathus A monotypic genus contain-ing only *I. werneri* from Sumatra. A small burrowing snake that has only rarely been collected. Nothing is known of its natural history.

Imantodes Five species found in Central and South America. Medium-sized but exceed-ingly elongated snakes with long tails.

Their heads are broad and rounded and the eyes are large and conspicuous, with vertically elliptical pupils. Totally arboreal, and capable of bridging huge distances between branches. During the day they usually coil within bromeliads and other epiphytes, and are found only in humid rainforests. They feed mainly on small lizards and frogs. Oviparous, laying small clutches of elongated eggs.

Ithycyphus Fives species from Madagascar. Medium-sized snakes with enlarged rear fangs, though not likely to be of danger to humans. Not well known. Mostly arboreal but *I. goudoti* is terrestrial. They eat lizards, especially chameleons.

Lampropeltis (kingsnakes and milk snakes)
Upwards of seven or eight species: there is some confusion over the status of several species-groups. For instance, the *mexicana* group is sometimes regarded as a single variable species and sometimes divided into *L. alterna* and *L. mexicana*. The common kingsnake, *L. getulus*, has a wide range over most of North America, including northern Mexico, and several subspecies are recognized. *L. triangulum* has an even larger range, from Canada well into South America and, at present, 25 subspecies have been described: several of these are of rather dubious status. Milk snakes are brightly coloured 'false coral' snakes, as are three species of mountain kingsnakes (*L. ruthveni*, *pyromelana* and *zonata*). All species are medium-sized snakes with smooth shiny scales and cylindrical bodies. They are powerful constrictors of mammals, birds and other reptiles, including venomous snakes. Most are nocturnal but they may be active during the day during cooler weather. All species are oviparous, with

▼ Sinaloan milk snake, *Lampropeltis triangulum sinaloae*, from Mexico.

clutches ranging from three or four in mountain kingsnakes to over 20 in some of the large forms of the common kingsnake.

■ *Captivity* Very popular species. All adapt very well to captive conditions without elaborate requirements. They will eat rodents readily, with the possible exception of newly hatched mountain kingsnakes, which tend to be small and may require lizards at first.

Lamprophis **(house snakes)** Thirteen species. Small to medium snakes known as house snakes and found mainly in Africa and Arabia, although one species, *L. geometricus*, is found on the Seychelles. They are powerful constrictors and eat rodents and lizards. Oviparous.

■ *Captivity* Several species are rare and some are unsuitable on account of their preference for lizards. The brown house snake, *L. fuliginosus*, is by far the most widely kept species. It eats small rodents quite readily and is undemanding regarding temperature. It lays up to 16 eggs per clutch and will often breed continuously throughout the year in captivity. The other species, which are not frequently bred, lay smaller clutches.

Langaha Three bizarre tree snakes from Madagascar. All species have nasal appendages, the purpose of which is probably cryptic but the shape and size varies between males and females.

▼ **Madagascan hognose snake,** *Leioheterodon madagascariensis.*

▲ **Fisk's house snake,** *Lamprophis fiskii*, **the rarest member of its genus.**

Leioheterodon Three species from Madagascar. Medium-sized snakes with powerful bodies and slightly upturned snouts. Found in forested areas, where they actively hunt for a variety of prey, including buried amphibians. Oviparous.

Leptodeira Nine species from North, Central and South America. Medium-sized snakes with slender, laterally compressed bodies, wide heads and large eyes. Found in a range of habitats, from semi-arid scrub to rainforests. Mainly nocturnal and arboreal. They feed on a variety of vertebrates, and some species eat the eggs of leaf-nesting frogs. Rear-fanged species which probably present no danger to humans. Oviparous.

Leptodrymus A monotypic genus cont[ain]ing only *L. pulcherrimus* from Cen[tral] America. A medium-sized snake foun[d in] rainforests up to 1,300 m (4,300 ft). [...] common and poorly known.

Leptophis Seven species from Mexic[o to] Argentina. Medium-sized to large sna[ke] with slender bodies and narrow he[ads]. Usually bright green in colour and so[me]times known as 'parrot snakes'. W[hen] alarmed they hold their mouths o[pen] displaying the bright blue interior. Arbor[eal] though also found on the ground. Diur[nal] and fast moving. Thought to feed ma[inly] on lizards, probably also snakes, birds [and] small mammals. Oviparous.

Lepturophis A monotypic genus contain[ing] only *L. borneensis* from Borneo. A medi[um-] sized snake that is arboreal but is other[wise] poorly known.

Limnophis A monotypic genus contain[ing] only the striped swamp snake, *L. bic[olor]* with a small range in southern Africa. T[his] small species feeds on fish and amphibi[ans] and is oviparous. Otherwise poorly know[n].

Lioheterophis A monotypic genus cont[ain]ing only *L. iheringi*, from Brazil. A small sn[ake] that is found in damp places and feeds [on] frogs. Poorly known.

Liopeltis Nine species from southern [and] south-east Asia. Small to medium-s[ized] snakes with slender bodies. Terrestr[ial,] found in forests, usually close to wa[ter.] Thought to feed on amphibians and liza[rds.] Oviparous.

Liophidium Seven species from Madagas[car] and neighbouring islands. Small snakes w[ith] slender, cylindrical bodies. Found ma[inly] in forested regions but otherwise very po[orly] known.

...*phis poecilogyrus* from the Amazon Basin.

...*his* Thirty-five or more species from ...ral and South America and the West ...es, including species previously placed ...e genera *Dromicus*, *Leimadophis* and ...*phis*. The three species from the ...pagos Islands are still referred to as ...*nicus* by some authors. Small to ...ium-sized snakes with cylindrical bodies ...smooth scales. They are found in a ...ty of habitat types, including swamps, ...slands, rainforests and cloud forests. ...e and nervous snakes that bite when ...lled. Rear-fanged but not considered ...erous. They feed on lizards, fish, frogs ...the eggs and larvae of frogs. Oviparous.

...*holidophis* Six species from Mada- ...ar. Small to medium-sized snakes about ...h little is known.

...*don* Five species from Central and ...h America, formerly known as *Siph-* ...s. Small to medium-sized snakes with ...ler bodies, wide heads and large eyes ...vertically elliptical pupils. Arboreal ...nocturnal and thought to feed mainly ...rogs and lizards. Rear-fanged snakes ...se bite can cause pain in humans. ...arous.

...*donomorphus* Six medium-sized species ...d in central, East and southern Africa. ...-aquatic snakes that tend to be noctur- ...feeding on frogs, tadpoles and fish. ...arous.

...*dryas* Eight species from Madagascar ...the Comoros Islands. Small to medium- ...snakes from forested situations. ...ler, arboreal species with large eyes ...vertical pupils.

...*gnathophis* A monotypic genus ...aining only *L. seychellensis* from the ...helles Islands. A medium-sized snake ...is thought to be diurnal and terrestrial, ...s otherwise poorly known.

...*phidion* (wolf snakes) Twelve species ...d in Africa south of the Sahara. Medium ...snakes that feed primarily on diurnal ...ls which they catch while they are ...p at night. Oviparous.

...*rophis* Three species from South ...rica, as far south as Argentina. Small ...edium-sized snakes with thick bodies ...an upturned snout, similar in build to ...*odon*, to which they are closely related. ...*micinctus* is a brightly banded species ...may mimic coral snakes. *L. dorbignyi*

is less colourful (and may mimic terrestrial pit vipers), while *L. histricus* has coral markings when young but later becomes brown. Diurnal and crepuscular snakes that feed mainly on toads. Oviparous.

■ *Captivity* Only occasionally available. Potentially interesting captives but often difficult to feed unless toads are available. Probably not bred in captivity.

Lytorhynchus (leaf-nosed snakes) Four species from North Africa, the Middle East and central Asia. Small snakes with an enlarged rostral scale. They live in arid places, including sand dunes and gravel deserts. They are nocturnal and eat lizards, especially geckos. Rare and poorly known.

Macropisthodon Four species from India, Sri Lanka, southern China and south-east Asia. Medium-sized, stocky snakes that are terrestrial or semi-aquatic. Rear-fanged species that mimic Asian pit vipers of the genus *Agkistrodon*. Diurnal or nocturnal, preferring open country and feeding mainly on frogs. Oviparous.

Macroprotodon A monotypic genus containing only the false smooth snake, or cowled, snake, *M. cucullatus*, from south-western Europe, North Africa and the Near East. A small, secretive snake with a flattened head and small eyes. It feeds mainly on lizards which are captured at night when they are hiding, especially in old stone walls. Rear-fanged but much too small to be of any danger to man. Oviparous.

Madagascarophis At least four species from Madagascar. Medium-sized, arboreal species with slender bodies, wide heads and large eyes. They apparently feed on arboreal lizards and frogs. Oviparous.

Malpolon Two species, *M. moilensis* and *M. monspessulanus*, found in southern Europe, North Africa and the Middle East. Large, fast-moving, diurnal snakes with slender bodies and a narrow head. They feed on other reptiles, small mammals and birds, especially ground-nesting and burrow-nesting species, such as bee-eaters. Rear-fanged and aggressive. The effects of the

▼ *Malpolon moilensis* from Egypt.

venom on man vary with the severity of the bite but can produce localized swelling and nausea. Oviparous.

■ *Captivity* Rarely kept on account of their fierce temperament and tendency to damage themselves by racing around the cage and striking at the glass.

Manolepis A monotypic genus containing only *M. putnami*, from Mexico. A small, terrestrial snake about which little appears to be known.

Masticophis (coachwhips) Eight species found from southern North America down into northern South America. Fast-moving diurnal snakes with long, slender bodies and streamlined heads. They are active hunters of lizards and small mammals, often quartering the ground with their heads raised slightly. They usually attempt to escape by fleeing, but, if cornered, they bite fiercely. Oviparous, laying clutches of up to 20 eggs.

■ *Captivity* Not very suitable as captives due to their nervous and aggressive disposition. They tend to rush wildly around their cages when disturbed and frequently damage their snouts on the sides.

Mastigodryas Eleven species from Central and South America (Mexico to Argentina). Closely related to *Coluber* and *Masticophis* and there is some confusion over which species should be included here. Medium-sized snakes with slender bodies, narrow heads and large eyes. Rapid, diurnal hunters, feeding on amphibians, lizards, other snakes, reptile eggs, birds and small mammals. Oviparous.

Mehelya (file snakes) Ten species found throughout Africa south of the Sahara. Their body is almost triangular in cross-section and their scales are heavily keeled, hence the common name. They feed on snakes and other small vertebrates, which they constrict. Oviparous.

Meizodon A genus of three species, found in Africa. Small, secretive, diurnal snakes that feed on small lizards and frogs. Oviparous.

Micropisthodon A monotypic genus containing only *M. ochraceus* from Madagascar. A small snake about which little is known.

Mimophis A monotypic genus containing only *M. mahfalensis*, from Madagascar. Closely related to the African genus *Psammophis*. A medium-sized snake with a narrow head and keeled dorsal scales. Diurnal and terrestrial. Thought to feed on lizards.

Montaspis A monotypic genus containing only *M. gilvomaculata*, from Natal. First discovered in 1990, and known only from three specimens. A small snake, black in colour with cream spots on the lips and a cream chin. Found near cold mountain streams at high altitude. Rear-fanged and thought to feed on frogs. Oviparous, otherwise poorly known.

Myersophis A monotypic genus containing only *M. alpestris*. This medium-sized snake is known only from Banaue, the Philippines and is rare. Its biology is completely unknown.

Myron A monotypic genus containing only Richardson's mangrove snake, *M. richardsoni*. A small snake found in New Guinea and along the northern coast of Australia, this rare species inhabits the intertidal zone on mudflats and in mangrove forests. It feeds on crabs and small fish. Viviparous but otherwise poorly known.

Natriciteres (marsh snakes) Three species, found in tropical Africa. Small snakes that feed on frogs and fish. Unusual among snakes in being able to break off their tail if grasped. Oviparous, laying up to eight eggs per clutch.

Natrix Four species found in Europe, North Africa and western Asia. Formerly included a great many additional species now placed in various other genera such as *Nerodia* (North America) and *Rhabdophis* (Asia). Medium-sized to large snakes that live in damp situations. Two species, *N. maura* and *N. tessellata*, are practically semi-aquatic but the grass snake, *N. natrix*, may sometimes be found away from water. All species eat amphibians, including tadpoles, and fish. The grass snake also takes small mammals and birds occasionally. Oviparous.

■ *Captivity* Quite easily maintained in captivity on live or prepared fish, but with a rather nervous disposition. They rarely bite but may release an obnoxious fluid from their cloacal glands. Captive breeding is possible but rarely attempted.

Nerodia (American water snakes) Eight species found in North America: mostly in the south-east, but *N. valida* occurs on the Pacific side of northern Mexico and in Baja California. Medium-sized snakes with thick-set bodies and heavily keeled scales. Highly aquatic species that swim well and are rarely found more than a few metres (yards) away from water. They feed mainly on amphibians and fish. When captured, they

often bite and invariably release a fo smelling fluid from the cloacal glar Viviparous, giving birth to up to 30 yo (although litters of almost 100 have b recorded).

■ *Captivity* Easy to keep in captivity, some species settle down well. Others, h ever, do not and remain bad-tempe They can be fed on whole or sliced f which should be supplemented with v mins. Because their metabolic rate is fa than that of most other snakes, they req frequent feeding if they are to remain good health and, especially, if they ar breed. Captive breeding takes places q frequently and the young will often small pieces of fish as well as tadpoles, e

Ninia Eight species found in Central northern South America, including Tr dad. Small, secretive snakes that live on rainforest floor among leaf-litter, presu to feed on invertebrates, small lizards small amphibians. They flatten their bo and may raise their head and neck w alarmed. Oviparous.

Nothopsis A monotypic genus contain only *N. rugosus*, from Central America the Pacific coastal region of north-wes South America. A small species whic found in warm, humid forests. Poss aquatic or semi-aquatic. Nothing is kno of its diet or reproduction.

Oligodon (kukri snakes) A very la genus, containing over 50 species. Sma medium-sized snakes found from Cer Asia and the Middle East, India, Bur southern China into Indo-China and so east Asia. May be nocturnal or diu and feed on invertebrates, lizards, frogs reptile eggs. Their scales are smooth their rostral scale is enlarged and slig upturned. Enlarged and recurved fang the rear of their mouth are used to slit shells of reptile eggs and may also hel grasping smooth or slippery prey. They said to resemble the kukri knives used the Gurkha troops. Some species are kn to be oviparous, and the others are assu to be. Recorded clutches tend to be sm usually six eggs or less.

■ *Captivity* Rarely available but some spe appear to be quite easily cared for, ea small rodents, etc. *O. formosanus* has bred in captivity.

Opheodryas (green snakes) Two spe found in North America. Small to medi sized, slender snakes that differ f each other in having keeled (*O. aestivu*

oth (*O. vernalis*) scales. Mainly terres-
, living among low vegetation, where
feed on insects and spiders. *O. aestivus*
iparous, laying clutches of up to 15 eggs
O. vernalis may be viviparous, or lay
near to hatching, in the northern parts
range.

aptivity The rough green snake,
odryas aestivus, usually does very well
cage with plenty of cover. It should be
yed occasionally to raise the humidity,
a constant supply of insects, including
rpillars and moth larvae should be
lable. Specimens have been known
ve for many years and breed annually.
ernalis has similar requirements but,
ome unknown reason, does not appear
lapt as well to captivity.

ites About 17 species of small to
ium-sized snakes found throughout
h of Asia. Formerly known as *Lycodon*, a
e now restricted to five species of South
rican snakes. Terrestrial, although
e species also climb. Sometimes associ-

ated with human habitations. Nocturnal
species that feed mainly on other reptiles but
may also take frogs and small mammals.
They have enlarged fangs at the rear of
their mouths but do not produce venom.
Reproduction not known.

Opisthotropis Eleven species found in
southern China, Indo-China, and on some
Indo-nesian islands. Some species are
known from very few specimens. Small to
medium sized snakes which may be totally
aquatic or semi-aquatic, depending on
species: several are found in or around fast,
clear, mountain streams. Their scales are
smooth to strongly keeled. Nocturnal, feeding on fish, amphibians including tadpoles,
freshwater shrimps and earthworms.
Oviparous, laying small clutches of eggs
close to water. Generally poorly known
snakes.

Oreocalamus A monotypic genus containing only *O. hanitschi* from Borneo. A small
species that has only occasionally been
collected and about which little is known.

Oxybelis (vine snakes) Four species from
southern Arizona to Brazil, Bolivia and

Peru. Medium-sized, slender snakes, with
elongated, pointed heads. Their eyes are
large and have round pupils. Brown or
green in colour. Highly arboreal species
from moist forest habitats. Rear-fanged
snakes that may open their mouths widely
when threatened, sometimes biting as a
last resort. Diurnal hunters that prey
mainly on lizards. Oviparous.

Oxyrhabdium Two species, *O. leporinum* and
O. modestum, endemic to the Philippines.
Medium-sized snakes with cylindrical bodies
and smooth scales. They have pointed
snouts and burrow in rotting logs, leaf-litter
and forest debris. Presumably nocturnal
but their habits, including diet and reproduction, are poorly known despite their
common occurrence.

Oxyrhopus Eleven species found from
Mexico to South America as far south as
Peru and Brazil. Medium-sized snakes with
smooth scales. Brightly banded in red and
black or red, white and black, like coral
snakes. Terrestrial and diurnal, feeding on
rodents, lizards, amphibians and other
snakes. Rear-fanged but not aggressive.
Oviparous.

Parahelicops A small genus, possibly monotypic, from south-east Asia. Very poorly known.

Pararhabdophis A monotypic genus containing only *P. chapaensis*, from Indo-China. A medium-sized snake about which almost nothing appears to be known.

Pararhadinaea Two species, *P. albignaci* and *P. melanogaster* from Madagascar. A small burrowing species whose natural history is poorly known.

Pareas About 15 species from China, Indo-China and south-east Asia, including Borneo. Small snakes with short, wide heads and blunt snouts. Their skulls are modified to enable them to extract snails from their shells. Oviparous.

Perinetia A recently described, monotypic genus containing *A. conlangesi* from Madagascar. Nothing is known of its natural history. *Note*: Genus recently changed to *Brygophis*.

Philodryas Sixteen species found throughout South America. Medium-sized snakes with slender, graceful bodies and narrow heads. Many are green in colour. Arboreal or semi-arboreal, diurnal in habits feeding on birds, bats, frogs, lizards and snakes. Oviparous.

Philothamnus (**green snakes and bush snakes**) Eighteen species found in Africa south of the Sahara. Slender, diurnal snakes with large eyes that feed mainly on frogs. Most species are green and live among low vegetation. Oviparous.

Phimophis Four species from Central and South America. Small to medium-sized snakes with modified rostral scales, which are turned up and overhang the lower jaw. Terrestrial and burrowing snakes that live in open situations and are thought to feed mainly on insects and their larvae. Oviparous.

Phyllorhynchus (**leaf-nosed snakes**) Two species, *P. browni* and *P. decurtatus*, from south-western North America, including Mexico, confined mainly to the Sonoran Desert region. Small snakes in which the rostral scale is enlarged and modified and may be used to protect the snout as it is pushed into crevices in search of food, consisting mainly of lizards and their eggs.

Pituophis (**gopher, pine and bull snakes**) Three species, *P. melanoleucus*, *P. deppei* and *P. lineaticollis*, found in North America,

▲ Natal green snake, *Philothamnus natalensis*, from south-eastern Africa.

including northern Mexico. *P. melanoleucus* has a large range and a number of subspecies, formerly regarded as full species, are recognized. Medium-sized to large snakes with keeled scales, and powerful, muscular bodies. May hiss loudly and strike aggressively if cornered, although their temperament varies. Diurnal, becoming nocturnal during hot weather, and feeding almost entirely on small to medium sized mammals. Oviparous, laying clutches of up to 24 eggs.

■ *Captivity* Popular snakes with amateur snake keepers. They normally settle d[ ] well and feed readily although some fo[ ] can be somewhat irascible. Bred in f[ ] large numbers, especially several of [ ] rarer forms. A number of colour and pat[ ] variations are known.

Plagiopholis Four species found in Ch[ ] Burma and Thailand. Small snakes, te[ ] trial but otherwise poorly known.

Platyinion A monotypic genus contai[ ] only *P. lividum* from Brazil. A small sp[ ] about which virtually nothing is know[ ]

Pliocercus Four or more highly vari[ ] species found from Mexico to the Am[ ]

n. (Seven species according to some orities.) Medium-sized snakes, some hich (or some forms of which) are oured or tricoloured 'false coral' snakes. live in tropical lowland forests and mainly on frogs.

ilopholis A monotypic genus, contain- only *P. cameroensis* from Cameroon. r relationships are unclear although are possibly related to *Aparallactus* actaspididae). Natural history poorly vn.

ymna (**shovel-snouted snakes**) Twelve es found in Africa south of the Sahara. are small, burrowing species that in loose soil. They feed on reptile eggs, h they swallow whole. Oviparous, g a few elongated eggs.

mmodynastes (**mock vipers**) Two es of small snakes from south- Asia, Indo-China and the Philippines. lverulentus is a common, wide-ranging es throughout southern China, south- Asia and the Philippines and has been d at altitudes over 2,750 m (9,000 ft) 'alaysia. *P. pictus* is less common and a more limited range in Malaysia. atra and Java. Both have angular s and large eyes with vertical pupils. r scales are smooth. Mainly nocturnal, ng on lizards and frogs. Viviparous, ucing small litters.

mmophis (**sand snakes**) A genus of over pecies found throughout Africa and Near East but *Psammophis condanarus* rs in Burma and Thailand and *P. line- s* ranges into western China. A single d from Indonesia is probably in error based on an accidental introduction. l to large in size, these fast-moving, 1al snakes feed mainly on lizards, h they run down. They live on the

mmophis sibilans leopardinus, from bia and southern Angola.

▲ Spotted skaapsteker, *Psammophylax rhombeatus*, a rear-fanged colubrid from southern Africa.

ground, or in low vegetation, usually in arid environments. Rear-fanged and veno- mous, their bite may cause local swelling and pain in man. At least some species will discard their tail as a defensive measure, although it is not completely regenerated. Oviparous.

Psammophylax (**skaapstekers**) Three species found in central and southern Africa. Medium-sized snakes that feed on small mammals, lizards and frogs. They are rear- fanged but rarely bite. Although the venom is highly toxic, it is released in such small doses that skaapstekers are not considered dangerous to man. Their reproduction is variable: *P. tritaeniatus* and *P. rhombeatus* are oviparous, but *P. variabilis* may be oviparous or viviparous, depending on subspecies.
■ *Captivity* Not readily available, but good captives, they usually settle down well and feed readily on small rodents. Not widely bred in captivity and feeding the small hatchlings could be a problem.

Pseudablabes A monotypic genus contain- ing only *P. agassisi*, from southern South America. A small burrowing snake about which hardly anything is known.

Pseudagkistrodon A monotypic genus from eastern Asia.

Pseudaspis A monotypic genus containing only the highly variable mole snake, *Pseuda- spis cana*, which is found throughout almost the whole of the southern half of Africa.

A large, bulky species, growing to over 2 m (6½ ft), it feeds mainly on small mammals. Viviparous, with litters of up to 100 young.
■ *Captivity* The mole snake makes a good pet. Freshly caught specimens may be aggressive but they soon calm down. Newborn young may refuse to eat rodents, preferring small lizards to start with.

Pseudoboa Four species from Central and South America, including Trinidad and Tobago. Medium-sized, terrestrial snakes that are found in rainforests, often near water. The pupils are vertically elliptical. Nocturnal, feeding on lizards, amphis- baenians, snakes and small mammals. Rear-fanged species that nevertheless constrict their prey. Oviparous: *P. neuwiedii* sometimes lays its eggs in ant nests.

Pseudoboodon Two species, *P. boehmi* and *P. lemniscatus*, both from the highlands of Ethiopia. Related to house snakes, *Lam- prophis*, but poorly known. *P. lemniscatus* is viviparous: *P. boehmi* is only recently described and its method of reproduction is not known.

Pseudocyclophis A monotypic genus con- taining only *P. persica*, from the Middle East and into central Asia. Formerly placed in the genus *Eirenis*, from which it differs mainly in having a combination of 15 scale rows around its midbody and a slightly different arrangement of scales on top of its head. A small, secretive snake, probably oviparous but otherwise poorly known.

Pseudoeryx A monotypic genus containing only *P. plicatilis*, from Brazil and Paraguay. A medium-sized aquatic species that is thought to eat fish and amphibians. Poorly known.

Pseudoficimia A monotypic genus, containing *P. frontalis*, from Mexico.

Pseudoleptodeira A monotypic genus containing only *P. latifasciata*, from Mexico. Similar to *Leptodeira*, in which genus it is sometimes placed. A small terrestrial snake about which little appears to be known.

Pseudorabdion Eight species (including two formerly placed in *Idiopholis*, three in *Agrophis* and one in *Typhlogeophis*). Distributed throughout south-east Asia and the Philippines. Small burrowing snakes with cylindrical bodies and smooth scales. Usually found among leaf-litter and beneath rotting logs, coconut husks, etc. They probably eat earthworms and other soft-bodied invertebrates and are thought to be oviparous. Otherwise very poorly known and, in several cases, rarely collected.

Pseudotomodon A monotypic genus containing only *P. trigonatus*, from South America. Viviparous, otherwise very poorly known.

Pseudoxenodon Nine species from China and neighbouring regions, the Malaysian peninsula (Cameron Highlands) and parts of Indonesia. Small to medium-sized snakes. Terrestrial and nocturnal, feeding on amphibians and lizards. Reproduction unknown.

Pseudoxyrhopus Ten species from Madagascar. Small to medium-sized snakes whose natural history is poorly known.

Pseustes Four species from Central and northern South America, including Trinidad. Medium-sized to large snakes with slender bodies and large eyes. They are terrestrial but climb occasionally and feed on birds, lizards and frogs. Oviparous.

Ptyas Three species found throughout much of central, southern and south-east Asia. Large snakes with powerful bodies, wide heads and large eyes. Diurnal snakes that adapt to a wide range of habitats and conditions. Often found around human habitations, where they feed on rodents, although amphibians, birds, lizards and snakes may also be eaten. Oviparous, producing clutches of up to 20 large eggs.

■ *Captivity* Impressive snakes for large cages, but with rather unpredictable temperaments. Wild specimens are likely to be infested with parasites but, other than this, they are hardy and adapt quite well to captivity. Captive breeding has not taken place on a regular basis.

Ptychophis A monotypic genus containing only *P. flavovirgatus*, from Brazil. A small snake with keeled dorsal scales. Rear-fanged and possibly of some danger to humans. It feeds on frogs and fish. Viviparous.

Pythonodipsas A monotypic genus cont[aining] only the western keeled snake, *P. [cari-]nata*, from south-western Africa. A s[mall] nocturnal snake with fragmented sc[ales] on the top of its head, and nostrils that [are] directed upwards. It lives in rocky de[serts] and often shelters under the prostrate le[aves] of the strange *Welwitschia* plant. Noctu[rnal,] feeding on small lizards and rodents. Re[pro]duction unknown.

Rabdion A monotypic genus contai[ning] only *R. forsteni*, from the Celebes. A s[mall] snake about which little is known.

Regina Four species from North Ame[rica,] related to the North American w[ater] snakes, *Nerodia*. Small to medium-s[ized] species that may have smooth or he[avily] keeled dorsal scales. *R. alleni* and *R. r.[igida]* are sometimes placed in a separate ge[nus,] *Liodytes*, but this is not widely accep[ted.] Semi-aquatic snakes that are found i[n] rivers, lakes and swamps and feed [on] amphibians, fish, crayfish and aqu[atic] invertebrates such as water snails [and] insect larvae. Viviparous, producing li[tters] of up to 40 young.

Rhabdophis About 12 species widely di[stri]buted throughout central Asia, I[ndia,] China, Indo-China, south-east Asia [and] Japan. Closely related to *Natrix*, with w[hich] they were formerly classified. Medium-s[ized] semi-aquatic snakes that feed on frogs [and] fish. Rear-fanged and considered dange[rous] to humans: at least one fatality has [been] recorded from *R. tigrinus*. Oviparous.

Rhabdops Two species, *R. bicolor* an[d *R.*] *olivaceus*, from India, northern Indo-C[hina] and China. Small to medium-sized sna[kes] thought to be nocturnal and to feed on [soft-] bodied invertebrates. Natural history po[orly] known.

Rhachidelus A monotypic genus contai[ning] only *R. brazili* from Brazil and Argentin[a. A] medium-sized, stocky snake that is diu[rnal] and terrestrial and eats mostly b[irds.] Oviparous.

Rhadinaea Up to 40 species, although [the] taxonomy is in some confusion. W[ide]spread, as currently understood, found [in] North America, through Central Am[erica] and into South America as far sout[h as]

◄ Western keeled snake, *Pythonodipsas carin[ata].* This species is unusual among colubrids in ha[ving] small fragmented head shields, more typical o[f] members of the Boidae. It is found in desert re[gions] of Namibia and Angola.

entina. Small snakes with cylindrical
ies and smooth scales. They live in a
iety of habitats but are invariably secre-
 species, often found among leaf-litter
 other debris. They eat earthworms,
phibians, including their eggs, and small
tiles. Oviparous, laying small clutches of
s.

idinophanes A monotypic genus from
th America. Poorly known.

mphiophis (beaked snakes) A genus
three species found in Africa. Large,
vy-bodied snakes that eat a wide range of
y, including small mammals and other
tiles. Oviparous, laying up to 17 eggs per
ch.

nobothryum Two species, *R. bovalli* and
lentiginosum from Central and South
erica. Medium-sized snakes with slender
ies, blunt heads and slightly keeled
es. The eyes are large and have vertical
ils. Both species are boldly marked with
 white and black bands and look like
al snakes, especially *R. bovalli*, which is
ost indistinguishable from a common
ies, *Micrurus alleni*. Nocturnal, arboreal
kes. Reproduction unknown.

Rhinocheilus (long-nosed snakes) One or
two species. *R. antoni* may be a subspecies
of *R. lecontei*, the long-nosed snake, which
is, in any case, variable. Medium-sized
snakes from southern North America
including northern Mexico, found mainly in
desert or semi-desert situations. Moderately
slender with a narrow head and pointed
snout. The upper jaw extends further
forward than the lower jaw. Brightly marked
in some parts of the range, where they
may mimic venomous coral snakes. Mainly
nocturnal, although active by day in the
cooler months of the year. Terrestrial
although capable of burrowing and even
climbing into low vegetation. They eat
mainly lizards although small mammals,
and perhaps birds, are taken by some
individuals. Oviparous, laying clutches of up
to 12 eggs.
■ *Captivity* Attractive and well mannered,
long-nosed snakes make good captives
provided they can be persuaded to accept
small rodents. Unfortunately, most will
not.

Rhynchocalamus A monotypic genus containing only *R. melanocephalus*, from the
Middle East. A small snake with a slender

▲ Long-nosed snake, *Rhinocheilus lecontei*, from
North America.

body, found in arid habitats. Thought to
feed on invertebrates and small reptiles.

Rhynchophis A monotypic genus containing only *R. boulengeri* from China and
northern Vietnam. A medium-sized snake
with a slender body, pointed head and an
upturned rostral appendage of unknown
function. Bright green and arboreal but
otherwise little known.

Salvadora (patch-nosed snakes) Up to eight
species from North and Central America.
Medium-sized snakes with slender bodies
and narrow heads. The rostral scale is
enlarged. Diurnal, fast-moving hunters of
lizards and snakes, although small rodents
are also eaten. All species are pale in colour
with a series of longitudinal lines running
along their dorsal surfaces. Oviparous.

Saphenophis Five species from north-
western South America (Colombia, Ecuador
and Peru). Small snakes from humid
regions. Thought to be diurnal but their
natural history is practically unknown.

Scaphiodontophis Five species from Central America. Small snakes with slender cylindrical bodies. *S. annulata* is a coral snake mimic. Found in forests and thought to eat lizards and other snakes. Oviparous.

Scaphiophis A monotypic genus containing only *S. albopunctatus*, from central and West Africa. A medium-sized snake with a modified rostral scale that is thought to be used for burrowing through loose, dry soil. Oviparous. Biology otherwise poorly known.

Scolecophis A monotypic genus containing only *S. atrocinctus*, from Central America. A small, nocturnal snake, usually found among leaf-litter and under forest debris. A brightly marked 'false coral' snake. It eats centipedes. Biology poorly known.

Seminatrix A monotypic genus containing only *S. pygaea*, the black swamp snake, found in the south-eastern corner of North America. A small, brightly marked snake, being glossy black with a red or pink belly. It is restricted to aquatic habitats, especially where the introduced water hyacinth occurs in large quantities: the snakes like to hunt among the crowns and roots of the floating plants for their prey, consisting of small fish, tadpoles, salamanders and leeches. Viviparous, giving birth from five to 15 young.

Senticolis A monotypic genus containing only *S. triaspis*, the neotropical rat snake, formerly placed in the genus *Elaphe*. It occurs in North and Central America, and just enters the United States in southern Arizona. A medium-sized, moderately slender snake with a narrow head. It has slightly keeled scales and a long tail. A semi-arboreal species that feeds on lizards, birds and mammals. Oviparous.

Sibon Ten species, including several formerly placed in the genus *Tropidodipsas*, found in Mexico, Central and South America. Medium-sized but very slender snakes with laterally flattened bodies, relatively wide heads and large eyes. Arboreal species from rainforests. Slug and snail-eating snakes that have specialized jaws for drawing snails out of their shells. Oviparous.

Sibynomorphus Eight species found in South America. Small to medium-sized snakes with cylindrical, moderately stout, bodies and blunt heads. Snail-eating snakes, closely related to *Sibon* but more terrestrial, found under stones in fields, etc. Presumed to be oviparous but rare and poorly known.

▲ *Stegonotus parvus*, **from New Guinea.**

Sibynophis Seven species found in India, Sri Lanka, Indo-China, southern China and south-east Asia, including the Philippines. Small to medium-sized snakes with slender bodies. Poorly known snakes that have been collected from lowland and montane rainforests. Apparently oviparous.

Simophis Two species, *S. rhinostoma* and *S. rhodei*, from Brazil and Paraguay. Small to medium-sized, slender species with smooth scales. Found in open fields and thought to feed on small mammals *S. rhinostoma* is claimed to be a false coral snake. Oviparous.

Sinonatrix Five species from China and Indo-China. Closely related to *Natrix*. They are semi-aquatic and are thought to feed on fish and amphibians. Two species, *S. percarinata* and *S. trianguligera* are oviparous, *S. annularis* is viviparous, while the reproductive mode of the other two species is unknown.

Sonora Up to six highly dimorphic species from North America. Two of them, *S. episcopa* and *S. semiannulata*, occur in the United States and the remainder are from Mexico. Small, terrestrial species that are restricted to arid desert and semi-desert habitats. Some forms are brightly coloured with rings of red, black and white. They eat invertebrates, including scorpions and spiders. Oviparous.

■ *Captivity* Not popular, but quite easily k in small cages with a dry substrate a some flat rocks under which the snakes c hide. A variety of cultured and collec invertebrate food can be offered, includ crickets and spiders. Captive breeding probably not been achieved, at least intentionally.

Sordellina A monotypic genus contain only *S. punctata* from Brazil. A very sn snake that is found near water and app ently eats frogs and tadpoles. Oviparous.

Spilotes (**tiger snake, chicken snake**) monotypic genus containing only *S. pullat* from Mexico to Argentina. A large, powe snake with highly variable markin The body is flattened from side to side, head is narrow and the eyes large. Unus in having an even number of dorsal sc rows (also found in *Chironius*) and theref without a vertebral row. Found in scrubby habitats, often near human set ments. Arboreal, feeding on amphibia birds (including their eggs), mamm and other reptiles. Often very aggressi Oviparous.

■ *Captivity* Attractive specimens ma impressive displays in large cages. Fai easily maintained once they have acclim tized but rather nervous. Regular capt breeding appears not to have taken plac

Stegonotus About 10 species found throu out south-east Asia, the Philippines, N Guinea and northern Australia. Mediu sized to large snakes with cylindrical boc and smooth shiny scales. Found in a vari of habitats but mostly terrestrial, feed on fish, amphibians and tadpoles, lizar snakes and small mammals. Oviparous.

Stenorrhina Two species, *S. degenhardtii* a *S. freminvillii*, from Central and north South America. Small, cylindrical sna with smooth scales and small hea Nocturnal or diurnal in habits and thou to feed on spiders. Oviparous.

Stilosoma A monotypic genus contain only the short-tailed snake, *S. extenuat* with a very limited range in central Flori This species is very small and slender spends most of its time beneath the surf in dry sandy soils. It apparently eats sn snakes, which it constricts. Lizards may be taken. Oviparous but otherwise a poc known species.

Stoliczkia Two species, *S. borneensis* fr Borneo and *S. khasiensis* from India. Sn snakes about which very little is known

eria Two species, *S. dekayi* and *S. occipito-ulata*, found in North and Central erica. Small, secretive snakes with keeled es, usually found in damp situations, re they search for slugs, snails, earth-ms and other invertebrates. Viviparous, ng birth to litters of up to 15 young.
aptivity Although there is very little rest in these small species, they will quite well in a vivarium with a damp strate, not too much heat and a constant ply of earthworms and slugs.

phimus A monotypic genus containing *S. leucostomas*, from Mexico. A small ke that is found in dry environments. It id to burrow and to feed on lizards but atural history is poorly known.

pholis A monotypic genus containing *S. lippiens*, from Mexico. A small species alse coral' snake, with yellow and black ds on its body. Fossorial and secretive. ogy poorly known.

ophis Three species from Colombia and ador. Small to medium-sized snakes slender bodies, narrow heads and large s. Terrestrial and diurnal, often found amp habitats and thought to feed on hibians and small lizards. Oviparous.

Tachymenis Six species from western and northern South America. Small snakes that are found in dry habitats, some-times at moderate altitudes. Terrestrial species, thought to feed mainly on lizards. Viviparous.

Tantalophis A monotypic genus containing only *T. discolor* from Mexico. A small, terres-trial snake that is poorly known.

Tantilla **(black-headed snakes or crowned snakes)** A large genus of about 50 similar species found from southern North America to Argentina. Very small, secretive snakes, with cylindrical bodies and smooth scales. They are characterized by a black patch on the top of their heads. Found in a wide variety of habitats, and usually nocturnal. They feed on insects and larvae and in some cases, apparently, small fish. The Rim Rock black-headed snake, *T. oolitica*, is classed as endangered and several other species have very small ranges. Oviparous, laying small clutches of up to three eggs.

Tantillita A monotypic genus containing only *T. lintoni* from Central America. Closely related to the black-headed snakes, *Tantilla*, which it resembles.

Telescopus **(tiger snakes and cat snakes)** Six species distributed throughout Africa, south-eastern Europe and the Near East, mainly in arid situations. Slender, noctur-nal snakes with large, prominent eyes and vertical pupils. They feed mainly on diurnal lizards, which they seek out in crevices while they are sleeping, but also take birds and small mammals. Rear-fanged but not dangerous to man. Oviparous.
■ *Captivity* A few species are occasionally kept in captivity, where they usually fare quite well. Small individuals of some species can be difficult to feed but adults usually take mice. Probably not bred with any degree of regularity.

Tetralepis A monotypic genus containing only *T. fruhstorferi* from east Java. A small snake, found only at high altitudes with a cool, seasonal climate. Natural history poorly known.

Thamnodynastes Six species from South America (but under revision). Small to medium-sized snakes with stocky bodies, wide heads and large eyes that have vertically elliptical pupils. Terrestrial and

▼ Namib tiger snake, *Telescopus beetzi.*

arboreal snakes that tend to be nocturnal. Thought to eat small lizards. Rear-fanged species whose bite may produce local pain and swelling in humans. Viviparous.

***Thamnophis* (garter snakes and ribbon snakes)** About 18 species found throughout North and Central America. Small to medium-sized snakes with slender bodies and heavily keeled scales. Most species are marked with a series of longitudinal lines running the length of their bodies. Diurnal species invariably found near water or in damp situations. They feed largely upon amphibians although some also take earthworms, fish and small mammals. Viviparous, with litters ranging in size from less than 10 to almost 100, depending on species. The San Francisco garter snake, *T. sirtalis tetrataenia*, is one of the rarest snakes in North America and is legally protected.

■ *Captivity* Attractive snakes that have long been popular with enthusiasts although not always as easy to keep in good health as is often thought. Due to their rapid metabolism, they require frequent feeding and, if fish is used, vitamin and mineral supplements are advisable. If rodents are accepted, these form a better diet. Breeding takes place regularly in captivity and the young are easily reared on a diet of earthworms at first, later graduating to slices of fish. Ribbon snakes (three species) make less satisfactory captives as they prefer amphibians and often refuse to eat fish.

***Thelotornis* (bird or twig snakes)** Two species, *T. kirtlandii* and *T. capensis*, found in tropical and southern Africa. Extremely slender arboreal snakes with long pointed heads growing to over 1 m (3 ft 4 in) in length. Their eyes have horizontal pupils, shaped like keyholes and they feed on lizards and small birds, relying on their cryptic coloration to ambush their prey. Rear-fanged and potentially dangerous to man. Oviparous, laying narrow, elongated eggs.

Thermophis A monotypic genus containing only *T. baileyi*, from Tibet. Natural history poorly known.

Thrasops Four species from tropical Africa. Large snakes with elegant heads. Black or green in colour with large black eyes. Arboreal, feeding on lizards, frogs and small mammals. Oviparous.

■ *Captivity* Good captives provided they are given a large cage with plenty of branches on which to climb and rest. Rodents are

usually accepted in captivity. Breeding has taken place but only occasionally.

Toluca A monotypic genus containing only *T. lineata*, from Mexico. A small, terrestrial snake that comes from cool, montane habitats. Viviparous.

Tomodon Two species from south-eastern South America. Small snakes that are thought to be terrestrial or semi-arboreal, feeding on lizards and small rodents. Viviparous.

Trachischium Five species from northern India and neighbouring countries. Small snakes that are terrestrial and probably nocturnal. Poorly known.

Tretanorhinus Four species from Mexico to north-western South America, Cuba and some smaller West Indian islands. Small snakes that are totally aquatic. Nocturnal, feeding on small fish. Oviparous. Poorly known.

Trimetopon Ten species from Central America. Small snakes that live in rainforest habitats but which are otherwise poorly known.

***Trimorphodon* (lyre snakes)** Up to 11 species from North and Central America although some forms are probably best regarded as subspecies. Medium-sized snakes with slender bodies, wide heads and large eyes. The pupils are vertical. Totally nocturnal, feeding on lizards, snakes and small mammals. Usually terrestrial. Oviparous.

Tripanurgos A monotypic genus containing only *T. compressus*, with a wide range in Central and South America, including Trinidad. A medium-sized but very slender snake with laterally compressed body. The head is wide and flattened, and the large eyes have vertical pupils and are red in juveniles. A nocturnal and arboreal snake that feeds mainly on frogs. Oviparous.

Tropidoclonion A monotypic genus containing only the lined snake, *T. lineatum* from North America. A small species, similar to a miniature garter snake. Often found around houses and in parks but also in open woodland and agricultural situations. Thought to feed mainly on earthworms. Viviparous.

Tropidodryas Two species found in south-eastern Brazil. Small snakes that are semi-arboreal and probably diurnal. They feed on frogs, lizards, birds and rodents. Biology poorly known.

Tropidonophis Eighteen species from Cen and South America, including five spe formerly placed in the genus *Macropop* Medium-sized to large species with hea keeled scales. Semi-aquatic species inv ably found near water, including strea rivers and swamps. Diurnal snakes that f mostly on amphibians. Oviparous.

Umbrivaga Two species from north South America. Small, terrestrial sna that feed on small amphibians and rept Natural history poorly known.

Uromacer Four species from Hispaniola its surrounding islands. Medium-sized large snakes, three with extremely slen bodies and narrow, pointed heads and other, *U. catesbyi*, heavy bodied with a bl snout. Diurnal and semi-arboreal, feed almost entirely on terrestrial and arbo lizards.

Uromacerina A monotypic genus cont ing only *U. ricardini* from Brazil. Clo related to *Uromacer* and similar to members of that genus. A very rare, arbo species that eats lizards. Poorly known.

Virginia Two species of earth snakes striatula and *V. valeriae*, from North Amer Small, secretive snakes that are found un rocks and debris. They like moist situati and feed largely on earthworms. Vivipar producing small litters of young.

Waglerophis A monotypic genus cont ing only *W. merremi*, from South Amer sometimes placed in the genus *Xeno* A medium-sized, thickset snake, resemb a terrestrial pit viper. A terrestrial spe that may be active by night and by day lives in damp habitats, near water, feeds mainly on amphibians. When thr ened it flattens its head and neck and ra them off the ground. A very aggres species with enlarged rear fangs, thou to be used to puncture the bodies of to The effects of its bite on humans is known. Oviparous.

Xenelaphis Two species, *X. ellipsifer* an hexagonotus, found in Thailand, Borneo Java. Large snakes, semi-aquatic, feed mostly on frogs.

***Xenochrophis* (keelbacks)** Five species piscator has a large range, from Afghanis right through to south-east Asia and Indonesian Archipelago. The other spe have more limited ranges within the s region. Medium-sized snakes, closely rel to *Natrix*, that live near water and mainly on fish. May be very numerou

able habitats. Rear-fanged species that
y give a painful, though probably not
gerous, bite.

ptivity One species, *Xenochrophis piscator*,
ften imported as 'Asian garter snakes'.
very suitable for captivity as they often
to feed properly.

odermus A monotypic genus contain-
only *X. javanicus* from the Malaysia
insula, the Indonesian archipelago
Borneo. A small snake with three rows
ubercules running down its back. The
aining dorsal scales are keeled and
se on the head are small and granular.
s species often burrows and is always
nd near water. It is thought to feed
nly on frogs. Oviparous.

odon (false vipers) Seven species found
n Mexico to Argentina. Medium-sized to
e, heavy-bodied snakes with broad
ds. Their markings and behaviour are
ilar to several species of terrestrial pit
rs, *Bothrops* and *Porthidium* species,
ich share their range. Sedentary rain-
st species that live on the banks of rivers
feed mainly on toads. Rear-fanged and
igerent; not thought to be particularly
igerous to man but capable of giving a
nful bite. Oviparous.

opholis One or, possibly, two species,
ich are not well known. *X. scalaris* is
n the Amazon Basin, and northern
th America. It is a small, slender species,
rnal in habits and found in damp forests.
eds mainly on small frogs. Reproduction
nown.

ophis Two species from southern
ia. Small snakes that are probably semi-
orial but whose natural history is almost
nown.

cys (Asiatic rat snakes) Six species found
ndia, China, Indo-China, south-east Asia
the Philippines. Closely related to *Ptyas*.
dium-sized to large snakes which may
e keeled or smooth scales. Slender-
lied diurnal species with large eyes. They
mainly terrestrial but sometimes take to
ter. Frogs, reptiles and small mammals
eaten. Oviparous.

▲ Duerden's burrowing asp, *Atractaspis duerdeni*,
from southern Africa, a member of the small and
poorly understood family Atractaspididae.

The Atractaspididae is a problematical group
of colubrid-like snakes from Africa and the
Middle East. It contains a small assemblage
of snakes that seem to have affinities with
one another but which cannot be easily
linked by any single characteristic. It may be
that there is more than one lineage involved.
For this reason, previous authorities have
been in considerable disagreement over
where the various genera fit into the scheme
of snake evolution and relationships. They
have been variously treated as colubrids,
vipers or elapids in the past. The current
feeling is that they constitute either a subfamily of the Colubridae or a family in their
own right. If they constitute a separate
family, which seems likely, there will still
be disagreement over which genera should
be placed in it and which should remain
within the Colubridae.

The Atractaspididae, as regarded here,
contains eight genera. Members of the
genus *Atractaspis* are venomous and the
others have Duvernoy's glands, extending
a long way back into the front half of
the snake's body. The venom-delivering
apparatus varies from genus to genus,
however. *Atractaspis* has large erectile
fangs on the front of its maxilla and no
other teeth. *Amblyodipsas*, *Chilorhinophis*,
Macrelaps, and *Xenocalamus* all have a short
maxilla bearing three to five normal teeth

and a pair of grooved fangs under the eye.
Most members of the specialized genus
Aparallactus also have enlarged fangs below
the eye: in some species the fangs have no
grooves and in *A. modestus* they are lacking
altogether.

Amblyodipsas Nine species from Africa
south of the Sahara. Small to medium-sized
snakes with cylindrical bodies, small eyes
and smooth, shiny scales. They burrow
in loose soil and feed on other burrowing
reptiles, amphibians and small mammals.
Nocturnal. Mostly oviparous, but *A. concolor*
may give birth to live young.

Aparallactus (centipede eaters) Eleven
species found throughout Africa south of
the Sahara, sometimes included in the
Colubridae. Small snakes with cylindrical
bodies and smooth scales. Their venom
apparatus is variable: back fangs may be
present or absent. They are burrowers often
associated with termite nests, rotting logs,
etc., and feed exclusively on centipedes.
Mostly oviparous, but *A. jacksoni* gives birth
to live young.

Atractaspis (burrowing asps, mole vipers)
About 12 species found throughout much of
Africa and with one species, *A. engaddensis*,
in the Middle East. Small snakes with small
heads, cylindrical bodies and smooth scales.
Their hollow fangs may be erected while
the mouth is closed, an adaptation to feeding in confined spaces. They are all burrowing snakes that may be seen on the surface
at night. They feed on other burrowing
reptiles and small rodents. Difficult to handle
safely, and capable of giving potentially
dangerous bites. Oviparous.

Chilorhinophis Three species from East
and central Africa. Medium-sized snakes
with small heads, small eyes and slender
bodies. The tail is rounded and the same
colour as the head, and is used to deflect
attacks. Burrowing snakes that feed on other
burrowing reptiles. Oviparous.

Macrelaps A monotypic genus containing
only the Natal black snake, *M. microlepidotus*. A medium-sized snake with a
thick, cylindrical body and smooth scales. A
burrowing species that feeds on a variety
of other reptiles, amphibians and small
mammals. Its bite is potentially dangerous
but it is normally docile. Oviparous.

Micrelaps Two species, *M. boettgeri* and *M.
vaillanti*, from central Africa. Small snakes
with cylindrical bodies, small heads and
smooth scales. Biology very poorly known.

Polemon Twelve species, including those previously assigned to *Miodon*, from West and central Africa. Small to medium-sized species with cylindrical bodies and smooth scales. Biology very poorly known.

Xenocalamus **(quill-snouted snakes)** Five species from central and southern Africa. Small to medium-sized snakes with unusual, pointed heads and tiny eyes. The body is cylindrical and the scales are smooth. They burrow in sandy soils, feeding only on amphisbaenians. Oviparous, laying small clutches.

ELAPIDAE Coral snakes, cobras, kraits, mambas and sea snakes

The Elapidae includes some of the best known, not to say notorious, snakes. It also includes a large number of small, generally inoffensive species, and the sea snakes, which are sometimes regarded as members of a family in their own right (occasionally two families), but are here placed in two separate subfamilies.

Members of the Elapidae share the same general body form and scalation as the colubrids, to which they are undoubtedly very closely related and there is some dissent as to which family is the more primitive of the two. The conservative view is that the elapids evolved from colubrids or colubrid-like species and this arrangement is maintained here.

The elapids have an almost global distribution but are better represented in the southern hemisphere than the northern. They occur in southern North America, Central and South America, most of Africa excluding the most arid parts of the Sahara Desert, the whole of southern and southeast Asia, and Australia, but are absent from the mainland of Madagascar. Marine elapids (sea snakes) are present to some extent in most tropical oceans but are absent from the Atlantic Ocean and the Caribbean. With one exception, they are most commonly found in coastal waters.

Differences between the colubrids and the elapids are limited to the arrangement of the teeth. The elapids have a pair of fixed fangs attached to the maxillary bone at the front of their upper jaw. There are no maxillary teeth immediately behind the fangs although there are teeth on the posterior part of the maxilla in most genera. The fangs are hollow, and venom can be for through the central canal.

Like the colubrids, members of this far have radiated into many ecological nicl including the marine environment. has led to the evolution of a varied se characteristics in size, shape and colc Most notable has been the converge evolution of certain Australian forms to the niche left vacant by the absence of vi on that continent: some Australian spe are so viper-like that they are commo known as 'adders'.

There are a number of schemes for s dividing the Elapidae. McDowell (1987) proposed six subfamilies and this arran ment is followed here: as it differs somew from previous ones, it is worth summariz it first. The subfamilies are:

The Bungarinae, comprising African Asian elapids, including the typical cob *Naja* species.

The Calliopheinae, comprising three of species in the genus *Calliophis*. Remain species previously assigned to this ge have been reclassified.

The Elapinae, comprising the New Wc species (*Leptomicrurus*, *Micruroides* *Micrurus*), a species previously assigne *Calliophis* but now moved to a separ genus, *Hemibungarus*, and one other sn southern Pacific genus, *Parapistocalamus* **The Hydropheinae**, comprising the vivi rous sea snakes and all the Austral elapids. Due to their very obvious ecolog differences, it is convenient for our purpc to deal with the Hydropheinae in two pa the Australian terrestrial elapids and the snakes. It seems likely that future resea

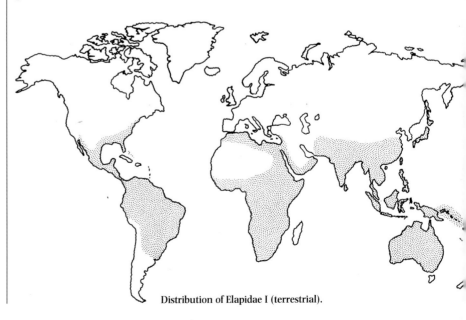

Distribution of Elapidae I (terrestrial).

will clarify the relationships between these groups of snakes.

The Laticaudinae, comprising the oviparous sea snakes, or sea kraits.

The Maticorinae, comprising only the Asian genus *Maticora*, expanded to include two species previously placed in the genus *Calliophis*.

BUNGARINAE

Typical African and Asian elapids, including most of the well-known species such as the cobras, mambas and kraits.

Aspidelaps Two species from Africa. Short, stocky snakes with enlarged rostral scales. One species, *A. lubricus*, is a brightly marked 'coral' snake whereas the other, *A. scutatus*, is a camouflaged, burrowing species. Nocturnal, feeding mainly on other reptiles. Moderately dangerous to man. Oviparous.

Boulengerina (**water cobras**) Two species from central Africa. Medium-sized snakes with moderately heavy bodies. They are unusual among elapids (except the sea snakes) in being largely aquatic in habits and feeding on fish. Potentially dangerous to humans but not normally aggressive. Oviparous.

Bungarus (**kraits**) Twelve species from India, Sri Lanka, China, Indo-China and other parts of south-east Asia. Medium-sized to large snakes with large shiny scales. Their bodies are slender and many are characteristically triangular in cross-section. Other species, though, are cylindrical or laterally compressed. The vertebral scales (those running down the centre of the dorsal surface) are large and hexagonal in shape. Most species are boldly banded in black and white or black and yellow but some are more

◀ Black Indian cobra, *Naja naja*.

▼ Red-headed krait, *Bungarus flaviceps*.

uniformly coloured. Kraits are nocturnal and terrestrial snakes that occupy a variety of habitats. They feed almost exclusively on other snakes and are often found around human settlements. Their venom is very toxic and potentially fatal to humans. Oviparous.

***Dendroaspis* (mambas)** Four species found throughout tropical and southern Africa. Medium-sized to large snakes (occasionally over 4 m (13 ft) in the case of the black mamba, *D. polylepis*) with narrow heads. The black mamba is terrestrial but the other three species are arboreal and green in colour. Fast-moving, diurnal hunters which run down their prey, consisting of birds and small mammals. Extremely dangerous to man. Oviparous.

***Elapsoidea* (garter snakes)** A small genus of seven species found throughout Africa south of the Sahara, including Somalia. Small, burrowing species that are often brightly coloured as juveniles. Nocturnal, feeding mainly on other reptiles. Potentially dangerous to man but unlikely to be fatal. Oviparous.

Hemachatus A monotypic genus containing only *H. haemachatus*, the rinkhals or spitting cobra. A medium-sized, stocky snake that may be plain or brightly banded. It is nocturnal and feeds on a wide range of vertebrates, especially toads. Its bite is potentially fatal to man, and venom sprayed into the eyes causes intense pain and sometimes blindness. Viviparous, with litters occasionally numbering 50 or more.

***Homoroselaps* (harlequin snakes)** Two species, *H. dorsalis* and *H. lacteus*, from southern Africa. Small, slender-bodied snakes with small heads and shiny scales. Both species are brightly coloured with yellow and orange markings. There are two hollow fangs at the front of the elongated maxilla. Burrowing species, sometimes associated with termite nests, and feeding on other small, burrowing reptiles. Too small to be very dangerous to humans although bites may produce discomfort. Probably oviparous, but poorly known.

Note: Members of this genus are grouped with the Atractaspididae by some authors.

***Naja* (cobras)** About 15 species, seven of which occur in Africa. The wide-ranging Asiatic cobra, *N. naja*, has now been separated into at least seven distinct species. Medium-sized to large snakes with stocky, cylindrical bodies. Their heads are narrow

and elegant but the most characteristic feature is the area immediately behind the head, which can be spread to form a wide hood that is almost unique among snakes. Cobras are terrestrial hunters, and may be nocturnal or diurnal. They feed on birds, small mammals and other reptiles. Some species from Africa and from Asia spit venom as a method of defence. All species are potentially dangerous to man. Oviparous: egg-guarding has been observed in some species.

Ophiophagus A monotypic genus containing only the king cobra, *O. hannah*, found from India, through Indo-China to southeast Asia and the Philippines. The world's largest venomous snake, at a maximum recorded length of over 5 m (16½ ft). Most specimens, however, are under 4 m (13 ft). The body is moderately slender, the head narrow. A narrow hood is spread when the snake rears up. Normally found in wooded, humid habitats but also on occasion near human settlements. The king cobra feeds only on other snakes, especially other cobras and kraits. It is exceedingly dangerous to humans, though not especially aggressive unless disturbed. Oviparous, laying large clutches of up to 40 eggs in a nest of dead leaves and other debris. Both sexes remain in the vicinity of their eggs and guard them until they hatch.

Paranaja A monotypic genus containing *P. multifasciata*, from West Africa. A medium-sized, slender snake which is mainly terrestrial. Its biology is poorly known.

Pseudohaje Two species from West and central Africa. Large cobras with slender bodies, large eyes and narrow hoods. Apparently arboreal but habits and biology very poorly known.

Walterinnesia A monotypic genus containing only the desert cobra, *W. aegyptia*. It is found in Egypt, the Middle East and the Arabian peninsula, especially near oases and human settlements. A medium-sized, fairly stout snake with glossy black scales. It has no hood, nor does it rear up when disturbed. It feeds largely upon lizards, especially *Uromastyx* species, in whose burrows it sometimes lives. Dangerous to humans but bites are rare.

CALLIOPHEINAE

A recently proposed subfamily containing only three species, all belonging to the genus *Calliophis*.

Calliophis Three species as currently rec nized (*C. bibroni*, *gracilis* and *melanu* occurring in India, the Malayan penin and Indonesia. Small snakes with sler bodies, and small heads and eyes. Noctu species that live in forests and feed on o small reptiles, including burrowing sna such as *Typhlops* species. Oviparous wh known, although there are suggestions some species may be viviparous.

ELAPINAE

The snakes in this family include the N World species as well as some from the World.

Hemibungarus Four species, including th that were formerly included in *Callio* (*japonicus*, *kelloggi* and *macclellandi*) and previously monotypic *H. calligaster*. They found in south-east Asia and the Philippi Small snakes with narrow heads. The b of *H. calligaster* is boldly marked with rings on its back and it is locally kno as a 'coral' snake. Secretive species fo in rotting logs and other debris in fore areas. Thought to be oviparous and to on other small reptiles but biology po known.

Leptomicrurus Three species of coral sna from South America. Similar to *Micr* species and regarded as part of that ge by some authorities. Slender snakes w small heads. Burrowing, and found in l litter, decaying logs, etc. Thought to ea range of small prey, including invertebra caecilians and amphisbaenians. Ovipar

Micruroides A monotypic genus contair only the Sonoran coral snake, *M. eury* *thus*, from the south-western United Sta and north-western Mexico. A small sn with typical 'coral' coloration of black–w –red–white–black bands around its bod differs from the *Micrurus* species in mi details of scalation. A secretive, noctu snake, often found in river washes. It feed lizards and other snakes and is gener inoffensive to humans. There are recorded fatalities from its bite. Ovipar laying small clutches of eggs.

***Micrurus* (coral snakes)** At least 50 spe (as many as 62 according to some auth ties) from southern United States, thro Central America and into South Americ far south as central Argentina. A variet habitats are used, from deserts to trop rainforests. Small to medium-sized sna with moderately slender bodies and sm

ads. Most coral snakes are brightly
rked, typically with rings of red, black
d yellow (or white). The sequence of the
gs varies somewhat and a few species
ve red and black rings only. Coral snakes
y be active by night or by day, although
rnal species tend to be restricted to areas
h plenty of cover, or they are active only
ring the early morning or late evening,
after heavy rain. They feed largely on
er reptiles and some specialize in eating
various species of burrowing amphis-
nians that share much of their range.
hough their fangs are short, coral snakes
duce a potent venom. Bites from some
cies can be fatal to humans unless anti-
om is available. Oviparous.

rapistocalamus A monotypic genus con-
ning only *P. hedigeri* from New Guinea
d Bougainville in the Solomon Islands. A
all snake with a slender body. It occurs in
ist forests and is secretive, living under
ting logs and leaf-mould. It is rare and its
logy is very poorly known although it is
ught to feed on the eggs of large land
ils.

DROPHEINAE (sometimes spelled
drophiinae)

e Hydropheinae are, traditionally, the
snakes and in the past they have been
arded as a separate family, the Hydro-
idae (or Hydrophiidae according to some
hors). Although there is some doubt
ut their true relationships, it is generally
epted that the differences between them
d terrestrial elapids are due to modifica-
s made necessary by their specialized
-style, i.e. they are adaptive.

As explained on page 232, the species in
s family are dealt with in two ecologically
arated groups.

Marine species

dyptophis A monotypic genus contain-
only the horned sea snake, *A. peronii*
m off-shore waters around northern
stralia, Indonesia and adjacent parts of
th-east Asia. A medium-sized snake with
ender forebody and stout hindbody. The
d is small and the tail is laterally flat-
ed. It prefers seas with sandy beds and
al reefs and apparently feeds on small
such as gobies. Viviparous, producing
10 young.

ysurus Seven or eight species found
shallow waters between the northern

Australian coast, Indonesia and New Guinea.
Three species have slightly more extensive
ranges into the South China Sea. Small to
large (mostly medium-sized) snakes with
quite stout bodies and laterally flattened
tails. They are found in the vicinity of reefs
and most species eat small fish. *A. laevis* also
takes crustaceans and fish eggs, while
A. eydouxii seems to take only fish eggs and
its venom apparatus is not well developed.
Viviparous, producing small litters of young.

Astrotia A monotypic genus containing
only Stokes' sea snake, *A. stokesii*. This
species has a large range, from the seas
around India, through south-east Asia as
far as northern Australian waters. A large,
heavy-bodied sea snake with a deeply
flattened tail and a keel-like row of ventral
scales. It feeds on slow-moving fish and
may be aggressive to humans. Fatalities
have resulted from attacks by this species.
Viviparous, producing one to five large
young.

Disteria Four species, one of which, *D. kingii*,
comes from northern Australia, whereas
the others are from India, the Malayan
peninsula and south-east Asia. Similar to
Hydrophis, in which genus they are included
by some authorities.

Emydocephalus Two species of sea snakes,
E. annulatus from the seas around northern
Australia, and *E. ijimae*, from the region of
Taiwan and the Ryukyu Islands, Japan.
Medium-sized snakes with slender bodies
and only moderately flattened tails. Their
heads are short, rounded and covered with
large scales. The rostral scale is conical in

shape and the general appearance has led
to the common name of 'turtle-headed sea
snakes'. Both species feed exclusively on
the eggs of fish. Their venom apparatus is
poorly developed and they do not pose a
threat to humans. Viviparous.

Enhydrina Two species, *E. zweifeli* and *E.
schistosa*, sometimes placed in the genus
Disteira. They are distinguished by a specialized scale at the front of their chin, thought
to be an adaptation to their diet of catfish
and puffer fish. *E. schistosa* is a widespread
species, living in shallow waters, especially
those of estuaries and tidal bays, from the
Persian Gulf to the South China Sea and
northern Australia: *E. zweifeli* is restricted to
the coasts of New Guinea. Medium-sized
snakes with elongated bodies. Because of its
habitat preference, *E. schistosa* is sometimes
trodden on in shallow water. It bites when
provoked and is the cause of most sea snake
mortalities. Viviparous, producing litters of
up to 34 young.

Ephalophis A monotypic genus containing
only *E. greyi*, found around the north-west
coast of Australia. A small species with
cylindrical body and slightly flattened tail. It
lives only among the tidal mangrove creeks
and flats, where it feeds on gobies in shallow
water. This species is relatively agile when
out of the water and may remain in the
intertidal zone at low water. The effects of
its venom on humans are unknown.
Probably viviparous.

Hydrelaps A monotypic genus containing
H. darwiniensis, from the coasts of north-
western Australia. A small species, similar

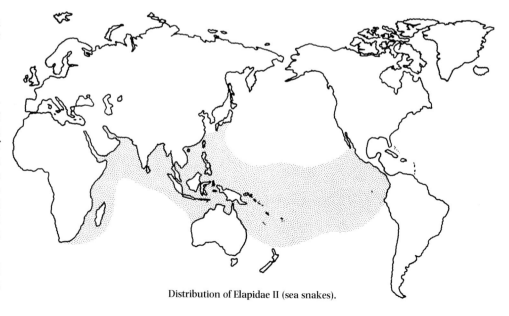

Distribution of Elapidae II (sea snakes).

in shape and habits to *Ephalophis greyi*, foraging in shallow water for small fish living in crab burrows of the intertidal zone. Inoffensive but potentially dangerous to humans. Presumed to be viviparous.

Hydrophis Thirty species, and therefore the largest genus of sea snakes. Found from the Persian Gulf to the western Pacific and northern shores of Australia. One species, *H. semperi*, is unique among hydropheine snakes: it is found only in the freshwater Lake Taal on Luzon Island, the Philippines. Small, medium-sized or, occasionally, large snakes, with small heads and relatively slender bodies, although the hindpart becomes progressively bulkier in some species. Apart from the freshwater species mentioned above, the members of this genus are found in shallow seas and coastal waters although they have also been recorded at great depths. They feed mostly on eels, although some species also eat fish eggs. Their venom is potent and human fatalities have occurred. Viviparous.

Kerilia A monotypic genus containing only *K. jerdoni*, from south-east Asia. Medium-sized with a compressed body and tail. Biology poorly known. Assumed to be viviparous.

Kolpophis A monotypic genus containing only *K. annandalei*, found in the coastal waters from Thailand to Indonesia. Further details of this newly described species are lacking.

Lapemis A monotypic genus, containing only *L. curtus* from the Persian Gulf, and the coasts of western India, south-east Asia and northern Australia. Two races are recognized. A stout species with a large head. The scales on the body become progressively more keeled towards the middle of the belly and are spiny in the case of adult males. (Note that these are not the ventral scales, which are reduced in size in these and all sea snakes.) It lives in coastal waters, especially in and around estuaries and river mouths where the water is turbid, and feeds on small fish. It bites readily if handled and human fatalities have occurred. Viviparous, producing small litters of young.

Parahydrophis A monotypic genus containing only *P. mertoni*, found around the northern coasts of Australia and the southern coasts of New Guinea and neighbouring islands. A small species with moderately slender, cylindrical body and smooth scales. It is found in tidal estuarine waters, among

mangroves and feeds on small fish. Potentially dangerous to humans. Viviparous, producing small litters of young.

Pelamis A monotypic genus containing only the pelagic sea snake, *P. platurus*. This species has a huge range, larger than that of any other snake. It is truly pelagic and is found in the surface waters off eastern Africa, southern Asia as far north as Japan, and northern Australasia, occasionally reaching round to Tasmania in the south. In addition, it crosses the Pacific and can be found along the Pacific coast of Central and northern South America. Fears that it may pass through the Panama Canal and establish itself in the Caribbean appear not to have been realized. Its body is slender and the head is long and narrow. Its coloration is variable but is normally some combination of bluish black and yellow. Entirely yellow individuals are also known. Despite its wide distribution, it is rarely seen away from the continental shelf. Hundreds, if not thousands, of individuals sometimes join forces to form huge 'slicks' extending over great areas. The apparent shelter afforded by these aggregations may attract the fish on which they feed. Liable to bite, although fishermen often handle them with apparent impunity. Their venom is very toxic, however, and they are potentially dangerous to humans. In tropical waters, reproduction probably occurs throughout the year. Litters of two to six young are born.

Thalassophina A monotypic genus containing only *T. viperina*, previously assigned to the genus *Praescutata*, among others. It is found from the Persian Gulf, through the South China Sea as far as Indonesia. A medium-sized species with very rough scales. Viviparous.

Thalassophis A monotypic genus containing only *T. anomolus*, found in the coastal waters of Thailand and Indonesia.

2. Australasian terrestrial species

Acanthophis (death adders) Three (possibly four or five) species found in Australia and New Guinea. Medium sized but very bulky snakes, with heavily keeled scales, that are counterparts of the vipers (which are absent from the region). They are found in a variety of habitats and eat lizards, birds and small mammals, which may be lured within range by means of the brightly coloured tail tip. Potentially dangerous to man: fatalities have occurred. Viviparous, with up to 30 young per litter, depending on species.

Aspidomorphus Three species from N Guinea and neighbouring islands. Sn snakes with rounded snouts and small ey Nocturnal, burrowing species about wh almost nothing is known.

Austrelaps (copperheads) Three species medium-sized snakes restricted to Austra including Tasmania. Cylindrical snakes t may flatten their heads when corner Diurnal, favouring moist situations a feeding mainly on small lizards and fro Viviparous, producing litters of three to young, depending on species. They potentially dangerous to man: fatali have occurred.

Cacophis (crowned snakes) Four spec found only along the eastern coastal zon Australia. Small to medium-sized cylindri snakes with a characteristic dark cap on of their heads. Their main food is lizar especially skinks, which are hunted at ni while they are asleep in crevices, etc. Th bite is not considered especially danger to man. Viviparous.

Cryptophis Five species found in north and north-eastern Australia and N Guinea (but see the note under *Rhino cephalus*). Small to medium-sized sna with cylindrical bodies and smooth, sh scales. Nocturnal hunters of diurnal lizar which they hunt and capture while t are asleep. Viviparous, producing litters up to eight young. Only the largest spec *C. nigrescens*, is regarded as potenti dangerous to man.

Demansia (whipsnakes) Nine species fou in Australia and southern New Guin Small to medium-sized snakes with lo slender bodies, narrow heads and large e They look superficially like the Europe and North American whipsnakes a coachwhips, and have a similar life-sty feeding on diurnal lizards, which t run down. Some species also eat frogs, a reptile eggs have also been found in stomachs of two species. Oviparous, lay clutches of up to 12 eggs. A communal r of the yellow-faced whipsnake, *D. psam phis*, has been found, containing ab 600 eggs. Reluctant to bite but potenti dangerous to man.

Denisonia Five species found only Australia. Small to medium-sized sna which may be slender or moderately sto The scales are smooth but coloration va and their eyes are large and have vert pupils. Nocturnal, terrestrial snakes

copperhead, *Austrelaps superbus*, from south-ern Australia.

mostly on frogs and lizards. Viviparous, [pro]ducing litters of three to seven young. [Lar]ge specimens are potentially dangerous [to m]an.

[Dri]*sdalia* Three species from southern [Aus]tralia, sometimes placed in the genus [Elap]*ognathus*. Small snakes with cylindrical [bod]ies and narrow heads. Secretive species [that] live beneath debris and feed on lizards, [whi]ch they hunt mainly during the day. [Inof]fensive and effectively harmless to [hum]ans. Viviparous, with small litters of up [to 1]0 young.

[Ech]*iopsis* A monotypic genus containing [only] the bardick, *E. curta*. This small, stout [sna]ke is found around the south-western [part] of Australia, where it inhabits localized [mois]t habitats. It is crepuscular and noctur-[nal] feeding mainly on frogs and lizards but [also] taking small mammals and birds. When [cornered] it flattens its body and will bite [if pro]voked. Potentially dangerous to man [altho]ugh probably not fatal. Viviparous, [with] clutches of three to 14 young.

Elapognathus Five species found around the southern coasts of Australia, including one species in Tasmania. Small snakes with cylindrical bodies and smooth scales. Terrestrial snakes that may be diurnal, crepuscular or nocturnal, depending on temperature. They feed mainly on lizards but may also take frogs. Not considered dangerous to man. Viviparous, producing small litters of up to 10 young. In cooler regions, females may breed every second or third year.

Furina Two species, the red-naped snake, *F. diadema*, and the orange-naped snake, *F. ornata*, from Australia. Small snakes with cylindrical bodies and smooth, glossy scales. Young specimens are brightly coloured with distinctive coloured patches on the tops of their heads. Nocturnal species that feed on lizards, especially skinks, which are caught while in their night-time retreats. Not considered to be dangerous to man on account of their small size. Oviparous, laying small clutches of one to six eggs.

Glyphodon Three species found in north-eastern Australia and southern New Guinea. Small to medium-sized species with slender bodies and a narrow head. The scales are smooth and shiny. Nocturnal and terrestrial, probably feeding mainly on skinks and geckos. Oviparous, laying clutches of six to 10 eggs.

Hemiaspis Two species found in eastern Australia. Small to medium-sized snakes with cylindrical bodies and smooth, shiny scales. Terrestrial species that may be crepuscular or nocturnal. *H. damelii* feeds almost exclusively on frogs whereas the other species, *H. signata*, eats frogs and lizards. Their bites may be painful but are not considered dangerous to man. Viviparous, producing litters of three to 20 young.

Hoplocephalus Three species restricted to eastern Australia. Medium-sized snakes with elongated bodies and broad heads. The ventral scales have a ridge along either side to assist in climbing. Specialized snakes that may be arboreal (*H. bitorquatus*), saxicolous (*H. bungaroides*) or both (*H. stephensii*). They feed mainly on lizards but frogs, birds and small mammals (including bats) are also taken. Potentially dangerous to man. Viviparous, producing litters of two to 12 young every other year.

Loveridgelaps A monotypic genus containing only *L. elapoides*, from the Solomon Islands. A medium-sized snake with slender, cylindrical body and bright 'coral snake' coloration consisting of white and black bands. The dorsal parts of the white bands are suffused with bright yellow. A very rare snake that occurs in forest areas, especially near streams. It is nocturnal and secretive and feeds on lizards, blind snakes and, probably, frogs. Possibly dangerous to humans but not aggressive. Reproductive habits unknown.

Micropechis (small-eyed snake) A monotypic genus containing only *M. ikaheka* from New Guinea and some neighbouring islands. A medium-sized to large snake with a stocky body. The eye is very small.

◄ Mainland tiger snake, *Notechis scutatus*, found in south-eastern Australia.

▼ Inland taipan, or fierce snake, *Oxyuranus microlepidotus*, from the arid centre of Australia.

▲ Mulga, or king brown, snake, *Pseudechis australis*, found throughout Australia.

Ogmodon A monotypic genus containing only the Fijian species *O. vitianus*. A small snake, rarely collected and found only on the island of Vitu Levi. A secretive, fossorial species that lives in mountain valleys. It apparently eats earthworms and other soft-bodied invertebrates.

Oxyuranus (**taipans**) Two species, the inland taipan, *O. microlepidotus*, found in central Australia and the Taipan, *O. scutellatus*, from northern Australia and southern New Guinea. Large, moderately slender snakes with large heads and prominent eyes. Mainly diurnal but becoming nocturnal in hot weather. Taipans of both species feed on mammals including rodents and bandicoots. Large prey is bitten then released, to be tracked down later, but small prey may be held while the venom takes effect. Extremely dangerous to man, although rarely encountered. The inland taipan produces the most powerful venom of any land snake in the world. Oviparous, laying clutches of up to 22 eggs.

Pseudechis Six species, found in Australia (five species) and New Guinea (one or two species). Large, moderately slender snakes with smooth glossy or matt scales and variable coloration. They all flatten their neck when cornered. Terrestrial snakes that may be diurnal, crepuscular or nocturnal, depending on the weather. A wide range of prey is taken, including frogs, lizards, other snakes, birds and small mammals. Not normally aggressive but potentially very dangerous to man. Reproduction variable: *P. porphyriacus* is viviparous, but the others are oviparous, with clutches of up to 19 eggs.

Pseudonaja (**brown snakes**) Seven species found throughout Australia (although some have limited ranges) and with one species ranging into eastern New Guinea. The western brown snake, *P. nuchalis*, occurs in several forms, some of which may later be described as distinct species. Small, medium-sized or large snakes with moderately slender bodies and smooth scales. They have small heads but their eyes are fairly large. Terrestrial species that are active mainly in the day, chasing and running down their prey of lizards, birds and small mammals. Irritable and aggressive snakes that may flatten their necks when annoyed. Potentially dangerous to man. Oviparous, sometimes laying clutches of over 30 eggs (larger species) but usually somewhat less.

Rhinoplocephalus Eight species as currently recognized although species have been

ecretive species that lives beneath forest ris in rainforests, swamps and other st habitats. Largely nocturnal, probably ling on other reptiles, frogs and small mmals. A dangerously venomous species ose bites can produce symptoms similar hose of sea snakes (myotoxic).

echis (**tiger snakes**) Two variable species, ater and *N. scutatus* with restricted ges along southern Australia. Forms of black tiger snake, *N. ater*, also occur on mania and several small offshore islands. lium-sized to large snakes with powerful ies and smooth, shiny scales. Variable in ration but with a tendency to become melanistic, especially in cooler localities. When disturbed, they inflate and deflate their bodies, while giving a loud hiss. The neck and front part of the body is flattened to a considerable degree and the snake may strike repeatedly. They are terrestrial and diurnal for most of the year, becoming nocturnal during hot weather. Their diet consists of fish, frogs, lizards, birds and small mammals – in fact almost anything that will fit into their mouths. Very dangerous to man: fatalities have occurred.

shuffled between this genus and *Cryptophis* in the past. Species previously known as *Unechis* are also included here. Found in desert or semi-desert regions in various parts of Australia. Small snakes with stout, cylindrical bodies, short tails and small, flattened heads. The scales are smooth and shiny. They are active at night, foraging for small sleeping lizards. Not considered dangerous to man on account of their small size. Viviparous, producing small litters of relatively large young. The biology of some species is poorly known.

Salomonelaps A monotypic genus containing only *S. par*, from the Solomon Islands. A medium-sized snake with variable coloration and markings. It is found in forested areas and is mainly diurnal, feeding on frogs and small reptiles. Potentially dangerous to humans, though not normally aggressive. Reproduction unknown.

Simoselaps At least 14 species found throughout Australia, restricted mainly to arid parts. Small, burrowing snakes that move beneath the surface, swimming rapidly through loose sand or soil. Their scales are smooth and highly polished and a number of species have shovel-shaped snouts (and are therefore known as shovel-nosed snakes). Several species are brightly marked with transverse body bands or annuli. In many of these features they parallel the habits and appearance of snakes of the North American genera *Chilomeniscus* and *Chionactis*. They come to the surface at night. Some species eat small lizards (skinks) while others eat reptile eggs. A few species eat both. Some, probably all, species are oviparous, laying clutches of three to five eggs.

Suta A monotypic genus containing only *S. suta*, sometimes placed in the genus *Denisonia*. Medium sized with a stout body and small head and eyes. A secretive snake from mainly dry areas which feeds on small lizards, snakes and mammals. Viviparous, producing litters of up to seven young.

Toxicocalamus About nine species found only in New Guinea and neighbouring islands. Small to medium-sized snakes with small eyes. They live in rainforests and montane forests and are nocturnal and perhaps semi-burrowing. Otherwise their biology is poorly known.

Tropidechis A monotypic genus containing only the rough-scaled snake, *T. carinatus*, restricted to a small area of south-eastern

Australia. A medium-sized snake with a moderately slender body and heavily keeled scales. It is nocturnal and partially arboreal, feeding on treefrogs and arboreal mammals, but it may also descend to the ground to forage. Potentially dangerous to man. Viviparous, producing up to 18 relatively large young.

Unechis Eight species, widely distributed throughout Australia. Small snakes with smooth scales and small heads. They are mostly uniform in colour although several have black patches on the top of their heads and some have a dark vertebral line. Shy, nocturnal snakes that occupy a variety of habitats but are most often associated with moist woods and grasslands. Their prey consists almost entirely of small skinks. Viviparous, with litters of one to 11 young.

Vermicella (bandy-bandies) Two species, found in Australia. Both are regarded as

▲ Bandy-bandy, *Vermicella annulata*, a secretiv elapid from Australia that feeds entirely on worn snakes.

rare, and have suffered from habi destruction, especially through agricultu practices. Small to medium-sized sna with slender, cylindrical bodies, smoo shiny scales and small eyes. Both spec are boldly marked with white rings arou an otherwise black body. Burrowing spec that appear on the surface only at nig in warm damp weather, in search of bli snakes (*Ramphotyphlops* species), on wh they appear to feed exclusively. Not regard as particularly dangerous to man, althou bites have occurred. Oviparous, with clutc of up to 13 eggs.

▼ Yellow-lipped sea krait, *Laticauda colubrina*, from Indian, south-east Asian and north-east Australian waters.

...ICAUDINAE

...members of the Laticaudinae are all sea ...es but are different from both the ...rophiine sea snakes and the terrestrial ...ids. They are less well adapted to ...ine life than other sea snakes. ...here is a single genus in the subfamily.

...auda (**sea kraits**) Five species of primarily ...nakes, although one species, *L. crockeri*, ...und only in the land-locked Lake Te- ...ano, Rennell Island in the Solomon ...ds, where the water is brackish. ...y are found around the shores of south- ...ern Asia, including those of the many ...e and small islands in the south-western ...fic. Two species reach the northern ...tralian coast. Medium-sized snakes with ...idrical bodies and a flattened tail. All ...ies are distinctively banded in black ...dark brown) and white, but *L. crockeri* is ...ned to become melanistic and may be ...ormly dark brown in colour. Apart ...t *L. crockeri*, the sea kraits are found in ...low water over coral reefs and outcrops. ...ess to exposed land appears to be a ...ssity, for shedding, drinking and egg ...ng. They feed on fish, especially eels. ...parous, laying clutches of up to 20 eggs ...revices in exposed coral and rocky out- ...s. There is some doubt surrounding ...reproductive mode of *L. colubrina* and ...rockeri*: there are unconfirmed reports ...ve-bearing in these two species. *L. colu-* ...n, however, lays eggs in at least parts of ...ange.

...TICORINAE

...Maticorinae consists of the genus ...icora.

...cora Five species, including two previ- ...y assigned to *Calliophis*. Found in India, ...o-China and south-east Asia including ...Philippines. Small to medium-sized ...es with very slender bodies and small ...ds. The venom glands are huge, extend- ...for about one-third of the length of ...body. Some are brightly coloured: *M.* ...gata* is the blue Malayan coral snake, ...ch has a dark blue dorsal surface, light ...flanks and orange underside. The head ...tail are also orange. Semi-burrowing ...es that are sometimes found in forests ...agricultural areas. They feed on other ...es. Generally inoffensive but possibly ...gerous to humans. Oviparous.

The vipers form a well-defined and advanced family of snakes found throughout much of the world but absent from Madagascar and Australia. Their most distinctive characteristic is a pair of shortened maxillae to each of which is attached a single long fang. Each maxilla is hinged so that the fangs can be folded back when not in use. The fangs have an enclosed canal through which venom is forced.

Vipers are typically short and stocky with broad heads. The scales are usually heavily keeled (except night adders, in which they are smooth) and the head is covered with small irregular scales: the night adder is, again, an exception and there are a few others. They are mainly terrestrial or arboreal but there are a few burrowing species and some are semi-aquatic. They may be diurnal or nocturnal, depending largely on their distribution: several species come from cold environments and are then mainly diurnal. Many are well camouflaged snakes that ambush their prey, which consists mostly of warm-blooded vertebrates, although some also eat reptiles and a few are partly insectivorous. Most species are viviparous but a few lay eggs.

The family is divided into four subfamilies: the Viperinae and the Crotalinae each have many species whereas the Azemiopinae and Causinae have few. The Crotalinae are unique among snakes in possessing a pair of large heat-sensitive pits between the eye and the nostril.

AZEMIOPINAE

This subfamily contains a single species. There are no heat-sensitive pits, while peculiarities of the skull separate it from the true vipers.

Azemiops A monotypic genus containing only *A. feae*. This rare and poorly-known snake comes from the Himalayan foothills of Burma, Tibet, central and southern China, where it lives in cloud forests. It is a medium-sized snake with smooth dorsal scales, large scales on the top of its head and short fangs. Its coloration is particularly striking, consisting of narrow orange rings on a dark grey or black background. The head is also orange. It is a terrestrial montane species, found up to 2,000 m (6,500 ft), and hibernates during the winter. Its eats small mammals and possibly other types of prey. Otherwise, little is known of its biology.

CAUSINAE Night adders

This subfamily contains a single genus, from Africa. Primitive vipers, with large scales on their heads.

Causus (**night adders**) Six species, found in Africa south of the Sahara. Small to medium-sized snakes with moderately stout bodies. They have smooth or weakly keeled scales and short tails. The snouted night adder, *C. defilippi*, has an upturned snout but the head is blunt in the other species. Nocturnal snakes that live in forests or grasslands and feed on amphibians, especially toads. Although their venom glands are large, the venom is not very powerful and their bites are not normally considered dangerous to humans, although there have been occasional fatalities. Oviparous, with clutches of over 20 eggs in some species.

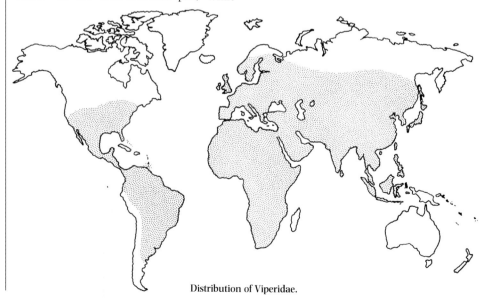

Distribution of Viperidae.

VIPERINAE 'True' vipers

Members of the Viperinae are foun[d] Europe, Asia and Africa, but not M[ada]gascar. They lack facial heat-sensitive [pits]. They tend to be heavily built though [not] especially long. Their heads are broad [and] covered with small scales and their tails [are] short. A variety of habitats are used [and] they may be diurnal or nocturnal. Usi[ng a] conservative arrangement, there are [ten?] genera and about 54 species.

Adenorhinos A monotypic genus cont[ain]ing only *A. barbouri*, from Africa. [The] species was previously placed in the ge[nus] *Atheris*. Poorly known but assumed t[o be] viviparous.

Atheris (**bush vipers**) Nine species [in] central and West Africa. Two species [*A.*] *hindii* and *A. superciliaris*, are under rev[iew] and may be removed to a new genus. S[mall] to medium-sized snakes with strongly ke[eled] scales. The heads are covered with m[any] small scales. Found in tropical forests [and] mainly arboreal, although the two sp[ecies] mentioned above are terrestrial. They ap[par]ently feed on frogs, lizards, small birds [and] mammals. The effects of the venom on [man] are not known. Viviparous, giving birt[h to] up to 10 young.

■ *Captivity* Rarely available and rather [deli]cate for reasons not yet fully underst[ood.] They require a tall cage with branche[s for] climbing and a humid environment. F[eed]ing can be a problem as not all specim[ens] will accept rodents and alternatives, in [the] form of lizards and frogs, have to be fo[und.] Captive breeding has occurred but is a [rare] event.

Bitis Thirteen species found through[out] Africa south of the Sahara. Small to l[arge] species (mostly medium sized) but [all] massively built with broad, triang[ular] heads. All species are terrestrial, and t[hose] from desert regions, of which Peringu[ey's] viper, *B. peringueyi*, is the best known, [are] efficient sidewinders. Other habitats inc[lude] mountains, rocky hillsides, forests and [?]

◄ (top) Fea's viper, *Azemiops feae*, a primitive [and] unique member of the viper family, from Chin[a,] Burma and Tibet.

◄ (centre) *Causus maculatus*, a night adder fr[om] Central Africa.

◄ (bottom) A common night adder, *Causus rhombeatus*, found over much of Africa south [of] the Sahara, eating a toad, its preferred prey.

young puff adder, *Bitis arietans*.

...rses. The small species prey mostly on ...rds but the larger ones eat birds and ...mmals. The large species are cryptically ...oured and epitomize 'sit-and-wait' ...dators, while small species may bury ...mselves beneath sand and loose soil in ...er to ambush their prey. All species ... dangerous, especially the larger ones ...h as the puff adder, *B. arietans*, and ... Gaboon viper, *B. gabonica*. Viviparous, ...ducing from four to almost 100 young. A ...r of 154 young *B. arietans* has been ...orded.

...*aptivity* Not often kept because of the ...ger to human life. Most species fare well ... captivity, however, with the possible ...eption of the rhinoceros viper, *B. nasi*-...nis, which has proved rather delicate. ...e small species may require a diet of ...rds. Captive breeding of *B. arietans* and, ...a lesser extent, *B. gabonica*, takes place ...ly regularly and the young are easily ...red.

...*astes* Three species from North Africa ...l the Middle East. Small vipers with ...derately slender bodies, broad heads ...l rounded snouts. *C. cerastes*, the desert ...ned viper, and *C. gasparettii* may have prominent horns or spines over their eyes but they are sometimes small or lacking in some populations. The other species, *C. vipera*, lacks horns. Confined to desert areas with loose sandy substrates, which they move across by sidewinding. They feed by ambushing their prey from a buried position with just their eyes showing. Lizards probably form the bulk of their prey although small mammals may also be taken. They have serrated lateral scales with which they produce a rasping sound when disturbed. Bad-tempered and dangerous to man, although their bites are rarely fatal. Oviparous, laying up to 25 eggs.

■ *Captivity* The horned viper, *Cerastes cerastes*, fares quite well in captivity provided it can be persuaded to accept rodents. It requires a cage with a substrate of sand, which should be deep enough for the snake to shuffle down into.

Echis (carpet or saw-scaled vipers) Six to eight species from North and West Africa, the Middle East, India and Sri Lanka. Small to medium-sized snakes with heavily keeled scales. When threatened, they will coil up and rub their scales together to produce a rasping sound. Mostly found in arid habitats, including sandy deserts, where they may move by sidewinding. They feed on lizards and small mammals. Dangerous to man because of their abundance in populated areas and their aggressive temperaments. They are the main cause of death by snake bite in some areas. Viviparous, producing small litters of young.

Eristocophis A monotypic genus containing only McMahon's viper, *E. mcmahoni*, from Afghanistan and northern Pakistan. Found in high deserts among sand dunes. It buries itself rapidly by shuffling down into the sand. It is probably nocturnal or crepuscular and feeds on lizards and small mammals. Although it is docile and not inclined to bite, it is potentially dangerous to man. Rarely collected and poorly known.

Macrovipera A recently resurrected genus containing four species previously regarded as belonging to *Vipera*. They are found in North Africa, south-eastern Europe and western Asia: *M. schweizeri* is confined to a few small islands in the Cyclades group. The other species are *M. deserti*, *M. lebetina* and *M. mauritanica*. Medium-sized snakes with thick bodies and broad heads covered with small scales. Terrestrial species that feed mainly on small mammals. Their venom is more toxic than that of the *Vipera* species and they are potentially dangerous to man. Unlike the *Vipera* species, they are oviparous.

Pseudocerastes A monotypic genus containing only *P. persicus* from the Middle East; there are several geographical races that are sometimes regarded as full species. Medium-sized snakes with moderately heavy bodies

▼ **Desert horned viper, *Cerastes cerastes*.**

▲ Wagner's viper, *Viperus wagneri*, from Turkey.

and keeled scales. There is a group of raised scales over each eye, forming a horn, but not spine-like as in *Cerastes*. They move by sidewinding in suitable areas, and feed largely upon lizards. Viviparous.

Vipera Currently about 22 recognized species ranging from northern Scandinavia, where the adder, *Vipera berus*, extends into the Arctic circle, east to Japan and south to Taiwan where a form of Russell's viper, *V. russelli formosensus*, lives. This species is also found throughout the Indonesian archipelago with *V. russelli siamensis* on Java and Sumatra and *V. r. limitis* on Flores and Timor. One or two species are found in North Africa. Many species are found in Turkey and the Middle East, where the most recent discoveries have been made (*V. wagneri* was described as recently as 1984, *V. pontica* and *V. albizona* in 1990). These tend to live in montane habitats, as do several of the European species: *V. aspis* in the Alps and other mountain ranges of central Europe, *V. ursinii* in scattered colonies in mountain ranges throughout southern and eastern Europe and western Asia, etc. Other species are found in a variety of habitats, including arid regions around the Mediterranean, heathlands, moors and lightly wooded regions. Small to medium-sized snakes with moderately thick bodies. The top of the head may be covered in many small scales, e.g. *V. ammodytes*, or with several large plates, e.g. *V. berus*. Some species have upturned or horned snouts – these are formed by groups of small scales rather than a single spine.

Predominantly terrestrial, although some species may climb occasionally. They feed on lizards and small mammals and, apparently, invertebrates. The venom of the European species is not particularly toxic and, although they are slightly dangerous to man, few fatalities have been recorded. The Asian Russell's viper, *V. russelli*, however, is large and produces a toxic venom that causes many fatalities.

Note: There is a strong case for resurrecting the older generic name of *Daboia* for Russell's viper.

■ *Captivity* A number of species are regularly kept and bred in captivity, especially in Europe. They adapt well and are usually trouble-free, although feeding juveniles, and the adults of smaller species, can sometimes present something of a problem as their natural prey is lizards. European and Middle Eastern species breed regularly, mating in the spring and giving birth in late summer. The young are easily reared once they begin to feed.

CROTALINAE Pit vipers

Species in this subfamily include the rattlesnakes and other pit vipers of North and South America, and a group of genera from south-east Asia. A large, prominent, heat-sensitive pit is situated on each side of the head, just below a line drawn between the nostril and the eye. It is larger than the nostril and the membrane lining can clearly be seen at the base. All pit vipers are potentially dangerous to man. Predominantly viviparous but members of a few genera lay eggs.

Agkistrodon (sometimes mistakenly spelt *Ancistrodon*) Ten species are recognized (11 if the dubious *A. affinis* is included), three from the New World (the cottonmouth, the copperhead and the cantil) and seven from the Old World. There is a likelihood that the Asian species will at some time in the future be removed to separate genera. The American species are distributed in the south-eastern USA and Central America, Asian species across central Asia (barely entering Europe in the Urals) and into northern China and Japan. Medium-sized snakes with relatively slender bodies (for vipers) with keeled scales. The tails may be brightly coloured in some species, and act as lures. Their heads are broad and roughly triangular in shape due to the large venom glands in the temporal region. The snout is pointed. A remarkable range of habitats is used, from freshwater swamps to deserts. *A. piscivorus* is found at sea-level on the Florida Keys, for instance, whereas some Asian species inhabit montane regions, and these include *A. himalayanus*, which occurs at up to 4,900 m (16,000 ft) in the Himalayan mountains. Prey includes items from most vertebrate groups, including fish and amphibians. Most, if not all, species give birth to live young, usually numbering about 10 per litter.

Bothriechis (palm vipers) Seven species, six of which occur in Central America and the seventh extends into northern South America. This is *B. schlegelii*, the eyelash viper, a polymorphic species with distinctive horn-like scales over each eye. Medium-sized, slender, arboreal snakes with keeled scales and prehensile tails. Mostly coloured green, with the exception of *B. schlegelii*, which may also be yellow or orange. Found in tropical montane forests, they feed on lizards, frogs, small birds and mammals. The bites of these species produces local pain and swelling but are not normally fatal to man. Viviparous.

Bothriopsis Eight species from South and Central America. Small to large, slender species, most of which are arboreal. They are found in a variety of forest habitats and several are very rare and are poorly known. Presumed to be viviparous.

Bothrops Formerly including practically all the Central and South American arboreal

▲ Black-speckled palm viper, *Bothriechis nigroviridis*, from Central America.

◀ Emerald pit viper, *Bothriopsis bilineata*, from the Amazon Basin.

semi-arboreal pit vipers, this genus is now reduced to 31 species, commonly known as lance-headed snakes, owing to the shape of their heads. Three species are found only on Caribbean islands. *B. atrox*, the fer-de-lance, is a dangerous species with a wide range over much of northern South America. *B. ammodytoides*, from Argentina, is the most southerly occurring snake. Small to large species with moderately stout bodies and keeled scales. All apparently terrestrial but occasionally climbing, and feeding on a variety of vertebrate prey. Dangerous snakes owing to their abundance and their aggressive natures. *Bothrops* species account for most of the snake bite deaths in South America. Viviparous.

Calloselasma A monotypic genus containing only *C. rhodostoma*, the Malayan pit viper. Found in Indo-China, the Malaysian peninsular and on Java. Apparently common where it occurs. Highly aggressive. Mainly nocturnal but sometimes diurnal, feeding on a variety of small vertebrates. This species is unusual among Asian pit vipers in laying eggs, with clutches of 20 to 40 eggs having been noted. The females coil around their eggs during incubation, apparently in order to protect them from predators.

Crotalus (rattlesnakes) The best-known genus of pit vipers. Twenty-six species are recognized, ranging from Canada in the north to Argentina in the south, and they include all of the rattlesnakes except the three species of *Sistrurus*. Adaptations to many environments have taken place but there are no arboreal species. Typically desert species although some are found in more humid environments, even rainforests. Others occur in scrub, grasslands and prairies. Nocturnal or diurnal, according to distribution and season – even primarily nocturnal species will become diurnal during cool weather. They feed on a variety of vertebrate prey, small species mainly on lizards and the larger species on ground-nesting birds and mammals up to the size of rabbits. All species are viviparous, giving birth to a variable number of young, depending on species and size.

■ *Captivity* Several of the more common species are kept by specialists. They present no obvious problems but should be kept dry at all times. Some species need a period of cool conditions in the winter.

Deinagkistrodon A monotypic genus containing only *D. acutus*, from south-eastern China and Taiwan. A large, heavy-bodied species with a characteristic upturned snout. Found in wooded mountains and hills. A variety of prey is taken, including amphibians, lizards, snakes and mammals. A highly venomous species whose bite often proves fatal to man – the local common name of 'hundred-pace snake' refers to the distance covered by victims before they succumb. Oviparous, like *Calloselasma*, laying around 20 eggs which the female guards.

Hypnale (hump-nosed vipers) Three species, found in Sri Lanka and south-western India. One of these, *H. walli*, may be a subspecies of *H. nepa*. Small snakes with short tails and keeled scales. Found in dry and moist habitats, often wooded and sometimes in association with human settlements. They feed on frogs, lizards, snakes, reptile eggs and small mammals. Although venomous and therefore dangerous to man, they are generally inoffensive. Viviparous, bearing four to 17 young.

Lachesis A single species, *L. muta*, the bushmaster, forms this genus. This is the largest pit viper, growing to 3 m (10 ft) or more. It has a disjunct distribution, in Central America, the northern part of the Amazon Basin and coastal Brazil. Nocturnal in habits and terrestrial, it is more or less confined to forested habitats. Although highly dangerous, this species is rarely aggressive. Unique among the American pit vipers in laying eggs.

Ophryacus This genus comprises a single species, *O. undulatus*, with a patchy distribution in southern and central Mexico. Medium-sized and rather stout, with keeled scales and spines or 'horns' over its eyes. Terrestrial or semi-arboreal. Viviparous.

Porthidium Fourteen species found in Central and northern South America. One species, *P. hyoprora*, is found in the Amazon Basin. Small to medium-sized, terrestrial pit vipers, including several chunky 'jumping' vipers such as *P. nummifer*. Mostly stout-bodied but some species are quite slender. Mainly nocturnal in habits but several species are poorly known. Dangerous to man though not usually fatal. Viviparous.

▼ Hognosed viper, *Porthidium nasutum*, from Central and northern South America.

Sistrurus The three species in this genus known as the massasauga (*S. catenatus*) a the pygmy rattlesnakes (*S. miliaris* and *ravus*). They are found in North Amer and Mexico. Although they have ratt they differ from members of the ge *Crotalus* in having several large scales on tops of their heads. A variety of habitats used, from wetlands and coniferous fore to deserts to cloud forest, depending species and location. They are all terrestr feeding on small vertebrates such as liza and rodents. Although bites are pain they are not normally con-sidered a dan to life. Viviparous.

Trimeresurus About 30 species from Ne China, Indo-China, India, Sri Lanka, sou east Asia and Japan. Small to medium-si vipers, with broad heads and modera stout bodies. Most are arboreal althou there are some terrestrial species. They in a variety of habitats, including ra forest, cloud forest, mangrove swar and mountains. Some are commonly fou around human settlements. The arbor species are often green in colour wher the terrestrial ones are usually brown, w a variety of markings. They feed on lizar frogs and small mammals, and possi birds. Bites from these species are pain and can be potentially dangerous, caus local tissue damage at the least. All spe are viviparous as far as is known.

■ *Captivity* Several of the arboreal spe in this genus are kept in captivity. Th usually adapt well and are easily cared in tall cages with branches for them to r Tropical temperatures of about 25–3(

(77–86°F) should be provided and the cages should be sprayed occasionally. Adults will usually eat rodents but the young, which are small, require small frogs or lizards.

Tropidolaemus A monotypic genus containing only Wagler's pit viper, *T. wagleri*, from south-east Asia. A medium-sized, arboreal species that changes its colour as it grows: the young are mainly green with spots of white and red, sometimes arranged into short crossbars, whereas the adults have a complicated pattern of scattered greenish-yellow spots, arranged into pale crossbars, on a black background, and pale green flanks. Arboreal, feeding on lizards, birds and rodents. Viviparous.

◀ McGregor's pit viper, *Trimeresurus mcgregori*.

▼ Wagler's pit viper, *Tropidolaemus wagleri*, from south-east Asia.

BIBLIOGRAPHY

There has been a minor explosion of books about snakes in recent years. The coverage has not been even, however, as some areas, such as North America and Australia, are now very well covered, whereas others, such as parts of South America, central Asia and, especially, central Africa, are hardly covered at all. Furthermore, many important books are out of print, and some have become collectors' items. In order to accumulate a comprehensive library of books about snakes on a worldwide basis, it is therefore necessary to be moderately wealthy. Being multilingual is also helpful, although many foreign books have English summaries and, in any case, latinized names are universally recognized.

The following list is not totally comprehensive. Where several books deal with essentially the same subject matter, the most recent or most readily available title has been given.

Snake Natural History and Biology

Burton, John A., *Snakes: An Illustrated Guide*, Blandford Press, London, 1991.

Coborn, John., *The Atlas of Snakes of the World*, TFH Publications, New Jersey, USA.

Mehrtens, John., *Living Snakes of the World*, Sterling Publishing Co., New York, and Blandford Press, London, 1987.

Parker, H. W. and Grandison, A. G. C., *Snakes – a natural history*, British Museum (Natural History), London, 1977.

Porter, *Herpetology*, W. B. Saunders Company, 1972.

Seigel, Richard A., Collins, Joseph T. and Novak, Susan S., *Snakes: Ecology and Evolutionary Biology*, Macmillan Publishing Company, New York, 1987.

Seigel, Richard A. and Collins, Joseph T., *Snakes: Ecology and Behaviour*, McGraw-Hill, New York, 1993.

Regional Accounts and Identification Guides

NORTH AMERICA

Behler, John L. and Wayne King, F., *The Audubon Society Field Guide to North American Reptiles and Amphibians*, Alfred A. Knopf, New York, 1979.

Ashton, Ray E. and Ashton, Patricia S., *Handbook of Reptiles and Amphibians of Florida*. Part 1: *The Snakes*, Windward Publishing, Inc., Miami, Florida, 1981. (Of more general interest than its title suggests because Florida has such a rich snake fauna.)

Conant, Roger, *A Field Guide to the Reptiles and Amphibians of Eastern and Central North America*, Houghton Mifflin Company, Boston, second edition 1975.

Stebbins, Robert C., *A Field Guide to Western Reptiles and Amphibians*, Houghton Mifflin Company, Boston, second edition, 1985.

Tennant, Alan, *The Snakes of Texas*, Texas Monthly Press, Austin, Texas, 1984. (Of general interest because Texas has such a rich snake fauna. Also available in an abridged form as *A Field Guide to the Snakes of Texas*, 1985.)

Wright, A. H. and Wright, A. A., *Handbook of Snakes*, two volumes, Comstock Publishing Associates, Ithaca, 1957. (The standard work on the snakes of North America.)

SOUTH AND CENTRAL AMERICA

Amaral, Afrânio do, *Serpentes do Brasil (Brazilian Snakes): a color iconography*, Ministry of Education and Culture, São Paulo, Brazil, 1977. (In Portuguese and English. Rather dated in its treatment and layout but still the most complete account of the snakes of this herpetologically important country.)

Cei, J. M., *Reptile del Centro, Centro-oeste y Sur de la Argentina*, Museo Regionale di Scienze Naturali, Turin, 1986. (In Spanish.)

Chippaux, Jean-Philippe, *Les Serpents de la Guyane Française* (The snakes of French Guiana), Institut Français de recherche scientifique pour le développement en coopération. Collection Faune Tropicale No. XXVII, Paris, 1986. (In French.)

Henderson, Robert W. and Schwartz, Albert, *A Guide to the Identification of the Amphibians and Reptiles of Hispaniola*, Milwaukee Public Museum, Special Publications in Biology and Geology Number 4. 1984.

Pérez-Santos, Carlos and Moreno, Ana G., *Ofidios de Colombia*, Museo Regionale di Scienze Naturali, Turin, 1988. (In Spanish.)

Pérez-Santos, Carlos and Moreno, Ana G., *Serpientes do Ecuador (Snakes of Ecuador)*, Museo Regionale di Scienze Naturali, Turin, 1991. (In Spanish.)

Rivero, J. A., *The Amphibians and Reptiles of Puerto Rico*, Universidad de Puerto Rico.

Rose, Janis A., *La Taxonomia y Zoogeographia de los Ofidios de Venezuela*, Universidad Central de Venezuela, Caracas, 1966. (In Spanish.)

Schwartz, Albert and Henderson, Robert W., *A Guide to the Identification of the Amphibians and Reptiles of the West Indies Exclusive of Hispaniola*, Milwaukee Public Museum, 1985.

Wilson, Larry D. and Meyer, John R., *The Snakes of Honduras*, Milwaukee Public Museum, 1985.

EUROPE

Appleby, L., *British Snakes*, Baker, 1971.

Arnold, E. N. and Burton, J. A., *A Field Guide to the Reptiles and Amphibians of Britain and Europe*, Collins, London, 1978.

Boulenger, G. A., *The Snakes of Europe*, Methuen and Company, Ltd., London, 1913. (Hopelessly out of date taxonomically, but the first book to deal with the European snakes in a readable style. A collectors' item.)

Dimitropoulos, A., *Snakes in the Cyclades*, (In Greek with English summaries.)

Frazer, D., *Reptiles and Amphibians in Britain*, Collins, London, 1989.

Steward, J. W., *The Snakes of Europe*, David and Charles, Newton Abbot, England, 1971.

ASIA AND THE MIDDLE EAST

Alcala, Angel C., *Guide to Philippine Flora and Fauna*. Volume X: *Amphibians and Reptiles*, Natural Resources Management Centre, Ministry Natural Resources and University of Philippines, 1986.

Cox, M. J., *The Snakes of Thailand and their Husban* Krieger, Malabar, Florida, 1991.

Latifi, M., *The Snakes of Iran*, Society for the Stud Amphibians and Reptiles, Oxford, Ohio, 1991

Leviton, Alan E., Anderson, Steven C., Adler, K and Minton, Sherman A., *Handbook to Middle Amphibians and Reptiles*, Society for the Stud Reptiles and Amphibians, Oxford, Ohio, 19 (Covers part of the Arabian peninsula, Kuv Iraq and a small part of Iran.)

Lim, Kevin K. P. and Lim, Francis L. K., *A Guide to Amphibians and Reptiles of Singapore*, Singa Science Centre, 1992. (A small but useful b with excellent colour photographs of the r common species found in Singapore.)

Maki, M. A., *Monograph of the Snakes of Japan*, 3 umes, Dai-ichi Shobo, Tokyo, 1931. (In Japan A valuable collectors' item.)

de Silva, Anslem, *Colour Guide to the Snakes of Lanka*, R & A Publishing Limited, Avon, Engla 1990.

Tweedie, M. F. W., *The Snakes of Mal* Government Printing Office. Singapore, 19 (Becoming rather out of date now but still most detailed account of the snakes of Malaysian Peninsula and Singapore.)

Wall, Colonel Frank, *Ophidia Taprobanica or Snakes of Ceylon*, Government Printing Of Colombo, Ceylon (Sri Lanka), 1921. (Rather of date taxonomically but very valuable owir the wealth of first-hand observations repo here. A collectors' item.)

Zhao, Er-mi and Adler, Kraig, *Herpetology of Ch* Society for the Study of Amphibians and Rept Oxford, Ohio, 1993.

AUSTRALASIA

Cogger, H. G., *Reptiles and Amphibians of Aust* (5th edition), A. H. and A. W . Reed Pty L Sydney, 1992.

Ehmann, Harald, *Encyclopedia of Australian Anim Reptiles*, Angus and Robertson, Pymble, N South Wales, 1992.

Glasby, C. J., Ross, G. J. B., and Beesley, P. L. (e *Fauna of Australia. Vol 2A Amphibia and Rep* Australian Government Publishing Serv Canberra, 1993.

Gow, G. F., *Complete Guide to Australian Sna* Angus and Robertson, Sydney, 1989.

McCoy, Michael, *Reptiles of the Solomon Islands*, V Ecology Institute Handbook No. 7, Wau, Pa New Guinea, 1980.

O'Shea, Mark, *A Guide to the Snakes of Papua Guinea*, Independent Publishing, Port More: Papua New Guinea (in press).

Shine, Richard, *Australian Snakes: a Natural Hist* Reed Books, Balgowlah., NSW. (Describes the r ural history of the rich Australian snake fau Not an identification guide.)

Weigel, John, *Snakes of South-East Aust* (Australian Reptiles Park's Guide to), Austra Reptile Park, Gosford, NSW, 1990.

AFRICA

Branch, Bill, *Field Guide to the Snakes and o Reptiles of Southern Africa*, New Holland, Lonc 1988.

Buys, P. J. and Buys, P. J. C., *Snakes of South West Africa*, Gamsburg Publishers, Windhoek, no date (1980s).

Broadley, D. G., *FitzSimon's Snakes of Southern Africa*, Delta Books, 1983. (A revised version of the original book by Vivian FitzSimons, which is hard to obtain now.)

Broadley, D. G. and Cock, E. V., *Snakes of Rhodesia*, Longman, Rhodesia (Zimbabwe), 1975.

FitzSimons, V. F. M., *Snakes of Southern Africa*, Purnell and Sons, Cape Town, 1962. (Becoming rather dated but still of value owing to the great amount of detail.)

Isemonger, R. M., *Snakes of Africa, Southern, Central and East*, Nelson, 1962.

Morais, Johan, *A Complete Guide to the Snakes of Southern Africa*, Southern Book Publishers (Pty) Ltd., South Africa, 1992, and Blandford Press, London, 1993.

Patterson R., *Reptiles of Southern Africa*, C. Struik, Cape Town, 1987.

Pitman, C. R. S., *A Guide to the Snakes of Uganda*, Wheldon and Wesley, Hertfordshire, 1974.

Spawls, Stephen and Branch, Bill, *The Dangerous Snakes of Africa*, Blandford Press, London, 1995.

Accounts of Families and Groups of Species

Armstrong, Barry L. and Murphy, James B., *The Natural History of Mexican Rattlesnakes*, University of Kansas, Lawrence, 1979.

Brodman, Peter, *Die Giftschlangen Europas und die Gattung Vipera in Afrika und Asien* (The poisonous snakes of Europe and the genus *Vipera* in Africa and Asia), Kümmerley and Frey, Bern, 1987. (In German.)

Campbell, Jonathan A. and Lamar, William W., *The Venomous Reptiles of Latin America*, Comstock Publishing Associates, Cornell University Press, Ithaca, 1989. (An authoritative guide to the heloderms, coral snakes and vipers of the area, with nearly 600 colour photographs.)

Gloyd, Howard K. and Conant, Roger, *Snakes of the Agkistrodon Complex: A Monographic Review*, Society for the Study of Amphibians and Reptiles, 1990. (A very detailed account of the genera *Agkistrodon*, *Calloselasma*, *Deinagkistrodon* and *Hypnale*.)

Heatwole, Harold, *Sea Snakes*, New South Wales University Press, Australia, 1987.

Klauber, Laurence M., *Rattlesnakes: Their Habits, Life Histories and Influence on Mankind*, two volumes, University of California Press, second edition, 1972. (A wonderfully thorough and readable account of this fascinating group of snakes.)

Lowe, Charles H., Schwalbe, Cecil R. and Johnson, Terry B., *The Venomous Reptiles of Arizona*, Arizona Fish and Game Department, 1986.

Mao, Shou-Hsian and Chen, Been-Yuan, *Sea Snakes of Taiwan*, NSC special publication number 4. The National Science Council, Taipei, Taiwan, 1980. (In English with Chinese summaries.)

Phelps, Tony, *Poisonous Snakes*, Blandford Press, London, revised edition 1989.

Pope, Clifford, H., *The Giant Snakes*, Routledge and Kegan Paul, London, 1961. (A popular account of the six largest species of snakes.)

Rossi, Roger, *Garter Snakes: Their Natural History and Care in Captivity*, Blandford Press, London, 1992.

Tolson, P. J. and Henderson, R. W., *The Natural History of West Indian Boas*, R & A Publishing Limited, Taunton, Somerset, 1993.

Williams, K. L. and Wallach, V., *Snakes of the World*, Volume 1, *Synopsis of Snake Generic Names*, Krieger Publishing Company, Malabar, Florida, 1989. (A basic checklist of snake genera giving synopses and type species of each. A second volume, listing current species, is planned.)

Williams, K. L., *Systematics and Natural History of the American Milk snake, Lampropeltis triangulum*, Milwaukee Public Museum, second edition, 1988.

Snake Hunting

Kauffeld, Carl, *Snakes: The Keeper and the Kept*, Doubleday and Company, Inc., New York, 1969. (Snake hunting in the United States, with some notes on keeping snakes in captivity.)

Wykes, A. *Snake Man: the story of C. J. P. Ionides*, Hamish Hamilton, London, 1960. (A biographical account of an eccentric and fascinating snake catcher.)

Snakes in Captivity

Mattison, Chris, *Keeping and Breeding Snakes*, Blandford Press, London, 1988.

Ross, Richard A. and Marzac, Gerald, *The Reproductive Husbandry of Pythons and Boas*, Institute for Herpetological Research, Stanford, California, 1990.

Note: There are literally dozens of books and booklets dealing with the care and breeding of snakes in captivity and there is not room to list them all.

PHOTOGRAPH ACKNOWLEDGEMENTS

249

Photographs have been provided by a number of photographers, who are credited below. Since the value of a natural history book is often judged by its visual appeal, their contributions are gratefully acknowledged here. My own photographs have been taken with the help of numerous people who have loaned or located specimens for me over the years. Many others have accompanied me on field trips to a variety of places on several continents. Their help has always been given freely and cheerfully and their company has greatly added to my enjoyment of snakes and my determination to find out all that I can about them.

William R. Branch: 20 (*bottom*), 24 (*top*), 31, 40, 60, 72 (*bottom*), 78 (*bottom*), 83, 93, 94–5, 98 (*top*), 99, 101 (*bottom*), 102, 105, 108, 120, 127 (*top right*), 134, 149 (*bottom*), 155 (*bottom*), 214, 220 (*top*), 224, 225, 226, 229, 231, 242 (*bottom*), 246

Nick Garbutt: 56 (*top*), 197

Koert Langeveld: 167

William B. Love: 35 (*top*), 68–9, 74, 83, 114 (*bottom*), 124 (*right*), 125, 126 (*top left*), 127 (*top left*), 128 (*bottom*), 131 (*top left and right*), 132, 151, 159 (*bottom*), 162, 173 (*left*), 245 (*top*)

Chris Mattison: 2–3, 8–9, 10, 12–13, 16–17, 20 (*top*), 21, 22, 23, 24 (*bottom*), 25, 26, 27, 28, 30, 32, 33, 34, 35 (*bottom left and right*), 36, 41, 42–3, 43, 44, 45, 55 (*top*), 58, 64 (*bottom*), 66, 70, 71, 72 (*top*), 73, 75 (*top*), 76 (*top*), 78 (*top*), 79, 81, 82 (*top*), 92, 97 (*right*), 98 (*bottom*), 107, 109, 110, 112 (*top*), 114 (*top*), 116, 118–19, 129 (*top and bottom right*), 130, 131 (*middle and bottom*), 136–7, 141, 142, 143, 147 (*top*), 157, 158, 160 (*top*), 164–5, 166 (*top and middle*), 169, 174, 175 (*top*), 178, 180, 182–3, 184, 187, 188–9, 192–3, 196, 199, 201, 204 (*bottom*), 206, 213, 215, 216, 218, 219, 220 (*bottom*), 223, 227, 243

William B. Montgomery: 80, 127 (*bottom*), 153 (*top*)

Mark O'Shea: 18, 29, 35 (*middle*), 52–3, 75 (*bottom*), 77, 82 (*bottom*), 91, 111 (*left*), 115, 122 (*top left*), 126 (*top right*), 128 (*top*), 133 (*bottom*), 135, 156, 159 (*top*), 172, 175 (*bottom*), 179, 202, 204, (*top*), 207, 217, 221, 228, 233, 240 (*bottom*), 245 (*bottom*)

James Savage: 126 (*bottom*)

John Tashjian: 122 (*bottom*), 129 (*bottom left*), 145, 160 (*bottom*), 173 (*right*), 205, 242 (*top and middle*), 244, 247

Geoff Trinder: 87, 146

John Weigel: 55 (*bottom*), 56 (*bottom*), 62, 64 (*top*), 67, 75 (*middle*), 76 (*bottom*), 91 (*left*), 100, 101 (*top*), 104, 111 (*right*), 112 (*bottom*), 139, 150 (*bottom*), 155 (*middle*), 166 (*bottom*), 170, 177, 200, 203, 237, 238, 239, 240 (*top*).

INDEX